The Goddesses' Henchmen

The Goddesses' Henchmen

Gender in Indian Hero Worship

LINDSEY HARLAN

OXFORD
UNIVERSITY PRESS

2003

OXFORD
UNIVERSITY PRESS

Oxford   New York
Auckland   Bangkok   Buenos Aires   Cape Town   Chennai
Dar es Salaam   Delhi   Hong Kong   Istanbul   Karachi   Kolkata
Kuala Lumpur   Madrid   Melbourne   Mexico City   Mumbai   Nairobi
São Paulo   Shanghai   Taipei   Tokyo   Toronto

Library of Congress Cataloging-in-Publication Data
Harlan, Lindsey.
The Goddesses' henchmen : gender in Indian hero worship / Lindsey Harlan.
    p. cm.
Includes bibliographical references and index.
ISBN 0-19-515425-8; 0-19-515426-6 (paper)
1. Rajasthan (India)—Social life and customs.   2. Hero worship—India—
Rajasthan.   3. Nationalism—India—Rajasthan—Religious aspects   I. Title.
DS485.R24 .H38 2003
306'.0954'4—dc21   2002071520

9 8 7 6 5 4 3 2 1

Printed in the United States of America
on acid-free paper

For Devon and Kirin

Acknowledgments

Writing this book, I benefited from the help and advice of many people. I am especially indebted to Gregory Nagy for his encouragement and advice as I first began outlining this manuscript while living in Cambridge during an academic leave from Connecticut College. I am equally grateful to David Shulman for his instructive observations during our many discussions of narrative framing—in the United States, over the Internet, and ultimately in Jerusalem. Cynthia Read provided gentle guidance through the editorial process, as did Theo Calderara and Stacey Hamilton. I also benefited greatly from thoughtful feedback on the entire manuscript from John Hawley, Alf Hiltebeitel, and Susan Wadley. For invigorating exchanges on specific aspects of this project, I thank Alan Babb, Ali Asani, Peter Claus, John Cort, Katherine Ewing, Joyce Flueckiger, Ann Gold, Don Handelman, Stephanie Jamison, Helen Lambert, Julia Leslie, David Lorenzen, Rebecca Manring, McKim Marriott, Asko Parpola, William Pinch, Velcheru Narayana Rao, Kevin Rhinehart, Richard Saran, William Sax, John D. Smith, and Joan Taylor.

For their support as department colleagues, I thank Garrett Green, Gene Gallagher, Roger Brooks, and Patrice Brodeur. I am also grateful for the encouragement I received from Nelly Murstein and Julie Rivkin, colleagues in other departments. For editing assistance, I thank my students Mark Douton and Georgia Shaw. For help with preparing my manuscript for review, I thank Diane Monte.

It would be impossible to name all the people who provided technical or moral support during my various research stints in India. Those to whom I owe a special debt for sustained assistance include various members from the royal families of Jodhpur and Udaipur, as well as the noble families of Amet, Bansi, Bari Sadri, Bassi, Bathera, Bedla, Delwara, Devgarh, Ghanerao, Jilola, Kanor, Kanota, Pipliya, and Salumbar. As always, I am indebted to long-time colleague Komal Kothari, who has always stimulated my interest in folklore. I acknowledge sustained assistance from Akshay and Jai Shri Delwara, Amarendra Singh and Raju Bai Sa Salumbar, Chandranath Dashora, Dhruv Singh Shivrati, Gopi Nath Sharma, Jagat Mehta, Lokendra Singh Ghanerao, Madhav and Kirin Bai Sa Bedla, Mahendra Singh and Pratap Bai Sa Ghanerao, Mohan Singh Kanota, Mohan Singh Osian, N. Tomar Singh Chauhan, Nahar Singh Jasol, Prabhuprakash and Anand Bai Sa Amet, Prakash Dashora, Pranavanand Saraswati and Numrta Nand Saraswati Kanor, Prem Shankar Sharma, Shil Sharma, and Veer Vijay Singh (Ricki) and Gayatri Ummaidnagar. For inspiration and for wonderful companionship in Chittor, I thank Susanne and Lloyd Rudolph.

I wish to make special mention of my gratitude to R. S. Ashiya, who recently passed away. Employed at the Bharatiya Lok Kala Mandal, he also served for many years as my language teacher and patiently guided me through various dialects. He sometimes accompanied me on short research trips and facilitated various travel arrangements. I am indebted, as well, to his son Manvendra Singh Ashiya, who helped me with stray details while I prepared this manuscript for publication and who has facilitated my ongoing research on hero cults. I also received help on hero cults from many other people, who will find themselves acknowledged when I publish my work on cults, though, of course, I feel gratitude at this moment. For permission to photograph, I thank the Eklingi Temple Trust and Arvind Singh, Mewar. To the various people whom I have mentioned I owe this book's successes, and not its shortcomings.

For financial support during my research, I am indebted to the National Endowment for the Humanities and the American Institute of Indian Studies, whose director general, Pradeep Mahendiratta, has facilitated my work in many ways over the years. For financial support but also for providing a wonderful environment for reflection on my research, I thank the Women's Studies in Religion Program at Harvard Divinity School, which was directed during the term of my fellowship by Constance Buchanan. Finally, I thank my home institution, Connecticut College, for providing support from the Frank Johnson Development Fund and for allowing me to pursue my research interests both in the field and at Harvard.

This list of acknowledgments would not be complete without mention of dear friends and relatives who provided encouragement in many ways. I feel grateful to my good friends Cynthia Atherton and Julie Hiebert, who have always understood and shared my love of India; to Judy Oat, Donna McNeill, Camile Burlingham, and Blair Eddy for timely diversion; to Dinos Santafianos for his thoughtfulness; to my sister Sarah, whose strength I admire and whose friendship I treasure; and my parents, whose commitment to education instilled in me the value of curiosity, which led me to take up a career of doing what I love.

Contents

Illustrations

Note on Transliteration

The system of transliteration I have used avoids diacritics and allows for approximate pronunciation for readers who are unschooled in the mysteries of diacritical marks. I have provided diacritics as well as definitions of important and frequently used terms in the glossary. Respecting different decisions on transliteration made by other authors, I have retained diacritical marks in quotations as well as in the titles of books and articles.

Relying on government maps, I have adopted typical, if not universal, spellings and transliterations of geographical names. I have also adopted what I believe to be the best-known spellings and transliterations of people's names. This has resulted in some inconsistencies, especially in the variant spellings of names that use retroflex consonants (for example, the consonants ḍ and ṛ).

Utilizing various languages and dialects, this book, which is based on fieldwork, privileges Hindi forms over Sanskrit ones (thus *Ramayan* rather than *Ramayana*). To avoid confusion, it also uses standard Hindi forms of terms from Rajasthani dialects (Marwari, Mewari, and so on) when they are available (thus *purca* instead of *parco*), except when providing direct quotation from Rajasthani dialects. Because many of the conversations that served as sources for the book were conducted in standard Hindi, which serves as a sort of *lingua franca* in Rajasthan, many direct quotes include standard Hindi terms. I use Rajasthani dialect terms (such as *malipannau*) where standard Hindi ones are lacking or where a standard Hindi equivalent differs markedly from the Rajasthani dialect term.

Transliteration of Hindi accords with accepted conventions. These include the dropping of unpronounced final *a*, the representation of the vowel ṛ as ri. The Rajasthani dialects' retroflex ḷ appears as l (and so the Rajasthani dialects' *kuḷ* becomes *kul* in the text and glossary). The Hindi v is represented as v except where conventional proper noun transliterations utilize *w*. The Hindi ś and ṣ appear as *sh*. The Rajput designation Singh appears in this conventional English form, except in the transliteration of authors' names from Hindi and Rajasthani sources. Note that c is always pronounced ch.

The Goddesses' Henchmen

I

Introduction

Arrival

Like many travelers in India, I have spent long hours in battered
taxis bumping along single-lane highways. During the past ten years
I have crisscrossed the state of Rajasthan many times on such
highways and watched its rocky yellow landscape speed by as my
intrepid drivers played chicken with oncoming cars, scattered
inattentive pedestrians, and sliced through herds of sheep and sleepy
buffalo. It is impossible to nap in these taxis: crackling radios blare
popular film anthems, dusty air roars in through rattling windows,
and high-pitched horns broadcast insults and indignation. And so I
have watched the desert lands and parched farms stream by while
slipping into fantasies about long cool showers and sweet hot tea.

Frequently my reverie has been interrupted by shocks of color
from roadside shrines displaying images adorned with shiny silver,
magenta, and aqua foil or with flecks of real silver strewn across
encrusted vermilion. Situated between scraggly cactus fences and
gritty road shoulders, the shrines are modest structures—usually
slightly elevated cement platforms bearing crudely carved stelai or
aniconic rock images—but finding them compelling, I have
annoyed more than a few drivers by pleading, "Stop! Back up!
Seriously! Let's see those images!" Not sharing my enthusiasm, the
drivers have inevitably muttered something like, "Nothing to see,
madam, just some village gods and goddesses or someone's
ancestors." No doubt they have wondered: Why waste time on
these meager monuments when we were off to see some grand
ancient temple or maharaja's palace?

Bored or intrigued, some have followed me from the car and, with evident amusement, listened to me grill hapless passers-by about the identity of the divinities and the particulars of relevant ritual activity. Noting my special interest in shrines that commemorate the violent death and deification of heroes, they have sometimes informed me about heroes worshiped in their families or villages. Many drivers have identified themselves as Rajputs, members of the martial caste that governed much of the area now known as Rajasthan, and have been quite ready to recite tales of heroism from their families' ancient or recent past. Their accounts were often much more detailed and animated than those given by the poor passers-by I accosted, most of whom knew little or nothing about the images near which they happened to be standing when we arrived. From these drivers I heard about decapitated warriors who killed many, even hundreds, of assailants before stumbling and sanctifying the earth with their blood; I heard about opium-sated youths who single-handedly rescued cows from tribal rustlers and returned them to crying calves; I heard about "freedom fighters" who preserved Hindu *dharm* (religion, law, and custom) or *Hindutva* ("Hinduness") from menacing Muslim invaders.

Whereas my attraction to roadside shrines stemmed from a desire for diversion on long trips, my fascination with hero memorials developed out of the research on the religious narratives of Rajput women that I conducted during my first long research stint in Rajasthan, eighteen months in 1984–1985.[1] In the early days of my research, when I called on Rajput women with letters of introduction in hand, I was usually greeted by men, who were understandably curious about the nature of my work. When I explained that I was interested in women's religious traditions, they often expressed disappointment. My project, they indicated, was unimportant: Why not forget women's religious traditions and write about something that mattered, like Rajput history and heroism? Frequently they went on to narrate stories about ancestral heroes worshiped in their household shrines or at monuments on the borders of the estates (*thikanas*) their families once ruled. While waiting to interview women in their comfortable and sometimes elegant Rajput homes, I collected many tales of headless horsemen, cattle thieves, and marauding Muslims.

As a strategy for getting past these guardians at the gates of *parda*, but also because of a genuine fascination with their stories, I said that the next time I came to work in Rajasthan I would try to do something that they felt was important: I would write on heroes. Meanwhile, I decided to record all the heroic narratives that came my way and visit hero shrines that belonged to the families I visited. Slowly I came to realize that although the men with whom I spoke tended to represent heroism as a subject that concerned and appealed to men, women also tell hero stories, and they perform rituals for heroes. Unlike men, the women with whom I spoke did not readily volunteer hero stories or use the stories to demonstrate the illustriousness of lineage and family. Rather, they narrated brief hero narratives, if asked, and focused overwhelmingly on ritual.[2] From them I learned about offerings and the rewards of ritual veneration.

---

1. This research was published as Harlan, *Religion and Rajput Women*.
2. Telling tales of heroism from one's illustrious past has been a common pastime among older Rajput men in Rajasthan. At social gatherings, men tell such stories and also tell tales that taunt other men about

Moreover, because the women in the household tended to be responsible for maintaining household shrines, they were frequently more knowledgeable about ritual than men were. Whereas women often suggested that I talk to men in the family if I wanted to learn the details of a hero's history, men often recommended that I talk to the women in the family to find out what offerings are suitable for various household deities, including heroes.[3] Women usually made the offerings themselves, though sometimes they gave the offerings they had prepared to husbands or sons who were particularly devoted to a household hero, or to Brahmins, in the few families that still regularly employed Brahmin *pujaris* (priests) to service household shrines.

Finally, I learned from women about the hero songs women sing during *ratijagas* (wake rituals) that accompany auspicious occasions such as birth and marriage.[4] In these songs are found depictions of heroes that differ significantly from the images of heroes found in other contexts and in genres performed overwhelmingly by men. In short, my work on women revealed clearly that hero worship was not simply something about or for men.

Research: Lacunae, Foci

In 1990 I returned to Rajasthan to keep my promise. I spent the academic year researching hero worship. I also returned to the field in 1998–1999, 2000, and 2002 to update my findings. As I gathered my data, I was continually struck by how little we actually know about hero worship in India. As archaeologists and classicists avidly continue to piece together the traditions of cultic hero worship in ancient European cultures, and as Indologists continue to speculate about kingship and heroism in ancient India from representations in literature and art, Rajasthan continues to offer an abundance of thriving hero cults and active hero shrines presenting splendid opportunities to collect heroic narratives and songs, observe ritual performances, converse with devotees, and confront tradition unfolding and changing moment by moment.

In a 1973 article entitled "The Folk Hero and Class Interests in Tamil Heroic Ballads," Stuart Blackburn bemoans the paucity of research and reflection on hero worship in India. His essay identifies various historical factors that contribute to neglect.[5] For one thing, those scholars who were initially interested in Indian concepts of heroism hailed from a background in or were very much interested in classics. Blackburn's article speaks of the "established cultural hegemony"

---

improprieties allegedly committed by their ancestors. Good-humored insults about possible illegitimacy and cowardice are traded as men sip scotch in the late evening hours. Much more is to be said on insults in chapters 2 and 3.

3. For reflections on the brevity of such accounts, see Harlan, *Religion and Rajput Women,* and "Heroes Alone and Heroes at Home," as well as Ramanujan, "Two Realms of Kannada Folklore."

4. For a selection of *ratijaga* songs, see Harlan "Women's Songs for Auspicious Occasions." I am grateful to Princeton University Press for allowing me to reprint some of these songs in chapter 5. Another occasion for which *ratijagas* are sometimes performed is the consecration of a new home or place of business.

5. "The Folk Hero and Class Interests in Tamil Heroic Ballads," 131.

effected by Greco-Roman biographical paradigms presented by Hanh, Rank, Raglan, Campbell, and others, and shows how heroic biographies from around the world have come to seem incomplete or deviant when measured against those of classical heroes such as Achilles, Odysseus, and especially Oedipus, the only hero to merit full marks according to Raglan's twenty-two-point hero paradigm.[6] Aptly demonstrating that the construction of the scale serves as a commentary on the constructors' social orientation and class interests, says Blackburn, is the fact that Raglan's scale affords the fewest points to Robin Hood, the social bandit. Moreover, he continues, "The bias of these 'comparative' studies was demonstrated without even crossing the Bosporus when Alfred Nutt applied Hahn's criteria to Celtic material and found it wanting."[7]

As non-European heroes once failed to measure up to classical European standards, Indian folk heroes have often failed to measure up to Indian classical standards gleaned from ancient Sanskrit texts. Blackburn refers rather loosely to the typification of these standards as the "puranic hero," that is to say, the courtly hero who predominates in myth compendia known as *puranas*. In a heuristic typology, he distinguishes these heroes from "local heroes," who are far more likely to be protagonists expressing what we have come to refer to as "subaltern" values and interests.[8]

In the decades since Blackburn's article, there has been a significant eruption of interest in folk heroes, which has manifested in some superb studies of folk epic.[9] A major moment in the study of heroes arrived with the publication of an edited volume entitled *Oral Epics in India*.[10] There have also been some intriguing epic studies, including a fine introduction to and translation of *Pabuji*, an oral epic about a popular Rajasthani Rajput hero.[11] Most recently there is Alf Hiltebeitel's ambitious and provocative volume, *Rethinking India's Classical and Oral Epics*, which, inter alia, critiques Blackburn's theory that marital epics develop in predictable paths from cults of deified heroes and proposes various ways in which oral epics "reenplot" classical epics.[12] These works have demonstrated

6. Blackburn, "The Folk Hero and Class Interests in Tamil Heroic Ballads," and Nutt, "The Arayan Expulsion-and-Return Formula in the Folk and Hero Tales of the Celts." On life pattern, see also de Vries, *Heroic Song and Heroic Legend*, as well as discussion in Beck, "The Hero in a Contemporary, Local Tamil Epic."

7. Blackburn, "The Folk Hero and Class Interests in Tamil Heroic Ballads," citing Nutt, "The Arayan Expulsion-and-Return Formula in the Folk and Hero Tales of the Celts," 132.

8. Blackburn, "The Folk Hero and Class Interests in Tamil Heroic Ballads." See also his "Patterns of Development for Indian Oral Epics" and "Death and Deification." For a thorough critique of Blackburn's ideas on development and spread, see Hiltebeitel, *Rethinking India's Oral and Classical Epics*.

9. A list of major works that consider epic and/or cultic context includes, inter alia, Beck, *The Three Twins*; Blackburn, Claus, Flueckiger, and Wadley, eds., *Oral Epics in India*; Flueckiger and Sears, eds., *The Boundaries of the Text*; Ann Grodzins Gold, *A Carnival of Parting*; Hiltebeitel, *Rethinking India's Oral and Classical Epics*; Hitebeitel, *The Cult of Draupadī*, vol. 1, *Mythologies* and vol. 2, *On Hindu Ritual and the Goddess*; Lutgendorff, *The Life of a Text*; Miller, "The Twenty-Four Brothers and Lord Devnārāyaṇ"; Richman, ed., *Many Rāmāyaṇas*; Roghair, *The Epic of Palnāḍu*; and Sax, *Dancing the Self*. There is also ongoing work by John D. Smith on folk *Mahabharat*s and by Susan S. Wadley, whose title for a book manuscript is currently "Raja Nal and the Goddess: Inscribing Caste and Gender in the North Indian Oral Epic *Dhola*."

10. Blackburn et al., eds., *Oral Epics in India*.

11. Smith, *The Epic of Pābūjī*.

12. Smith, *The Epic of Pābūjī*. For concise presentation of these arguments, see Hiltebeitel's second chapter "Oral Epics," 11–47. For application of his theory in the Rajasthani context, see his third chapter, "The Epic of Pābūjī," 88–120.

the variety and complexity of heroic scenarios in the Indian context and have proven time and again another of Blackburn's points: heroes under investigation cannot be understood without taking into account the social location and strategic interests of performers.[13]

Although the work on oral epic has done much to broaden our understanding of hero veneration in India and to correct the elitist bias that results from inordinate attention to upper-class traditions, especially those transmitted by Brahmins, in some ways the work has inadvertently bolstered another old standard, which is also troublesome. Because so much of the literature on heroism has been located in the sphere of epic, scholarly focus on epic has tended to render the paltry research on nonepic hero veneration as background or context.[14] There are some good treatments of epic narrative that do seriously explore, or even privilege, cultic context, and they are all the richer for it (Philip Lutgendorf's *Life of a Text* is a prime example), but they are limited by the scope of inquiry, which is determined by a primary interest in epic and its tellings. In most cases, expanding the focus to explore at length nonepic heroic traditions in the area would render any such study an unwieldy and unmarketable tome.[15] One exception to the tendency to focus predominantly on epic is work on hero memorials, but the studies on commemorative stones have generally been preoccupied with iconography or with speculation about patterns of diffusion in martial cultures.[16] These works have not been able to tell us much about narrative representation or ritual veneration.

Understanding more fully the range and depth of the heroic requires that our gaze shift every so often to inspect sources inadequately investigated or utterly ignored or, best yet, previously unknown. In my work I have chosen to utilize epic as context and focus on two subjects, which are too vast to be treated adequately in a single volume. Following the advice of colleagues and editors, I have therefore decided to treat them separately. The first subject, which I address in this volume, comprises largely Rajput ancestral or domestic hero traditions in which Rajput women typically serve as performers of rituals for deceased heroic family members. The second is the intricate constellation of cultic hero traditions performed either by *bhopas* (loosely translated as "mediums" in that they communicate with divinities, in this case through possession), who hail from a variety of caste and class backgrounds, or by Brahmin priests, who are few and far between but quite visible in their association with the royal hero cult in Udaipur.[17] Shrines that service hero cults draw devotees from a variety

13. The point is made frequently in recent folklore studies. See, for example, Narayana Rao, "A Rāmāyaṇa of Their Own," 115.

14. A good example of exploration of the heroic outside the epic context is the much-cited work by K. K. N. Kurup, *The Cult of Teyyam*. See also Peter J. Claus, "Heroes and Heroines in the Conceptual Framework of Tulu Culture," and his essay, "The Siri Myth and Ritual." Stuart Blackburn's work on epic development is related to work with bow songs; see his *Singing of Birth and Death*.

15. Or multiple volumes in a series, such as Alf Hiltebeitel's Draupadi volumes.

16. Good examples are Settar and Sontheimer, eds., *Memorial Stones*, and Thapar, "Death and the Hero."

17. Another term that might be used loosely is "shaman," but this term is troublesome in that it tends to connote otherworld journeys, which are not made by *bhopas*. For recent reflection on the difficulties of employing the term "shaman" interculturally, see Smith, "The Disappearance and Recovery of Possession in Sanskrit

of backgrounds, but are considered déclassé by many members of high castes, including Rajputs. Although these subjects merit separate volumes, however, I want to make some preliminary observations about them both by way of providing a foundation for this two-part project.

Domestic and cultic traditions portray heroes and heroism in ways that diverge considerably from the representations that proliferate in epic. For example, they often feature themes that are either muted or absent in epic. Looking at cultic and domestic traditions enables us to expand our notion of the heroic and of "what counts" as heroic; those whose enduring interest is epic can thereby understand more fully the choices made by epic performers, who are doubtless familiar with many of the constructions of heroism contained in their mothers' and fathers' stories and with cultic depictions by priests or by *bhopas* as they compose and relate their songs.[18] The sexy bejeweled bridegroom hero of whom women often sing in *ratijaga* rituals (the lovely man with dangling *lalas* [glass turban pendants], an alluring pajama string, and luxurious velvet slippers) may also be an epic's saffron-donning ascetic who dies with detachment but, while alive—and this is often deemphasized in epics devoted to deified heroes and may be altogether lost in the scholarship on epic—is intermittently, ambivalently, or poignantly lovesick.[19] Such themes, however faintly whispered or even explicitly and heartily denied in some epics, presumably resonate with women who hear epic performances, and even with men who have had their mothers' songs reinforced in their memories by the repeated performance of women's *ratijaga* songs on auspicious occasions.[20] In cultic traditions as well, eroticism finds expression. In this vein I might mention that one of the major duties of heroes is to cure female infertility—a duty that has often resulted in accusations of improper client-patient relations.[21]

Epics and other narrative traditions largely concerned with war frequently thwart relationships between men and lovers or wives and affirm the values of renunciation expressed metaphorically (by the hero's saffron turban) or contextually, as when the hero is initiated by an ascetic, or he is disguised for a time as an ascetic, or he is reluctantly dragged into marriage and then fortu-

---

Literature." I use the term here to refer to a professional healer ritually possessed by a hero. Further discussion on usage follows in my forthcoming volume on cultic hero worship.

18. On the matter of "what counts" and "who counts," I thank Joyce Flueckiger for her oral communication, February 12, 1997. For extensive discussion of women's voices and intertextuality, see Harlan, "Heroes Alone and Heroes at Home"; Wendy Doniger, *The Implied Spider*, 79–107; and Ramanujan, "Toward a Counter-System" as well as his "Two Realms of Kannada Folklore."

19. On "the celibate body" evoking "a divine and heroic mystique of epic proportions," in the context of an illuminating discussion of colonialism, nationalism, and asceticism, see Joseph S. Alter, "Celibacy, Sexuality, and the Transformation of Gender into Nationalism in North India," especially pp. 45–46.

20. For an interesting discussion on Pabuji's struggles with asceticism, see Hiltebeitel, *Rethinking India's Classical and Oral Epics*, 96–105. For reflection on the notion that epic is not read, or heard for that matter, for a first time, see Ramanujan, "Repetition in the Mahābhārata," 419, cited in Hiltebeitel, *Rethinking India's Oral and Classical Epics*, 44–45.

21. For instructive conversation on this point I thank Helen Lambert, personal communication, January 1996.

nately liberated by a call to arms just before consummating wedlock.[22] Typically the women in such epics are invested with desire to which the men fall prey or which they are somehow obligated to satisfy.[23] The tendency to portray women as invested with carnality and as romantically aggressive or dangerous has a hoary heritage. Stephanie Jamison has shown how many ancient texts, including epics, represent men as the passive victims of unrestrained female lust.[24]

Moreover, in epics representations of women are frequently unflattering in a variety of other ways. In epics that feature martial heroes (as in many contemporary American action films) women distract, interfere, and make trouble. Pabuji, who is repeatedly referred to as an "ascetic of the desert" but who marries the love-struck woman pursuing him despite his initial disinclination, is called away from his marriage ceremony by a village woman (a goddess incarnate) who wants him to get back her stolen cows, even though she knows he will be killed. In this epic, again as in many action films, women tend to appear at dramatic moments to distract or waylay heroes, instigate conflict, and/or ruin the best-laid plans. And here, as in other epics concerned with war, representations of male heroes and their female relations often reveal a general disinterest in women and an antipathy toward particular women. As John D. Smith has observed, the perspectives offered in epics are overwhelmingly male, and they are at times inarguably misogynist.[25]

Some of the scholarship on epic reinforces the tendency to minimize or marginalize women characters. For example, the informative and otherwise valuable introduction to the volume *Oral Epics in India* presents a typology of oral epic that sets out three models of what epics are "about": the martial epic, the romantic epic, and the sacrificial epic.[26] According to this scheme, martial epics feature male heroes who die in battle and then are worshiped; romantic epics relate romances between men and women who are not worshiped, as well as other romantic matters such as journeying and miracle working; sacrificial epics tell of women who are victimized by injustice and who are worshiped as divinities (goddesses or *satis*). In many cases, assigning one of these genres to specific epics requires a bold determination of what is central to epics. Although designed to present ideal types to which real epics do not adhere perfectly, the typology tends to essentialize, to rob epic of its complex plot, which often includes multiple heroes, some of whom express ambivalence about their roles

---

22. A frequently cited typology of such traditions is Jason, *Ethnopoetics*.

23. *Pabuji* is a case in point.

24. Jamison, *Sacrificed Wife, Sacrificer's Wife*. See also Harlan, "Nala and Damayanti's Reversals of Fortune"; Shulman, "Battle as Metaphor in Tamil Folk and Classical Traditions" and *Tamil Temple Myths*, 105–130; and Anand Pathwardan's film, *Father, Son, and Holy War*, in which a seller of semen-thickening medicine claims that women are nine times more sexually driven than men are. The more typical and conventional/legal (*dharmashastrik*) ratio is 3:1.

25. See Harlan, "Heroes Alone and Heroes At Home," 240, and Smith, "Scapegoats of the Gods," 188.

26. Other typologies utilize these titles but explore different relationships. For example, Heda Jason classes romantic epics as a subgenre of historical epics in *Ethnopoetics*.

and actions. The typology therefore distracts attention from somehow secondary or "nonessential" elements that do not fit the model, however integral and
persistent they might be. Thus *Dhola* is romantic whereas *Pabuji* is martial,
despite the fact that war, dominance, and territory are salient motifs in *Dhola*,
and *Pabuji* contains two key marriages: one for the hero who is much loved and
who displays at least fleeting hesitancy about leaving his bride (he complains a
bit to the goddess), and one for Gogaji, an ascetic hero who has his own epic
but makes an appearance here as the eager suitor of Pabuji's sister. So important are these marriages that each functions as a *parvaro*; Smith translates this
term as "epic episode" but notes that its primary meaning is "battle." The weddings are listed as two of the twelve *parvaros* that structure the singer's performance and help guide the singer "through the complexities of the story."[27] The
commonplace association between war and marriage, which is represented as
inherently dangerous for men, is also to be found, as David Shulman has noted,
in a variety of Tamil myths.[28]

The designation "sacrificial" is also misleading. As to what constitutes sacrificial epic, the authors of the typology suggest only that sacrificial epics portray
sacrifice outside the martial context as performed, typically, by south Indian
women, who metamorphose into divinities.[29] Yet, as is so well known as to hardly
bear repeating, epics that are very much given over to the martial often represent both battle and heroic death as sacrifice.[30] A case in point is the self-sacrifice
of the hero Dhebo to Pabuji's hungry goddess, a vulture who (along with other
vultures) consumes his entrails as hors d'oeuvres well before he dies in battle
and makes available the rest of his flesh and blood.[31]

Having wrestled with this typology, Alf Hiltebeitel has gone on to argue
that Smith's translation of *Pabuji* distorts the epic by leaving out crucial frame
stories, all of which are concerned primarily with women.[32] Smith has reason

27. Smith, *The Epic of Pābūjī*, 19–20. On narrative punctuation and chronotopes, see Ramanujan, "A
Flowering Tree," 239.

28. Shulman, "Battle as Metaphor in Tamil Folk and Classical Traditions," 124. See also Sax, *Mountain
Goddess*, 71.

29. More specifically, the category comprises women who die as sacrificial victims of injustice as they
metamorphose into goddesses and *satis*, women whose sacrifice typically occurs on the pyres of their deceased
husbands. For further reflections on this typology and its challenges, see Shulman, "Outcaste, Guardian, and
Trickster," 114, and Gold, *A Carnival of Parting*, 15.

30. See, for example, Hiltebeitel, *The Ritual of Battle*.

31. This is Dhebo, whom Alf Hiltebeitel describes as *bhomiya*-like, although he denies the claim by Stuart
Blackburn, John D. Smith, and Komal Kothari that the epic developed out of a *bhomiya* cult and that it is, as
Kothari maintains, "an elaborated story of a *bhomiya* god," in "Performers, Gods, and Heroes in the Oral Epics
of Rajasthan," 110, quoted in Hiltebeitel, *Rethinking India's Classical and Oral Epics*, 25. An informant told him
that the epic *Alha* takes up the matter of a goddess's need for heroic blood and her dissatisfaction on this count
in the *Mahabharat*: "Because the Pāṇḍavas were not killed, therefore their blood couldn't be utilized to propitiate Devī. Like Sītā, Draupadī was also the avatar of Mahādevī. The blood of the five Pāṇḍavas had to be utilized to propitiate Mahādevī, who was Draupadī herself. But this could not be fulfilled because the Pāṇḍavas
were not killed. And therefore she remains dissatisfied as Draupadī, and comes as Belā"; *Rethinking India's
Oral and Classical Epics*, 496.

32. *Rethinking India's Oral and Classical Epics*, 115.

to see these stories as peripheral: the *bhopa* performer with whom Smith worked knew only one of the stories and did not include any of them in his performances.[33] Thus Smith does not include them in the text proper. Hiltebeitel, by contrast, sees the marginal stories as key. He uses them to decode matters of utmost import in the epic. Suggesting that the stories depict the affairs of goddesses who are very much integral to the "unfinished business" that the oral epic accomplishes, he maintains that oral epics tend to reenplot classical epics, if also to complete or recode their messages.[34] Hiltebeitel's work conveys clearly the idea that what appears in the margins or may seem a peripheral concern in the midst of a narrative can often illuminate and define themes that are crucial.[35]

Another illustration of the tendency of scholarship to emphasize or accentuate features sharply chiseled in dominant imagery and to miss or ignore fainter features—and softer voices—is the omission in Smith's translation of the ten songs that are sung in the context of the weddings of Pabuji and Gogaji. Smith explains that the songs, which "in one form or another" are known to all *bhopa*s with whom he worked, are "non-narrative" songs. By this characterization he presumably means not that the songs are devoid of narrative but rather that they do not advance the narrative of *Pabuji*. He explains that they "resemble independent folksongs, with a single, more-or-less fixed form" and so "differ radically from the narrative songs."[36] Persuaded by their evident distinctiveness, he puts them aside, explaining that he is "concerned only with the epic *parvaro*s proper," but that "the non-narrative material would repay study."[37] He delivers a tempting invitation![38]

Performed as songs of praise inviting deities to the weddings, these songs are an epic's representation of women's *ratijaga* songs. As I have said elsewhere, I see these songs as significant intertextual referents. Sung at auspicious occasions, *ratijaga* songs celebrate domesticity and fertility, themes that are subdued or disparaged elsewhere in the text.[39] It strikes me that Smith's decision to exclude the songs and treat them as not integral to the narrative has the effect of enhancing the narrative's recurring characterization of Pabuji as a warrior-ascetic and an incarnation of Ram's brother Lakshman from the epic, *Ramayan*.[40]

---

33. Such performances, of course, are never all-inclusive: each performance is conditioned by context, including patronage, and individual inspiration, including both the performer's personal interpretation/understanding of his "text" and his inclination (even whim) in any given performance. The term *bhopa* is used to refer to a *Pabuji* performer. When used in this context, it does not designate a medium who becomes possessed by a cultic hero.

34. Hiltebeitel, *Rethinking India's Oral and Classical Epics*, 44. Hiltebeitel borrows the term "unfinished business" from Smith, *The Epic of Pābūjī*, 93.

35. Hiltebeitel, *Rethinking India's Oral and Classical Epics*, 114–120.

36. Smith, *The Epic of Pābūjī*, 20, where he also notes that they are sung to different tunes.

37. Smith, *The Epic of Pābūjī*, 20.

38. Response to this can be found in Harlan, "Heroes Alone and Heroes at Home."

39. Harlan, "Heroes Alone and Heroes at Home."

40. See Hiltebeitel's discussion of Lakshman as an ascetic in *Rethinking India's Oral and Classical Epics*, 97–99.

श्री पाबू जी   SHRI PABU JI

FIGURE I.I. Pabuji at Mandore

Withholding the songs eliminates hints of ambivalence and silences whispers of alternative or countervailing value.

Much more can be said about the complex ways in which epic traditions absorb and refract perspectives from variant sources and the myriad ways in which epic has been constructed in scholarship, but to do so here would be to privilege epic traditions, counter to the agenda proposed, and to distract from the pressing

FIGURE I.2. Equestrian hero image

business of filling in gaping and hazardous ethnographic potholes.[41] Starting from the periphery, most visible at the roadside memorials to fallen heroes, this book delves into hero worship at home, a milieu in which both men and women tell narratives about the glorious sacrifices of heroes from yesteryear and in which, generally speaking, women perform rituals expressing their values, their desires. Using narratives and rituals as sources, this study examines the ways in which ancestral heroes encapsulate and express the ideals of perfection and masculinity, articulated most clearly against the backdrop of domesticity, householdership, and femininity. Moreover, it considers how representations in hero stories and songs are deployed by men and women to bolster varying agendas.

Researching Heroes: Environs and Genres

While conducting my research I lived Udaipur, the city in southwest Rajasthan where I had previously done research, and spent my days visiting domestic and cultic hero shrines in Udaipur and its environs, that is to say, the area formerly

---

41. See also Hiltebeitel, *Rethinking India's Oral and Classical Epics*, and Harlan, "Heroes Alone and Heroes at Home" and "Tale of a Headless Horseman."

known as Mewar.[42] Wandering the alleys of the old walled city in Udaipur, strolling along the broad streets of its fashionable central bazaar, and riding in autorikshaws through the suburbs and nearby villages, I discovered shrines with stelai that feature visages of heavily mustached and turbaned heroes and silhouettes of equestrian warriors.

I also made numerous trips to countryside shrines about which I learned while collecting narratives in Udaipur. Some of these were located in elaborate pavilions on the premises of palatial, if often crumbling, estates owned by members of the erstwhile aristocracy. Others were crude stelai located on the borders of fields or alongside roads. Still others were simple whitewashed temples tended by *bhopa*s or by priests, the vast majority of whom are Brahmins. Meandering through Mewar, I repeatedly visited the fortress at Chittor, the medieval capital of Mewar before it was moved to Udaipur. At the gates of Chittor are located some of the best-known hero memorials, which are dedicated to Mewari soldiers killed while defending the fortress against attacks by Muslim armies. These receive regular ritual veneration and special attention during the festivals of Navratri and Dashara, which celebrate the victory of the goddess Durga over her demon foe, and during Jauhar Mela, an annual festival celebrating the three legendary mass immolations of women as their husbands defended the fortress against Muslim conquerors.

Finally, I made long trips to Jodhpur and visited shrines in nearby villages around Jodhpur, in other words, the area formerly constituting Marwar. Many of the women who married into Mewar estates were raised in Marwar. From them I initially learned of the heroes worshiped in their natal families. As with my travels in Mewar, as I visited each village I met many women who hailed from villages elsewhere, and my list of shrines to visit continually grew. At many cultic shrines, moreover, I learned of other shrines dedicated to the same hero. Some of these shrines were said to be located at the places where the heads of decapitated warriors fell, while others were held to be situated where the bodies eventually came to rest.

During my travels I became familiar with three recurring epithets designating heroes (*virs, surs*) who are worshiped.[43] Whereas the first two, *jhunjharji* and *bhomiyaji*, refer to heroes whose actions conform closely to the same scenario, the third, *sagasji*, indicates heroic status despite deviation from that sce-

---

42. For more detailed description of Udaipur and its environs, see Harlan, *Religion and Rajput Women*, 4–6.

43. I have chosen to use the term *vir*, rather than *sur*, when possible in my analysis for many reasons, some of which were suggested in my prefatory note on transliteration. First, *vir* is the term that arose most commonly in conversation, whereas *sur* appears more commonly in Rajasthan's poetic traditions, though *vir* is used there as well. Second, I tend to use the standard Hindi, rather than Rajasthani forms of words because these forms are better known by people (including scholars and students) who know Hindi spoken outside Rajasthan. *Vir* works well for Hindi or Rajasthani, whereas *sur* (in Hindi, *shur*) has variant forms, such as *suro*, *sura*. Third, even if I were to use terms from what is typically called Rajasthani, they would be Marwari, as opposed to Mewari, the dialect spoken in Mewar, where I did most of my work. Fourth, in Mewar, there are many dialects spoken. This is especially true in the case of Rajput women, many of whom marry into households there from other parts of Rajasthan and beyond. Moreover, bardic poetry I have cited is composed in Dingal. Fifth, because of this complex linguistic situation (and most certainly because of the influence of various Hindi media, including films) Hindi is the lingua franca for many living in the urban Udaipur context. I

nario. The *jhunjharji* (also *junjharji*)—the hero most frequently encountered in Mewar, but also appearing in Marwar and eastern Rajasthan—is a warrior who loses his head in battle but manages to continue fighting and to kill many enemies before falling to the ground. The term derives from the reduplicative verb *junjhuno*, "to struggle," which summarizes the desperately difficult situation of the headless warrior striving to achieve his goal of revenge, justice, or reunion with a loved one after suffering the normally fatal wound of decapitation.[44] In some narratives, the struggler's chest develops eyes that guide him; this unsubtly suggests that the warrior "sees" with his heart. The "struggler" is also represented as sprouting a lotus stalk from his neck, which signifies his transcendence of ordinary human existence and experience.[45]

The decapitated struggler is a transitional, metamorphosing being who is still alive in the sense that he has not stopped fighting, yet also beyond life and even death. According to pervasive Hindu beliefs about mortality, death is absolute when the inner self or *atman* of the deceased departs the body during a cremation ritual.[46] In the case of a *jhunjharji*, the *atman* has been liberated from the body (a situation made clear in representations with lotus imagery), yet the body has not yet fallen. In all cases, the body will eventually fall, which will indicate the end of his headless struggling. Typically, the *jhunjharji* fights until he happens to encounter at the edge of some village a woman strolling alone or, more typically, in the company of a female friend. Surprised by the *jhunjharji*, she exclaims, "Look, he has no head!" Instantly the warrior stumbles and falls or tumbles off his horse. Finally he rests. That arriving in female company terminates the warrior's drive is surely related to the widely dispersed notion that heroic (martial or athletic) vigor (*virta*) and contact with women do not mix: even the thought of women can cause distraction and sap a warrior's strength.[47] The convention of encountering women after furious fighting serves as punctuation

---

have used Rajasthani dialect terms where common Hindi cognates are lacking and when they are used in references to quotations from Rajasthani dialects, and in scholarship on poetics. Having said this, I should caution that the term *vir*, which Rajputs use along with *sur* for their ancestral heroes, is the same term that is used to designate a hero who does not die in battle and is not worshiped as *vir*. It also designates a separate class of divinities that are identified as companions of various well-known deities, especially Shiv and Hanuman (as Balaji or Langur Vir). Unlike the metamorphosed *vir*s discussed here, many of these *vir*s can be controlled by tantric praxis. One *thakur* characterized worship of these beings as "a very low sort of worship" in which "someone uses mantras to control them." Explaining that this kind of *vir* is "generally used for bad purposes," he said that control of them "is magic (*jadu*) use [that is] tantric," and "low-grade tantric" practice at that. He explicitly distinguished them from *jhunjharji*s and other heroic beings studied here. Like the term *shakti*—which can be used for a human (especially a woman) having "power," as an epithet for a goddess, or as a class of bloodthirsty female beings—the term *vir* has a wide semantic range.

44. This word comports nicely with Gregory Nagy's characterization of the ancient Greek hero as "off balance" and in search of equilibrium; remarks in his "heroes" class at Harvard, fall 1996.

45. The lotus is an ubiquitous symbol of transformation and transcendence in Hindu and Buddhist traditions. For an interesting parallel, note the case of Indra. After he slays the demon Vritra, but before he ascends to his position of king in heaven, he sinks to the depths of a lake, where he abides in lotus root. See the discussion of Indra (especially in the context of the fifth book of the *Mahabharat*) in Dumézil, *The Destiny of the Warrior*, 124–125.

46. On the social construction of death and sacrificial cremation, see Knipe, "Sapiṇḍīkaraṇa," and Parry, "Sacrificial Death and the Necrophagous Ascetic."

47. The notion that contact with women can sap men's strength in war or games is, of course, prevalent in many cultures.

at the end of a socially approved period of supermundane martial miracle work-ing. It occurs after the warrior has achieved his military goals and before he manages to return home.[48] Termination of the berserk hero's killing frenzy is clearly a point at which closure is socially beneficial: the warrior "drops dead" outside society, which the women represent and demarcate.[49] The shrine for the *jhunjharji*'s body is generally understood to be located at the edge of soci-ety, and he is considered to be a guardian of the village, estate, or city on whose border his shrine is located. It is not surprising, then, that some *jhunjharji*s are homologized to the deity Kshetrapal, "Protector of the Field," himself iden-tified with the god Bheruji.[50]

The homology with Kshetrapal points to the connection between the *jhunjharji* of Mewar and the *bhomiyaji*, an epithet more commonly employed in Marwar. The term derives from the word *bhumi* or "land, earth" and es-tablishes the hero as a protector of property and soil. The term designates the hero's role as protector of the land, which is in a sense his land: he is a lord or master of the land.[51] Although the derivation of the term points to a different emphasis in the nature of heroism, it signifies the same type of hero known in Mewar as *jhunjharji*. Like the *jhunjharji*, the *bhomiyaji* loses his head in battle but struggles to fight on. In conversations with pilgrims, devo-tees, and scholars in Rajasthan, there emerged no criteria that would distin-guish one of these heroes from the other. Occasionally people made a stab at differentiating the two, but their efforts bore no fruit. They would imme-diately think of exceptions and realize that the two shared the very charac-teristics that at first seemed to distinguish them. For example, some initially ventured the idea that *bhomiya*s were primarily concerned with protecting the land, whereas *jhunjharji*s were more typically occupied with returning stolen cows, but would then think of examples in which the category with which they, being Mewaris or Marwaris, were more familiar, contained ex-amples of both activities.[52] The narratives of *jhunjharji*s and *bhomiyaji*s both include numerous instances of heroes who return cows stolen by rustlers, and contain stories in which the heroes defend land against assault by in-vaders, either rival Hindu kings or Muslim emperors. Moreover, many people use the terms interchangeably. Interviews with wives who married out of one region into the other suggest that women may well contribute to the ten-dency to translate the terms one into the other. For both types, the scenario that entitles the heroes to the epithet is bloody, sacrificial death in battle.

---

48. On the problem of the berserk warrior's threat to peaceful society in ancient Indo-European cultures, see Dumézil, *The Destiny of the Warrior*, 115–137.

49. On the myth of Cuchulainn, whose warrior wrath is partially calmed by (naked) women when he returns to the capital, Emain Macha, from Ulster's frontier, see Dumézil, *The Destiny of the Warrior*, 134–135.

50. In Banaras, heroes are often also homologized to the directional guardians or *dih-palas*. See "The Bir Babas of Banaras," 79–84.

51. The term is also used to refer to a category of landlord. Laḷas's *Rājasthānī Sabd Kos* provides as a syn-onym *bhumidhari*, s.v. This dictionary also defines *bhomiya* as someone who, protecting cows, Brahmins, *dharm*, a village, or land, dies fighting and attains paradise (Virgati), s.v.

52. On *bhomiya*s and cattle, see Kothari, "Performers, Gods, and Heroes in the Oral Epics of Rajasthan," 110.

The other epithet that is commonly employed for heroes is *sagasji*. This term, prevalent in Mewar, includes heroes who are not killed in combat. Many are murdered while relaxing at home or praying at the entrance to a temple. Most are stabbed to death, but some inadvertently consume poison, which causes agonizing pain and can impell them to run about crazed and yelling furiously like a warrior in battle.

There is disagreement about the provenance of the term *sagasji*. The most common etymology links the term to *sagati* (Hindi and Sanskrit: *shakti*), a power that is often embodied in martial goddesses such as Kali and Durga, as well as Rajput lineage goddesses or *kuldevis*, and which here refers to the power of a warrior engaged in warfare.[53] Others relate the term to the Urdu word *saksh*, "person"; the etymology implicitly likens the *sagasji*, who is typically known by epithet rather than name, to a sort of "unknown soldier" epitomizing violent death.[54] Like the word *vir*, which means both man and great man or hero, the term *saksh*, in this context means both person and great person, one who has realized innate potential as a person.[55]

In Udaipur, the most visible hero shrine is the two-story Sagasji Bavji temple in Sarv Ritu Vilas, located near the massive City Palace and served by Brahmin priests. It commemorates the death and transformation of Surtan Singh. This hero was stabbed to death by order of his father, the much-revered Maharana ("Great King") Raj Singh, who had been told (many versions say wrongly) that his son was misbehaving in his father's harem. Whereas some variants hold that Surtan Singh (who is also often referred to as Sultan Singh) was accused by a scheming royal advisor of engaging in illicit relations with one of his mother's co-wives, some say he was charged with fancying his own mother. Because the Maharana ordered the assassination, to this day reigning *maharanas* have been barred from entering the temple, which is an extraordinarily busy one. Devotees visit daily, but on Friday the temple is crowded with hundreds of visitors seeking the hero's blessings.

Surtan Singh's brother Sardar Singh also became a *sagasji*. He is worshiped in a private shrine located in the royal family's quarters in the City Palace as well as in a public *sthapana* (shrine) that bears a large painting of Sardar Singh on a wall, not far from the entrance to the City Palace. These *sagasji* brothers are but two of a group of *sagasjis* who died at different times because of palace intrigue and who are worshiped at shrines throughout the city. Some are served by Brahmin priests; others are maintained by *bhopas* haling from various caste backgrounds. Just outside Udaipur in the royal *mahasatiyan* (cremation ground), the shrines of which are generally maintained by a Brahmin household, there are two *sagasji* shrines: one is attended by *bhopas*, who bless and cure devotees

---

53. On *shakti* and female divinities in the context of western India, see Babb, *Absent Lord*, 143–160; Gold, "Gender, Violence and Power"; Tambs-Lych, *Power, Profit, and Poetry*, 108–109 and 186–187; Harlan, *Religion and Rajput Women*, 52–61; Hiltebeitel, *Rethinking India's Oral and Classical Epics*, 38–43 and throughout; and Kothari, "Performers, Gods, and Heroes in the Oral Epics of Rajasthan," especially p. 115.

54. See Laḷas, *Rājasthānī Sabd Kos*, s.v., and Gold, *Fruitful Journeys*, 40.

55. *Saksh*, unlike *vir*, lacks the gender assignment: it can designate a man or a woman. I am grateful to Ali Asani for discussion of the Persian derivation and gender of the term.

FIGURE 1.3. Udaipur City Palace

on a weekly basis. The other (said by some devotees to be Surtan Singh's, by others to be Sardar Singh's, and by still others to be Surtan and Sultan Singh's) recieves routine attention from priests but also annual veneration by the *bhopa* from Sarv Ritu Vilas.

All these heroes—*jhunjharjis*, *bhomiyajis*, and *sagasjis*—are considered to have died exceptionally violent deaths and so have come to be identified with violence. Victims of violence, they have also conquered death, their excruciating initiation into divinity investing them with the power to control life and death. Their death manifests their *sat*—goodness or trueness (hence the term *sat* is sometimes equated with the term *sattva*)—as warriors, but also their *rajas*, their kinetic force or passion, a quality (*gun*) most commonly identified with the warrior class (Kshatriya *varn*).[56] As divinities, the heroes continue to be associated with these qualities. The *sattvik* (pure, good, true) character is most fully evident in the divine heroes whose natures, on balance, are thought to be peaceful. They take food offerings such as sweets and milk concoctions, which are thought to be cooling and pacifying. (*Sattvik* cultic heroes who possess *bhopas* manifest themselves in *shanti bhav*, peaceful influence, mood: their

56. These are two of the three *guns* (qualities): *sattva, rajas, tamas* (lethargy, torpor, inertia). Perhaps the best-known discussion of these is found in the *Bhagavad Gita* within the *Mahabharat*. Rajputs often consume food and other substances generally classified as *tamasik*, but which may effect in Rajputs a *rajasik* response. For discussion of the *guns* on this point, I thank McKim Marriott, October 18, 1997. On the *sattvik* and *rajasik* natures of Kshatriyas, see Davis, *Rank and Rivalry*, 49–51. On the dual nature of Kshatriyas, see also Goldman, "Rāmaḥ Sahalakṣmaṇaḥ."

FIGURE I.4. Brahmin priest at Surtan Singh's temple, Sarv Ritu Vilas, and, above, a portrait of Maharana Raj Singh

bhopas sway gently and speak softly.) The *rajasik* character is most apparent in those warriors whose overall nature is thought, on the whole, to be irascible. They take offerings such as alcohol, opium, and tobacco, which are thought to heat the body and inflame the passions. (*Rajasik* cultic heroes who possess *bhopas* manifest themselves in *ugra bhav*, fierce influence, mood: their *bhopas* shake violently and shriek with utter abandon.) Characterized as predominantly fierce or as peaceful, all heroes, domestic and/or cultic, are both *sattvik* and *rajasik*. Even the most pacific are testy at times, and even the most volatile are calm enough to find pleasure and be judicious in their dealings with devotees. For the most part they are helpful if properly fed, irritable if kept waiting for offerings.

Heroes Empowered and Heroes Devoured: The Goddesses' "Goats"

Whatever their preference in terms of food offerings, the heroes themselves are food offerings. Like all Rajputs, every hero is a devotee of a *kuldevi*, a *devi* or

Saptamatrikas or "Seven Mothers" of Sanskrit literature) depicted along with Bheruji on the embossed pendants many Rajput women wear. A similar "appetizer scene" is also found in the *bhomiya* song that is included in the ten songs sung before the marriages of the heroes Pabuji and Gogaji, who weds Pabuji's sister.[62] In many such narratives and songs, the hero is explicitly identified as or likened to a goat who offers himself to his goddess or goddess substitute (bird, which may have yet another identity, as in the case of the vulture/mother). Thus Pabuji's *bhomiya* song images the hero as a goat killed by enemies as the hungry she-vultures (who are pervasive in this Rajasthani poetic tradition and others) circle above, waiting to feast on their tasty "goat" flesh after having sampled one of his organs.[63]

The correlation between the battling hero and the sacrificial goat is articulated with striking clarity in the goat sacrifice rituals that occur on Navratri. In the spring of 1991, I spent much of this festival visiting the palace belonging to an aristocratic family that once governed Amet, a *thikana* granted by the Mewar Maharana.[64] During Rajasthan's vernal Navratri, goat sacrifices were performed on the seventh, eighth, and ninth days for three different goddesses: one for Karni Mata, the chosen deity (*ishtadevta*) of the family; one for Naganechaji, a goddess that had been imported into the family generations ago by a bride; and the last for Ban Mata, the family's official *kuldevi*. For Ban Mata, a special tantric ritual was performed in which she was offered bits of spiced goat heart and liver.

My Rajput host, Prabhuprakash Singh, explained to me that Navratri is a festival in which the Rajputs of times past worshiped the goddess so that they would be successful in military campaigns launched on Dashara. Even today, after sacrificing goats for the goddess, the Rajputs spend Dashara cleaning and worshiping their weapons. When I asked my host whether Navratri and Dashara didn't also have something to do with Ram's war with and victory over the demons as told in the *Ramayan*, he said that some people in Rajasthan had come to think of the holidays as being mostly about Ram, but that this was the fault of the British, who wanted to subdue Rajputs by convincing them to worship docile, pastoral deities like Vishnu, of whom Ram and also Krishna are incarnations.[65] He stressed then—and affirmed again in a recent trip, which coincided with fall's Navratri—that for Rajputs Navratri and Dashara are both for the goddess Durga (to whom tutelary goddesses are homologized), and that the

---

62. For detailed exegesis of this song, see Harlan, "On Headless Heroes"; see also Smith, *The Epic of Pābūjī*, 20.

63. For anaysis of this popular song, which is also sung independently of *Pabuji*, see chapter 4.

64. Navratri is celebrated during the fall and spring. The vernal Navratri is often called "little Navratri" as opposed to the more prominent one celebrated in autumn.

65. Having observed the ritual cycle in a Rajasthan village in the 1960s, Brij Raj Chauhan remarks that Dashara was not a major holiday in the village and that "Ram's victory over the demon king Ravan is not celebrated on this day in the part of the country, and Ram Lila in the form one sees it in Uttar Pradesh is hardly observed in that form in southern Rajasthan. Essentially Navratra not Dashara is the festival enjoyed by the villagers as a community," 199. During Navratra (Navratri) and only during Navratra all the deities of the village are worshiped, the Rajputs perform animal sacrifices, and the *bhopas* in the village goddess's shrine become possessed and offer predictions for the coming year, 185–189.

chief event of the holiday period occurs on Mahashakti Navmi (the final day of Navratri), the date on which is made the final goddess sacrifice, the one for the *kuldevi*.

It is widely believed that feeding the goddess, who embodies *shakti* (power) and indeed bears the epithet Shakti, enables devotees to wield weapons infused with *shakti*/Shakti. As we shall see, the sword itself is often referred to as a *shakti* and identified with and as the goddess. Moreover, swords and other sharp weapons drink blood, chew and spit *pan* (a concoction with various ingredients including betel nut, which dyes lips and saliva blood red), and so forth. Weapons that have tasted blood acquire blood lust. Craving more victims and prepared for carving, they are worshiped with special reverence on Dashara. Such powerful and hungry weapons have protected and empowered the many devotees who feed the goddess and from among whom she receives her special protégé-victims, who choose to offer themselves as *balidan*, a sumptuous meat sacrifice.

The word "choose" is key. Whereas enemies are assumed to die and be devoured by the protagonists' goddesses counter to their desires—they worship another *kuldevi*, if they worship a goddess at all—heroes who die in battle are represented as desiring their heroic death, which brings them and their descendants glory and fame.[66] In narratives, their choice is indicated in two ways. As we have seen, some heroes are explicitly proclaimed to be saffron-donning, which means that they have put on a saffron turban (and perhaps other saffron garments as well), in anticipation of certain death in an unwinnable war. This type of war is called a *saka*, literally a "cutting down"; its outcome is sure enough that it is frequently preceded or accompanied by a *jauhar*, a mass immolation of women (*satis*) and often their children as well.[67] Putting on saffron is an act analogous to the choice made by a goat to become the goddess's offering. Rajputs and others commonly believe that the goat indicates willingness to be a victim by twitching or shivering in front of the goddess's shrine or icon. In the goat sacrifices I have witnessed, several goats have been set loose in the courtyard in front of a sacred icon. The one who faces the altar and twitches has been deemed to have expressed his desire to be sacrificed.[68]

The second way in which such a choice is indicated is even less ambiguous. The hero slices off his own head—and usually offers it directly to the goddess—before beginning or rejoining a battle. The best-known example of this is that of the hero Kallaji, a published song for whom exclaims, "You cut off your head and offered it to the feet of [the goddess] Jagadamba!"[69] In cases such as this, a warrior is most succinctly identified as the sacrificer as well as victim. With one stroke of his sword, he cuts and renders himself the goddess's goat.

66. Greek heroes, such as Achilles, seek *kleos* (glory), which Achilles earns, as well as a homecoming (*nostos*), which Achilles is denied; Gregory Nagy, remarks in his "heroes" class, Harvard, fall 1996.

67. On *saka*, see Ziegler, "Action, Power and Service in Rajasthani Culture," 69, and Harlan, *Religion and Rajput Women*, 122–123.

68. On an animal shaking (or nodding) in the context of sacrifice and the myth of the buffalo Mahisha, see Biardeau, "Brahmans and Meat-Eating Gods," 25.

69. This song is found in a pamphlet published by Śil Śarma, *Ārati*.

FIGURE 1.6. Kallaji image, Chittor

Some Rajputs have said that this gesture precludes the humiliation or emasculation that results from decapitation by an enemy. Moreover, when heroes are fighting Muslims, self-decapitation precludes decapitation by an "unclean" hand that might have once killed cows or desecrated sacred images.[70]

Whether the result of an enemy blow or of a self-inflicted wound, the hero's death is death at the perfect time: in the heat of battle and while in the service of the goddess. It is also in the perfect place: the battlefield, in the imagination of Rajputs and many other Rajasthanis, is, as the *Bhagavad Gita* terms it, the *dharmakshetra*, "field of duty." Dying at the time, and in the place, of duty makes the hero's death the perfect death and evinces the Rajput's fitness as a perfect sacrificial victim. As we shall see, even the *sagasji*, who dies after being ambushed or poisoned, is construed as implicitly adhering to this paradigm of martial perfection. Perfection, however, is a construction rendered by persons from different social locations and with diverging interests. Any notion of perfection reveals different orientations, beliefs, and values, even as it presumes, and perhaps challenges, a certain continuity of perspective arising from what is often termed the "dominant discourse."

Gregory Nagy has described the hero as a "mirror of experience."[71] Clearly, studying heroes provides access to the ideals cherished, the desires pursued, and the anxieties experienced by the people basking in their reflective glow. Focusing on heroism is an excellent point of departure for a study of culture and its past, for heroes reflect ever-changing valuations of history and serve as sources of inspiration for facing contemporary challenges and concerns about the future. Asking "for whom is the hero heroic" and "how is the hero heroic" while encountering heroic narratives, songs, and rituals directs attention to the various tensions and shifting alignments between persons with different levels and kinds of status and authority.

Pressing these questions, this study is devoted to offering new ethnographic findings on ancestral hero worship, about which little has been written, with the aims of broadening our understanding of heroism and of celebrating some of the rich variation revealed by sequential focus on everyday domestic worship and local hero cults, which are considered by many upper-caste people déclassé. As we shift the spotlight away from those glorious well-known epics that are so appealing in terms of their complexity and scope, but also draw on them for context when helpful, we encounter some "unknown soldiers" who are as often hailed by epithet as by name, and who are assuredly unfamiliar to most, if not all, scholars of Indian culture. Examining some salient and subtle ways in which these heroes reflect, but also refract, the ever-shifting and indefinite spectrum of cultural meaning, we will encounter some heroic henchmen who are recognizable as the goddess's willing victims, but whose "goatliness" lies in the eye of the beholder.

Before I sketch the plan according to which analysis will proceed, let me say a word or two about some decisions I have made about sources. Some of

---

70. On contagion and Muslim stereotyping, see chapter 2.
71. Comment from his "heroes" class, Harvard, fall 1996.

the narratives to be discussed arise from interviews I conducted during my previous work on religion and Rajput women. I promised anonymity to those
women, most of whom then observed some form of *parda*.[72] Many of the women
whom I initially encountered as informants eventually became friends who
helped facilitate my work in many ways.[73] Because I never formally advised them,
"we are now on the record," I will honor the initial terms of cooperation.
Throughout the pages that follow, then, I characterize women informants in
terms that suggest their "positionality," and do not use their names unless they
gave me permission during my subsequent trips.[74]

Even during my initial interviews, women clearly knew that some of the
details in their stories (including place and family names, as well as the identity
of the heroes) would narrow down the list of possible informants, but were satisfied with the possibility of a limited number of possible sources. The characterizations of them I provide here are not enough to single them out from among
this limited number but, I believe, sufficient to convey their personhood, if you
will, and not represent them as disembodied abstractions or shady voices stripped
of physicality.[75]

This issue of anonymity did not present itself in the case of the professional
singer who performed many songs analyzed in the final chapter. She was eager
to see her fame spread! I should not, and will not, however, reveal the names of
the other singers, who were obviously shy about performing for a microphone,
if also concerned about possible imperfections in their performances.

The texts offered by men present different challenges. Because men have
always operated in the public sphere, I did not offer them anonymity when I
interviewed them about heroes. Nevertheless, when men spoke up while I was
interviewing women to whom I had promised anonymity, I extended anonymity to them if identification would tend to reveal the identity of the women (typically wives) I came to interview. Finally, I have withheld the names of some few
informants who did not want to be identified as the source of certain evaluative
remarks made about others in the context of informal and often wide-ranging

---

72. During the interviews many worried that they would make mistakes, a concern expressed by many
nonscholars who do not share the scholar's delight in textual variants; this was especially clear to me in cases
where women sought initially to refer me to their husbands for the official stories. Taking seriously the wish of
many women to retain their privacy, I have not revealed their names, even though many now undertake more
public activities than they did previously, and some would probably feel comfortable claiming their words, especially words offered during later talks, when they knew that heroes were my primary interest. For a full account-
ing of the "nuts and bolts" of my initial research among Rajput women, see *Religion and Rajput Women*, 14–24.

73. Some of the ways in which I have benefited include introductions to knowledgeable people, tips on
research sites, company on some trips, and moral support during times when circumstances such as rioting
and ill health made research difficult.

74. I was tempted to try to secure their permission to use certain quotes, but then would have an odd,
and seemingly arbitrary, mixture of revealed/unrevealed sources that would be distracting. I decided against
pseudonyms because these often carry unintended connotations that can cause offense.

75. Although my training is in the history of religions, I realize that any book based on fieldwork will
interest anthropologists, who quite rightly insist on this much. I am indebted to Susan Wadley for inspiring
me to render these decisions explicit in the context of an introduction.

conversations.[76] Having specified the terms of engagement, let us ponder momentarily the plan according to which analysis of ancestral hero veneration will proceed.

Strategy and Synopsis

Because heroes do serve as "mirrors of human experience," it is important to have a basic familiarity with some contours of the environment in which hero worship occurs. Before turning to an examination of domestic traditions of hero worship, I thus provide a chapter that provides ethnographic context. Chapter 2 introduces the readers to Rajasthan not as an objective geographical entity but as a subjective and various construct. Its regional "reality" is informed and shaped by a historical legacy that has commonly privileged the actions and interests of Rajputs, the dominant caste in this part of India. The chapter examines the stereotype of the "martial Rajput" over the span of the past few centuries and explores the inevitably imprecise but evocative concepts of "martial ethos" and "Rajputness" as construed by Rajputs and others, including scholars. From the ranks of these "martial Rajputs" come the overwhelming majority of the heroes worshiped by Rajputs in Rajasthan.[77]

The book then devotes two chapters to domestic hero narratives. These chapters ponder scenarios in which the slaughter of heroes by enemies constitutes sacrifice to protective goddesses who are emblematic of their bloodlines but also identified with the interests of society, which is represented as the protégée of Rajput heroes dying in battle and is rendered feminine in relation to their evident masculinity. Chapter 3 investigates consistent and divergent ways in which men and women understand heroes who die fighting enemies as bequeathing to Rajput families glory and status. It then suggests that to the extent that females are conceived as requiring sacrifice by males, men and women are envisioned as having inimical interests. More specifically, it looks at narrative representations of women who demand, if also dread, heroic sacrifice and whose mere presence at the margins of society dispatches heroes to heaven and denies them their desired, but potentially dreadful (headless), homecoming. In so doing, it discerns another alliance between inimical others, in this case the women with whom men are most intimate and hostile men.

Arguing that heroic death transcends distinctions of good/bad character and timely/untimely death, chapter 4 contemplates the relationship between hero-*balidan* and blood-loving goddess, who protects and is protected by her hero

---

76. My hope is to remain worthy of the epithet *bholi*, an epithet given me as a compliment by one of the women I have now known over twenty years. Although I had read Ann Gold's work and learned that this term is in fact a compliment (its connotation being one of nonduplicity or nonmanipulation rather than one of simple-mindedness or stupidity), I asked her what she meant. She replied that it meant that what I said to people's faces is what I said behind their backs.

77. The others (non-Rajputs) are considered to conform to the martial ideal that these Rajput heroes summarize.

consort. It examines the hero's assumption of the epithet Bheruji (Bhairava), which expresses his achievement of divine status through sacrifice but also states his continuing intimacy with the goddess he served as self-sacrificing soldier. This chapter examines his dual incarnation as Kalaji-Goraji, "Dark-Light" Bheruji, whose persona both distinguishes and unites opposed attributes or tendencies such as salaciousness and sexual restraint. It then considers the characterization of hero-goat as Bheruji in the context of other constructs with which heroes are associated, whether in narrative or informal discourse. Analyzed first are ancestors and ghosts; then ascetics and criminals, both considered, like ghosts, to be actively or potentially threatening outsiders.

Chapter 5 investigates the verbal iconization of heroes in women's songs, which, picking up where stories leave off, move the hero from past to present and celebrate his return to devotees in the context of *ratijagas*. Thinking through these songs' scant but significant references to, and dense condensations of, narrative, it argues that women's ritual hospitality resocializes heroes once banished by women and renders them well-disposed and much-desired guests with whom various forms of social intercourse is expected and accepted. Songs express what women want and suggest how men who have sacrificed themselves can be put to good use as providers and guardians of the good life, with its abundance of progeny, provision for material needs, satisfaction of sensual longings, and manifestation as social order. Having examined songs for heroes, the chapter situates them in relation to songs for the other main recipients of *ratijaga* hospitality. Treated first are ancestors, with whom heroes are identified and from whom heroes are also distinguished by virtue of their perfection. Next come Bherujis. frolicking in gardens and inciting the passion of women, who want to see their *lala*s "all night long." Then there are the *sati*s, rendered in memorial stelai and lyrical icons as heroes' human complements and understood as figures whose death synchronizes and unites human and divine femaleness. Finally, we arrive at goddesses. The placation of these most ultimate females requires not only sacrifice by men but also hymns of praise by women, whose interests, like their goddesses', may ultimately render men divine henchmen.

2

The Land of Heroes

Rajasthani Soil and Rajput Blood

As anyone who has glanced at the tourist literature on India doubtless knows, Rajasthan is famous for its martial heritage and traditions of heroic sacrifice. In the images offered for public consumption on the state's web page, in the tourist pamphlets produced in India and abroad, in the copious collections of armor and antique weaponry displayed in public museums and private homes, and on the inscriptions and plaques on heroic monuments, Rajasthan's military history finds current expression. Elegant *havelis* (urban mansions) and even modest homes sport decorative images of guardian figures with horses or elephants on entryway walls.[1] The silhouettes of crenellated walls and crumbling battlements snake along the rocky Aravalli Hills, never letting the visitor forget that Rajasthan, literally "Land of Kings" is a space organized by centuries of martial challenge.

Analyzing the idea of Rajasthan as an imaginative construct, Derick Lodrick has argued that Rajasthan has been perceived and organized as a discrete region by outsiders for the past four centuries. Having traced the administration and conceptualization of the territory roughly demarcated by Rajasthan's contemporary borders through periods of Muslim and British rule and having surveyed Indian nationalist writing, he shows how Rajasthan has been constructed as an area dominated by Rajput political and cultural hegemony.[2]

Although fleshing out the idea of Rajasthan as a subjective reality is an unsatisfactory sort of business—there are, after all, at

---

1. Examples of guardian figures and some fascinating iconographic innovations are to be found in Wacziarg and Nath, *Rajasthan*.

2. Lodrick, "Rajasthan as a Region," 1.

least as many subjective Rajasthans as there are people who have lived in or known of Rajasthan—it is not wholly inaccurate to observe that much of the imagery in the plethora of Rajasthani expressive traditions reflects Rajput heritage, dominance, and patronage. In Rajasthan, members of other castes have had to take account, in their cultural representations and their political struggles, the great power of Rajputs to affect and control their lives. Moreover, the conceptualization and naming of Rajasthan as the "land of kings," who were overwhelmingly Rajput, reflect the orientation that Rajasthanis from all castes have for centuries internalized, enacted, appropriated, confronted, and in various ways resisted.[3]

In an essay entitled "Becoming Rajasthani: Pluralism and the Production of *Dhartī Dhorāṅ Rī*," Joan Erdman has described various ways in which folk and classical artists as well as their governmental and private patrons in the decades since Independence have sought to represent Rajasthan as a state that combines both nationalist, patriotic fervor and regional, cultural sensibilities, which are predicated on a shared perception of martial heritage and esprit. To illustrate these commitments, Erdman analyzes the composition and performance of the 1970s multimedia extravaganza entitled *Dhartī Dhorāṅ Rī* (Desert Land) in Jaipur, the state capital.[4] A cursory glance at salient motifs of this program, which was attended by prominent politicians and members of the business community in Jaipur as well as by villagers during its tour through the countryside, indicates the intimate connection between patriotism and cultural preservation on the one hand and the figure of the Rajput on the other. Dated roughly midway between Independence and this writing, the program explicates the linkage between legitimacy of authority and a cultural heritage dominated by Rajputs that is simply assumed or implicit in much of contemporary Rajput political thought and rhetoric.

Dhartī Dorāṅ Rī begins, perhaps predictably, with the lines: "This land of heroes, Rajasthan!"[5] The next few lines portray the land itself as a "tale of bravery" that has "reverberated with the sounds of battles" in which "Rajputs have donned the sacrificial orange" (saffron). It goes on to describe the beauty of the Rajput hero, with special attention to the magnificence of his mustache. Even in this representation of Rajasthan as a modern secular state that embraces various communities, the stalwart mustached Rajput remains an imposing and focal representation of virtue and heroism, while the land, Rajasthan, is portrayed as the locus for the enactment of Rajput bravery.[6]

3. For an example of resistance in Rajasthan, see Harlan, "Satī: The Story of Godāvarī," where I also note that the area roughly delineated by the term Rajasthan was previously known as Rajputana, which makes explicit the link between land and Rajput rulers.

4. According to Erdman, the phrase "dhartī dhorāṅ rī" juxtaposes two images, *dharti*, or "land, earth" (illustrated in the program with slides of the immovable Aravalli Mountains) and *doran*, "desert" (illustrated with slides of shifting sand dunes). These images convey twin commitments to retain heritage and welcome innovation; Erdman, "Becoming Rajasthani," 70.

5. The line recalls the opening sentence of a comic book devoted to the Mewar hero Maharana Pratap: "Rajasthan in western India was the home of the valiant Rajputs"; *Rana Pratap*, 1.

6. For a general discussion of the sacrality of geography in Hindu nationalist discourse, see Varshney, "Contested Meanings," 238. Sudhir Kakar also cites Varshney and addresses this theme in *The Colors of Violence*, 30–40.

This covalent imaging of Rajasthan and Rajput is suffused with gendered nuance. Having starkly summarized Rajasthan through verbal iconization of the Rajput heroic man, the production then turns to treat Rajput women. It pays special tribute to Hadi Rani, the Mewari Rajput queen who cut off her head so that her husband would not be distracted by thoughts of her while he was off at war.[7] In this context, the text proclaims that if a Rajput man can frighten lions, a Rajput woman can "roar like a lioness"; it then identifies Rajput women as "the secret of Rajput honor."[8] Elsewhere I have had much to say about the representation of Hadi Rani as an exemplar of Rajput feminine virtue and wifely duty.[9] Here what is important is the way in which the glorification of a region is clearly tied to images drawn from the dominant caste, the Rajput, together with the way in which those images are starkly gendered. In this performance piece, as in the many Rajput comic books readily available in bazaars, the writings of local historians, the speeches of politicians, and the tales told by parents to their children, Rajasthan's history, its well of inspiration, is one of Rajput heroes who lived way back then, "when men were men" and "women were women."[10] In sum, in this politico-poetic text, regional and Rajput-caste identity are construed, conjoined, and conveyed in heavily gendered idioms. As "the land of heroes," Rajasthan is portrayed as the theater of masculine virtue and performance, distinguished from, if also at times complementing, the enactment of femininity and subjugation.

As is well known, the British tended to imagine India and Indians as weak and effeminate, the exception being members of the "martial races," with whom the rulers often felt a special affinity.[11] The respect due Rajputs as embodiments of martial and masculine virtue was argued vividly by Col. James Tod in his *Annals and Antiquities of Rajasthan* (1829), where he surveyed and evaluated Rajasthani history and culture. An agent much celebrated to this day in Rajasthan, Tod was especially enamored of Mewar, which remains famous throughout India as a bastion of resistance to Muslim authority.[12] Like his compatriots, Tod found in the Rajputs kindred souls who were adept at horsemanship and blood sports ranging from tiger hunting to pig sticking.[13]

7. Hadi Rani is frequently transliterated as Hari Rani in English writings.

8. Erdman, "Becoming Rajasthani," 68. On the "contemporary lionization of women" by Christian fundamentalists, see Randall Balmer, "American Fundamentalism," 49.

9. *Religion and Rajput Women*, 160–169, 198–202.

10. On the deployment of "Rajput war cries" in right-wing electoral strategy, see McKean, *The Divine Enterprise*, 38.

11. On assigning purely masculine qualities to warriors (Kshatriyas) and the colonialist appreciation of "hard masculine valour," see Nandy, *The Intimate Enemy*, 76. Nandy contrasts this perspective with an indigenous construction of the Brahmin as masculine and the Kshatriya as feminine; he says the "Brahman in his cerebral, self-denying asceticism was the traditional masculine counterpoint to the more violent, 'virile' active Ksatriya, the latter representing—however odd this may seem to the modern consciousness—the feminine principle in the cosmos"; *The Intimate Enemy*, 10. For further discussion of martial masculinity, also see pp. 20–21, 54–55, 76–87, 80. On hardness and the "softness" of the secular state in contemporary Hindu nationalist discourse, see Hansen, *The Saffron Wave*, 8. For reflections on similar notions in the context of Bengal, see Mrinalini Sinha, *Colonial Masculinity*.

12. On this point, see Rudolph and Rudolph, "The Political Modernization of an Indian Feudal Order," 41–43.

13. Susanne Hoeber Rudolph and Lloyd I. Rudolph describe such sports as "feudal play." See their "Rajput Adulthood," 179.

Tod portrayed the Rajputs as embodying vigor and boldness, revealed through bloody deed and attitude, but also evident in their choice of deity. He understood the bellicose Shiv or Har, widely worshiped by Rajputs and resplendently enshrined in Mewar at the royal Eklingji Temple at Kailashpura, as a deity befitting the martial Rajput.[14] To Tod, the Rajput way of life, epitomized by war, wine, women, and faith in Shiv, distinguished Rajputs from other Indians to such an extent that he could scarcely think Rajputs Hindu. Rather he compared them to mighty heroes from Europe.

> The religion of the martial Rajpoot, and the rites of Har, the god of battle, are little analogous to those of the meek Hindus, the followers of the pastoral divinity, the worshippers of kine, and feeders on fruits, herbs, and water. The Rajpoot delights in blood: his offerings to the god of battle are sanguinary, blood and wine. The cup (cupra) of libation is the human skull. He loves them because they are emblematic of the deity he worships; and he is taught to believe that Hara loves them, who in war is represented with the skull to drink the foeman's blood, and in peace is the patron of wine and women. With Parbutti [Shiv's wife] at his knee, his eyes rolling from the juice of the p'fool and opium, such is the Bacchanalian divinity of war. Is this Hinduism, acquired on the burning plains of India? Is it not rather a perfect picture of the manners of the Scandinavian heroes?[15]

Tod's admiration for the Rajput code inhering in their battle god, together with his flattering exclusion of Rajputs from "meek Hindus" who are "worshippers of kine," comports closely with the perspective on British strategy propounded by my Navratri host, who remarked that fearing Rajput strength, the British wished to render Rajputs docile worshipers of a Vaishnava divinity.[16]

Tod's appraisal of manly Rajasthani Rajputs is also affirmed by another well-known British observer, William Crooke, who wrote toward the end of the nineteenth century. Like Tod and my Rajput host he portrays them as embodiments of boldness and masculine virility. He claims the "dry air of the desert has hardened the muscle and strengthened the chivalry of this most interesting people in Northern India." Contrasting the Rajputs living east of Rajasthan with "their brethren" to the west, he deduces that the "life of the Rajput in the British districts is not calculated to develop the manly virtues." He first links their lack of manliness to domination of those Rajputs by the British: colonial subjugation has deprived each of them of the opportunity to "serve as a soldier of fortune" and so denied him a "fitting occupation." Crooke supports his thesis of flawed masculinity, however, with the observation that the Rajput "despises trade and industrial pur-

---

14. On the identity of "the ancient Rajput and the Shaivite warrior-ascetic" in Mewar and elsewhere, see Kolff, *Naukar, Rajput, and Sepoy*, 81–82. On the Eklingji Temple, see Henri Stern, "Le temple d'Eklingji et le royaume du Mewar (Rajasthan)."

15. *Annals and Antiquities*, vol. 1, p. 57.

16. On the Vaishnava deity Ram and effeminacy, see Nandy, *The Intimate Enemy*, 20. On Shaivism and Vaishnavism among Rajputs in Kathiawar, see Tambs-Lyche, *Power, Profit and Poetry*, 84–86.

suits" and that Rajputs lack "the standard of education which fits them for civil employment."[17] Thus disinterest in education and disdain for technology also effect a lack of masculine vigor in these eastern Rajputs. These charges resonate with the pervasive industrial-era notion of masculinity as manifest in conquest of nature.[18] With this assuredly inferior nature the "backward" Rajputs are identified. Although Crooke's characterization of the plains Rajput is unflattering, it is not utterly disapproving: although the Rajput's "house is pretentious" and "badly kept," and the Rajput "dispenses a rude hospitality," still, his "dignity of manner, his courtliness of address and his *bonhomie* make him a pleasant companion and a favourite with the British officer."[19] And so affinity is preserved.

The observations offered by Crooke seem to have left little impression on Rajputs, wherever their domicile. Rajasthani Rajputs, in any case, hardly speak of Crooke; what need is there when Tod so thoroughly eulogized them? Moreover, in the well-known 1950s essay entitled "The Idea of the Martial Rajput," John Hitchcock describes the martial Rajputs of Uttar Pradesh (a state bordering Rajasthan on the east) in terms reminiscent of Tod's. Although emphasizing that not all Rajputs could be properly understood as martial—for example, those influenced by the Arya Samaj movement or by Gandhian principles—Hitchcock says that for Rajputs inhabiting the village he studied, Tod's admiring characterizations of martial Rajputs has remained both apt and influential.[20] He characterizes them as confident in their innate talent as warriors and leaders as well as in their duty to teach members of lower castes how to behave.[21] Summing up the pervasive stereotype of the in-charge "martial Rajput," he speaks of a "tendency to overweening ambition, extreme pride, and rashness" as well as a "code of revenge and the tendency to rely on force as an instrument of policy."[22] His reflections comport generally with the more detailed characterization of "Rajputness" found in G. Morris Carstair's well-known psychoethnography, *The Twice-Born*, written at approximately the same time about residents of a Mewari village. Early in his description of the Rajput community, Carstairs quotes a Rajput named Amar Singh, who conjoins patriotism for Mewar or Virbhumi ("Land of Heroes") and loyalty to the newly formed Indian nation within the fierce Rajput persona:

17. *Races of Northern India*, 91. Tod describes Rajputs in Rajasthan as "destitute of mental pursuits"; *Annals and Antiquities*, vol. 1, p. 59.

18. Extensive reflection on the identification of femininity with nature is found in Sherry B. Ortner's classic essay "Is Woman to Nature as Man Is to Culture?" See also Nandy, *The Intimate Enemy*, 32.

19. *Races of Northern India*, 92.

20. Hitchcock, "The Idea of the Martial Rajput," 10, 16. On the Arya Samaj and hero worship, see also Lapoint, "The Epic of Guga," 285. On Kshatriyas and Arya Samaj reform, see Pinch, *Peasants and Monks in British India*, 107–109.

21. Hitchcock, "The Idea of the Martial Rajput," 11, 13. About Rajputs in Kalu and Kangra, Crooke says, "They are keenly jealous of their dignity, insisting on receiving a special form of salutation from those of a lower grade, the unauthorised assumption of which was in former days punished by fine and imprisonment"; *Races of Northern India*, 53.

22. Hitchcock, "The Idea of the Martial Rajput," 13. On revenge as a common theme in north Indian "martial epics," but an uncommon one in south Indian ones, see Narayana Rao, "Tricking the Goddess," 113.

Mewar is the best land in all India, the *Vir-bhumi*, of India. . . . We are proud to be men of the *Vir-bhumi*, and I'm ready to fight for religion and for my country—who knows when the need may arise? I'm ready, and all Rajputs are the same. Panthers and tigers don't eat grass and that's what Rajputs are, a carnivorous race.[23]

The comparison of Rajputs to feline predators, especially lions, but also tigers and panthers, is to be found throughout depictions of Rajputs in narrative and lyrical traditions. Moreover, it is evident in the title Singh (Lion), which is borne by every male. In fact, many Rajputs have more than one such cat name: Sher Singhs (Lion Lions) and Bagh Singhs (Tiger Lions) abound. Like the feline hunter, Rajputs tend to be, as Carstair's informant explains, carnivorous. They are not, as Tod so disparagingly noted, "feeders on fruit, herbs, and water." Like alcohol, which many Rajputs drink and which all consume in at least ceremonial sips at weddings, meat is believed to embolden and so enhance martial and sexual performance. Both meat and drink are thought to enrich sperm, enhance physical strength, and fortify martial resolve.[24]

Carstairs goes on to describe the tendency of Rajputs to brook no insult and to demand submission from inferiors.[25] Today Rajput tales of umbrage and retribution for disrespect or insolence abound. Represented as particularly offensive in such accounts are remarks that suggest cowardice among male ancestors or accusations of improper dalliances by female progenitors. Although trading insults of this nature is common sport among men at social gatherings, an insult at the wrong time or place can spark a long-standing grudge, if not speedy retribution. In fact, one Rajput youth, who was discoursing on the subject of avenging insults, noted that grudges resulting from insults are so prolific among Rajputs that at any gathering someone will have refused to come because someone else is there. He offered his personal opinion that all Rajputs require vengeance, and went on to be more specific: "Udaipur Rajputs get you so that you won't know it," while "Jodhpur Rajputs get you so that you do know it," an approach he clearly admired. He then narrated accounts of recent incidents in which Rajputs succeeded in wreaking revenge.

In one story, many variations of which reached my ears during stays in Udaipur, a young Rajput lord from a prominent *thikana* shot out some lights in town. The police sent a messenger to tell him that they were going to arrest him, but the Rajput shaved half the messenger's head and mustache before sending

23. *The Twice-Born*, 108.

24. Ann Gold describes an incident in which Rajput men threatened a woman whom they believed was bringing shame to the community by abandoning *parda* to perform worship of the cultic hero Devnarayan. Before confronting her, Gold says, they cooked meat and drank liquor, activities "appropriate to the nature of Rajput males, as warriors and hunters." These activities are gender-ladened; "Purdah Is as Purdah's Kept," 177–178. On meat eating and Kshatriya ranking, see Dumont, *Homo Hierarchicus*, 74–75.

25. The propensity for avenging insults is pithily summed up by the following couplet: "Don't annoy a Jat in the jungle or a Bania in his shop; Don't provoke a Rajput, who will bring trouble sometime or another." This appears in Singh, *The Castes of Marwar* (with an introduction by Komal Kothari), which is an edition of the *Census Report of 1891* commissioned for Jodhpur Foundation Day, 39. On insults and grudges outside the Rajput context, see Wadley, *Struggling with Destiny in Karimpur, 1925–1984*, 100–102.

him back. Shaving or cutting off an opponent's hair, a common element of battle ritual in Rajput war stories, is an index of triumph and the superior virility to which it attests. The same nobleman (who recently died under much disputed circumstances) is featured in another widely circulated story (again, with multiple versions) that I heard recited by Rajputs while in Udaipur. The gist of the story is that he sought to buy petrol on account at a filling station, but the attendant had orders not to give him any more until he paid his previous bills. The attendant ended up with a bullet in his leg. Although Rajputs I knew tend to represent this alleged shooting as extreme, I have heard it deployed on various occasions to illustrate real "Rajputness." As my raconteur noted, no Rajput boys he knows can stand to be made light of. He said that when he was in school, Rajput boys stood together in redressing a slight to any one of them.[26]

Needless to say, insults are frequently catalysts for combat in many hero stories. A good example is a story narrated to me by the priest at a *bhomiyaji* shrine on the outskirts of Udaipur. His version, along with versions narrated by family members who live with him near the shrine, holds that two Chauhan Rajputs had trouble with their bullock cart right at the spot where a guru had predicted they would ultimately be worshiped. One of them took up the reins in his mouth to pull it and the other chided him, saying, "you're a Rajput, not a Balai [member of a lower caste]!" The result was a fight to the death, and led eventually to the establishment of a cultic shrine in Hiranmagri.

Not only accusations of cowardice and insults to genealogical purity but also actions, including and especially decapitation, prompt bloody struggle and retribution. The *jhunjharji* may have various sorts of unfinished business when his head is severed, but one of them is inevitably giving at least as good as he got.

Two decades after Carstairs, the task of decoding Rajput ethos was taken up with enthusiasm by political scientists Susanne and Lloyd Rudolph, who distinguished the Rajput martial code instantiated in Mewar and glorified by Tod from the more practical and strategic code exhibited in Jaipur, located perilously near Delhi, the imperial capital. The Rudolphs' work notes the benefits that flowed to Jaipur because of its cooperation with the indomitable Moghal rulers, and contrast the Jaipur rulers with those of Mewar, famed and now glorified for their "valor without regard to consequences."[27] It observes that the result of the Mewari rulers' resolve to resist domination was recurrent depopulation and impoverishment, whereas the Jaipuri rulers, allied with their emperors, prospered.[28]

Describing this more pragmatic Rajput sensibility once prevalent in Jaipur, the Rudolphs have outlined a strategy of military alliance supported by and also implemented through marriage alliance, the giving of daughters in wedlock to the Moghal court—a measure signaling both intimacy and security of compact.

---

26. He was referring to his days in Mayo College, but I have heard similar stories from other schools in the area.

27. "The Political Modernization of an Indian Feudal Order," 41.

28. Ruminating on the "Rajput ethic," Ann Grodzins Gold describes Mewar as "the kingdom most perfectly epitomizing the nonpragmatic standards of Rajput valor"; *Fruitful Journeys*, 26. See also pp. 24–25.

Work by Dirk Kolff demonstrates that such military alliances, symbolized and also effected through marriage, were integral to the mode of Rajput adventurism that predominated in the era that ended with the seventeenth century.[29] During that era, he argues, Rajput status was based largely on the enactment of a military, and overwhelmingly mercenary, mode of existence. Conformity to a code of martial plunder, with women as the spoils of conquest and pawns in the game of negotiation and alliance, determined "Rajputness" in northern India. Young Rajput men (jawans), living as mercenaries, styled themselves ascetics for the duration of their martial pursuits but through their martial asceticism earned booty that included women, a homecoming, and its rewards of settled life.[30] Although often hereditary, Rajput status was thus open to recruitment. It could be earned.[31]

Like the Rudolphs, Kolff contrasts this more pragmatic strategic code with the hereditary code articulated most strictly in later centuries by the Rajput denizens of Mewar, for whom impeccable genealogy was the sine qua non of Rajput status. Kolff says that by the middle of the seventeenth century, the "new Rajput genealogical orthodoxy" exhibited in Rajasthan and "particularly Mewar" held sway.[32]

Commitment to the principle of "genealogical orthodoxy" has continued to characterize Rajasthani Rajputs in more recent times, as is illustrated by the comments of the diarist Amar Singh, a member of the Jaipur nobility, who remarked that if he were to be asked to write a history of Jaipur, he would have to "leave out that part which deals with the marriage of Akbar with Raja Man Singh's daughter.[33] Still more recently, the Rudolphs, commenting on rhetoric in nationalist speeches made in Jaipur during the struggle for Independence and also on narratives told later by Rajput men throughout Rajasthan, explain that the "favored tales . . . are not stories of great military victories, but of disasters, and Udaipur, which frequently sacrificed its nobility and prosperity to the chivalric ideal, is still greatly admired even in sober history."[34] And in Udaipur today, the claim that Mewar's monarch is superior to all others (he alone bears the title "Maharana") because the royal family resisted more successfully than others the

---

29. *Naukar, Rajput, and Sepoy.* On Rajput marriage alliances and statecraft, see also Tambs-Lyche, *Power, Profit and Poetry*, 88; Henry Stern, "Le pouvoir dans l'Inde traditionelle"; and Jean-Claude Galey, "L'État et le lignage," as well as his more recent "Reconsidering Kingship in India: An Ethnological Perspective."

30. The commonly recognized period for adventure is twelve years; Kolff, *Naukar, Rajput, and Sepoy*, 81. Jawan (a term imported into Indian English with this spelling) status lasts until age forty; Kolff, 82. In this context, it is interesting to note that according to Jonathan Parry (who worked in Banaras), someone who dies before forty is destined to go to hell; "Sacrificial Death and the Necrophagous Ascetic," 84. As noted above, the goal of homecoming, *nostos*, is a well-known theme in the Greek epic cycle.

31. On the realization of "Rajputness" by various groups, see William R. Pinch's interesting chapter, "Being Vaishnava, Becoming *Kshatriya*," in his *Peasants and Monks in British India*, 81–114; also see Tambs-Lyche, *Power, Profit and Poetry*, 86; Fox, "Family, Caste and Commerce in a North Indian Market Town" (also cited in Tambs-Lyche, 86); and Ziegler, "Action, Power and Service in Rajasthani Culture," 18–26. On the abduction of women as indicative of heroic status in a lower-caste narrative from eastern India, see the tradition of Tulsi Bir in Prakash, "Becoming a Bhuinya in Eastern India," 160–161.

32. Kolff, *Naukar, Rajput, and Sepoy*, 73.

33. Amar Singh Diary, July–December 1933, Jaipur: Wednesday November 29, 1933, p. 411 (citation courtesy of Mohan Sigh, Kanota). For an abridged edition of the volume, which has an introduction and analysis, see Susanne Hoeber Rudolph and Lloyd I. Rudolph, with Mohan Singh, Kanota, *Reversing the Gaze*.

34. Rudolph and Rudolph, "The Political Modernization of an Indian Feudal Order," 42.

Muslim demand for its daughters by fighting recurrent losing battles that culmi-
nated in *jauhar* is proudly and frequently repeated in conversation, tourist tracts,
popular journalism, and ritual.

In western India, and especially Mewar, narration of tales of defeat is integral to the practice of hero worship. With few exceptions, the heroes whose monuments are found on the borders of estates and in public shrines are much-adored
losers. Victory in defeat by enemies is proclaimed incomparably glorious. It is a
scenario rehearsed in the self-sacrifice of heroes who, having earned violent death,
attain the power to grant life and control the lives of the living. Thus the three
sacks of the Mewari fortress of Chittor by Muslims are causes of celebration, and
have been commemorated annually by thousands of sword-wielding Rajputs
during the Jauhar Mela, the first liturgical event of which is formal worship of the
legendary hero Kallaji, whose monument graces the gates of Chittor. First celebrated in the 1960s, it quickly became an annual "family reunion" for Rajputs
seeking inspiration and meaning after their forfeiture of sovereignty.

Identity in the Post-Independence Era:
Nostalgia, Resistance, Adaptation

One often hears from Rajasthani Rajputs the lament that since the establishment of democracy in 1947, Rajput *riti-rivaj* ("code" or, literally, "norm-and-

FIGURE 2.1. Jauhar Mela procession, Chittor

FIGURE 2.2. Rajput boy watching television at Amet Haveli, part of which now contains paying guest rooms and a restaurant, Udaipur

custom") has deteriorated. Although, as in any culture and as in all periods of history, the code of *riti-rivaj* has always fluctuated and adapted, the relatively abrupt cessation of Rajput sovereignty and aristocratic service has mandated that Rajputs adapt quickly and accept the urgent necessity of earning a living that in many cases is felt to be incommensurate with Rajput status and self-image, and so to develop new strategies for achieving economic security while retaining self-respect. Although some have joined the army or police and others have become involved in the transportation industry (driving trucks is considered vaguely analogous to riding horses and guarding property), and more recently some have converted their homes (palaces, urban mansions, modern homes) into guest houses for tourists, many older Rajputs, especially those who feel too old or proud

FIGURE 2.3. Pichola Haveli/Hotel, Udaipur

to adjust, have simply sold possessions to meet expenses and left the sorry business of adaptation to younger generations.[35]

For many Rajputs, the sense of displacement by civil authorities and resentment toward businessmen who have been successful in the post-Independence
period has resulted in frustration, defiance, and nostalgia. Frustration, with its
concomitant demoralization, has been most evident in denunciations of government (generally portrayed as incompetent) and of businessmen, especially
Baniyas (as elsewhere frequently stereotyped as greedy and self-serving). Resistance is exemplified in various antinomian activities of some Rajputs, especially
young men; these range from game poaching to "bashing up" insolent subor-
dinates. It is also reflected in the bravado and approval with which accounts of
such activities are related. Nostalgia has been expressed with particular poi-
gnancy in reverie about adventure and luxury in the days of yore and in the desire
of many Rajput men to have histories written about their lineages or estates.
Stories of yesteryear, which express sadness about loss and evoke solidarity
through recitations of a shared past, are often also heartening. They illustrate
honor and fortify claims to superior social status, even as its achievement has
been to many increasingly elusive.

35. For reflections on adaptations among Rajputs in Kathiawar, see Singhji, *The Rajputs of Saurasthra*,
287–288.

One of the greatest challenges to *riti-rivaj* has been the erosion of *parda*, the custom of secluding women.[36] Among wealthy and aristocratic Rajputs, men frequented the *mardana* (male quarters), which women scarcely transgressed, and women lived in the *zanana* (female quarters), which was either a large section of the home or an entirely separate domicile, to which only family men had access.[37] In villages, Rajput men and women often occupied the same space inside the home, but men would entertain and conduct business with nonfamilial men outside the home in separate buildings or huts, thus effecting temporary partition. Without question, the manliness of the Rajput persona so admired by the British was accentuated by the strict segregation of the sexes in Rajput society. As in so many British colonial clubs, men reserved a space where men could converse without distraction and where the sensibilities of the weaker sex would remain inviolate.[38]

Today, few families continue to divide households into *zanana* and *mardana*. One reason is that the arrangement, which requires servants to do "women's work" in men's quarters and to perform "unladylike" tasks in women's, is now too costly. It also strikes most Rajputs as antiquated. Exposure to television, which arrived in the mid-eighties, and familiarity with the living situations of Rajputs who have migrated to big cities such as Mumbai and Delhi and of non-Rajput elites who have become neighbors in Rajasthan's cities have undoubtedly contributed to the sense that containment of women within the home is now impractical and outmoded. Nevertheless, virtually all Rajput women who live in villages and many Rajput women who live in towns and cities in western Rajasthan have continued to observe some form of *parda* or at least cover their heads, if not hide their faces, when they return to their villages to celebrate holidays or attend weddings. In some urban families, young women have taken jobs as primary school teachers, though most of the women who do so are expected to retire once their marriages are arranged. This decline of *parda* has been seen by some Rajputs, particularly men, as an index of the dissolution of Rajput society and what is generally referred to as "high" Rajasthani culture.

The tendency to point to lax observance of social norms by women as an indication of social decline is characteristic of cultures in which members feel threatened by rapid social change, an influx of new ideas, and norms considered dangerously modern and alien, that is, "Western." Time and again we have seen revivalist and fundamentalist movements target women's comportment as indicative of what is right or terribly wrong with society.[39] During the past decades in Rajasthan, Rajputs have been especially vehement in their denun-

36. On the elasticity of *parda* and its impact on men, see Gold, "Purdah Is as Purdah's Kept," and Harlan, "Abandoning Shame."

37. Exceptions were some trusted servants and some merchants.

38. Although practice varied among families, some unmarried girls and postmenopausal women in the family were allowed into male quarters. Dancing girls and other entertainers were also welcomed in this relatively public space.

39. See Hawley and Proudfoot, "Introduction," 4–5 and 27–32. This focus on gender adaptation as symbolic of social welfare is shared in colonialist rhetoric, as is made clear by the British condemnation of *sati* immolation, a practice they cited as an indication of India's need for foreign rule.

ciation of "love marriage," a practice that can sully genealogical purity, the sine qua non of Rajput status.[40]

Many Rajput men with whom I spoke also expressed concern that Rajput women's exposure to new and especially Western ideas might be tempted to smoke cigarettes and drink alcohol. Smoking cigarettes is generally thought unseemly. Moreover, one Rajput aristocrat, a *thakur* ("lord") from a prominent *thikana* with an impressive *haveli* (residence) in Udaipur, explained that women who smoke "look cheap." Another Rajput man associated smoking cigarettes with "loose morals." Far more vexing, however, is the idea of women drinking alcohol. The same aristocrat who said that women who smoke "look cheap" told me that "women can't hold their liquor." Whereas many Rajput men drink socially, and there are myriad drinking stories depicting an inebriated protagonist's adventures, I heard very little positive said about drinking by women.

Several generations ago, women both drank and smoked. Thus, the very practices condemned as modern in the case of women predate abstention. Moreover, many village women have never become "teetotalers"—an English word that often popped up in Hindi conversation. In fact, I attended an uproarious women's drinking party in one Rajput village I visited. Rajput village women downed shots of country liquor before becoming thoroughly embroiled in a villagewide water fight around the time of the Holi festival.[41]

Thus, as is often true of groups associated with that nebulous term "fundamentalism," the measures taken in the interest of getting back to "fundamentals" are sometimes notably innovative, even "modern." This is not to label Rajputs fundamentalists—though, as we shall see, the high visibility of Rajputs in some right-wing political activities has led many outsiders to associate Rajputs as a group with an inherently fundamentalist agenda—but rather to point out that during this period in which Rajputs feel their identity has been threatened, moves made to preserve identity, most poignantly articulated in martial tales of heroism in bygone days, are, like so many fundamentalist strategies, informed by contemporary constructions that tell us more about present desires than the past "realities."[42]

And so although many Rajput men speak with nostalgia and pride about the rugged and virile virtues of Rajputs, especially the "martial Rajputs" of yore, they freely and frequently compare Rajputs with American cowboys. Like many journalists and others who sell Rajasthan as a tourist destination to travelers, many Rajputs do not hesitate to package Rajasthan as India's "Wild West." One

40. There have been various well-known departures from the norm, including the recent well-publicized elopement of a young nobleman with a daughter from Mewar's royal family. Although this goes "against the grain" because of the daughter's superior status, the marriage is still intracaste and so not deemed particularly problematic.

41. During Holi celebrations, it is customary to behave in ways that are usually unacceptable. Nonetheless, engaging in unseemly behavior is voluntary, and many women choose not to transgress norms. The majority of high-ranking Rajput women decline to drink alcohol or the customary drink made from cannabis extract.

42. Like many Muslims, many Rajputs would distance themselves from the notion of "fundamentalism." To apply the label generally would distort evident polyvocality. On the use of the term "fundamentalist" in the context of Hinduism, see Hawley and Proudfoot, "Introduction," and Hawley, "Hinduism: Satī and Its Defenders."

young aristocrat told me that, like cowboys in America, Rajputs adore horses, and that a poster of the Marlboro man was a highly treasured commodity among his friends. Another place in which the comparison arises, albeit implicitly, is the video rental booth. In video stalls, which are sprinkled throughout neighborhood bazaars, one inevitably finds amid the limited foreign stock a selection of spaghetti westerns. Also to be found in these stalls are seemingly countless variations on what one might call "modern cowboy" films. "Dirty Harry" Eastwood movies abound, as do blockbuster hits by other weapon-wielding martial arts connoisseurs such as Chuck Norris, Charles Bronson, and Sylvester Stallone, whose performances, incidentally, inspired the naming of the Rambo Boutique, situated just outside the Udaipur Palace Gates.[43] The young man mentioned above surmised that Rajput boys like these films because the heroes never stand down from a challenge, are very brave, and always get revenge. Another Rajput man, who runs a successful Jodhpur inn that caters to foreign buyers from various internationally known furniture vendors, told me that in the recent Mr. Universe pageant held in Jodhpur's Umed Bhavan Palace, contestants were given a multiple-choice question about whom they would most like to spend an hour with. One of the options was President Clinton and another was Clint Eastwood.[44] Although no contestant picked Eastwood, my Rajput informant assured me that if there had been any Rajputs among the contestants, all of them would have picked him. In short, although Western values have been seen as possibly diluting moral fiber, young Rajput men seem to have interpreted at least some foreign imports to be commensurate with, if not directly illustrative of, Rajput sensibilities.

Having sketched with rough strokes some dominant elements in frequently rehearsed representations of Rajput ethos, I turn now to addressing directly, though expeditiously, the image of the Rajput that has become so familiar during the past decade of rapid political change and communal tension: that of Rajput as defender of *dharm* or preserver of the social order. I begin this task by addressing the well-known saga of Roop Kanwar.[45]

Rajputs and Hindutva

In the fall of 1987, a young Rajput woman living in a prosperous village just outside Jaipur burned to death on her husband's funeral pyre. Accounts of what exactly transpired have varied drastically. Some people have represented Roop Kanwar's immolation as utterly involuntary: she was pushed onto the pyre, perhaps after having been drugged. Others have held that whether or not she

---

43. At my local video stall, I noticed *Three Men and a Baby* and *Cocoon*. Surprised to find these among the hypermacho films, I asked the proprietor why he ordered them. His response: the orders were mixed up.

44. I confess that I have forgotten the name of the third candidate.

45. I will do so only briefly because this incident has been treated so thoroughly elsewhere. In fact, the literature on the Roop Kanwar controversy is enormous. Comprehensive analysis and an excellent bibliography are to be found in *Sati, The Blessing and the Curse*, edited by John Stratton Hawley. See also Hawley's essay "Hinduism: Satī and Its Defenders" in his edited volume *Fundamentalism and Gender*.

was physically forced onto the pyre, social pressure made her incapable of voluntarily choosing to immolate herself.[46] Still others have represented her death as completely voluntary: ardently desiring to join her husband on the pyre, Roop Kanwar was transformed into a *satimata*, a divinity whose abandonment of life makes her family illustrious and whose metamorphosis into a guardian deity assures the family enhanced prosperity.

Although not all Rajputs have favored the latter interpretation, many Rajputs did rally to champion the divinity of Roop Kanwar and to defend the practice of *sati* immolation as appropriate for Rajput women and as commensurate with Hindu *dharm*.[47] Moreover, in the pro-*sati* demonstrations that ensued, the *sati* came to serve as an emblem of resistance to what many considered an attack on Hindu *dharm* by misguided and decultured secularists and feminists.[48] Some of the defenders of *sati* immolation established a group entitled the Sati Dharma Raksha Samiti or Committee for Defending the Dharma of *Sati*. (The group dropped the word *sati* from its name, however, when members became concerned that the title could cause them to run afoul of recently enacted legislation prohibiting *sati* glorification.) The committee was able to mobilize about 70,000 demonstrators to counter a protest led by 3,000 feminists just two days earlier.[49]

As all these events transpired, a Rajput presence was highly visible. One of the most enduring photographic images to come from the period is that of the *sati sthal* (literally, "place of the *sati*,") ringed by mustached Rajput jawans donning turbans and wielding swords. Although they were banned by the government from celebrating the *sati*'s immolation with a *chunri utsav*, or ceremonial immolation of her scarf, these guardians of the *sati sthal* ensured that the ceremony would indeed occur and that the sacred space of the *sati*'s divine transformation would be preserved.

In the comments of Rajput defenders, as in those of politicians, journalists, and academics who tried to interpret the death and celebration of Roop Kanwar, one observation was passionately and frequently repeated: in the interest of defending the rights and well-being of women, the Indian state was prohibiting a well-precedented practice sacred to many Hindus, whereas the courts had recently upheld the right of Muslim men to divorce their wives abruptly in accordance with Muslim personal law. Thus Roop Kanwar, in this context emblematic of Hinduism, was compared with Shah Bano, a Muslim woman whose demand for an equitable divorce settlement was denied because the Indian constitution protects the tenets of minority religious traditions such

---

46. For a compelling discussion of *sati* immolation and agency, see Oldenberg, "The Roop Kanwar Case."

47. On *sati* immolation as a phenomenon primarily characteristic of martial groups, see Thapar, "In History," 14–19.

48. On this point, see Nandy, "Sati as Profit versus Sati as a Spectacle," 36.

49. The committee also organized a recitation of the *Bhagavad Gita*, one of the most widely revered texts for Hindus throughout India, at the *sati sthal* or "site" of Roop Kanwar's immolation. The recitation's completion coincided with a celebration of the first anniversary of the young woman's death. For visual documentation of the deployment of Roop Kanwar's image as emblem of Hindu *dharm* in the context of anti-Muslim agitation, see Anand Pathwardan's film, *Father, Son, and Holy War*.

as Islam; in Shah Bano's case, Islamic code was protected and enforced. The image of Rajput Roop Kanwar was thus deployed by some Hindus to convey the inequity they perceived between themselves and Muslims, whom they viewed as unfairly favored.[50]

As the controversy over Roop Kanwar continued, agitation increased over the proposal of some right-wing Hindu politicians to tear down the Barbari Masjid, a sixteenth-century mosque in Ayodhya.[51] They claimed that the mosque had been constructed on the site of the birth of Ram, hero of the *Ramayan* and, it should be noted, scion of the Rajput solar *vamsh* ("lineage") to which the Mewar *maharanas* belong. Proponents of the destruction, which finally occurred in the fall of 1992, often portrayed the plan as offering compensation for the desecration of this sacred Hindu site. Their processions throughout the country, as well as the eventual siege of the site, staged symbolic conquest over Islam and victory over the Muslims whose progenitors destroyed many temples and to whom, it was argued, the law has given preferential treatment. Demonstrations favoring temple demolition set off a series of bloody Hindu-Muslim riots throughout north India. The riots gave momentum to the demolitionist movement, which ultimately stormed the mosque.

Much of my research on venerated heroes, the vast majority of whom are Rajput, occurred during the tumultuous period leading up to the destruction of the Babari Masjid. Having settled in Udaipur during the summer of 1990, I faced a fall fraught with palpable Hindu-Muslim tension, which finally erupted in a week of sporadic rioting. In this city blood was shed after a rumor spread through the bazaar that Muslims had pulled the eyes off an image of the Hindu god Bheruji. The newspapers reported looting and stoning as various rumors of violence and violation made their way through my neighborhood.[52]

The day the rioting ended, I traveled to Jodhpur for a research trip twice delayed by curfew. The next day rioting broke out there. Burned vehicles littered nearby streets, and there were abundant rumors (rape, stoning, shrine desecration, poisoning) reported by neighbors and residents of the home in which I stayed. Curfew was lifted a week later, but, of course, anxiety and suspicion persisted.[53] Many residents had previously prided themselves on the absence of rioting in the city's history. Now in Jodhpur, as elsewhere in Rajasthan and north India, there was much talk of distrust and vulnerability in the newly renewed and fragile calm.

50. On the "figure of woman" acting "as a sign in discursive formations, standing for concepts or entities that have little to do with women in actuality," in the context of nationalism, see Chatterjee, *The Nation and Its Fragments*, 68–71.

51. For background on this controversy and issues of communalism, see Ludden, ed., *Contesting the Nation*, and van der Veer, *Religious Nationalism*.

52. One of the chief topics of discussion in the house where I lived was whether to drink the milk—might it be poisoned?

53. For an introduction to riots and rumors in Indian contexts, see Das, "Introduction: Communities, Riots and Survivors," 20, 28; Pandey, "The Colonial Construction of 'Communalism,'" 124; and Kakar, *The Colors of Violence*, 15. On the difficulties of substantiating the events of riots, see Pandy, "Community and Violence."

These feelings were clearly exacerbated during coming months by events that transpired thousands of miles away. The new year brought the Gulf War. In the weeks preceding the counteroffensive, there were posters of Saddam Hussein plastered throughout the Muslim sections of Udaipur. Many Hindus construed the posters as a challenge and an affront, even if they did not sympathize with or support the nations arrayed against Hussein.[54] For many Hindus his face served as a symbol summarizing "Muslim fanaticism," an English phrase pervasive in English and Hindi conversation.

The events I have just described figure as significant elements of the temporal context in which I gathered heroic narratives. Accounts of self-sacrifice by Rajput heroes, many of whom died while fighting Muslims and "defending Hindutva," certainly reflected the fears and prejudices of people living amid communal hostility and volatility.[55] Moreover, during and after the Gulf War, I found that as I pursued my research, some of the Hindus with whom I spoke assumed that because I was American, we shared a common enemy. Needless to say, my (post–September 11th) trip to Udaipur in summer 2002, a time of heightened tension between India and Pakistan, brought me into contact with many sharing this assumption.[56] Thus not only the Gulf War and the threat of new wars but also my nationality undoubtedly contributed to a tendency to depict Muslim enemies in heroic narratives as especially vile. There is, of course, no way to measure how much the representations of Muslim "others" were influenced by current events or how "communally biased" they were now as opposed to how much they would have been if related earlier. Unflattering characterizations are also to be found in accounts from previous decades and centuries. As is always the case, contemporary sympathies and animosities helped formulate constructions of yesteryear.

There are many blatant examples of incursions of present affect into the past to which I could point. One that readily comes to mind is a narrative performed by a shrine attendant at a roadside hero memorial just outside of Jodhpur. In the beginning of a story, which he later sang for me while he played his *ravanhattha* (stringed instrument common in the Marwar area), he described the hero's enemies as local tribal cattle raiders (Minas), but later on the villains are identified as Pathans, whom he called the "freedom fighter's" Muslim foe.[57] This kind of association between Muslim and cow-thieving tribal is not new or particularly unusual. In fact, in the legend of Kallaji recited to me by a Rajput

---

54. There was widespread criticism in local conversation, as in the Indian press, that the NATO campaign signaled its willingness to intercede in matters that it should not. India had denied refueling rights to NATO planes during the initial days of the counteroffensive.

55. On the invocation of heroes, as well as gods, as indicators "of the boundary of the Hindu community" in the rhetoric of the incendiary fundamentalist Sadhvi Rithamvara, see Kakar, *The Colors of Violence*, 156. For reflection on oral epics' demonstration of resistance to Sunni Muslim authority, see Hiltebeitel, *Rethinking India's Oral and Classical Epics*, 47.

56. This was an abrupt change of perspective for me: I was used to being called upon to explain American support for Pakistan and Muslims. I now gradually escaped lectures from taxi drivers about American support for Pakistan; perhaps now I could appreciate the peril that Hindus felt was ever present and even in their midst?

57. The musician identified himself as Deva Ram and his community as Padiyar.

bhopa at Kallaji's shrine in Rundela, the hero first earns the gratitude Mewar's Maharana Udai Singh by subduing the rancorous rustler Bhil population around Bari Sadri, an estate not far from Udaipur, and then is called away on his wedding day by this monarch, who needs reinforcements to defend Chittor from Akbar's siege. Defeating tribals unsubtly serves as evidence of an ability to rout Muslims, who are by implication the "ultimate" or "real" enemy.[58]

A similar, and perhaps more heinous, substitution process occurs in *Pabuji*, whose hero fights two separate campaigns. In the first he captures she-camels not from tribals but from the demon Ravan, ruler of Lanka. In the second he rescues cows stolen by a Pathan, a cow-killing villain. It could certainly be argued that together the episodes suggest identification of the demonic and the Muslim.[59]

Returning to our hero narratives, representations of the villainous Muslim nemesis of the "freedom-fighting" hero serve, among other things, to relocate animosity and fear to a temporally distant "place".[60] Given the right circumstances, however, such representations can also serve to ignite passions and justify conflict. In the hands of agitators who favor current conflict, the images may be deployed to express intolerance and incite violence.[61]

Throughout the period leading up to the destruction of the mosque and during the aftermath of the destruction, one Rajput hero's name reverberated throughout India: Rana Pratap. This medieval Maharana of Mewar and inveterate enemy of the Moghul emperor had been championed by Indian nationalists as a paradigmatic freedom fighter during their struggle for Indian independence from the British. With the British gone, Pratap had resumed his paradigmatic function of nemesis to Muslims (who today have often been portrayed by Hindu nationalists as foreigners). Indeed, a comic book (*Amar Chitra Katha*) devoted to Pratap eulogizes him at length on the inside of its cover, which, having detailed the specifics of Akbar's conquest and resistance by this "lone, unbending figure" whose "freedom was his honor," concludes, "In essence Rana Pratap's name is synonymous with the highest order of the revolutionary patriotic spirit of India."[62] Furthermore, in Pratap, whose equestrian statue dominates the Udaipur skyline and whose story has been inserted into the Ram Lila performances (which depict the feats of Ram) of some non-Rajput villagers near Udaipur, the idea of Rajput as defender of *dharm* has been powerfully packaged and dramatically deployed.[63]

58. In addition to using the word "tribal" as an adjective, here and throughout I employ the word, according to Indian English usage, as a noun to refer to persons belonging to tribes.

59. For an interesting, if somewhat antiquated, sketch on Pathan Muslims, see Singh, *The Castes of Marwar*, 224–226.

60. Gyan Pandy has spoken of the spatial displacement of violence in riot narratives in his address, "Community and Violence."

61. For allusions to the volatile and catalytic nature of heroes (particularly Rana Pratap) in contemporary discourse, see Kakar, *The Colors of Violence*, 73–74, 80; McKean, "Bhārat Mātā," especially, 250–251, 270–279; and Banerjee, "Masculine Hinduism, the Shiv Sena, and Political Mobilization."

62. "Rana Pratap," 1. For further reflection on Rana Pratap in the contexts of tourism and fundamentalist rhetoric, see Harlan, "On Hero Worship."

63. I was apprised of the insertion of the Pratap story by a Rajput noblewoman whose son's pony got loose during a Ram Lila and was then incorporated into the performance as Pratap's horse.

FIGURE 2.4. Maharana Pratap

Having noted Pratap's predominance in political discourse, I ask readers to recall that the heroes I treat in this book are worshiped as heroes. They are ritually venerated by descendants at home and at their erstwhile estates, or by various pilgrims in a cultic milieu. My goal is to understand hero worship primarily as a religious phenomenon. Many worshiped heroes are characterized as "freedom fighters" ridding India of invaders, but they are seldom the well-known heroes glorified in the rhetoric of right-wing politicians. In Rajasthan, the hero Ram, for example, is not worshiped as a *vir*: he is not a *jhunjharji*, *bhomiyaji*, or *sagasji*. Rather, he is worshiped by members of various communities as Vishnu incarnate.[64] Although Ram's struggles against the demons may function as a paradigm for resisting Muslims, as it has elsewhere in India, worship of him does not conform to the patterns we have been inspecting. He does not die in battle and he is not worshiped as a warrior per se.

64. The Jagdish Mandir, the most prominent Vaishnava temple in Udaipur, is typical in its focus on Krishna tradition and iconography. Three of the so-called *car dham* (the four great pilgrimage places in Mewar) are for Krishnite deities: Shri Nathji, Carbhuja, and Dvarakadish. The fourth site belongs to Eklingji, Shiv.

Nor is Rana Pratap. Greatly admired as the symbol of Hindu defiance and as the epitome of Mewari independence, this monarch did not die in battle.[65] Rather, he lived to tell the tale of the great battle of Haldighati, a much-visited tourist destination and the site of an annual fair. Pratap's mount Chetak is, perhaps, another matter.[66] This celebrated steed is easily assimilated to the paradigm of the ritually venerated hero. Chetak, for whom the express train between Udaipur and Jaipur is named, as is Chetak Circle, the shopping area in which the Government Tourist Emporium is located, died as he landed from an enormous leap that rescued his rider Pratap from the Moghul soldiers in pursuit. The sequence of events in the story of Pratap's rescue and Chetak's demise is portrayed in a series of monumental paintings in the Udaipur City Palace. Evidently, this celebration of Chetak is no new phenomenon: the place Chetak has had in the hearts of Mewaris was remarked upon almost two centuries ago by Tod, who claimed that half the houses in Mewar bore images of Chetak.[67]

Today, if one wishes to see active commemoration of Chetak's sacrifice, one can visit Chetak's imposing *chatri* (funerary pavilion), located near the battleground at Haldighati. This monument resembles the pavilions in which the stelai of royal and noble family members are situated.[68] Sequential visits to the *chatri* have revealed that the monument, which has received continuous maintenance, is an active shrine that receives offerings from pilgrims. The inscription on the pavilion reads as follows.

> Here fell dead on June 21, 1576, Chetak—the daring and devoted
> horse of Maharana Pratap. In spite of being badly wounded Chetak
> saved his master in his critical hour by carrying him from Raktatalai to
> the other end of Haldighati by jumping across the nearby stream. To
> cherish the loyalty and sacrifice of Chetak, this memorial was raised.[69]

My point here is not that Chetak is actually worshiped as a *vir* (which, after all, means "man" as well as "real man," that is to say, "hero"); it is simply that violent sacrificial death is a prerequisite for *vir* status and independent worship. Like the heroic-sacrificial dog and elephant we shall soon encounter, Chetak is honored as if or in the way of the hero. Moreover, this supermundane steed is

---

65. Writing before the agitation over Ram Janam Bhumi and the political success of right-wing parties in this decade, Susanne and Lloyd Rudolph observed: "Rana Pratap, because of his defense of the homeland against an 'alien' power, became a cultural hero not only for Rajputs but also for the incipient Indian nation"; "The Political Modernization of an Indian Feudal Order," 44. Also instructive are their reflections on the invocation of Rana Pratap as the "guarantor of Hindu Religion" by the Bhuswami Sangh, 64. On heroes worshiped and not worshiped in the epic context, see Hiltebeitel, *Rethinking India's Oral and Classical Epics*, 23 and Blackburn, "Patterns of Development for Indian Oral Epics," 16.

66. Popularly spelled this way in English, Chetak is properly transliterated "Cetak."

67. *Annals and Antiquities*, vol. 1, p. 270.

68. Royal ancestors are memorialized with cenotaphs identical to those of heroes. Quasi-heroic commemoration conveys and enhances the legitimacy of descent and inheritance from valiant ancestors. The association with ruling ancestors, in turn, stresses the royalty of "Rajput" heroes, who are, as the term Rajput conveys literally, "sons of kings."

69. Facing the shrine is a *cabutra* for the god Bheruji. This location near, and association with, Bheruji is common, as we shall see. In many cases Bheruji's location near a hero shrine conveys homology.

reminiscent of the special, and often magical, horses ridden by well-known medieval *jhunjharji*s and *bhomiyaji*s, which have shared in the sacrality of their masters' transformations. At least one such horse is considered the incarnation of a goddess.[70]

In sum, the much-invoked Ram is not worshiped in Rajasthan as a hero in the sense of domestically or culturally venerated *vir*; nor is Rana Pratap, who is greatly, even passionately, admired in Rajasthan, as he is throughout India. Understanding the respect and affection given each, however, can be deepened by familiarly with the logic and mechanics of locally worshiped heroes, who are on the one hand identified with a goddess (who generally appears as a *kuldevi* or "clan goddess") and homologized to Bheruji (Bhairava), and on the other hand viewed as glorious exemplars.[71]

In fact Tod, implicitly recognizing the reflective glory of Pratap and worshiped martyrs, juxtaposes Pratap with the fated heroes Jaimal of Badnor and Phatta (Fatta, Patta) of Kailwa, whose icons are ritually venerated at Chittor. Reflecting on his travels through Haldighati and Chittor, he says, "I have climbed the rocks, crossed the streams, and traversed the plains which were the theater of Pratap's glory, and conversed with the lineal descendants of Jaimal and Patta on the deeds of their forefathers, and many a time has the tear started in their eye at the tale they recited."[72] Jaimal and Phatta, who are still venerated by their descendants but also incorporated into the prolific cult of the legendary Kallaji and worshiped together with him and with all the *satis* of Chittor at the Jauhar Mela, are "freedom fighters" in the context of recent communal tension. In 1991, Chandra Shekhar, then prime minister, spoke at the Jauhar Mela, which is preceded by veneration at the Jaimal and Phatta memorials at the outer gates of the citadel. Equally worth noting is Prime Minister Chandra Shekar's participation in the celebration of the Rathor Rajput hero Amar Singh, who, as the *Indian Express* put it "was born on December 12 in the year 1613, fought valiantly against the Moghul empire and is a household name in Nagaur."[73] The Prime Minister is reported to have offered flowers at Amar Singh's memorial.[74] The contemporary relevance of such heroes is also apparent in the naming of the Vir Phatta Sarasvati Vidya Mandir, a school in Amet, the *thakur* of which descends from a common line and continues to contribute toward the upkeep of the Phatta Shrine at Chittor.

Thus, the climate and circumstances of communal hostilities doubtless informed the local hero narratives I gathered. At the same time, these narra-

70. Pabuji's magnificent mare, Kesar Kalami.

71. As Alf Hiltebeitel has shown, the legacy of stories found in the (Sanskrit) *Ramayana* is influence and infiltration: scenarios and personae from the epic have a way of popping up in all sorts of places, including local epics. The truth of this is patent, whether or not one agrees in every respect with his interesting, if debatable, thesis about "reenplotment." See his *Rethinking India's Oral and Classical Epics*. As to Pratap, this swashbuckling, Moghul-fighting king has come to serve as an emblem of Mewar. Presiding over Udaipur as a massive equestrian statue atop the city's highest peak, he is often held up as an incarnation of martial ethos and regional, as well as national, pride.

72. *Annals and Antiquities*, vol. 1, p. 265 note 1.

73. See "Prime Minister Takes Part in Rathore Celebrations" *Indian Express*, December 30, 1990.

74. See "Favorite of the Puppeteer," *The Hindu*, January 3, 1991.

tives provide scenarios that surely shape contemporary envisionings of recent events and continue to shuffle and deal new configurations of heroic and villainous, us and them, ours and theirs.

Before concluding this sketch of subjectivities, it is worthwhile to ponder briefly some of the ways in which these dichotomies may polarize and reflexively configure identities. Given salient folkloric and political representations of Rajput as defender of Rajasthan (and India) against Muslims, it makes sense to begin with the contrastive imagings of Rajput and Muslim. Such a project merits at least a book; here only some of the more striking aspects of construction, useful to us as we embark on an exploration of hero worship, can be treated. Although many Rajput heroes died fighting non-Muslims, the identity of worshiped heroes is informed by the history of war with Muslims that has led worshipers to routinely type heroes, whether *jhunjharjis*, *bhomiyajis*, or even *sagasjis*, as "freedom fighters."

It would be folly, however, to limit a discussion of reflexivity, however preliminary, to the topic of Rajputs and Muslims. The word "Rajput," whether deployed as noun or adjective, is informed by the mutual regard of Rajput and various other others, including members of indigenous tribes such as the Bhils, as well as Brahmins, Jains, and so on. Looking at some ways in which a number of these groups—which make various appearances in narratives we will be following—are imaged and positioned vis-à-vis the Rajput will avert an overly romantic characterization of Rajputs as the swashbuckling and freedom-fighting foe of Muslim conquerors; help convey the premise that Rajput is an imaginative and therefore fluctuating and contestable identity; and, most importantly in terms of this book's agenda, serve as background crucial for understanding a number of narratives to be presented in chapters following.[75] First, and appearing as verily synonymous with "other" in many contexts, is the Muslim.

Muslims and Other "Others"

I begin with a dark tale of a chance encounter with a Rajput man whose sister I had come to interview. I had been listening to her explain that there were three or four *jhunjharjis* commemorated at the familial *mahasatiyan* (cremation ground), and that her natal family, which governed a large *thikana*, goes to worship these heroes at weddings, in addition to making an annual pilgrimage

75. This discussion of others is not meant to be comprehensive. It is designed only to designate a few, albeit significant, ways in which Rajput identity is constructed in relation to identities of other groups, as represented by Rajputs in routine ways, deploying characterizations or tropes. For a recent and brief but interesting utilization of this strategy, which helps frame various essays on Jains, see Cort, "Introduction: Contested Jain Identities of Self and Other." As to romanticism, Rajasthan and its Rajputs are often portrayed by tourists and journalists as veritable embodiments of romanticism, a commodity that sells to tourists. See, for example, Apple, "India: Asia's Epic Adventure." For scholarly analysis of commodification, see two articles by Barbara N. Ramusack: "Tourism and Icons" and "The Indian Princes as Fantasy." For a powerful fictional representation of Rajput domination of subalterns, a subject not properly treated in this project on Rajput representations of ancestral heroes, see Devi, "Paddy Seeds." For a brief comment on subaltern representations of Rajput heroes, see below. More thorough treatment follows in my work on cultic veneration.

to offer them coconuts. She spoke to me only of rituals, and her brother, who had been listening, appeared increasingly frustrated with her comments. An impetuous young man, he emerged from the recesses of the parlor to expound upon the nature of *jhunjharjis*. He introduced his discourse on *jhunjharjis* with the following comments:

> *Jhunjharjis* adhered to the strict rule of Rajput *dharm*. They sacrificed their lives for their kings and maintained the honor of the family. When there was no other way, they would chop off their heads and give them to their comrades. Then they'd fights without heads. The enemies were Muslims and unclean. If Muslims cut off Rajputs' heads, they'd [Rajputs would] become unclean, as Muslims destroy *murtis* [icons] and cows. So they'd chop off their heads and could fight better.

These frank and unabashed remarks, which were made in the mid-1980s, a time not especially marked by communal tension and which seem surprisingly stringent given that fact, make a number of important points. First, as we have seen, such heroic narratives, and particularly the narratives recited by men, tend to link the sacrificial death of a hero with familial honor. The protection of this honor in the past implicitly accrues to the present generation; the young raconteur demonstrated evident pride as he spoke of his familial *jhunjharjis*. Second, it presents Muslims as threats to familial honor. Typically, when Rajput men or women speak of heroes as maintaining or defending honor, they indicate that the death itself conveys honor by demonstrating the courage inherent in the Rajput's bloodline. Often the sustaining of honor is also linked to the protection of familial women, who might be violated if their kinsmen fail to fight bravely; not all women are assumed to have the opportunity or inclination to immolate themselves so as to avoid violation.[76] In this quote honor is associated explicitly with the preservation of the warriors' purity.

The heroic narratives Rajputs tell about Rajputs are seldom concerned with matters of purity. As Kshatriyas, warriors, their *dharm* includes battle, which means among other things chancing bodily mutilation, a fate that typically renders a sacrifice unsatisfactory in Brahmanical circles. For example, mutilation is of great concern and cause for elaboration in an account of the death of the hero Kallaji composed and published by Shil Sharma, author of the previously mentioned song describing the self-decapitation of Kallaji Rathor.[77] A well-known Udaipur resident whom I visited on various occasions, Shil Sharma is, as his name would tend to indicate, a Brahmin. But let us recall that sacrificial heroes are frequently decapitated; their heads and trunks are frequently venerated in separate shrines. A violent and bloody death also presents the distinct possibility of being consumed as carrion by various scavenging beasts including the kite, which often appears as a theriomorphic form of the *kuldevi*. Thus

---

76. On mass self-sacrifice (*jauhar*, or as it is frequently spelled in English, "johar") as a defensive strategy, see Oldenberg, "The Continuing Invention of the Sati Tradition," 163–165, and Harlan, *Religion and Rajput Women*, 162–185.

77. See Harlan, "Tale of a Headless Horseman," and Śil Śarma's pamphlet, *Karmavīr Kallā*.

what looks like an unacceptable form of death is revalued by Rajputs as just the right sort of death—consumption by one's goddess. Death in battle typically renders the hero immune from impure contagion and so suitable for divinity and, it is also frequently said, enlightenment or *moksh*, liberation from rebirth; the two transformations are held not to be mutually exclusive.[78]

Here, however, there is concern that the touch of a Muslim might render the Rajput impure. The Muslim's sins of cow killing and icon smashing are so heinous as to render the Muslim polluting; he threatens the purity of both the hero and the family whose bloodline he shares. Implicit is the assumption that being killed by a Muslim may render the hero a victim of sacrifice unfit for the goddess, even as scavenging kite. The solution, self-decapitation, precludes the possibility of being sacrificed by an unfit sacrificer. In the myriad hero stories in which heroes cut off their own heads, the sacrificer and sacrificed are succinctly represented as one.[79] It should be noted, however, that in narratives in which the hero is decapitated by an enemy, the hero's voluntary assumption of the risk of death in war subtly but surely renders the hero not just a victim but a self-sacrificer. The venerated hero volunteers for sacrifice/*balidan*.

The Rajput aristocrat's comments quoted above single out the threat of contamination by the Muslims' polluting touch as the reason for *jhunjharjis'* self-decapitation, and so distinguishes Muslims from Rajputs on the basis of the Rajputs' relative purity. The remarks reflect presumptions about impurity that are asserted with special vehemence and passion during times of heightened communal tension. Hence, it should be observed, in such tales pollution may be temporally conditioned.

Before leaving this discussion of Muslims and contagion, I should note that in some narratives I collected, some on heroes and some on *satis*, another sort of contact with Muslims is said to pose a danger. In these stories, however, it is not a Muslim's touch but the splashes of the *nil* (bluing) that Muslim *Chipas* (printers) throw that are dangerous: the splashes cool the hero's *sat*, the moral fuel ("truth force" or "right stuff") that makes him an incomparable warrior while living and also enables him to fight on after decapitation.[80] *Sat* enables *satis* to bestow wondrous blessings, pronounce devastating curses, and combust spontaneously on the pyre.[81] Printers throwing *nil* effect the same result as the pervasive "two women" who point to a hero and exclaim, "Look! He has no head!"

78. On contextual shifts in the meaning of *moksh* according to Rajasthani villagers, see Gold, *Fruitful Journeys*, 3–5, 235–239, 262–263, and 287–288.

79. For representative reflections on a king's role as sacrificial agent and sacrificed victim, see Heesterman, *The Inner Conflict of Tradition*, 110; Hiltebeitel, *The Cult of Draupadī*, vol. 1, pp. 63, 77; Pierre Filliozat, "The After-Death Destiny of the Hero According to the Mahābhārata," 4; Visuvalingam, "Bhairava's Royal Brahmanicide," 165; Shulman, *The King and the Clown*, 36; and Beck, *The Three Twins*, 53. See also Parry, "Death and Cosmogony in Kashi," and Biardeau and Malamoud, *Le sacrifice dans l'Inde ancienne*, especially p. 146.

80. Not all Chipas are Muslim, but Chipas throwing *nil* at Hindu *satis* and heroes are typically presumed to be Muslim. For reflections on the valences of *nil* in the context of *sati* immolation, see Weinberger-Thomas, *Ashes of Immortality*, 24–34. On *sati* immolation, bluing, and childlessness, see Harlan, "Satī: The Story of Godāvarī," 229.

81. See Harlan, "Perfection and Devotion," 79–91.

It stops the hero cold.[82] He is not simply contaminated but rather arrested by contact with the inauspicious liquid sprayed by the inimical other.

Another way in which Muslim warriors are distinguished from Rajputs in contemporary lore is the typification of Muslims as hypervirile and lecherous predators. The emphasis on their sexual drive serves to support the appropriateness of *sati* immolation, the necessity for which is often attributed to Muslims. Indeed, many Rajputs believe that the custom of *sati* immolation originated in Rajasthan in response to invasions by Muslims, who might violate warriors' wives. Precedents in ancient epics are often brushed off as exceptions.

The tendency to attribute overdeveloped virility and sexuality to Muslims is not exclusively a Rajput predilection. It is commonplace in Hindu characterizations of Muslims (and characterizations of many inimical "others," including Hindus, throughout the world) particularly during periods in which fears of imminent rioting or memories of past rioting circulate rampantly.[83] Recent analysis of rioting connected with the Babari Masjid controversy has noted the tendency among Hindus to represent Muslims as dominant predators and to represent Hindus as emasculated by Muslim strength and by any actual, potential, or rumored violation of Hindu women.[84]

In stories that feature Rajput heroes, however, Rajputs are not portrayed as actually or inalterably emasculated by Muslims, or by any other adversaries, for that matter. Like threats of impurity and dishonor, the threat of emasculation is often asserted in accounts in which Muslims fight, but it is either not enacted or enacted but nullified by emasculating and bloody revenge. Precluding enactment is the premise that the heroes' very status as Rajputs, whom the British typed along with Muslim Pathans as belonging to the "martial races," makes them virile by nature: *virta* (virility) as manliness or heroism is their heritage, conveyed through blood. Second, the choice of death in battle as a sacrifice renders a soldier not the Muslims' victim but his goddess's. Finally, hero stories often include reference to the immolation of wives, which is understood to safeguard the heroes' virility. Indeed, one of the most famous and cherished tales of Rajput honor, a tale not of a hero but of a heroine, is the story of Padmini. This Mewari princess deploys a

---

82. In the myth of Cuchulainn in Ulster, the hero's progress to the capital is checked not only by women, whose nakedness causes him to divert his eyes, but by cold water, "which finally calms him," but not before his warrior heat causes the water to boil and the vat's staves and rings to burst. The warrior had to be dunked in three vats before his furor diminished; Dumezil, *The Destiny of the Warrior*, 134–135.

83. On the accusation of lecherousness in an "other," Slavoj Žižek holds: "We always impute to the 'other' an excessive enjoyment: s/he wants to steal our enjoyment (by ruining our way of life) and/or has access to some secret, perverse enjoyment. In short, what really bothers us about the 'other' is the peculiar way it organizes its enjoyment; precisely the surplus, the 'excess' that pertains to it"; "Eastern Europe's Republics of Gilead," 54, cited in Amrita Basu, "Feminism Inverted," 165. On Muslims and reputed sexual appetite, see Kakar, *The Colors of Violence*, 107, which also cites on this point S. C. Dube's vintage *Indian Village*, 187. On Hindus seen as lechers by Muslims in the context of Hindu-Muslim rioting, see also Kakar, *The Colors of Violence*, 71, as well as 107–108.

84. Hindus do not represent themselves as violators. Samuel Klausner has argued that rioting is a victim-defined arena of conflict, like assassination and massacre; see his article "Violence" in *The Encyclopedia of Religion*, cited in Kakar, *The Colors of Violence*, 70. If they speak at all of atrocities committed by other Hindus, they represent the violence as occurring not within the community but "outside." For reflections on the phenomena of dissociation and displacement, see Pandy, "Community and Violence."

sort of Trojan horse trick to liberate her husband, who has been abducted, the story goes, by the lecherous Ala-ud-din as part of a plan to obtain her as ransom for his release. Having liberated her husband and initiated battle, Padmini immolates herself to protect her family's honor.

In cases where emasculation by decapitation does occur, recall that decapitation is not the end of life but the beginning of heroism in Rajput hero narratives. Headlessly, heroes struggle until they achieve their desires, which inevitably include exacting revenge in the form of many, typically a hundred, enemy heads. Thus, the hero's decapitation enables him to demonstrate his superior virility as a *vir* or *sur*. All versions of the story of Kallaji, for example, represent him as decapitating the many Muslims pursuing him as he makes his way to reunion with his wife, who then becomes a *sati*.

A third stereotype that arises in Rajput characterizations of Muslims in hero stories is that of cheat.[85] In the Padmini legend, it is always clear that Ala-ud-din is illegitimately deceptive when, having used the pretext of wanting to negotiate peace, he steals her husband and renders her ransom. The abduction comes off as an underhanded and despicable trick, just the sort of thing one would expect from a lecher. A similar characterization is made in the story of Kallaji. There Kallaji's nemesis is the mighty Moghul emperor Akbar, who in the terms of one account "violates the rules of engagement" by shooting Kallaji's uncle, the Maharana's chief general at Chittor, after sundown.[86]

While portraying the villainy of the Muslim, both stories, ironically, exemplify the principle, one trick deserves another. Padmini fights fire with fire by tricking Ala-ud-din: she hides soldiers in compartments that ostensibly contain ladies-in-waiting. Moreover, Kallaji hoists his uncle, wounded in the foot by Akbar's bullet, on his shoulders, which fools Akbar into thinking that Kallaji and his uncle are in fact Carbhuja, a four-armed form of Vishnu. Terrified, Akbar flees to fight another day and to deploy another trick. He splatters cow blood on the ground so that no Hindu Rajput can cross over his nefarious "line in the sand."

Hence, trickery by the enemy is treacherous; trickery by the protagonist is clever. When the enemy tricks, he reveals the hero's honesty, simplicity, innocence, and guilelessness. This hero is the straightforward strongman, who, like Achilles, wins by strength and courage alone. But when the hero is clever, like Kallaji, the "Artful One," and like Padmini, her story's Odysseus, cleverness contrasts not with honesty, simplicity, innocence, and guilelessness, but with stupidity or even cowardice.[87]

In narrative representations, Rajputs and Muslims thus share a capacity for subterfuge, which is valued or condemned according to the perspective and

85. On the derision of Muslims in middle-period Rajasthani culture, see Ziegler, "Action, Power and Service in Rajasthani Culture," 63–64.

86. The inscription on Jaimal's memorial states, "While inspecting the repairs to a breach in the fort during Akbar's siege in A.D. 1568 he was shot by the emperor." The claim that Jaimal was shot unethically is, however, challenged by at least one Kallaji *bhopa*.

87. Kallaji, which is often written Kalaji, is popularly held to derive from the word *kala*, "art, craft." For interesting commentary on Athena's identification of Odysseus's deceptive nature, and its potential for trouble in his home country, see Bok, *Lying*, 29.

positioning of the beholder. As it turns out—to take a step backward—lust is another shared characteristic. Rajputs rulers are often celebrated for the immensity of their harems. Wives and concubines are sources of both pleasure and danger. The *zanana*, with its competing co-wives and concubines, is often depicted as a place of treachery. Control of the *zanana* indicates strength as a ruler, whereas lack of control inevitably leads to disaster.[88]

Furthermore, although Ala-ud-din's capture of Padmini is deemed illegitimate, marriage by abduction has been represented in Hindu legal thought, beginning with Manu's *dharmashastra*, as a legitimate form of union for warriors.[89] The perspective is also conveyed in epic. For example, Stephanie Jamison has compared the abduction of Helen by Paris as according with practice in the *Mahabharat*.[90] The Greek cycle also depicts Achilles as alienated from his peers because he has been denied his "prize," a woman he captured in battle. His act of abduction is represented as legitimate. His deprivation of the abducted woman is not. In Rajput rendering of history, obtaining women as trophies is typically deemed not dastardly but sensible. Thus the conquering monarch typically demands and receives in marriage the daughter of the defeated king. Such an alliance is simply good statecraft.

Although Rajput lore inherits this perspective on women as booty, Rajput heroes worshiped as heroes do not take women as prizes for an obvious reason: their heroic status arises from death. The *jhunjharjis* and *bhomiyas* who die in battle continue to kill and sometimes travel toward home, but they are in no position or condition to seek out any sort of material or strategic advantage through capture. Headlessly they win their individual battles with their assailants, but their wars are generally lost, and in any case they "drop dead" as soon as they achieve revenge or make it back to the outskirts of their villages or towns. And so, although heroes do not abduct, they are not represented as morally opposed to the practice of abduction. Desire for possession of the enemy's women is not exclusively a characteristic of the enemy. Again, as is so often the case in representations of opposed forces throughout the world, a trait condemned in the other is possessed by the subject, revealing that to some extent the enemy is the "us" of which the hero is emblematic. He appears to us, if darkly, in the hero's reflection.

Not all inimical qualities are to be found in the hero's reflection, it could be argued. Certainly Rajputs and Muslim diverge in their treatment of cows and their ideas about beef eating. As we have seen, the scurrilous Muslim foe of Pabuji must be defeated to save cows. To Hindus, the cow is "Mataji," mother,

---

88. There are plentiful stories of disaster incited by women's scheming in Rajput kingdoms, as elsewhere in India. One is reminded of the classic case of the Sanskrit *Ramayana*'s Kaikeyi, whose plot to exile Ram and have her son Bharat crowned king leads to her husband's blindness and death, the defoliation and degeneration of his kingdom and, later, to the abduction of Sita, as well as Ram's battle with Ravan.

89. For a translation of the well-known passage (3.27–43) on the eight allowable forms of marriage—one of which is abduction—see Wendy Doniger, trans., *The Laws of Manu*, 45–46. On the regular practice (among "middle-period" Rajputs) of taking daughters as tribute at the end of hostilities, see Ziegler, "Action, Power, and Service in Rajasthani Culture," 62.

90. "Draupadī on the Walls of Troy."

or rather more specifically the wholly beneficent, *dharmik*, and *sattvik* or "good, pure" Mother. The distinction between Rajput and Muslim, however, is not one of herbivore and carnivore. Unlike Brahmins and most other caste groups, Rajputs, as we have seen, typically eat meat, which is held to promote physical strength, blood lust, and virility. In fact, one young Rajput man, an accomplished polo player, told me one reason that his mare was so very talented at polo is that he mixed meat juices with her feed.

Like the killing toward which it conduces, meat eating is an exception to the principle of vegetarianism and *ahimsa* (noninjury) dear to other Hindu castes and especially Brahmins. The exception is indicative of the anomalous position of the warrior in the *varn* or class hierarchy. Whereas others are to observe the *sanatan* or "universal" *dharm* not to kill, warriors kill by profession and are deemed predisposed toward warfare by inherited disposition as well as lifestyle. As the famous warrior Arjuna learned from his divine charioteer Krishna in the *Mahabharat*, a warrior faced with battle must follow *svadharm*, the "personal" duty that derives from status as a warrior. Fighting and hunting, along with eating meat, are the bloody activities that display and contribute to martial character and disposition.

One other, perhaps obvious, point merits mention here. Rajput lore does not represent Rajputs as eating cows, but it should be recognized that appropriating others' cows has been a dimension of conquest not only by Muslims but also by Hindus since ancient times. Rajasthan is no exception.[91] In fact, the hero Pabuji is a consummate cattle raider, as is Ravji, the Rajput villain in the epic *Devnarayan*, which is told by and about herding-caste heroes.[92] As for the Rajput hero stories I collected, in ones that have anything at all to do with cows Rajputs are represented as cattle rescuers, as one might expect.[93]

In fighting fiercely and eating meat, the Rajput and Muslim, then, appear as mirror images, if also differently hued or somewhat distorted ones.[94] The cow, of course, remains sacred among and so protected by Rajputs; the bovine image frequently serves as an icon of *dharm* on memorial stelai commissioned and maintained by Rajputs. Yet in warfare and carnivorism, we see again images of Rajput and Muslim converging and making the Muslim comparatively familiar while rendering the Rajput comparatively inimical in the context of otherwise shared Hindu values.

---

91. On cattle raiding among Rajputs in recent times, see Hitchcock, "The Idea of the Martial Rajput," 15. On cattle raiding as "an invitation to war" in traditions of Saurashtra and elsewhere, see Sontheimer, *Pastoral Deities in Western India*, 71. On heroes and cattle throughout India, see Thapar, "Death and the Hero," 295. On ancient traditions, see also Lincoln, *Priests, Warriors, and Cattle*, as well as his *Death, War, and Sacrifice*, where he gives a pithy summation of the practice among Indo-Europeans: "Raiding is presented as a heroic action, sanctioned by divine approval, hedged with ritual, and open in its use of force to regain that which rightfully belongs to the Indo-European warrior and/or his people"; p. 11. For further comparison, see Wolcot, "Cattle Raiding, Heroic Tradition, and Ritual," and Brenneman, "Serpents, Cows, and Ladies."

92. See Smith, *The Epic of Pābūjī*, and Miller, "The Twenty-Four Brothers and Lord Devnārāyaṇ."

93. On heroes as "defenders against cattle raiders" in south India, see Blackburn, "The Folk Hero and Class Interests in Tamil Heroic Ballads," 135.

94. The metaphor of "fun house" mirror works well here.

Thus, although the very points of similarity (cleverness, lust, carnivorism, even transgression) are held as marks distinguishing foe from protagonist, there are ways and contexts in which the Rajput and Muslim are explicitly recognized as noninimical and even congenial. If the Muslim is a non-*dharmik* iconoclast, the Rajput defender of *dharm* is also, as we have seen, proudly antinomian. In fact, as John Smith recognizes in his study of Pabuji, who "plunders his way along" during his adventures, the word *dhoro* is glossed by the preeminent Rajasthani dictionary (*Rajasthani Sabd Kos*) as both "hero" and "brigand."[95] Furthermore, centuries back the term Rajput itself was once a title that designated not only the "trooper" but also the courageous "brigand."[96]

Today, as in times past, Rajputs youths often glorify the transgressive behavior of their comrades. Tales of retribution and game poaching abound. Some also relate with evident admiration tales of Rajput dacoits who have defied various constabulary forces. What might otherwise be assessed as wrongful behavior here comes off as rightful resistance to wrongful authority. A good example is another renowned Pratap, a *jhunjharji* from the Jodhpur area. This Pratap, whose story will be recounted more fully later, was killed by police who had hunted him down as a dacoit having begun his criminal career after killing another Rajput to attain vengeance for an insult. Col. Mohan Singh, the stately and elderly but exuberant Rajput who recited to me Pratap's story at his home in Jodhpur, was a retired army officer widely respected by Rajputs I came to know in Rajasthan. From many quarters I had heard about his adventures wrestling panthers, chasing crocodiles, and pig-sticking. With great relish Col. Mohan Singh recited to me Pratap's story, then went on to point out various similarities among Rajasthani dacoits and Rajputs. For example, in the context of affirming the Rajput respect for their women, he claimed that Rajasthani dacoits "have great respect for ladies: they'll loot a village, but will inform and advise" villagers beforehand so as not to catch women off guard.[97]

Further evidence is found near Jodhpur at a roadside shrine commemorating the death of a Rajput who, my Rajput taxi driver assured me, is a *jhunjharji*. This fellow, I was told, lived in a village outside Jaisalmer and prospered by smuggling along the Pakistani border, but actually died in a motorcycle accident. Hence the roadside shrine. In my taxi driver's view, a criminal life that risked death, not the technicality of actually being killed on a motorbike, made this Rajput a *jhunjharji*. The driver went on to say, however, that the hero's death was probably confrontational.[98] Among Rajputs, he stressed, it is shameful to yield the road to oncoming traffic. In short, although people killed in auto accidents are not generally classed as *jhunjharji*s, and the taxi driver's tale contained

---

95. Smith, *The Epic of Pābūjī*, 238 and 445 note 295. On Kshatriyas as brigands, see Dumont, *Homo Hierarchicus*, 74.

96. See Qanungo, *Studies in Rajput History*, 99, and Hitlebeitel, *Rethinking India's Oral and Classical Epics*, 92.

97. This brings to mind the protocol established by Phoolan Devi, the Bandit Queen, who is depicted in the film by that name as warning villagers by megaphone before entering a town to loot it. See *Bandit Queen*.

98. This characterization renders him a sort of "road warrior."

no evidence of the decapitation and "struggling" required of a *jhunjharji*, his characterization of Rajput smuggler as a *jhunjharji* represents an instance in which dacoity, combined with aggressive and lawless driving by a Rajput, demonstrates sacrality manifested and confirmed by violent death.

One other significant aspect of comparability is the embracing by Rajputs and other Hindus of Muslims who fought alongside Rajputs against forces from Delhi. Just as some Rajputs served as mercenaries in Muslim corps (though this service often required at least nominal conversion), some Muslims fought alongside their Hindu patrons.[99] Thus, for example, one of the *bhopas* who is routinely possessed by Kallaji is also at times possessed by various Muslim heroes or *pirs*.

Another intriguing, if somewhat more complicated, example of syncretism—this one referring to a Hindu warrior worshiped by Muslims—is to be found in the person of Naruji, a celebrated *jhunjharji*. Naruji was not a Rajput but a Caran, though many people with whom I spoke in the vicinity simply assumed that, being a *jhunjharji*, he must have been a Rajput.[100] The eminent Rajasthan historian Gopi Nath Sharma told me that Naruji was a Caran insulted by a Rajput, who said to him, "You get your reward at the time of marriage [a gift expected by Carans and other attendants during weddings]; you should get your reward at the time of war!"[101] As a result, he fought furiously. Situated just below the City Palace gates, where Naruji's body is supposed to have fallen, is a memorial with a plaque describing Naruji's defense of the icons in Jagdish's temple from Aurangzeb. Its inscription translates:

Sri Naru Ji's Memorial [Smarak]

In the time of M. R. Raj Singh, V.S. 1736 on the eighth of the dark half of the month of Magh, when Badshah Aurangzeb was advancing on Udaipur, he gave an order to break all the icons. When the foreigners began to enter the doors of the Jagnath Ray Ji Temple, Barath Naruji, joined by twenty soldiers, bravely fought against him and attained Virgati [heaven, paradise].[102]

Just yards down the hill, however, is a shrine for the place Naruji's head fell. This shrine is tended by Muslims. One of them explicitly described Naruji to

99. For examples of discussion of this point, frequently made in the context of contemporary rhetoric denouncing communalism, see the chapter "Medieval History and Communalism," in Engineer, *Communalism in India*, especially p. 16, and also Anand Pathwardan in his film *Father, Son, and Holy War*. Norman Ziegler's treatment of medieval Rajasthan discusses in depth the case of Muslim Rajputs, "who were not viewed by the Rajput as belonging to a separate and distinct *jati* or caste, but as Rajputs like themselves"; "Action, Power and Service," 58. According to the 1891 Census, some Muslims were referred to as Rajput-Muslims because they were regarded as Rajputs who converted to serve Muslim lords. Some practiced goddess worship. By the time of that census, however, this practice was declining, if not disappearing. This does not, as we have seen, negate the tendency of Rajputs (as opposed to "Rajput Muslims," who are generally termed simply Muslim or "Musalman" or sometimes Desi Musalman by others) to conceive of them as sources of contagion. See Singh, *The Castes of Marwar*, 41–43; for objections to the classification of these Muslims as Rajput, see Komal Kothari's introduction to this book.

100. Carans traditionally served as bardic panegyrists who accompanied Rajputs into battle.

101. Interview, December 22, 1987.

102. This term translates literally as goal or destination (*gati*) of warriors (*vir*).

FIGURE 2.5. Naruji

me as a "freedom fighter" who was a Muslim fighting in the Maharana's army against Aurangzeb. When I expressed surprise, he and some young Hindu men I would judge to be in their twenties laughed and agreed that it sounded odd now, but repeated that Naruji was a *pir*.[103] For offerings, he takes sweets and coconuts, items palatable to Hindu heroes. Thus although Naruji is identified by most people as a Hindu "freedom fighter" who defended the palace gates as well as the Jagdish Mandir (Vishnu Temple) slightly below them from the Moghul emperor Aurangzeb, he is routinely worshiped as a *pir* by Muslims at a shrine just yards away from the main monument, the base of which is adorned with painted Hindu imagery.

The terms *pir* and *vir*, in fact, are often used as synonyms and may denote the same person, although their semantic ranges diverge considerably. In general parlance, a *pir* is a teacher whose words or deeds help followers and guide

103. Dhabhaji, a senior administrator at the City Palace, told me that the first Muslim to venerate Naruji was a carriage driver (*kochvan*) who took up veneration after two or three decades; interview December 20, 1987.

them on the path of devotion.[104] Although some *pirs* are *shahids*, martyrs who died fighting and whose example of self-sacrificing devotion inspires faith in devotees, others have no martial experience. Otherwise exemplifying traits and virtues admired by Muslims, these nonmartial teachers little resemble the *jhunjharji, bhomiyaji,* or *sagasji*, who must fight and die violently, or even the Muslim *pirs* who die in battle. The similarity between Muslim *shahids* and Hindu *virs* is not lost on Hindus, who sometimes refer to Hindu *virs* as *shahid*, an Urdu term derived from Arabic.[105] I should also mention that I have also heard the world *bhomiya* used by a Muslim, over the windshield of whose autorickshaw was painted the words, "Victory to Bhomiya!" Surprised and assuming that he was driving someone else's rickshaw, I asked this young man (with whom I had just concluded a vigorous round of bargaining) if he had written those words. He said he had. When I asked who the *bhomiya* was, he said "Ram" and then noted, with a smile, "I'm a Muslim, there's just one god."

Whether Hindu or Muslim, the supplicants of a cultic hero may well include both Hindus and Muslims who mingle as pilgrims at shrines.[106] This is particularly interesting in that sometimes the troublesome and vile spirits possessing supplicants seeking exorcism at Hindu shrines are discovered to be Muslim, and the equally unpleasant spirits possessing supplicants at Muslim shrines turn out to be Hindu.[107] In this context, it is interesting to note that Mahendra Singh, a middle-aged Rajput man from Ghanerao, one of Udaipur's sixteen chief estates, described a Muslim healer as his spiritual guide and told me of various troubles through which this guide had helped him, including problems with ghosts that haunted a property that he wanted to develop. What seems to be of importance in such cases is not identity as a member of one community or another, but faith in the power of the divinity and his human agent or healer; efficacy is alluring. During one visit to a Hindu hero shrine, I met a smiling young Muslim woman who told me that Muslims could worship Hindu heroes if they brought no image of the heroes into their homes. She explained that it is perfectly acceptable to light a candle (*diya*) for a Hindu hero, and she does this routinely for her *sagasji* at her in-laws' home (*sasural*).[108] Another salient example is a Muslim devotee of the

---

104. In Arabic, *pir* originally meant "old man," one wise with experience, and later came to mean teacher generally; Kathryn Ewing, personal communication, October 18, 1998. The word also refers to martial heroes who die in battle and so presumably serve as paradigms of devotion and sacrifice. I thank both Kathryn Ewing and Kevin Rhinehart for discussion on this point. Joyce Flueckiger, who works on Muslim storytelling in south India, has confirmed Kathryn Ewing's observation from work primarily in Pakistan, that *pir* typically refers to teachers, and the martial meaning is subordinate or encompassed; July 29, 1997. On the worship of *pir* (and *vir* in the context of *pir*) see Lambert, "Medical Knowledge in Rural Rajasthan"; Coccari, "The Bir Babas of Banaras," 127–148; Roy, *The Islamic Syncretic Tradition in Bengal*; and Burman, "Hindu-Muslim Syncretism in India." Further discussion of Hindu-Muslim convergences is to be found in my next book project, on hero cults. See also Mayaram, *Resisting Regimes*, and Gottschalk, *Beyond Hindu and Muslim*.

105. Kevin Rhinehart apprised me of its derivation in a personal communication, July 30, 1997.

106. For example, the famous divinity Ramdev, whose main shrine is near Jaisalmer, is venerated by Muslims as a *pir* and by Hindus as a *vir*. Ramdev, who did not die a violent death, had a miraculous apotheosis. Many Hindus consider him an incarnation of Krishna.

107. See Kakar, "Some Unconscious Aspects of Ethnic Violence in India," 136–138, and also his essay "Lord of the Spirit World," 63–67, as well as his "Soul Knowledge and Soul Force," 25–58.

108. This hero died at the hands of family members, not Muslims.

dacoit *jhunjharji* Pratap.[109] The same retired colonel who told me Pratap's story revealed that he knew of a Muslim who "was not a fanatic" and had composed a song about Pratap that was well worth hearing.

In sum, although there is a prima facie tendency to conceive of Hindu hero-ism in the context of Muslim invasion and to understand heroes as defenders of the land (whether Rajasthan as Virbhumi or India as a whole) against Muslims (so often portrayed as alien and incomparably inimical) there is, at the same time, some evidence that Rajput and Muslim, in some contexts, represent codes bear-ing resemblance. As we have seen, the valuation of characteristics varies accord-ing to social location: Rajput trickery is clever, Muslim trickery is scurrilous.[110] At the same time, however, the "good guy" who defends against the alien others is also somewhat suspect. The good warrior is also antinomian and must break code to keep it. Guarding the perimeters of society, he threatens those without but also, at least potentially, those within. The two nameless women who appear in many *jhunjharji* or *bhomiyaji* stories and exclaim "Look! He has no head" will not allow the avenging hero back into town; his success in fighting enemies has made him far too dangerous. And, as the stories of Pratap, the Rajput turned dacoit, and of the Rajput smuggler-hero demonstrate, the representation of Rajput hero as "above" laws or even "criminal" is no obscure theme in Rajput lore. Finally, the attribution of heroic self-sacrifice to *vir* and *pir* may, in certain contexts, con-duce toward conflation, so that *vir* and *pir* may lose their force as opposing desig-nations and become epithets of one and the same hero.

To pave the way for representations of Rajputs and Rajput heroes vis-à-vis other "others," let me point out one final aspect of Rajput-Muslim resemblance. In various folkloric contexts it is clear that like the Muslim, the Rajput, who may at times and certain ways appear non-*dharmik* or even criminal, may be con-trasted with the Brahmanical and, more specifically the Brahmin, whose figure (like the cow's) sometimes serves as emblem for Hindu *dharm*. Rajput duty is often summed up as a twofold charge to defend Brahmins and cows, a task also frequently connected with a duty to protect women.[111] Brahmins and cows are conceived to be extremely *sattvik* (pure and good), and Rajput women, at least, are understood to be *sattvik* in relation to Rajput men, who are thought in all cases to be predominantly, though not wholly, *rajasik* (volatile, kinetic) and *ugra* (fierce). Recall that Tod's eulogy of Rajput warriors contrasted them with non-Rajput Hindus who are "meek . . . worshippers of kine." All three classes of protected being share aspects of "meekness" and are construed to be inherently less aggressive and heroic than Rajput men. Whether reflecting or merely agree-

---

109. For discussion of another Rajput turned dacoit, see Hitchcock, "The Martial Rajput," 15.

110. The detection of illegitimate cleverness or deviousness in the enemy is not limited to this context; according to Ashis Nandy, the British found the "inscrutable Oriental" to be "clever but devious"; *The Intimate Enemy*, 72.

111. Descriptions of heroes frequently make allusion to either all or some of these protégés. A good ex-ample is to be seen in some comments of Nahar Singh at the Museum in the Mehrangarh Fort in Jodhpur. He defined *bhomiyas* for me as "local people who fought to the death to save the honor of ladies, protecting them from Muslims, or who protected cows" (February 1990). For further exemplification, see Miller, "The Twenty-Four Brothers and Devnārāyaṇ," 442.

ing with the colonial attitude, Rajputs do readily distinguish themselves from Brahmins on these grounds. Thus, for example, they tend to bring up the physical weakness of Brahmins, who are apt to be "bookish" and who would, it is often said, make wretched soldiers.[112]

No doubt a major reason for the tendency to type Brahmins as dependents is that Brahmins once answered to Rajput kings as advisors and as priests who often relied on royal patronage. A number of times I heard the disparaging aphorism: "A Brahmin approaches with his hand up [asking for alms], a Rajput with his palm down." It occurs to me that this expression conveys less a general contempt for Brahmins than a specific conviction of relative superiority and an indication of unwillingness to follow unquestioningly the council of Brahmin advisors.[113] Noting with characteristic panache the tendency among the Rajputs of his day to withhold deference from Brahmins and to show them only "outward civility," Tod explains: "The Rajpoot slays buffaloes, hunts, and eats the boar and deer, and shoots ducks, and wild fowl (cookru); he worships the horse, his sword, and the sun, and attends more to the martial song of the bard than to the litany of the Brahmin."[114] Here Tod indicates that the Rajputs he knew were much more concerned with the opinions of the bards who recorded their deeds and recounted tales of ancestral glory (and sometimes dishonor) than they were with the opinions of their Brahmin "betters."

In Udaipur today, most of the Rajputs could hardly be described as antibrahmanical. Indeed Rajputs inevitably use the most polite forms of address when conversing with Brahmins, and they often turn to well-known Brahmin teachers and scholars for information about history and religion, and for advice.[115] It should also be said that although Brahmin heroes are scarce, one such hero has a memorial built by the royal family of Jodhpur and is ritually venerated along with other heroes on an annual basis with the celebration Jodhpur Foundation Day.[116] And yet they also frequently stress the fact that many of the Brahmins in Udaipur are "newcomers" from Gujarat. Having been in Mewar only for half a millennium or so, it is said, they tend to associate with each other (as members of many communities do), preserve Gujarati customs (especially Navratri rituals and dances), and speak Gujarati dialects at home.[117]

---

112. "A Rajput who reads will never ride a horse" is an aphorism often cited by the Rudolphs. See *Reversing the Gaze*, 3, and also the Rudolphs' article, "The Political Modernization of an Indian Feudal Order," 41, as well as Lloyd Rudolph's "Self as Other," 148. For familiarization with the different codes of warrior and Brahmin in history and elsewhere in India during different periods of history, see Heesterman, *The Broken World of Sacrifice*, and his book *The Inner Conflict of Tradition*; Dumont, *Homo Hierarchicus*; essays in Madan, ed., *Way of Life*; Raheja, "India: Caste, Kingship, and Dominance Reconsidered"; Dirks, *The Hollow Crown*; and Nandy, *The Intimate Enemy*.

113. For a note on Brahmins as "hirelings," see Tambs-Lyche, *Power, Profit, and Poetry*, 267.

114. Tod, *Annals and Antiquities*, vol. 1, pp. 25, 57.

115. Carstairs remarked that Rajputs accorded Brahmins "formal respect," but Brahmins "who entered politics or business . . . were intemperately abused"; *The Twice-Born*, 114.

116. According to the plaque there, the memorial was constructed by the Maharaja in gratitude. For discussion of this memorial and others venerated on Foundation Day, I thank Praladh Singh, October 23, 1990.

117. The tendency to focus on these "outsiders" rather than point to the Brahmins who have been in Mewar for a much longer period of time is probably indicative of a tendency to delegitimize Brahmin claims to status in Rajasthan.

The struggle between *Kshatriyas* and Brahmins to establish superiority has a history that stretches back to Vedic times: the "palms up" aphorism is but a variation on this ancient and familiar theme.[118] Tension between what are often termed Brahmanical concerns, such as asceticism in pursuit of liberation (rather than conquest) along with ritual purity, and values represented as Rajput by Rajputs and often by members of lower castes as well, pervades traditions of heroism.[119] Brahmins tend to construe Rajput heroes and the values these heroes embody as conforming relatively closely to the Brahmanical norms that they espouse and represent, whereas others, be they members of lower castes or non-Hindus, tend to depict Rajputs as poignantly unconcerned with these norms. Thus the "everyman's" Rajput of Rajputs, and the often even less refined (or Brahmanical) Rajput of subalterns, thrives on crude and polluting substances and pleasures. Such tensions suffuse the variant representations of Rajput heroism by Brahmins and various lower status *bhopas* and pilgrims. Thus, for example, the blood of the Rajput hero Pabuji, whose epic is recited by lower caste performers, admixes with the blood of his low-caste companions in arms. When the suggestion is made that the confluence ought to be prevented so that Pabuji's body will remain uncontaminated, the goddess steps in to thwart preventative measures. She does so at the request of Pabuji, who says of his companions, "If their blood remains separate then Bhīls will not protect Rajpūts and Rajpūts will not protect Bhīls, and nobody in the world will recognize Pābūjī!"[120]

Recall that the assessment of Rajputs as being unconcerned with pollution is always contextually conditioned, however. There continues to be anxiety about pollution by contact with Muslims, whose touch as well as their blood is represented by Rajputs and other Hindus as polluting in some, though by no means all, situations. Moreover, it is significant that Rajput heroes decapitated by Muslims are not themselves described as polluted, however much the threat of impurity through decapitation by Muslims is elaborated in narrative. Ultimately pollution is transvalued by the hero's voluntary commitments, first, to sacrifice himself for Brahmins-cows-women, *dharm*, Rajasthan, and India, and second, it almost goes without saying, to feed a hungry goddess.

Although Rajput identity is largely informed by notions of conquest, sovereignty, and superiority over inherently lesser subjects, comparative disregard for many Brahmanical norms has been accompanied by an easily detectable if sometimes diffuse or sentimental sense of solidarity with some peoples of much lesser status. The entryway to the City Palace in Udaipur sports a relief carving of the Maharana and a member of the Bhil tribe, which expresses unity and affinity between the Rajputs in the king's lineage and the Bhils who once protected from enemies the Maharana's ancestor Guha. Legend holds that the Bhils chose Guha, scion of the Guhilot line to which the maharanas belong, as their leader and placed upon his brow a *tika* or "mark" of sovereignty from the blood

118. Heesterman, *The Inner Conflict of Tradition*.

119. On the different commitments to asceticism, see Kolff, *Naukar, Rajput, and Sepoy*, 82.

120. Smith, *The Epic of Pābūjī*, 451. Pabuji performers are low-caste *bhopas*, a term that in this context does not refer to a healer possessed by a deity.

of one of their members. Also protected by Bhils was Maharana Bappa Rawal, whose mother placed him under the care of a Brahmin after her husband was killed and kingdom overrun. Before becoming a *sati*, she charged a Brahmin with raising her son, who was to disguise himself as a Brahmin so that no enemies would find him. This adoptive father, however, found raising the boy intolerable. The boy's Rajput blood made him miserable as a cowherd, the role he played as a Brahmin's son; it also made him kill small animals, revealing the Rajput's killer instinct. Ultimately Bappa went off to live among the Bhils, a situation that proved far more felicitous. Famous for their expertise in archery and their ability as hunters, the Bhils offered Bappa a life more compatible with Rajput sensibilities.[121] Accounts of Rajput ascendancy and state consolidation often provide reference to similar tribal alliances.[122]

Carstairs represented the Bhils as the "reverse of the metal" constituted by high-caste or "twice-born" (*dvija*) groups (Brahmins, Rajputs, and Baniyas), but Rajputs have referred to Bhils as rugged and as worthy opponents, and frequently expressed admiration for their ability as hunters, warriors, and bandits. Although Rajput domestic narratives, like the narratives of *bhopas* belonging to a variety of castes, frequently depict Bhils as scurrilous beef-eating cattle thieves, they also represent Bhils as brave and kindred martial spirits and even close companions to Rajputs.[123] Moreover, it has been argued that erecting the hero memorial stones that dot the Rajasthani countryside and are overwhelmingly Rajput is a practice that the Rajputs adopted from the indigenous tribes who once commemorated their heroes' deeds with wooden memorials.[124] In sum, although Rajputs, like members of other high-status groups, tend to see tribe members such as Bhils as inferior (one Rajput from Jodhpur referred to the Bhils of yesteryear as "sword fodder for Mewar") and comparatively unrefined or even unclean, Rajput imagery frequently reflects the resonance of Rajput and tribal norms. This compatibility is also demonstrated in the first narrative recited in the next chapter. There the mother of a Muslim general disguises herself as a Bhil to exact a boon from the especially well-disposed and magnanimous Rajput hero Maha Singh.[125]

Between Brahmin and Bhil lie the vast majority of communities in western Rajasthan. It is not possible to reflect on the subjective construction of "Rajput"

121. For the legends of Guha and Bappa, see Harlan, *Religion and Rajput Women*, 27–29, 124–125; and Tod, *Annals and Antiquities*, vol. 1, pp. 181–182. On Bhils as hunters, see G. Morris Carstairs, who quoted the Maharana of his time as saying that when the *maharanas* of yore went out hunting, "if they called for Bhils to act as beaters for them, for every one they summoned, two would come"; *The Twice-Born*, 108.

122. See Tambs-Lyche, *Power, Profit, and Poetry*, 267.

123. Writing in 1915, Sir Herbert Risley, who describes the Bhil as "hunter, blackmailer, and highway robber," also says, "we are told" that he is "the king of the jungle" and that he "is always ready for a fight"; *The People of India*, p. 141.

124. See B. D. Chattopadhyaya, "Early Memorial Stones of Rajasthan: A Preliminary Analysis of Their Inscriptions."

125. See Alf Hiltebeitel's discussion of the low-status identity of Pabuji's followers, who are by profession warriors and therefore represented as in some sense "Rajput"; *Rethinking India's Oral and Classical Epics*, especially 88–91. On Rajput leaders with tribal comrades, see also Khadgawat ed., *Rajasthan through the Ages*, vol. 1, p. 429. For conventional speculation on the tribal origins of Rajputs, see Surajit Sinha, "State Formation and Rajput Myth in Tribal Central India."

in the context of each of these groups or to comment on typifications of these groups circulating among Rajputs. It is necessary, however, to think briefly through the dynamics of association commonly referred to as "Rajputization."[126] The proliferation and predominance of Rajput elites in Rajasthan has made Rajputs, more than Brahmins, targets of identification and association. In some parts of India, lower-caste peoples have tended to adopt some Brahmanical behaviors in hopes that emulation of Brahmins will lead to respect and upward mobility for their group over time, but in Rajasthan lower status groups have been more likely to share Rajput values and aspire toward Rajput status.[127] This strategy is illustrated handily by the adoption of Rajput names (designating various kinship segmentation units, such as the *shakh* [branch] or *nak* [twig] of the patriline) by members of the low-status castes.[128] For example, some members of the Darzi or tailor caste go by the name Guhilot, a patronymic that designates Rajput descendants of Guha. Another example is to be found in the woeful origin myths of many low-status groups, who say that they were once (and are still and should be considered) Rajputs, but their ancestors were persuaded to become lowly farmers by Muslim conquerors who gave them land, or their ancestors disguised themselves as non-Rajputs to avoid capture by Muslims, thereby resulting in their loss of credibility.[129] One final illustration is the association of a group with Rajput male progenitors who united with low-caste women. Mers, members of a tribe with heavy representation in northwest Rajasthan, claim that their ancestors were Rajput lords who married Mina women. Like the Bhils, the Mers frequently appear as cattle raiders in Rajput hero narratives.[130]

At the same time, there have been some disadvantages in identifying with Rajputs and claiming lofty status despite lowly appearance. The central government's implementation of the so-called Reservation Policy, a sort of "affirma-

126. Such terms —particularly "Sanskritization," which refers to the appropriation and transvaluation of indigenous traditions expressed in the vernacular by Sanskrit-speaking elites (overwhelmingly Brahmin) who consume and produce Sanskrit texts—have fallen into disfavor because of their implicit tendency to posit a simplistic bipolar dynamic or relationship between "high" and "low" persons and their "great" or "little" traditions. The critiques have merit, but there is no need to throw out these babies along with their baths. If recognized as processes that operate in the midst of others, including resistance to Sanskritization and alternative or independent value transformation processes, and if deployed as concepts with mindfulness of their modest interpretive efficacy, these etic imports can shed some light. See Wagoner, "'Sultan among Hindu Kings'"; Pinch, *Peasants and Monks in British India*, 81–114; Kulke, "Ksatriyaization and Social Change"; and Staal, "Sanskrit and Sanskritization."

127. On "Rajputization" and tribes in central India, see Sinha, "State Formation and Rajput Myth in Tribal Central India." On mobility and the relative openness of Kshatriya status generally, see Dumont, *Homo Hierarchicus*, 74–75, 198.

128. On identical and similar strategies of identification, including those listed below, see Pinch, *Peasants and Monks in British India*, especially 81–114; Prakash, "Becoming a Bhuinya in Eastern India," 148 and 157; Davis, *Rank and Rivalry*, 58, 136; Cohn, "The Changing Status of a Depressed Caste"; and Rowe, "The New Cauhans." On the attractiveness of the Kshatriya norms, rather than the Brahmanical, over "the sweep of Indian history," see Rudolph and Rudolph, "Rajput Adulthood," 179. For reflections on transitional identification of a tribal group (the Rawats) with Rajput *riti-rivaj*, see Carstairs, *The Twice-Born*, 135–136. See also Kolff, *Naukar, Rajput, and Sepoy*, 82.

129. See, for example, Davis, *Rank and Rivalry*, 58.

130. The most famous such story is that of *Tejaji*. This hero pursued the Mers to return cattle to their Gujar (herder) owners. See census information in Singh, *The Castes of Mewar*, 50–51.

tive action" program that set aside quotas for members of "backward" groups, provided incentive to reject upper-crust values and to exhibit precisely those behaviors that indicate deviation from the norms of privileged groups and that signal deprivation and persecution. The strategy of accentuating lower status identity through dissociation from elite codes aims at access to educational benefits and greater employment opportunities.[131]

Identification with the martial ethos of Rajputs is not limited to members of Hindu castes and tribes that are in many, though not all, contexts represented as outside the Hindu social order.[132] Let us look at the Jains. Although Jainism is generally referred to as a religion separate from Hinduism, Jains have often been located by Hindus within the fourfold Hindu *varn* schema, which includes Brahmins, Kshatriyas, and Shudras (servants, members of the lowest castes), as well as Vaishyas (a group comprising farmers and merchants). In the Udaipur area and elsewhere in Rajasthan, Jains are often understood to be Vaishyas, or, more narrowly, as Baniyas, merchants. In fact, many Baniyas in this area are Jain, the two words often being used interchangeably. The Jain tenets of nonviolence and vegetarianism have made it easy to suppose that Jains identify with the Hindu code of conduct professed most vehemently and approximated most closely by Brahmins, their superiors in the Hindu status scheme. Recent fieldwork among lay Jains, however, demonstrates the importance of the Rajput martial ethos to lay members of this group.[133] Many heroes who are venerated by these Jains earn devotion not by adhering to Brahmanical norms, but by exhibiting martial violence and discipline, both of which shape their character and ultimately enable them to realize the higher *dharm* of nonviolence articulated by Jainism.[134] Moreover, Jains revere ascetics who have attained liberation as *jins*, "conquerors," so that asceticism, as Alan Babb puts it, "turns out to be a spiritualized martial virtue."[135] It should also be noted that members of some prominent Jain lineages, such as the Oswal, claim Rajput ancestry and boast of services rendered the Rajput aristocracy.[136] Moreover, there are Jain *bhopas* and devotees who participate routinely in the cultic worship of Rajput heroes.

Rajput characterizations of Baniyas, whatever their faith, are often derogatory. Stereotyped as voracious capitalists and vilified as moneylenders, Baniyas have often been targets of verbal abuse by Rajputs and others.[137] Yet there are

131. On this phenomenon in India generally, see Dirks, "Homo Hierarchicus." On "de-Sanskritization" in connection with a Hyderabadi community that derives its origins from Rajasthan Marwaris, see Kakar, *The Colors of Violence*, 89.

132. As we shall see, members of tribal groups are identified with or encompassed by the notion "Hindu" when juxtaposed with Muslim conquerors. The Hindu is, in such an instance, represented as the indigenous as opposed to the foreign.

133. Babb, *Absent Lord*, and Cort, "The Bell-Eared Great Hero."

134. For first bringing this to my attention and for continuing discussion of this point over several years, I thank John Cort.

135. *Absent Lord*, 82.

136. See Babb, "Rejecting Violence."

137. Typifying the tendency to degrade a class by impugning the reputation of its women, one of Harald Tambs-Lyche's informants said that "A Baniya or Patidar girl will sleep with anyone." Tambs-Lyche identifies the informant simply as a member of a "Rajput-allied caste"; *Power, Profit, and Poetry*, 105.

many tales of trusted Baniya *kamdars*, servants in charge of household management in royal and aristocratic lineages, and many Rajputs today express approval of the magnificent Jain temples (such as those at Ranakpur) gracing the Rajasthani countryside. Moreover, many are deeply respectful of the Jain monks and nuns who practice stark asceticism. Ascetic discipline is often understood by Rajputs and others as essential to the cultivation of martial character and the realization of military goals. Nevertheless, Rajputs often construct their identity by contrasting it with these particular others, and many eagerly distinguish Rajput *riti-rivaj* from that of Jain laity. In Udaipur, I heard more than one Rajput dismiss Divali, the festival devoted to the goddess of wealth, as a Baniya holiday and compare it unfavorably to two "Rajput holidays" that Rajputs considered most important, Navratri and Dashara, both of which celebrate martial conquest.[138]

In sum, the representation of Muslims in folklore and history needs to be located within the context of contemporary constructions of caste and issues of communalism: the rendering of Rajput and Rajput hero in heroic tales conjures up images of a number of others who challenge, alter, and sometimes also affirm the "Rajputness" of Rajput heroes. The configuration of Rajput code that emerges in any particular tale will reflect the dynamics of association between Rajputs and other groups. These dynamics will include conflict at times, but also moments of consensus so that Rajput heroes who appear in the ancestral narratives of Rajputs will share premises with other narratives, including those conveyed by pilgrims in cultic shrines for Rajput heroes. This dimension of consensus should not be dismissed or deemed unimportant.

Rosalind O'Hanlon has commented on some scholars' "demand for a spectacular demonstration of the subaltern's independent will and self-determining power," and Gloria Raheja has argued that this agenda "has meant that the continuities between hegemonic discourse and subaltern culture have generally been ignored."[139] Although reflection on voice in narrative is always a thorny speculative process, it seems necessary to note that alternative, nonsubaltern codes must be recognized and reckoned with. The Rajput is a dominant caste holding values that contain and co-opt, but also challenge, not only tribal but also Brahmanical norms. This is especially important to recall in the context of hero veneration by Brahmins, whether priests or devotees, at Rajput hero shrines.

Before leaving this cursory treatment of "otherness" and pressing on to focus directly on heroic text, be it domestic or cultic, one more matter should be considered. There is another "other" who remains as yet unattended: the hero himself. In Rajasthan, as elsewhere in India and the rest of the world, divinities, who are in some sense alien, must prove themselves. Recall that mention of hero worship often produces admissions of skepticism if not outright denunciation. Educated urbanites are especially likely to consider hero worship déclassé

138. Needless to say, the worship of wealth on Dan-teras is compared unfavorably with the worship of Devi and weapons on Navratri and Dashara.

139. O'Hanlon, "Recovering the Subject," 191; Raheja, "Introduction," 15. See also Raheja, "The Paradoxes of Power and Community" and "Negotiated Solidarities"; Gold, "Outspoken Women," 104–106; and March, "Two Houses and the Pain of Separation in Tamang Narratives from Highland Nepal," 136.

or superstitious. Particularly suspect among such people are the well-known cultic heroes such as Pabuji and Tejaji, as well as the village heroes. Chiefly suspect are the *bhopas* who claim to be possessed by heroes. Many Rajputs do not believe in possession, and group *bhopas* (whether hero *bhopas* or *bhopas* who are possessed by other divinities, such as goddesses or Bherujis) with false ascetics who beg for a living. Often I heard *bhopas* denounced as déclassé, but then I also heard some of the very people who denounced *bhopas* relate experiences in which they had actually sought aid from *bhopas* in a moment of desperation and then were disappointed with the results. For example, one Brahmin academician, who deemed my research on *bhopas* misguided (if I had to work on religion, I should study the *upanishads*), told me that he had taken a dying relative to such a shrine and it had done no good. For many, the *bhopa's* shrine is something of a court of last resort, a long shot for people in dire straits.

Many Rajputs share the general suspicion of *bhopas*. In fact, I met few Rajput pilgrims at the shrines I visited. I did, however, meet Rajputs who had made pilgrimages to the shrine of a *jhunjharji* at Nim ka Khera, a village near Chittor. This *jhunjharji* specializes in curing alcoholism. I know of one Rajput man who credits his sobriety to this *jhunjharji*, and another who sought sobriety there but failed. According to the *bhopa* at that shrine, those who seek to break the spell of addiction are supposed to bring a full bottle of alcohol, consume the liquor at the shrine, then leave behind the bottle and with it the addiction. His estimation of the *jhunjharji's* success rate is more optimistic than that of some others I encountered. In this vein I should also mention another hero shrine, located in the Pokran area and also specializing in curing addictions. It is well known for curing opium addiction as well as alcohol abuse.[140]

In addition to the general skepticism Rajputs direct toward these nonetheless popular shines, they sometimes demonstrate a certain bravado in their rejection of unknown or unproved deities. The following example, which demonstrates an especially vivid lack of receptivity, demonstrates the principle well.

> Just outside Jodhpur I was playing polo. I took a fall and saw that my horse's girth had broken. Then two more riders fell just around the same spot. Also the grooms, two or three of them, fell there. My friend, who lived there, said, "There's a *bhomiya* in the shrine [*sthan*] just near there. So he and some other people made offerings there. But this other friend said that he didn't believe in this *bhomiya* stuff, so he went over and urinated right at the *bhomiya*. Nothing happened to him. But then later he was sleeping and he jumped up having a fit; he was saying "he's coming, he's coming!" He thought that someone was coming to kill him. The fits continued for two or three days. Then he sent some offerings.[141]

---

140. Pokran appears on various maps with diverse spellings such as Pokaran and Pokhran.

141. During the past decade there has been a resurgence of interest in polo, which has become a tourist attraction as well as a local form of entertainment. Many Rajput boys have trained for the sport and numerous horse-raising facilities have been established. Matches are frequently televised.

The skepticism demonstrated here is not unusual for Rajputs. It surfaced whenever there were reports of a new deity. For example, during my stay reports circulated around Udaipur that a striking young Rajput woman from a nearby village had proven herself to be an incarnation of the goddess Avadi Mata, whose main shrine is located in a village not far from Chittor. Although pilgrims flocked by the hundreds to the village to receive her blessing, and her Rajput family was clearly profiting on that account, most Rajputs I knew challenged her authenticity. Many pointed to her history of mental problems and said that she was simply deranged.

Brij Raj Chauhan's classic ethnography, *A Rajasthan Village*, records the same kind of skepticism. When a new deity appeared in the village and a procession of tribute was arranged, some young Rajputs "wanted to test the bona fides of the new deity, and instigated a conflict." Afterward, "a spirited young Rajput said, 'I could have put the deity in its proper place.'"[142] Chauhan notes the tendency of Rajputs to be skeptical and attributes it to their education and experience in towns. There is, however, something else at work. Rajput skepticism reflects not just a skepticism about unfamiliar deities but a demonstration of challenge to deities that are not their own. These other deities represent implicit challenges not only to one's own deities but also to one's own power. Thus, according to Chauhan, the "spirited young Rajput" claims that he could have "put the deity in its proper place." While acknowledging the deity's existence, he is denying its power over him. I recorded a similar observation from Mahendra Singh of Ghanerao. It was made in the context of discussing not heroes or goddesses but ghosts, particularly those living in the wilderness areas around the Aravallis. He told of a meeting with a ghost during a stroll at night. He said that although he believed in some ghosts, he would not be intimidated by them. Having noted that the ghost he encountered was a Rajput, he smiled and exclaimed, "I am also a Rajput!" The implication was that he would not let that other Rajput push him around.

Hence the skepticism is linked to perceptions of status and power. Rajputs may venerate and eulogize divine warriors from their own lineages, but they do not typically or readily worship the ancestors of others. To do so risks conceding status, which is generally calculated according to the zero-sum principle. A similar dynamic can be seen in the worship of familial goddesses. I have already noted the tendency for households to have double *kuldevi* traditions. The "men's story" typically stresses the acquisition of a *kuldevi* through conquest: the dominant king takes both the losing ruler's daughter and the emblematic icon, the *kuldevi*. Whereas men are quick to tell of acquiring deities by conquest, they tend to dismiss stories women tell of importing *kuldevis* at the time of ordinary marriages.[143] Men either deny the importations or consider them to be secondary or insignificant, dismissible infiltrations. The principle that skepticism and

142. Chauhan, *A Rajasthan Village*, 187–188.
143. On alternative battle and ordinary marriage motifs in *kuldevi* foundation myths, see Harlan, "Battles, Brides, and Sacrifice," and also *Religion and Rajput Women*, 100–106.

acquisition by conquest both would seem to uphold: deities are, among other things, tokens in the game of status negotiation.

The next chapter takes up directly the ways in which Rajputs contend with their divine "hero others" and deploy their heroic narratives to demonstrate the quality of Rajput descent and the superiority of some Rajputs over others. Although conflicts with Muslims or tribal groups often set the scene for demonstration of "the manly virtues," the contest that appears preeminent in the narratives that Rajput men tell is one of status negotiation within Rajput ranks, where a historic heroic death embodies the *virta* that sorts rank and place. Together, the "historical" narratives reveal much about identity and stature in a world in which intracaste rank remains both a source of pride and a commodity that indicates privilege. The chapter compares the sorts of narratives men tend to tell with those generally told by women, who usually deploy them to demonstrate not relative but absolute status. Their interest lies less in contemporary rank than in the bare fact of heroic transformation, which makes available to them the power of a divinity whose worship is overwhelmingly their responsibility and domain.

3

Heroic Story

Slaughter and Glory

Go, ye heroes, go to glory.
Though you die in combat gory.
Ye shall live in song and story.
Go to immortality!

Go to death and go to slaughter
Die, and every Cornish daughter,
With her tears your grave shall water.
Go you heroes go and die!
Go you heroes go and die!

With these lines from Gilbert and Sullivan's operetta "The Pirates of Penzance," delicate but spirited daughters of a "modern major general" cheer on faint-hearted policemen who ultimately lament, "when constabulary duty's to be done . . . a policeman's lot is not a happy one." Seeking to embolden reluctant "heroes" preparing to fight pirates, these maidens, who have previously described themselves as "hardy little lasses," predict "death and slaughter" that will bring forth devotion from weeping "Cornish daughters" and earn the policemen "immortality" in the form of "song and story."[1] Here, death in battle brings glory and immortality through song and story, as well as the promise of life—the flora to arise from well-watered graves. A more concise summation of important principles of hero veneration, whether in Victorian England, ancient Greece, or contemporary India, could hardly be found.

The following chapters theorize about immortal heroes remembered through song and story. We begin with heroic stories that tell

1. Gilbert, "The Pirates of Penzance," 27, 37, 13.

in detail the accomplishment of divinity and the establishment of routine ritual veneration. Sampling narratives told at home by descendants and their relatives, this chapter and its successor chart the contours and characteristics of domestic veneration, while suggesting ways in which heroes who have gone to "death and slaughter" speak to the men and women invoking and vivifying heroic stories. Contemplating the stories presented in this chapter and the next allows us to understand scenarios in which death at the hands of an enemy and for the betterment of society constitutes sacrifice for and by a bloodthirsty goddess, who consumes her henchmen and renders them divine. As we shall see, both society, represented in variant modes as female, and the goddess who serves as guardian as well as emblem of society, require heroic death and slaughter; the hero-victim perfecting himself by fulfilling his duty as a male sacrificer preserves territory and, more important, those who must not be sacrificed. Achieving and conferring glory, the hero's sacrifice bears variegated fruit (*phal*). Glory is inherited by descendants, who may claim enhanced status and command deeper respect as generations proliferate and prosper.

I begin my treatment of heroic story with a sample selected because of its richness and explicitness, qualities that make it an excellent point of departure.[2] What follows, in this chapter and its sequel, is a close, if sometimes purposefully meandering, reading of the text, which comprises frame episodes that reveal, comment upon, and open up the text that they also preface and circumscribe. The episodes, together with that which they frame and engage, illustrate some recurrent elements of domestic hero worship and provide opportunities to elaborate upon these principles and introduce crucial context. In other words, the sample is to be used here not only as a scope for inspecting elements of culture that are significant and compelling but also as a springboard for going beyond the specifics of the text and exploring topics and perspectives that may complement the text or, at times, demonstrate divergence from it. In sum, the text is deployed as code or cipher.[3]

Despite analysis and utilization of the text throughout two chapters, my reading of it will remain incomplete. It goes without saying that analyses of text are inevitably incomplete in that they reveal any interpreter's (or narrator's) position and commitments at any given moment, and so are temporally bound and robbed of inherent, temporal fluidity.[4] But beyond this, there is the complexity of this multiply framed oral text, in which frame frames frame and subsequent/and or preceding text diachronically (that is to say, prospectively and retroactively) and also synchronically (with the various textual elements suggesting strikingly ambiguous and intersecting trajectories and points of closure). Although, as we shall see, there is some overt reckoning with ethnopoetics, the text is drawn upon here to suit this book's agenda: gendered analysis of heredi-

---

2. A portion of this narrative appears in Harlan, *Religion and Rajput Women*, 197–198.

3. Reflections on the functioning of this complex, doubly framed narrative are offered in Harlan, "On Being Framed in a Rajput Hero Narrative."

4. A good, if somewhat lamentable, example of the shifting nature of the interpreter's position and commitments is provided by a comparison of my discussion here and my fleeting utilization of the text in *Religion and Rajput Women*, 197–198. There, regarding the frames as extraneous, I omitted them.

tary hero veneration. This chapter utilizes the first frame, introduced in the first paragraph, as an emblem that reveals ways in which, first, both men and women attribute and configure the glory and status that heroic sacrifice confers, and second, men and women are understood as engaged in a battle of the sexes in which women, so often imaged as the Rajput equivalent of demure "little lasses," are rendered disturbingly "hardy." Attribution and configuration of glory and status are the subjects conjointly treated in the next two sections, whereas the battle motif is explored in the third. The next chapter focuses on the second (or framed) frame, which renders starkly explicit the often presumed and therefore invisible or translucent context in which heroic sacrifice is understood by Rajputs: the sacrifice of soldier to goddess, male to female, men to women.

The story was told to me by a middle-aged Rajput woman whose family governed one of the most prominent *thikana*s in Mewar. This woman is an enthusiastic storyteller as well as a devotee of both her ancestral hero and the cultic hero Kallaji, whom she credits with healing one of her children from a dire illness. During my interview with her, her husband, who was then writing a history of his *thikana*, interrupted regularly with approving affirmations of her narratives. Later he also rendered several hero narratives of his own. I use her version of the story, rather than his, for several reasons. First, although it is much shorter than her husband's, it makes more lucid than his does the frame episodes that will engage us throughout these two chapters. Its opening frame, for example, is a wonderfully concise demonstration of the special interest that men's narratives usually exhibit in relative status, particularly the relative status of Rajput families but also the relative position of Rajputs and members of other communities. The very economy that distinguishes this woman's telling from many men's tellings and that renders it in this respect more typical of women's tellings than men's makes especially evident what is often at stake and what is given special emphasis in men's tellings. Thus utilizing this narrative emphasizes the point that although, as I will argue, there are rather routine ways in which men's and women's narratives vary, men's and women's tellings are inevitably intertextual: there are no pure, unfiltered voices speaking, whoever the narrators and whatever their messages. Thus the comparisons I draw here should always be considered relative and fluid.

As I indicate below, it is evident to me that the husband's passion for history, so evident in his brimming library and in his display of Rajput artifacts, has informed her telling, which is much more concerned with history and status than the vast majority of other women's accounts I recorded. His presence during his wife's narration may have also heightened reflexivity and enhanced resemblance to his account. Although I am privileging her narrative, and not his, by reporting it in whole and by using it to frame two chapters, I will be resorting to his narrative when comparison is useful. With all these caveats in mind, then, let us attend her story.

This story is about Rana Maha, Rao Sahab of Bathera. A *rao* ["king": the title of a *thakur* from another estate] . . . came back from war: he was frightened.[5] He told a maidservant to get a coal for smoking a pipe. His wife said to the maidservant, "Don't take an iron thing for the coal, take a wooden thing. He's frightened of swords, so don't take an iron thing." He was so ashamed, he committed suicide.

Then Maha Singh went to war and did a lot of *puja* [ritual veneration] to Shiv and Mata ["Mother," meaning the Goddess].

The Rao Sahab Maha Singh was engaged in war with the Muslim Ranbaj Khan. The Rao Sahab had a custom of granting a boon to someone every morning. Ranbaj Khan's mother came to the king's court disguised as a Bhil woman and asked of him the boon that in the upcoming battle her son be allowed to strike the first blow. Thinking her son an ally, the king assented. Then the Bhil woman revealed her identity [as a Muslim], but the king had already given his word and was bound by it.

When the battle began, Ranbaj Khan charged toward the king and with a single slash of the sword removed his head. Outraged by the twin insults of trickery and decapitation, the king fought on brilliantly until he had revenge in the form of Ranbaj Khan's head. The decapitating blow he dealt also split in half his enemy's elephant and elephant saddle. To this day we worship the Rao Sahab's sword and shield on Dashara.

The two fought all the way to Bandanvara—all the way from Rundera—and there two ladies were passing and saw this man without a head and said, "Look! What kind of man is this?" And with these words he fell down.

There is a *chatri* in Bandanvara, where his body fell. There is also one in Rundera, where his head fell. When Ranbaj Khan and Maha Singh died, Maha Singh's dog kept their blood from mixing together and the dog died after this, so there's a memorial stone for the dog in Bandanvara.

Then Maha Singh had two sons: Sarang II, first ruler of Kanor, which split from Bathera, and Surat Singh, who ruled Bathera.

Frame One, Take One: Combat Gory's Glory and the Status It Confers

The account begins by delivering an insult, a *gali*. As we have seen, holding honor dear, Rajputs are easily affronted, but also frequently proficient at effrontery.[6]

---

5. His *thikana* name is deleted here, lest the incendiary insult this frame describes be launched at a specific party. Other renditions of this story I have collected do not assign a name to this character. See note 8.

6. Rajputs are by no means alone in their fondness for insults. Indeed, India has an abundance of derogatory expressive traditions. Among the best known to students of folklore are the insult songs (*galiyan*) that women sing during wedding festivities. Such songs proclaim, among other things, the sexual ineptitude of grooms and their male relations as well as the sexual voraciousness of their female relations, especially mothers. In Rajasthan, women perform such insult songs with hilarity not only weddings but also during the festival of Holi, in which hierarchical relationships are typically inverted. For examples of insult songs in Rajasthan, see Gold, "Sexuality, Fertility, and Erotic Imagination in Rajasthani Women's Songs."

During social gatherings, Rajput men regularly trade insults that serve as much-savored spice in their highly formal and polite social intercourse. Good-natured ribbings often communicate affection. They are expressions and agents of bonding. Not all insults, however, are intended or taken to be utterly, or even marginally, benign. Questioning honor, they may convey dishonor; implying convictions of superiority, whether slight or profound, they may irritate or even infuriate and prompt revenge.

This narrative's first mission is to deliver an accusation of cowardice in the line of another prominent family. Prefacing the account of Maha Singh's transfiguration into a *jhunjharji*, the *gali* frame story effects a stark contrast between Maha Singh's heroism and the cowardice of this Rajput from a purportedly lesser family. Whereas the convention of contrasting hero with coward (or heroic with cowardly attribute) is commonly employed in a variety of expressive genres (for example, the aphorism about the child destined to be a hero: "the hero plays alone, the coward must have company"), in this case the frank assignment of cowardice to the ancestor of a specific family unsubtly suggests an agenda.[7] This "coward episode" illustrates well the principle that heroic narratives, and particularly the stories men tell, continue to sort out social relationships and further claims to status. Like the hero memorial that once delineated the border of one's territory as opposed to others', the heroic "memories" conveyed in such accounts of glory negotiate or establish the possession of relative as well as absolute illustriousness.

If the point is not crystal clear in the variant we have before us, it is absolutely adamantine in the narrative of our raconteur's husband, a middle-aged mustached Rajput. His account renders this coward frame story in such detail that it veritably overshadows the Maha Singh vs. Ranbaj Khan story, which is a good bit shorter. If the gusto with which he delivered it doesn't leap forth from the page, the completeness of detail cannot but help convey his sense of enthusiastic mastery as well as historic import.

> Maharavat Maha Singh, forefather of Kanor, was a Sarangdevot [a Rajput *kul*]. In his time there was no Kanor: he was in Bathera. During his time in Mewar the *jagirdars* [*thakurs*] were transferred from one *thikana* to another; they were not fixed to any *thikana*. So there was a famous warrior Ranbaj Khan. He and his soldiers attacked Mewar side, so while he was entering Mewar, His Highness Maharana Udaipur sent . . . [another estate's *thakur*], who was quite a young man. He went into the battlefield. He felt terrorized by the

---

7. A version of this aphorism was incorporated into the lyrics from the impromptu performance of a ballad for me by the previously mentioned Deva Ram. He described the hero he venerates as Hanslav Bhomiya. Accompanied by his *ravanhattha* in his modest home near the hero shrine, he sang, "What is it [that is, no matter] if the hero is alone, the hero *is* alone [*sūro to eklo ī*—in other words, that's what defines him]; the hero plays alone, the coward cannot." The hero's play may refer to his fun as child, but it may also suggests his future as a metamorphosed divinity; as we shall see, deceased spirits and deities are often also said to play, by visiting or possessing human beings. On possession play, see Gold, "Spirit Possession Perceived and Performed in Rural Rajasthan," 39 note 5; and Erndl, Victory to the Mother, 105–134.

soldiers or something came to his mind [for some other unknowable reason he became afraid] so he couldn't face Ranbaj Khan. He reached his place and he just got off his horse onto the ground, put his sword down, and sat down while his wife from the room above saw him sitting in an awkward way.[8]

At the same time he called his maidservant to bring fire for his *cilam* [pipe]—to smoke his *cilam* he wanted that fire. So his wife in a taunting way told his maidservant not to give fire to him [the warrior] in an iron pot, but [rather] in a wooden pot because "he's frightened of iron"—like a sword or anything else made of iron.

These words struck him badly and he took out his sword and cut his neck himself and died there.

This was reported to the Maharana and he became upset because Ranbaj Khan had entered Mewar.

The story goes on to tell of *puja*, the meddling Muslim mother, and Maha Singh's dramatic demise by Ranbaj Khan's sword. Like the wife's story, the husband's neatly contrasts the inglorious death of the coward and glorious death of the devout sacrificial soldier. Both stories deploy the *gali* to establish superiority, though typically stories sort out the relative status of rival Rajputs without resorting to such an obvious insult. Often the battle is not circumscribed by any frame indicating noncombatant competitors, and sometimes the battle account becomes a type of frame for the story of rivalry, the details of which are explored at length. Consider the following *jhunjharji* story, told to me by a Rajput from the ruling family of Amet and filled with such details. It begins with a battle frame, even as a second battle is folded into a reckoning of rivalry by way of support for the premise of superiority.

There's one [*sagasji*] at Jilola . . . the place from which we adopt if necessary. He died during a fight there.

There's also one in Amet, though not from our family. He was a Rajput killed during a succession battle here at Amet. It was during the Amet-Meja war for succession of the throne [*gaddi*]. His shrine is right in the granary, which is located in a part of the palace that has now been sold off to some *Baniyas*.

There is a sub-*thikana* of Amet called Vemali, a younger-brother *battis thikana* [an estate granted to a younger son; one of a group of thirty-two lesser states of Mewar].[9] Amet is the elder-brother estate.

The Rawat [king, *thakur*] of Amet died with no heir. His wife wanted a Vemali child to sit on the throne, but Jilola had always had

---

8. I have omitted the reference to the *thakur*'s name and *thikana* here, as above, because both identity and incident are contested. Although all writing inscribes perspectives, this is so blatantly prejudicial that I have decided to grant the characterization the same anonymity I originally assured to various informants. The alternative course would be to activate or aggravate, rather than simply acknowledge, a latent feud. The story of the cowardly lord, so well known among women, has typically been told to me without attribution to a particular person. Although I may be emulating their circumspection, I believe that the identity of the lord has become irrelevant in the story, which, we will see, women typically deploy to serve a different genre of rivalry.

9. On Mewar's political structure and *thikana* ranking, see Harlan, *Religion and Rajput Women*, 33–37.

first priority in terms of adoption. So she forcibly set the child on the throne.

There was a big battle and a warrior was killed and became a *sagasji bavji*. Everything was set on fire. Someone from Jilola was put on the throne but then the Maharana of Mewar granted the loser Meja. Amet was asked by him to give a few villages and 10,000 rupees cash per year. . . .

So Meja . . . was a new grant and it also became a *solah thikana* [one of the top "sixteen estates" in the three-tiered hierarchy of Mewari *thikana*s] with the same seat [as Amet], which is why to this day if they are at some function, we won't be and if we are there, they won't be.[10]

In this text, the hero's actions are almost wholly eclipsed by the mass of details on a political rivalry initiated generations ago—the raconteur identified his great-grandfather as the person adopted—but to this day continues to produce sparks. The death of the hero, who is not a familial hero but a hero fighting on behalf of the family's interests, is not explicitly represented in this context as bringing glory to the family, though, it goes without saying, the deaths of all martial agents are understood to enhance the glory of king and state. Nevertheless, the war in which he fought becomes the arena of status negotiation. Clearly the teller of the tale regards Amet's claim to the title of *solah thikana* as prior and exclusive. The peripheral *sagasji* fighting for Amet is rendered implicitly a martyr or witness to the claim's truth and authenticity—even if the "usurpers" did get their own *thikana*.

This hero, as we have noted, is not the only hero in the narrative, which begins with mention of a *sagasji* in Jilola. Taken together with the account's conclusion, which describes the establishment of Meja, the reference to the Jilola *sagasji* would certainly seem to fortify Jilola's claim to be the appropriate place of adoption and also to challenge indirectly Meja's claim to recognition as a *solah thikana*. Mention of a *sagasji* in Jilola supports the line's illustriousness and implicitly suggests that not only custom but also martial glory should be considered evidence of Amet's case for superiority.

Note that both of the *sagasji*s mentioned in the account die fighting an enemy. Whereas most *sagasji*s are victims of assassination stemming from political intrigue, these die in outright combat. They demonstrate the tendency, often found in *sagasji* stories, to make the *sagasji* not just an unwitting victim but also an aggressive agent who, like the *jhunjharji*, struggles on with superhuman determination. He may keep his head, but his struggle beyond death is shown to be analogous to, if not identical with, the *jhunjharji*'s or *bhomiya*'s. He is a willing sacrifice, and his will is strong enough to propel him forward despite mortal injury.

It is instructive to compare the Amet story, which so visibly uses heroes to prop up its case for superior status, with the story of Amet's most celebrated famil-

10. This narrative exemplifies a hoary theme in Indian narratives: dynastic conflict, which is very prominent in epic, from Sanskrit *Mahabharata* to vernacular *Gogaji*.

to demonstrate that the Baniya's loyalty was beneficial to her family, for which reason it continues to pay him respect (*dhok*).[11] She also betrayed ambivalence, however, about venerating such a figure. Having described him as a *kamdar*, she then immediately deploys the conjunctive "still" before saying that he "fought loyally." Here, at the very least, she presents this servant as exceptional.

Her account also suggests what I certainly interpreted as a keenness to explain that Rajputs are not possessed by this spirit. The claim that Rajputs do not get possessed is common among Rajputs, many of whom deeply dislike the idea of someone else controlling their bodies. Nevertheless, there are instances in which Rajputs, typically village Rajputs, rather than aristocrats, are represented by relatives as having been possessed by deceased family members, including heroes.[12] Moreover, some hero cults have Rajput *bhopas*. Here, however, the claim that Rajputs do not get possessed would seem to betray an even deeper conviction that Rajputs would be unlikely to be controlled by an outsider. At the same time, it certainly seems that here possession of Baniya family members is invoked as an index of the *kamdar* spirit's veracity.

The same kind of servant-master tension found in the *kamdar*'s story is revealed by this final narrative about a non-Rajput hero. Its narrator is a woman who hails from a Mewar *thikana* that was ruled by Sisodiya Rajputs and was living, at the time I interviewed her, in a modern house in Jodhpur. Like her elderly mother, whom I came to know well during my earliest days living in Rajasthan, she demonstrated a love of stories, and although she was young and dwelled in a city rather than on her husband's family property in Kushalgarh, she had stories galore to share about her *sasural*'s history and customs. She told me in a typically economical but nonetheless exuberant fashion not of a warrior who dies fighting alongside his Rajput patron but of a servant who dies at the hands of his master.

> There was a servant who was poisoned. This man had gained so much strength that the late His Highness Darbar had come to meet him.[13] His Highness had a silver coin in his hand. He gave it to this chap to see. The fellow felt it and pressed it and made it very long. When the Darbar saw this, he was afraid that the man had become too powerful and had poison given to him. He [the Darbar] used to sit on horseback. He'd grab a branch and do a pull-up and pull the horse up with him.
>
> His [the servant's] wife was a *satiji*. She put her palms on the front gate. You can still see the prints.

This narrative fails to provide a caste designation for the servant, who could well have been what Rajputs call a Daroga (the offspring of a union between a Rajput father and a woman from a lesser caste), but who could also have been

---

11. Another woman in her household told me that Vijayvargi (also referred to as Vijayvargiya) is commemorated with a *chatri* (funerary pavilion), located in front of a Shiv temple in Tilasma.

12. On distrust of possession among Rajputs, see Harlan, *Religion and Rajput Women*, 66–67, and on Rajputs' distrust of *bhopas* in particular, see Chauhan, *A Rajasthan Village*, 206.

13. Darbar, "court," is frequently used to refer to a king.

from any number of castes that typically attend a Rajput lord. The account illustrates concern that the servant posed a threat to the Darbar, who should be stronger than his servant to retain control over him. The solution is poison, which is consumed by many a *sagasji*, although in this case the *vir* is not explicitly referred to by that designation. Ironically the servant's strength is conveyed through hyperbole: he squeezes a coin until it becomes thin and long. Thus the account paints a glorious portrait of this hero-to-be, this match for a pull-up performing king.

Moreover, the account mentions that this strong man's wife became a *sati*, which is also considered a grand thing. Rajput women are usually reticent to attribute *sati* status to women of other castes, but here a Rajput woman unhesitatingly describes the servant's wife as a *sati*, whose auspicious red palm prints are represented on the front gate of the estate. Thus the narrator's account both illustrates a lesson given to an impertinent servant and the glory of a servant who attained transhuman status when he was assassinated. His demise resulted from conflict, an implicit challenge to the master's control, yet the Rajput account pays him tribute, albeit one that co-opts his challenge. The servant's defiance reflects positively on the king's line!

This narrative is unusual. Rarely does a non-Rajput challenge a Rajput and then earn a Rajput eulogy. In any case, it completes the brief list of narratives I collected about non-Rajput heroes celebrated by Rajputs. Revealing as these narratives are, they are overshadowed by the proliferation of Rajput hero narratives told by Rajputs about their own family members. The nonfamilial narratives are interesting not simply because they are exceptions to the principle that Rajputs worship their own heroes, who reflect and illustrate family status, but because they demonstrate that non-Rajput heroes' deaths can be and, in fact, are deployed by Rajputs as evidence of status. Even where the hero is victim not of a common enemy but of a Rajput, his illustriousness is refracted by Rajputs to illuminate Rajput glory. In sum, in such narratives Rajputs retain a proprietary interest, much to their benefit. To this day these heroes remain vibrant status markers for Rajputs.

One further point bears mentioning. Although the narrative clearly conforms to the principle that heroes' deaths reflect glory on Rajput lines, its content, as well as the tone with which it was delivered, also strikes me as betraying sympathy for the servant executed by the *thakur*. It could be that in this case the narrator, a young woman married into the family that venerates this hero, feels some sense of solidarity with the servant so severely treated. As I listened to her story, I had the definite impression that the servant's death was not simply a testimony to justice served upon an uppity underling but rather, or at least also, a tragedy.

This said, the narrative does not cast the king who ordered execution as a contemptible villain. In fact, this lord reminds one of the great Mewar monarch Raj Singh, who, although responsible for his son's execution, is described favorably by pamphlets dedicated to his son, as well as by Brahmin attendants and pilgrims at the Sarv Ritu Vilas Sagasji Bavji shrine.[14] He is especially praised in

---

14. Raj Singh is often described as one of the great kings of Mewar. Although having his son killed is viewed as a mistake, it is often dubbed understandable, for any king is seen as a target for sons who wish for premature succession. Patricide, by contrast, is seen as inexcusably "against the grain."

local histories for sheltering the icons of the Vaishnava deities Shri Nathji and Dvarakadishji from the Moghul emperor Aurangzeb when they arrived from Mathura and Dvaraka.[15] Nevertheless, stories about the execution of Raj Singh by his father often betray ambivalence about this monarch, who is quick to pronounce a death sentence and later learns that a scheming advisor or some other miscreant was to blame for the rumors of Sagasji Bavji's impropriety in the harem. The involvement of a miscreant may alleviate but not absolve the rash king's guilt. Because of the Maharana's mistake, temple attendants say, no *maharana* since his day has been allowed to set foot in Sagasji's Sarv Ritu Vilas temple.

Thus in cases where Rajput is not only lord but also executioner, the glory reflected in the lord's family may be tempered by discomfort over a divergent or even discordant tone of tragedy, folly, or injustice. The fact remains, however, that whatever else non-familial stories told by Rajputs may convey, the heroes' death in "combat gory" contributes to the glory of Rajput ancestors and their progeny down through the generations to the present, even while demonstrating Rajputs' superior place in the social order.

Beneficial as these rare nonfamilial hero stories may be, however, they do not tend to be as efficacious as familial ones. For one thing, nonfamilial heroes do not demonstrate the mettle of the family's bloodline, which is thought by Rajputs to pass on caste-specific traits such as courage, as well as its overall quality (*sat*).[16] For another, prior to Independence, self-sacrifice by ancestors in battle could be pointed to in support of familial claims to various benefits, including estate grants, income, and titles, from a king or overlord. Thus, for example, references to ancestral heroics in a text like Shyamal Das's *Vir Vinod*, published in 1887 by the Mewar Maharana, could be, and were, used to secure resources from the Maharana, whose family benefited from their self-sacrifice.[17] While descendants of a hero benefited from these resources, the Maharana's family benefited in terms of political power and resources accrued through conquest; both then continued to reap the glory of sacrifices by soldiers.

Resource claims based on heroic actions by predecessors are not innovations but rather extensions of the principle that heroic soldiers, whether dying or surviving, could expect to be rewarded for their evident willingness to die as heroes. Note the following account given by the vibrant but stately raconteur, Nahar Singh, formerly the director of the Museum and Research Center at the Mehrangarh Fort in Jodhpur and now chief administrator of the City Palace Museum in Udaipur. I interviewed Nahar Singh during my field research a decade ago and more recently during my latest trip to Udaipur.[18] In the narrative below he relates events in the history of his family's estate, Jasol.

15. This also appears on maps as Dwaraka.

16. On the transmutation of code and substance, see Marriott and Inden, "Towards an Ethnosociology of South Asian Caste Systems," and Harlan, *Religion and Rajput Women*, 32–33. On *sat* as quality as against *sat* as *a* quality in Rajput discourse, see Harlan, *Religion and Rajput Women*, 124–125.

17. See Sharma, *Maharana Raj Singh and His Times*, 8, which is cited in *Power, Profit, and Poetry* by Tambs-Lyche, who says, "We have every reason to suppose that a similar logic obtained in Saurashtra," p. 274 note 18. See also Shyāmaldās, *Vīr Vinod*.

18. I also heard similar versions of some of the narratives he told from his daughter, whom I visited in Bassi, a *thikana* near Chittor, and a site I have visited on a couple of occasions while scouting out hero shrines.

In Jasol there lived Surat Singh the head of the family [the oldest son, and therefore heir to the lion's share of his father's property]. The younger brothers [that is, other junior male relatives, including cousins and nephews] each took a [small] share. Jaswant Singh [a cousin] claimed a [bigger] share [than he was offered] but was told [by Surat Singh] he should take what was given to him. Jaswant Singh started looting the area and became a sort of dacoit and a big problem for Surat Singh, who was chief of Jasol.

So [the great general] Man Singh gave an invitation to Surat Singh help him in a crisis—there was a siege [going on at the time]. Surat Singh was really clever. He said, "My maternal uncle is the Pokran chief [Pokran being hostile to Man Singh], so I'll abstain. I must be excused: I cannot fight my maternal uncle." He [then] said, "Invite Jaswant Singh: he's an outlaw and a relation." His idea was that Jaswant Singh would be killed there and this thorn would be removed. He thought, "I'll be rid of him!"

Jaswant Singh accepted, thinking, "If I succeed, I'll be rewarded and if I die, I'll be a hero." He helped the Maharaja. The Maharaja said, "I'll give [you] a *jagir* [estate] and a *lakh* [100,000] of rupees to him." He [Jaswant Singh] refused and said, "I already have a *jagir* but he [Surat Singh] won't allow me to have it, so tell him to give me my share. So the Maharaja told Surat Singh to give it to him and his descendants.

Thus Jaswant Singh, who lived but was willing to die as a hero, at long last received his estate. In this case, what Jaswant Singh claimed, however, was not the superior rewards offered by Man Singh but rather the estate he claimed from his own family. The story illustrates not only that martial heroism could be profitable but, more important, that such heroism could support a claim to a share commensurate with the hero's perception of his status within his family. Typically, another male relative would avoid staking such a claim, but would venture out to serve another king with hopes of being rewarded for valiant service with an estate not associated with his father's.[19] Hence, for example, in the legend of Kallaji, Maharana Udai Singh grants this Rathor Rajput from the Marwar area an estate in Mewar, near Rundela, after he subdued tribal cattle rustlers. This claim is repeated to this day at Kallaji's Rundela shrine by the Rajput *bhopa*, whose family claims descent from Kallaji. In Jaswant Singh's case, however, receiving a share is not merely a matter of prosperity but also a point of honor, so much so that receiving honor is literally a matter of life and death. Pursuit of his stake provides the real possibility of attaining a hero's death, which the narrative clearly reckons a desirable end.

Another example of the tangible benefits gained from heroism is the case of Mewar's Man Singh, a Jhala Rajput said to have resembled his contemporary, Rana Pratap. Any descendant will eagerly tell how, when Pratap was fighting Akbar,

19. An exception would be Rajputs living in Shekhawati (also written Shekhavati), where primogeniture was not customary.

Man Singh served as a decoy. Leading the army and wearing Pratap's insignia, he was killed while Pratap was spared, on account of which Man Singh's descendants were given Bari Sadri, one of the sixteen foremost estates of Mewar.[20]

Today many of the benefits that are to be derived from glorious heroic sacrifices are comparatively subtle. In addition to furthering claims of relative status among Rajputs, stories of heroism by worshiped or even unworshiped heroes can, as we have seen, be used to boost the credentials and advance the agendas of politicians.[21] In short, hero stories both are and have political currency. They also sell well to tourists, who find the luxurious palaces (now hotels) but also the imposing fortresses, crumbling battlements, and memorial-filled cremation grounds of Rajput maharajas and aristocrats frightfully romantic. Indeed, the martial romance of Rajasthan has proven so alluring to tourists in recent years that the April 1997 "Special Travel Issue" of the hoary American magazine *Town and Country*, an issue containing articles on five desirable tourist destinations—France, Jamaica, England, Rome, and India—devoted most, if not all, of the nine pictures in the article "India: Asia's Epic Adventure" to Rajasthan. Needless to say, most of the photos feature contemporary Rajputs in antiquated dress.[22] Thus, given the recent boom in Rajasthani tourism and a political climate in which right-wing, and often fundamentalist, politics have been successful on the national, as well as local, level, status derived from the glorious self-sacrifice of forebears can be an efficacious and lucrative commodity.

If Rajput narratives continue to confer glory, negotiate status, and in some cases facilitate access to power and wealth, they also, as we have seen, continue to remind their narrators and audiences of past antagonisms. The extent to which bygones can be bygones and hostility can remain located in the past depends on the narrator's current perceptions of community, feelings of efficacy, and concerns about power and resource distribution. Although in many stories conflicts with external enemies such as Muslims and Bhils are more a peripheral concern than are conflicts among friends and relatives, the external enemies are represented in accord with, or at least, in the context of, prevailing stereotypes and tensions.

Thus our frame story, linked as it is to the Maha Singh saga, clearly makes a claim about the superiority of Maha Singh, and of course the family that basks in his glory, over Ranbaj Khan and his family, or at least his scheming, Bhil-impersonating mother. Maha Singh is patently glorious in that he died fighting

---

20. One woman from Bari Sadri added that Man Singh's heroism also earned his family Chattar and Chammar.

21. This subject deserves extensive treatment, which would require inappropriate digression here. Still, I cannot pass on without mentioning that the Bharat Mata Temple of Hardwar contains a "Hall of Heroes" among whom stands Rana Pratap, once Maharana of Mewar, and that the Maharana of Udaipur, until his death in 1984, served as president of the Vishva Hindu Parishad (VHP), a Hindu nationalist political organization. On his role in the "All-India Sacrifice for Unity" and its relevance to the Bharat Mata Temple, see McKean, "Bhārat Mātā," 256. Not a few Rajputs have stood for election and been active political organizers in recent years. Their activities have provided ample opportunity to invoke the martial Rajput past.

22. Apple, "India: Asia's Epic Adventure." I recognize many of the people in the photos. If there are any pictures from outside Rajasthan, they could just as well have been taken inside the state's borders, as the dress and scenery will reveal to anyone who has spent time there.

in an obviously voluntary manner (he could have conceivably gone back on his word once he realized that he had been duped, but his honor precluded it). His bravery in dying voluntarily while remaining true to his word is made even more manifest in the account by the narrator's husband. Picking up precisely where we left off, let us see how his account proceeds, then abruptly ends.

> So the Maharana sent a message to Maha Singh [in Bathera] to face Ranbaj Khan. Maha Singh was a great warrior. Ranbaj Khan's mother knew that. At the same time every morning after finishing his *puja* work, he fulfilled only one demand of anyone who could approach him at that time. So Ranbaj Khan's mother went before Maha Singh and told him that she was Ranbaj Khan's mother and that she wanted him to fulfill her wish.
>
> Then Maha Singh promised her, saying "You are not only Ranbaj Khan's mother but my mother. I'll fulfill your wish without fail." That old lady told Maha Singh that in the battlefield he should not take out his sword until Ranbaj Khan could strike first at Maha Singh. Until that time he was not to take out his sword.
>
> So Maha Singh promised to do the same. Then Maha Singh went straight to the battlefield and because he had all those bindings [his words], he did not wait so that his soldiers would die unnecessarily, so he told Ranbaj Khan to strike first and Ranbaj Khan took out his sword and cut Maha Singh crosswise, from neck to underarm.

In this account there is no disguise. Ranbaj Khan's mother is still portrayed as taking unfair advantage of Maha Singh's goodness, but in this case she does not fool him into thinking she is an ally. Rather, Maha Singh knows full well that she is inimical, and though he realizes that this mother, whom he respectfully calls his mother, will seal his doom, he cannot abandon his habit of doing good and deny her.[23] He then rushes headlong into sacrifice, so as to spare unnecessary bloodshed.

The variants share a depiction of Ranbaj Khan as a formidable enemy who kills the hero with a single slash of the sword, which ends the story as far as the husband is concerned. The wife, however, goes on to make the religious-ritual implications of the death manifest. These variants represent Maha Singh as strong and adept with his sword. The formidableness of the enemy renders the death of the hero all the more glorious.

At the same time, however, both accounts reveal ambivalence. If formidable, the Muslim is also flawed. In one way or another he "hides behind his mother's skirts" and so is clearly inferior to the magnanimous Maha Singh while being comparable to the frame's sorry male specimen (who is more of a contemptible counterpoint to the hero than another rival). Hero stories, in general, distinguish the hero through comparison with another who, if he has virtues, also embodies undesirable, inferior, and often unsavory qualities. This assignment of degenerate qualities is common when it comes to representing Muslims, who come

---

23. The implications of this identification of enemy and mother are discussed below.

off badly in much contemporary discourse, but it is also true for other enemies, whose descendants belong to communities considered less troublesome, such as Bhils and members of other tribal groups.

Rajput texts that tell of rivalries between Rajputs fighting a common enemy often deprecate the two who are inevitably inferiors (Rajput and non-Rajput), but, as in the ambiguous case of Ranbaj Khan, the inimical groups may not simply be parallel "others." In one notably humorous text, a Rathor Rajput tells the story of the Kachvaha Rajputs' conquest over tribals to belittle his Kachvaha interlocutor during a battle of wits performed before a British audience. This text is not one I collected but rather a passage from Amar Singh's diary, whose author, an educated and urbane nobleman who resided near Jaipur, reflected on his life in over ninety volumes. In the following excerpt (dated October 7, 1933), Amar Singh, a Rathor, recounts his conversation with the Kachvaha nobleman. Throughout the passage, Amar Singh baits his victim, first belittling the Kachvaha Rajputs for the cheap and easy way they won their Jaipur from a tribal group and then asserting that no Kachvaha could ever be a sacrificial hero.

> Then the Thakur of Joabnir came and as is his habit started showing his knowledge. He told Col. Cole that this was the place where the Kachwahas had won a great victory. I had not heard of this and asked who they had won this against. He said the Meenas [Minas]. I laughed at this and told him that he ought to be ashamed of giving out these things. They ought rather to be hidden. The Kachwahas had given the Meenas a feast and plied them well with drink and then butchered them in their unconscious sleep. . . . He said that the Rathors had done the same when they took Pali from the Brahmins. I said they had done nothing of the sort. They had been asked by the Brahmins to become their rulers and even if what you say is true they do not at least brag of it as a victory. Then he asked me how the Rathors had taken Mandore. I said that it was given to Chundaji in dowry. He said that such things were not accepted in dowry. I said that everything was acceptable that a father-in-law would give. Had he not accepted a dowry when he was married? He said that was different. I said that it was not. On this he began talking about a Kachwaha that had fought after his head had been cut off. I said that no Kachwaha could do that. It was a made up story. It was the Rathors only who had done it and that is why they had earned the title of Kabondhas.[24]

In this passage, Amar Singh represents himself as winning his own little victory over the Kachvaha *thakur*, whose family, he argues, defeated such an

---

24. Amar Singh's diary, 339. For access to portions of the diary and permission to cite it, I thank Thakur Mohan Singh of Kanota. The Sanskrit term *kabandha* appears in the *Devimahatmya* and is applied to slain demons who stand back up and resume fighting after losing their heads in battle. I thank Rebecca Manring for pointing this out to me, September 20, 1998. Asko Parpola has said, "this usage in the *Devimahatmya*, in turn goes back to Ṛgvedic *kavandha-* or *kabandha-* 'barrel, water vessel with a large belly,'" and also has "the meaning of 'cloud' as well as of 'belly' and [is used] as an epithet of the storm god Marut [with the adjective *urine* 'watery']." He adds that in the Sanskrit *Ramayana*, *kabandha* is an epithet of the demon Danu. Personal communication, September 21, 1998. See also Monier-Williams, *Sanskrit-English Dictionary*, s.v.

unworthy enemy, and through trickery at that! Having stripped conquest and conqueror of glory, he asserts that no Kachvaha could ever fight as a *jhunjharji*, a conclusion linked directly (formally, if not also causally) with their conduct vis-à-vis the Minas. Moreover, Amar Singh is not content to stop here. Just a few lines later he points out that the Kachvahas acquired from the conquered Minas their tutelary goddess Jamvai Mata. He says that they "had adopted [her] as their own mother" and goes on to gloat over the embarrassment that calling a Mina deity "mother" causes his conversation partner by telling him "there was no getting away from the facts."[25] Clearly Amar Singh felt triumphant. Sitting across from the Kachvaha *thakur*, he converted the Kachvaha *thakur*'s "loss"— the Kachvahas' purportedly unseemly victory against the lowly and inebriated Minas—into his gain. It is hard to resist surmising that this round of insults, like agonistic athletic competitions, brings new life to this nobleman living in the dull and peaceful days of the late British Empire.

To sum up: all the hero stories encountered thus far in one way or another tell of struggles that yield glory, in which current generations do their best to bask. Not all hero stories convey or emphasize all the same messages, however. I have used narratives that reveal dominant or recurrent motifs, but as yet have failed to focus specifically on ways in which the narratives diverge. It would be absurd, in fact impossible, to undertake the task of showing all the ways that all the narratives depart from one another. What makes sense in light of this volume's abiding interest in gender, is to look at divergence, or more precisely the tendency or impetus toward divergence, in the context of gender. This purpose is to be pursued in the following section, which focuses on the question of voice: it takes up the matter of who is narrating, men or women, and comments on the different ways in which men and women tell hero stories. Its analysis is formal, but as always, form has everything to do with substance, and most significantly for our purposes, for the ever-abiding battle of the sexes.

Telling Hero Stories: The Long and Short of It

Let us return to the fact that our initial (coward) sample text was delivered by a woman and that the status-sorting insult episode in a hero narrative is very unusual in that it *was* told by a woman. Such blatant disparagement of another lineage in a hero story is common in heroic narratives recounted by men, who make frequent allusions to lineage development and historical rivalries, but atypical of women's accounts. It is not that women would necessarily disagree with the sorting out of status such episodes are so often deployed to accomplish, but rather that their interest in heroic narratives is generally directed elsewhere.[26]

25. Image appropriation is generally intended to heighten, not reduce, prestige. For reflections on images as "trophies of war," see Davis, *Lives of Indian Images*, especially, pp. 51–87; and Sax, *Mountain Goddess*, 167–168. For comparison, see Geary, *Furta Sacra*.

26. On variance of interest between men's and women's accounts in other contexts, see Kakar, *The Colors of Violence*, 101, 115–118, 124; Ramanujan, "Two Realms of Kannada Folklore"; and Harlan, *Religion and Rajput Women*, 52–90.

For one thing, women's narratives tend to cut to the chase and begin not with the intergroup politics that lead to confrontation but with the confrontation, which is but a prelude to the death that delivers to the family a divine hero. Women typically regard death not as testimony from the past that supports a claim to status now but as a beginning of the hero's availability to the family in succeeding generations, including and especially the present generation, to which the hero continues to bestow blessings, and by which the hero continues to require propitiation.[27]

For another thing, as I have said repeatedly, women tell relatively concise hero stories. Scholars working on folklore in various parts of India have noted that women often tell stories that vary from men's, not only in content but in scope. In part, this is connected to women's comparative lack of concern for the politico-historical context. In fact, women frequently refer to their husband's knowledge and recitation of heroic stories as *itihasik* or "historical" (though here I should caution that the *itihasik* in no way excludes the mythic).[28] It may be that men, whose ancestors once routinely heard bards sing of the heroic (and sometimes the less glorious) exploits of the patriline, retain a sense that among the purposes of recitation are the preservation of a sort of family history and the continuous vivification of glory down through the generations.

In part, however, women's economy is also sometimes related to a lack of knowledge about and interest in that which they conceive to be *itihasik*. Shifting residences and acquiring new deities through marriage, women tend to receive less long-term exposure to familial traditions. Marrying in, they learn rituals and hear stories of the benefits to be derived from continuing to perform the rituals. The details of the historical occasion for the performance of rituals is simply not as important as the present expectation of rewards from continuing veneration.

The following text conveys a sense of the parsimony that typifies women's accounts. It was told by a young Rajput woman about Maha Singh, the subject of our rich initial narrative.

> In my father's family was a *jhunjharji*. He was fighting for Jodhpur against a Musalman. In the fight, his head was cut off. His wife got this information and became a *sati*. Maha Singh was his name.[29]

27. Comparing narratives recited by men and women in south India, A. K. Ramanujan has noted that men's narratives tend to end with the prince's marriage, but in women's stories marriage is only the beginning. See "Toward a Counter-System," 52.

28. A. K. Ramanujan has noted that women's stories, or "granny's tales," tend to be more focused on the household and less concerned with public events than men's, and has shown how this divergence of concern is reflected in the distinction made in ancient Tamil literature between *akam* (home) and *puram* (city) genres. See "Two Realms of Kannada Folklore," 41–75, and also "Toward a Counter System," 33–55. See also Gold and Harlan, "Raja Nal's Mistake," especially p. 160, and Narayana Rao, "A Rāmāyaṇa of Their Own." In previous work I have contrasted the concise, domestically focused *kuldevi* stories narrated by women with the more *itihasik kuldevi* stories narrated by men. Women's stories often speak of relationships between daughters and *kuldevis*, who accompany them to their conjugal home—though this importation transgresses the dominant convention that women must worship their husband's *kuldevi*, who is represented in men's accounts as a martial predator, typically a kite; *Religion and Rajput Women*, 115–118.

29. The narrator then goes on immediately to talk about *satis*. She notes that Maha Singh's wife pronounced a curse: no one in the family would be able to buy material for a *sati* monument. For information on *satis*' curses, see the following, by Harlan: "Perfection and Devotion," 84–89; "Satī: The Story of Godāvarī," 229–230, 238–239; and *Religion and Rajput Women*, 139–146.

This bare-bones account shares very little with the first Maha Singh narrative (and, of course, even less with the second)—just the point that Maha Singh is a *jhunjharji*, which is reiterated by the statement that "his head was cut off," and the fact that he fought for Jodhpur against a Muslim. It lacks the insulting frame story, as it does many other features, including the worship of Shiv and Mata, the masquerade by Ranbaj Khan's mother, and the heroic death of Maha Singh's dog.[30]

One *itihasik* detail that this brief account does provide, and which the opening narrative fails to give, is the immolation of the hero's wife as a *sati*. Both men's and women's accounts often make mention of *satis* who follow the hero to the afterlife: *satis'* deaths, like heroes', make their families illustrious. As has become clear, the *satis* of heroes compound heroic glory: the wives' devotion to their husbands shows possession of *sat-sattva*, and having *sattvik* wives reflects well on the men to whom they were joined as they circumambulated their marriage fires. Men, however, are far less likely than women to isolate the wives' deaths from the heroic context and tell independent *sati* stories, in which the actions of a hero are either eliminated or reduced to context.[31] Unlike hero stories, independent *sati* stories seldom sort out the relative status of competing Rajput families. It is often said that *satis'* deaths make their families illustrious. Their deaths, however, are not typically connected with tales of martial struggle and political intrigue. Moreover, the families maintaining *sati* shrines venerate wives married into the family. As the ballad *Sati Godavari*, about which I have written previously, and the recent case of Roop Kanwar make explicit, a *sati* makes not only her husband's family (*sasural*), but also her natal family (*pihar*), resplendent.[32]

Viewing the first narrative in light of the second, which is more typical of women's narratives in its length and dearth of *itihasik* detail, allows us to see that its specificity, as well as its concern for status, makes it unusual. Both factors indicate that as narrative it shares territory predominantly, though not exclusively, occupied by men.[33] As we saw, the interest of the raconteur's husband in family history, along with his presence at her performance, were influences that probably shaped her story. Further support for both speculations is provided by my experience with another aristocratic couple. The wife's rendering of a hero story, which was attended by a husband who, like the previously mentioned husband, had been working on his family's history, contains far more *itihasik* detail than is usual. Although the account does not specifically name the hero, this *jhunjharji* is Bagat Singh (also referred to as Bhagwat Singh), whose

30. The dog is reminiscent of the hound who accompanies the Deccan god Khandoba. That canine laps up any drops of demon blood that eludes blood-thirsty goddesses. See Stanley, "The Capitulation of Mani," 280, 282.

31. Most *sati* stories do not involve heroes; in fact, little if any information is typically given about the husband. For extensive treatment of *sati* narratives, see Harlan, *Religion and Rajput Women*, 112–181; Weinberger-Thomas, *Ashes of Immortality*; and Paul B. Courtright, *The Goddess and the Dreadful Practice*.

32. See Harlan, "Satī: The Story of Godāvarī," 229 (in this case even the *momal*, mother's family, is made illustrious); and Anand Pathwardan's film, *Father, Son, and Holy War*, in which the male relatives of Roop Kanwar are interviewed.

33. It is nevertheless necessary to warn against merely reducing this woman's story to an example of "dominant discourse," and to recall A. K. Ramanujan's pithy observation that "genders are genres," in "Toward a Counter-System," 53.

remote shrine is thriving. The wife's story, which comports in all major respects with the one I heard from Mangilalji, the Pilva shrine's *pujari*, goes like this.

> There was a *jhunjhar*, who was the elder grandson of the *thakur* of Pilva [village in Marwar, in the vicinity of Jodhpur], but his uncle was jealous. He had a habit of going to listen to *Pabuji* in any village it was being performed and to stay the whole night listening to the performance. His uncle told his grandfather that the boy was going to other women. The uncle gave the same message to the boy's wife. The grandfather gave permission to finish the boy off. The uncle wanted control [power].
>
> That night the boy came home after *Pabuji*. His wife was angry and didn't open the door for him. She was on the upper story [of the house]. He slept on the ground floor room, a very small room. His uncle had foreseen this happening and tied the boy, who had very long hair, to a bed leg and then three or four persons attacked him. The uncle cut the boy with a sword. After his head was chopped off, the boy got up and killed one or two of his uncle's followers, then died.

Although certainly not as detailed as our first narrative, this account is one of the longer and more specific narratives I collected from women. Unlike those narratives, it is almost completely given over to the actions of the hero. Unlike most men's narratives, which so frequently open and close with intrigue and status struggle, it vaguely sums up politics with one sentence, "The uncle wanted control." Moreover, we never learn whether or not he got it, and the relative status of the fraternal lines is left unclear. The *jhunjharji* dies a glorious death, which is attested to by his headless revenge, but the death is not explicitly deployed to sort and rank Rajputs.

The divergent focus and scope of women's narratives are illustrated nicely in another sample text, which treats this same hero. It was recited to me by a reserved aristocratic Rajput woman in her mid-fifties. Although women, who grow up in their father's household (mother's *sasural*) and then marry into their husbands' homes (their *sasural*s), typically know few stories about divinities worshiped by their mother's natal families, this woman spent an unusual amount of time during childhood years in her mother's natal household and so had many stories to contribute about its traditions. Once again, this well-known hero story is slightly longer than is common. Its unusual detail, however, demonstrates clearly a tendency in terse accounts: it makes explicit reference to present practice, particularly contemporary ritual.

> There were three Champavat sons: one at Kanota, one at Naila, and one at Santa. Their grandfather, Bhagwat Singhji, had long hair, which was typically worn by all Rajputs then. His enemies got him while he was on his cot and they tied him to his bed by his hair. He tried to get free. He jumped up to try to free himself and blood splattered up to the roof. So now they [male family members] keep their hair very short [and will wear] not even a *chotu* [bit of hair

worn longer than the rest in back]. The enemy slit his throat—the enemy who tied him to the *palang* [cot].

A *ratijaga* is done for him on *purnima* [full moon night]: for sleeping and all the good things.[34] The *chatri* is in Jaipur near the central jail and the family still goes there.

Beginning with a vague nod to history and the never-explained division of Champavat lineages, the account moves quickly to action, but then relates all the action to men's current custom of wearing short hair. More important, the account ends by bridging narrative and ritual, the *ratijaga* or night-wake performed by women. Thus the actions serve as raison d'être for the *ratijaga* songs women regularly sing. As we shall see shortly, they are little concerned with the *jhunjharji's* past. They generally fail to provide biography and focus largely on posthumous appearances and blessings. In short, the narratives generally provide an explicit segue to what is of great concern to women, the good things to come from ritual praxis. The hero's presence signifies benefits: a good night's sleep, health, wealth, progeny, and so on. Status is largely an unspoken concern.

Having argued the point about status so strongly, I should reiterate that the divergence of focus in women's and men's narratives does not indicate women's lack of concern with relative social status. Rather, women's narratives are, generally speaking, not the place where such status sorting tends to occur. One reason, perhaps, is that heroic narratives tell of men in a patriline that men join through birth and in which they remain throughout life.[35] These men are by extension the "sons of heroes," just as Rajputs are the "sons (*put*) of kings (*raj*)." Women's interest in sorting out status within the Rajput community more typically centers on marriages between members of this patriline and other groups. Proposals are the very stuff of status negotiation in this hypergamous community. Who is or who is not acceptable for sons and daughters is a favorite topic among women. They discuss proposals made by the families of prospective brides to their sons with great relish and worry about the prospects for their daughters as they wait to hear on proposals they have sent.

Another possible reason why women may fail to emphasize relative status in their hero narratives is that sometimes the Rajputs who appear as inimical losers (whether in the midst of text or in frame stories of hero stories told by men, or occasionally by other women) may hail from lines in which female narrators, or their mothers or sisters-in-law, have been raised or into which their sisters have been married. In such cases, it might well be in their self-interest or simply good form not to dredge up unflattering episodes. This is a very different take from that evinced in the second Maha Singh story, whose male raconteur repeatedly named the coward and greatly embellished the details of his infamy.

In sum, in hero stories women focus less than men on elements that may be deployed to defend or assert relative status and more than men on ritual detail. Typically making scant, if any, references, to politics, women would seem ei-

---

34. I take this reference to the benefit of sleeping to mean that unlike the *jhunjharji*, who was attacked in his sleep, one can rest easily.

35. Exceptions to this scenario are adoption and ascetic renunciation.

ther to neglect the historical circumstances described in men's accounts or else to build on the hidden or barely exposed foundations these circumstances constitute by moving on to matters of greater concern to women. Exemplifying clearly women's tendency toward brevity, paucity of *itihasik* detail, and predilection for referencing ritual is the following account. It celebrates the heroism of Man Singh, and was recited by a vivacious and gracious middle-aged Rajput woman who was described to me by many men and women in the community as knowledgeable about matters of *dharm* (religion) and *riti-rivaj* (customs). She is the wife of the *thakur* who recited the previous Man Singh account.[36]

> Man Singh was an Amet ancestor, an eldest son who was fighting with his father. His father went for a shoot and went into the area where his son was staying. The father arranged for someone to assist him. When the son entered a tent to meet the father, someone chopped off his head. The son had no sword. He ran back with his head chopped off. Back in Kailva, his wife had a delivery. That son became *thakur* of Amet anyway.
>
> When a son has his haircutting [tonsure ceremony], it takes place there [at Man Singh's memorial]. We worship at [the time of] marriages too.

The account "explains" the filicide with the fleeting reflection, "That son became *thakur* of Amet anyway." It includes a few other details, such as the wife's delivery. It provides a pretext for entering the son's territory—not a pilgrimage to the Carbhuja temple, but a shoot. The discrepancy does not appear to be significant. In any Rajput pilgrimage or travel for whatever purpose, men would inevitably hunt animals for food and entertainment. Another variant element is the observation that the son was unarmed, which could indicate the woman's sympathy for this son, who is, in this text, relatively innocent. Her husband's account makes the father's actions more defensible. It emphasizes that the son came with others and was perceived to have hostile intent. In short, the wife's account seems to exculpate the son and so enhance the tragedy of execution. At the same time, however, it also softens the guilt of the father. Here not the father but "someone" kills the son. This felicitous imprecision effectively diminishes her husband's indictment, so that the account delivers a kinder, gentler portrayal of both parties. Thus, again like the filicide Raj Singh, the executioner in the intrafamilial struggle is rendered not utterly inimical.

Having summed up the *itihasik* situation, the account then specifically relates the actions within the text to two types of ritual events, both rites of passage. The first involves tonsure (*mundan*), which some families perform for daughters but most do only for boys. The ritual typically occurs at a goddess temple, but in many families it takes place at a hero shrine instead. In either case, the tonsure dedicates the child to a goddess. It represents a direct dedica-

---

36. From this woman, whom I have come to regard as one of my closest friends in Rajasthan, I learned an enormous amount about women's traditions. She also taught me basic but invaluable rules of comportment during my earliest days as a doctoral student, and invited me to observe many religious rituals during my various stays in and around Udaipur.

tion of the child via an offering of hair (substituting for head), or else an indirect dedication through identification of the child having his hair cut with the hero who offers his head to the goddess in battle.

The second rite of passage is marriage, which requires a *ratijaga*. *Ratijagas* propitiating a variety of deities, including heroes, are performed by women at marriages, as they are for births, or at least the births of sons. Thus in this hero text, as in the previous account, there are indexed or intertextual references to ritual and, more specifically, women's songs.

Many women's accounts of heroes actually contain only references to ritual and no specific scenario of events. For example, one woman in her twenties said that there is a *jhunjharji* in her father's family and a *chatri* for him. At weddings and also annually, she said, her family goes there to pay homage. This was all she had to say, except that there were "three or four" more memorials for *jhunjharjis* at the cremation ground. Her lack of detail was sufficiently irksome to her brother, who was listening to her account from a short distance that he cut in to offer the comments about *jhunjharjis* cited in the previous chapter: these heroes "adhered to the strict rule of Rajput *dharm*" and chopped of their heads to avoid becoming "unclean, as Muslims destroy *murtis* and cows." In this case, neither youthful narrator provided *itihasik* detail about the specific *jhunjharji*, but the woman's emphasis on ritual drove her brother to supplement her account with action, albeit in this case a general "historical" scenario rather than a specific account of the particular hero's deeds.

Another instance in which a man stepped in to render more complete a woman's account demonstrates a telling exception to this tendency. Let us revisit the woman who narrated in front of her husband the notably *itihasik* account of the Pilva *jhunjharji*, who was murdered while tied to his bed. When she ended her account without reference to ritual, her husband stepped in to make the reference for her. He noted that there were two shrines for the *jhunjharji* in Pilva, one where he lived and one in the cremation ground. He then noted that his family worships the *jhunjharji* on various occasions, though he mentioned specifically only one, the full moon night. He went on to say that when his "great, great grandfather came to Jaipur and was in charge of the camel stables, they [the family] made a small *cabutra* [platform] for him and placed an image in the *sthan* [shrine] near Police Lines for the *jhunjhar*." He also said that he and his family still worship there and that its *pujari* (temple servant) goes there. Finally he noted that his family keeps an image of *jhunjharji* in a box at the place where Ganesh *puja* [ritual veneration of the elephant-headed, obstacle-removing deity Ganesh] is observed during weddings. There both bride and groom worship the hero before actually going to his *sthan*. Here, it seems, we have an exception that implies, if it does not prove, the rule. The husband so conversant with *itihas* may inform and extend his wife's account, while her performance of ritual and knowledge of its benefits may inform and extend her husband's account.

Thus it seems that whereas some women's accounts resemble the more detailed men's accounts, men may well know more about household ritual than they typically include in their accounts. Both men and women generally consider this ritual knowledge to be primarily women's knowledge—even in the case of male heroes, whom, as we have seen, men tend to think of as being particularly important to men.

When men do include references to ritual, their references are generally not to routine veneration. Men seldom mention the veneration of heroes at weddings, and when they do they tend not to refer specifically to women's *ratijaga* songs. Moreover, like our initial Maha Singh story, they often relate the hero's death to Dashara, because the hero's weapons are specially worshiped on that date.[37] As one senior Rajput man explained in reference to Dashara, weapons that have "tasted blood" are especially venerable and efficacious. As elsewhere in India, these tested deadly implements are often said to be infused with *shakti*, power. Moreover, swords and knives are frequently identified directly with the goddess in that they "drink blood."[38] On Dashara, men worship these weapons and give special reverence to the weapons of heroes who have fought, killed, and died in battle.[39] Women are typically admonished not to touch these weapons, which are ritually cleaned on that day.[40] The weapon rituals are thus literally out of their hands. Thus references to Dashara—or to Navratri, with which Dashara is often conflated—do not point toward women's ongoing rituals, whether routine household worship or rite-of-passage performances. Rather, the Dashara ritual, which is also referenced in women's accounts, reconfirms a bond between Rajput men (generations of them) and their goddesses. A fine example of this is our initial narrative about Maha Singh, the devout hero whose sword bisected the enemy before becoming an object of veneration on Dashara.

One final significant aspect of women's references to ritual is that, as in the case of so many women's *sati* stories and unlike most men's stories, they are accompanied by references to miracles, about which women sing in their *ratijaga* rituals. The following narrative is a good example, and serves as a remarkably rich summation of tendencies and exceptions already given. This is an account given by a Rajput woman raised in the Jaipur *thikana* of Ladana. She initially, but quickly, provides some *itihasik* details of intrigue and status struggle within her father's family, before turning to discuss ritual and its efficacy at length.

37. On the veneration of weapons as an expression of solidarity among men in successive generations of their patrilines, see Sax, "Fathers, Sons, and Rhinoceroses." Of special note is Sax's description of Pandav Lila performance in a Himalayan context.

> The old weapons, taken out from under the eaves and present on the altar for the duration of a performance, represent the previous generation, now mostly deceased. The ancestors are thus virtually present on the central altar, in the weapons with which they once danced.
>
> In effect, the interrelated patrilines of the village are substantialized in the weapons, which are explicitly linked to the principle of agnatic descent. The martial energy of the deceased fathers is recycled through these weapons to their adult sons who dance the main roles. (289–290)

38. A legend of Shivaji, the seventeenth-century Maratha king, holds that the goddess Bhavani entered his sword. See photograph and caption by Eleanor Zelliot, in Zelliot and Berntsen, eds., *The Experience of Hinduism*, 173.

39. As we have seen, on this day too occurs the worship of all weapons and horses, who are typically adorned with elaborate antique bridles and saddles.

40. This stricture, of course, is prevalent in many hunting and martial cultures throughout South Asia and the world.

Our *rajkumar* [heir apparent] was a *jhunjharji*. There was a battle in which our families were going [involved]. There were two brothers: the little brother stayed in Jaipur and the big one was given the village of Ladana. The younger one said, "Why do I have to stay in Jaipur?" [This] younger one wanted to stay in Ladana. So the older one left his seat and gave it to his brother. The older [one] went to Jaipur.

The elder one's son was a *jhunjhar*. His name was Bharat Singh . . .[41] He went to fight in Tonk. His head was cut off and he fought eight hours after that. Two girls were getting water from a well and pointed it out [to others nearby] that he had no head, so he died. From there his head took off and flew to Ladana—from Tonk.

A man never believed in this story. A *purohit* said, "don't drink and go there," but he did it [drank alcohol anyway] and his arm started to hurt, so people began to believe the story. He was a servant in the household.

Another *purohit* told this man, "Take one rupee and twenty-five pice to the *jhunjhar*. He did and the pain stopped.

There's a *mandir* [temple] where a *purohit* [Brahmin priest] and a family member do the worship. No one pays attention to this, but it is very important. We go there for weddings, births, and tonsure. Men wear a *madaliyau* [amulet] for him. When a son is born, they give the amulet [to the boy]. They used to keep [wear] it, but now they put it in a drawer afterward. But it must remain there for him: all boys must do this.

There's *puja* on the fourth of the bright half of the month for him.

This account succinctly identifies the benefits of venerating this hero, as well as the dangers of failing to be respectful of that ritual. The drunken man who goes to the shrine is injured. Returning with an offering, he is cured. The narrative predictably mentions rites of passage, including those for which *ratijagas* would be performed. It also refers to a monthly ritual, this time one performed on the fourth. *Jhunjharjis* are typically venerated on full moon nights, but some are worshiped additionally or alternatively on death anniversaries. The narrative also mentions another ritual, however. Whereas virtually all Rajput women either wear or keep in special boxes amulets of *kuldevis* worn by familial *satis*, men in this family wear, or more commonly these days keep in a box, a hero amulet, indicating not only protection by but also identification with this familial hero.

The narrator is evidently apprehensive that ritual veneration is now not all that it should be. Before mentioning men's and women's rituals, she laments, "No one pays attention to this, but it is very important." No doubt the ritual veneration of heroes, like the ritual veneration of other familial deities, is not all it once was. As Rajput resources have declined, so have expenditures on rituals. Gone are the days when every family employed Brahmins for routine functions. Meanwhile, women have increasingly assumed more ritual responsibility,

---

41. Unfortunately, I cannot read this name in my notes. It appears to be Naruka.

especially as the line separating men's and women's quarters (*mardana* and *zanana*) in the household has disappeared and women travel more freely, albeit often veiled and escorted, than they did just a few years ago. In many respects functioning as the domestic analogues of Brahmin priests, women have often also served as substitutes once hiring priests became too expensive for families. Women make offerings within the home and also send or even deliver offerings to shrines located on the borders of erstwhile estates or in ancestral cremation grounds.

In a nutshell, whereas men's and women's domestic hero narratives share much, including an interest in demonstrating familial glory, and whereas they are surely influenced by each other, they also differ from each other. Women's narratives that specifically address status considerations, for example, are more typically concerned than men's narratives with absolute rather than relative status. As we have seen, they also tend to have different points of departure. In men's stories conflict leads to glorious self-sacrifice, which is the end conveying contemporary glory, whereas in women's stories conflict, if mentioned at all, tends to become merely the circumstance of the hero's death, which is the beginning of routine ritual veneration and its tangible rewards. Ritual veneration is taken up by women in the performance of auspicious *ratijaga* songs, which begin where the story ends, and have much to say about rewards not just of the death of ancestral heroes but also of their routine veneration. Men's accounts that do mention ritual veneration usually refer not to *ratijaga* performances on auspicious occasions such as births and marriages or to the routine veneration that women generally perform, but to Navratri and Dashara. During these days goddess worship includes goat sacrifice, a rite of passage for Rajput boys, and veneration of weapons by men.

If men's and women's hero accounts tend to diverge in ways that reflect their interests and duties as men and women, they also reflect tensions between men and women. In these hero stories is to be found a theme that runs throughout other heroic genres, as it does in folklore the world over: the battle of the sexes.

Frame One, Another Take: Gendered Damnation in the Battle of the Sexes

Aside from serving as a means for launching an investigation of ways in which men's and women's hero narratives treat glory as a relative or absolute status determinant and as a cause for ritual commemoration and veneration, our coward frame story illustrates another theme that frequently arises in folklore, as well as in general conversation among Rajputs: the relative status and ability of Rajput men and women. In the ordinary day-to-day relations between Rajput men and women, there can be little question as to who is superior. The system is extraordinarily patriarchal. More than other groups, Rajputs have observed *parda* and limited the mobility and influence of women. Nevertheless, as one Rajput man informed me early in my first research visit, "Rajput men and women are always arguing about who is stronger: men say, 'we are stronger as we are the ones who have our heads chopped off in battle,' and women say, 'we are stronger, as jumping onto a fire is more difficult than that.'" He went on to repeat a saying that settles the matter in favor of women: "The sari is more powerful than the *sapha* [turban]."[42]

Rajput men and women seldom argue the point directly. Unlike men gathering to socialize and unlike the wife in this first frame story, living women tend not to challenge men directly, much less insult them to their faces. For one thing, contact between men and women is limited by the legacy of *parda*, which mandates that women demonstrate respect and modesty to men. For another, such an overt affront by a woman would be deemed particularly unseemly and out of place. Rather, women's challenges have been more safely implicit and targeted on comparatively remote male figures, including those frequenting folklore, which, as we know, sometimes constructs alternative hierarchies based on divergent values and agendas.[43] Stories can be strategized and shaped by those with inferior status, power, and authority (i.e., subalterns) in a mode of or as the basis for "everyday resistance."[44] Hence in stories and song, women may subtly or even blatantly subvert artfully rendered representatives of men in charge and/or build solidarity among other subordinate companions and family members.

Our initial narrative, although providing evidence for the narrator's conviction that Bathera is better, delivers a blatantly gendered indictment of a man in charge. A wife calls her husband a coward. Her taunt is obviously counterhierarchical. Wives are not supposed to insult husbands. Yet here a wife not only insults but also humiliates her husband in front of a lowly maidservant. Like the story of the Hadi Rani, which, as we have seen, locates the "secret" of Rajput honor in women, the story provides an illustration of women motivating, and indeed having to motivate, men to be brave. Hadi Rani insults and inspires: she decapitates herself so that her charms will not distract her husband from martial duty. In one version Hadi Rani first says to her husband, "Wear my bangles, and give me your sword, and sit secure in the circle of these four walls: and don't ever call yourself a Rajput."[45]

---

42. These are the observations of N. Tomar Singh Chauhan, Tamla House, Udaipur, during an interview on January 17, 1985.

43. It is worth noting that the convention of contrasting a demanding wife who challenges her husband's performance in battle with a defective husband is also to be found in a well-known *khyat* (a collection of stories and genealogies). In one vignette, the *khyat* contrasts the Muslim Daulat Khan with his wife, who greets him after battle with a barrage of questions. She asks him how many elephants he captured, and he replies that the Hindu king (Rao) took all the good ones and left "only those which resembled male buffalo calves." The wife then asks him how many men he converted to Islam, and he says that he "had graves dug for those" and then "handed over" the graves "to the Rao in battle." *Mumhtā Nainsī rī Khyāt*, vol. 3, p. 90, cited and translated in Ziegler, "Action, Power and Service in Rajasthani Culture," 69.

44. On "everyday resistance," see Haynes and Prakash, "Introduction." See also the other essays in their volume, *Contesting Power*, as well as Raheja "Introduction," 1–29, and Scott, *Weapons of the Weak*.

45. This translation appears in Gold, "Gender, Violence, and Power: Rajasthani Stories of Shakti."

The frame story's insulting wife, however, motivates her husband not to attain glory but to commit suicide, a compensatory gesture. His demise is no heroic death.[46] In her demand for honor, the wife is, apparently, ruthless—justifiably ruthless, but ruthless nonetheless. Although heroes who die honorably do not necessarily in life always exemplarize honor, a virtue that conveys glory, it is always true that dishonorable conduct will diminish glory. As in the case of Gilbert and Sullivan's modern major general, who tells a falsehood to rescue his daughters from abduction but of whom his daughters then sing, "He is telling a terrible story, which will tend to diminish his glory, though they [the pirates] would have taken his daughters over the billowy waters," Rajput men who comport themselves dishonorably, and particularly those who display cowardice, reduce familial luster.[47] And so, this frame's highly annoyed woman, like Hadi Rani, would prefer a dead husband, ordinarily a considerable liability, to a living husband who shies from duty and strays from the course of honor. In both cases, the wives ridicule men with the desire to effect compensatory rectitude. In the case before us, the compensation is suicide, which is ordinarily deemed dishonorable and even cowardly. Under the circumstances, however, self-inflicted death conduces to a noble end and is penitential in the mode of asceticism.

It is widely accepted in India that an ascetic's self-sacrifice in a sacred river delivers him from rebirth and gives him salvation. Self-sacrifice by satis and heroes also conveys liberation. For less fully realized people, self-sacrifice can vitiate/ameliorate the inglorious and embarrassing effects of substandard behavior. The angry wife's husband sacrifices himself for an unselfish cause that, like the other modes of self-termination explored, conduces toward a definite and desirable benefit. It is not deemed cowardly, sinful, and wasteful. Moreover, the coward's suicide demonstrates courage, the virtue he previously and shamefully lacked. Hence his demise is clearly restorative in this regard, as well. His case is reminiscent of the heroine in one of the chapters of Gita Mehta's *A River Sutra*. In this novel, set in south India, a young dancing girl is abducted by a bandit but then willingly becomes his bride and takes to worshiping with him at a sylvan hero shrine. After he is killed, she drowns herself in the sacred Narmada River. Her death allows her to rejoin her husband in the afterlife, but also purges her of sin. The river, represented throughout the text as the goddess Narmada, is an eager consumer of sacrificial victims.[48]

The case also brings to mind the situation of Mewar's Maharana Raj Singh, who killed his son. According to some versions of the story, Raj Singh was consumed by guilt after killing his son and asked a Brahmin how to free himself of his burden. The Brahmin replied that he could burn himself to death in a sa-

46. On compensatory suicide, see Jean Filliozat, "The Giving up of Life by the Sage," 146. See also comments on the exculpatory suicide or *atmahatya* recommended to Raj Singh for his executing his son later in this chapter. In the south Indian context, there is the example of the tragic king who, having learned that he has ordered the execution of an innocent man, Kovalan, proclaims, "There is no way left open to me save to give up my life," and then swoons and dies; Daniélou, trans., *Shilappadikaram*, 129. For background, see also Coomaraswamy, "Atmayajna."

47. Gilbert, "The Pirates of Penzance," 23.

48. Mehta, *A River Sutra*, 162–190. A Naga ascetic offered his adoptive daughter to the Narmada; 254.

cred *pipal* tree, or [even better] die a hero's death in battle. If neither option appealed, said the Brahmin, Raj Singh could perform a great work of charity. Raj Singh opted for charity and as a result, the story goes, we have Raj Samand, Mewar's great artificial lake.[49] This penance is said to have absolved the king of his sin and so removed a stain from a man who is otherwise lauded as a strong ruler and valiant nemesis of Moghuls.

In our frame, the husband performs a most radical compensatory gesture. Nevertheless, the narrative emphasizes not compensation but cowardice. One reason, as we have seen, is surely that the story is situated to effect a contrast between the husband and the never-flinching and oh so honorable Maha Singh, who will not behave dishonorably even if tricked into dying by a dishonorable woman, the villain's mother (disguised or not). Thus, compensation cannot stand on its own merit; it is rendered a feeble accomplishment by comparison with the realization of heroism in Maha Singh's performance of self-determined heroic sacrifice.

More important in terms of our current agenda, however, the claim of cowardice is bound to remain emphatic because of the narrator's identification with the frame's female protagonist, who represents honor (relative to her husband) and demands honor (in the form of her husband's dead body). Here the demanding wife is the "secret" of any honor her husband can eventually muster. His compensatory death is evidently more to her credit than his. Thus wife, not husband, is the guardian and guarantor of honor. From this perspective, however, glory reflects not primarily (if even minimally) on family but on gender: the protagonist embodies women's need for "death and slaughter" as index of, as well as occasion for, glory.

Like the story of Hadi Rani, this story is one that women love to tell. Often stripped of familial identities, accounts of the woman who shames her husband appears in a variety of other contexts. This intrepid wife's taunt typically serves in other situations to illustrate the wife's indomitable martial spirit or, more specifically, her daring, resolve, and honor. Thus if the comparison between hero and coward is conventional, so is the comparison between Rajput man and woman. One aphorism, expressed in a *doha* (couplet) told to me by the Rajput aristocrat and history buff who recited the sari/*sapha* aphorism above, holds that although the lion, unlike other animals, will circle a fire, a lioness will jump right in it.[50] The message: a Rajput man (a Singh) may approach death in battle, but he defends himself as he fights for victory, whereas the Rajput wife whose husband has died ascends the pyre as a *sati* to embrace the certain death. The comparison unequivocally suggests that the courage of the Rajput woman is both comparable to the courage of a Rajput man— they are both lions—but also ultimately superior.

It appears that where the Rajput hero compares most fully to the *sati* is in the arena of legend. The hero depicted as unambiguously declaring sacrificial status

---

49. According to Col. Tod, however, this project was undertaken for famine relief; *Annals and Antiquities*, vol. 1, p. 454.
50. N. Tomar Singh Chauhan, interview on January 17, 1985, Tamla House, Udaipur.

by decapitating himself before battle is the indisputable counterpart of the woman represented as choosing to burn on the pyre. In each case the death is manifestly sacrificial. The hero's self-decapitation also represents most clearly his *sat* or substantive goodness, which is also the fuel that produces spontaneous combustion of the *sati's* body.[51] The hero whose head is sliced off by another is still a sacrificial victim, and his death is deemed voluntary because he chose to fight. Nevertheless, as the lion couplet shows, the claim of female superiority because of the *sati's* immediate and unmediated embrace of death is still forceful.

Domestic narratives, unlike the nameless *bhomiyaji* song sung in *Pabuji* and unlike the legend of cultic hero Kallaji, infrequently feature heroes who slice off their heads before battle. Rather, domestic narratives represent the hero's death as occurring more naturally—at the hands of an enemy—and postpone manifestations of the miraculous until after decapitation, when the hero's last activity is vengeful headless struggling. One reason may be that *itihasik* ancestral narratives, in comparison with epics and cultic narratives, typically keep supernatural motifs to a minimum; while living, the hero remains pretty much a human being, albeit a dashing, daring, courageous one. Moreover, some men appear willing to deemphasize or rationalize the fantastic nature of the hero's post-decapitation struggling. Several Rajput men with whom I spoke volunteered a quasi-scientific comparison between the post-decapitation twitching of a goat's body and the post-decapitation fighting of the hero during his final moments. Like the *sati*, whose surfeit of *sat* manifests as superhuman power to curse, bless, and feel no pain after she takes a vow to ascend the pyre, the hero's surfeit of *sat* manifests in his final moments as superhuman power to achieve glorious vengeance while disregarding pain after decapitation. Thus these "last moment" accounts, during which time the *sati* and hero are metamorphosing into divinities, seem to stretch credulity less than the more mythic nonancestral accounts in which goddesses appear on the battlefield to accept a self-decapitated head or in which (as in epic) a decapitated hero's neck sprouts a lotus shoot and his chest develops eyes to direct his fighting.[52]

In short, women, particularly those who become *satis*, are often shown to be unambiguously unafraid of and unmoved by the prospect or experience of death, whether their own or that of their beloved sons and husbands. Like the lioness jumping into the fire, they are incomparable. One possible objection to reading

51. On the veneration of heroic woman as *satis*, not as *viranganas* ("heroines"), whose actions require transgressing gender code, see Harlan, *Religion and Rajput Women*, 182–204. With regard to the analogy between heroic death and the death of the *sati*, Tryambaka, having argued that general rules may be amended by supplementary ones (such as those allowing certain animal sacrifices), says that the rule against suicide is modified by "the warrior's deliberate courting of death in battle" as well as the "self-sacrifice of the *sati*." The only other exception listed is the "ritual suicide of the ascetic in a sacred place"; Leslie, "A Problem of Choice," 49, citing *Strīdharmapaddhati* IV.8.2.1–20. On the association between heroes who die for their king and *satis* who die for their husbands in Kannada traditions and, more generally, in south Indian iconography, see Filliozat, "The Giving up of Life by the Sage," 151–152. Of particular interest are sculptures that depict *satis* severing their heads in the manner of warrior husbands; see Filliozat, "The Giving up of Life by the Sage," 152 figs. 14–15.

52. In *Devnarayan*, Nevo is depicted on the *par* (illustrative scroll used in performance) with a lotus sprouting from his neck and two eyes on his chest. See Smith, *The Epic of Pābūjī*, 100 note 6. These characteristics are also found, in the version of the *bhomiya* wedding song that John D. Smith collected, though his singer argued that the description should not be taken literally; 100. The *bhopa* from the hero shrine at Maithaniya also incorporated this motif into his lyrical rendition of this hero's saga when he sang for me during a visit to his home.

our frame element as demonstrating the superiority of Rajput women might be that in the context of this particular story, which implicitly contrasts the frame's coward with Bathera's glorious hero, the superiority of the woman demonstrates not the superiority of women in general but the inferiority of this man and his family, given that a woman seems to be "wearing the pants." Even if this message is implied by the narrator or inferred by listeners, the "battle of the sexes" motif is sufficiently common to allow to stand the conclusion that women are better. Both resonances, contradictory as they may be, can coexist, just as the claims in folklore that women are better coexist with the general conviction that men are better, which is illustrated in myriad ways including preference for sons, comprehension of women (along with Brahmins and cows) as requiring male protection, and worship of heroes while heroines are worshiped not as heroines but as *satis* (through immolation, re-reversing the gender hierarchy they transgressed by fighting).[53] Like people, the folklore that people generate tolerates and often artfully conjoins or transcends many contradictory and conflicting notions.[54]

Another anticipated objection is that the "woman is stronger" (and so better) claim, like representations of insurgency in much of folklore, defuses commitment in that folklore and serves as a valve that allows oppressed groups to let off steam. According to this logic, superiors merely tend to co-opt challenges and so reduce their force and effect. I will not disagree with the observations that any expressive tradition can function to reduce pressure and that subalterns' challenges can be co-opted. Nevertheless, letting off some steam does not necessarily mean letting off all of it. Expressed through performance of various folkloric genres, "everyday resistance" can continue to keep up the pressure and conduce toward change.[55]

To this I add that co-opting resistance in itself may indicate change or at the very least recognition that the resistance is significant enough to co-opt. Moreover, if men do represent women as superior, and if their representation indicates some co-opting of resistance, then resistance has at least made some impact. That uppity women transgress the gender code on occasion and are celebrated for it by men and women alike can be used by women as charter for sundry challenges. The stories of counterhierarchical heroines such as Padmini, for example, have been deployed to legitimize transgressing *parda*. Various Rajput women who had previously adhered strictly to the rule of *parda* left their homes to "campaign" for their husbands and other male relatives who were fighting political battles. For them the examples of Padmini and other martial heroines have served as legitimizing and inspiring paradigms.[56]

Whether invoked by men or women, however, the image of the braver or more militant woman has a dark side. For example, it is often deployed to demonstrate not the inferiority of Rajput men vis-à-vis women but the inferiority of

---

53. See Harlan, *Religion and Rajput Women*, 181–204.

54. On the coincidence of opposites in Hindu myth, see Wendy Doniger O'Flaherty's *Śiva: The Erotic Ascetic*. On opposition appearing as split imaging, see Gold, "The 'Jungli Rani' and Other Troubled Wives in Rajasthani Oral Traditions."

55. See Raheja, "Introduction," 26.

56. Examples of other martial heroines include Tarabai and the Rani of Jhansi.

others in relation to Rajputs. Again one thinks of Roop Kanwar. Her immolation is frequently represented by many *sati*-supporting Rajputs as an act of paramount bravery that demonstrates Rajput superiority in general. Thus, she has
become for many emblematic of Rajputness, a fact demonstrated strikingly in
Pathwardan's well-known film about contemporary masculinity in India.[57]
Moreover, she is an emblem not only of Rajput code and its celebration of women
who follow men in death as in life but also of Hindutva. Thus a number of
Pathwardan's subjects invoked Roop Kanwar's name in the context of legitimat-
ing their support for the demolition of the Babari Mosque in Ayodhya and the
building of a Hindu temple. In their fundamentalist agendas, the *sati* who is so
fully *sattvik* and superior also connotes control of women by men in charge of
an ideal social order.

Our story, of course, does not represent the husband-demeaning woman as
a *sati* who dies on the pyre. It does, however, represent her as a "good woman"
relative to her man, precisely because of her demand for battle, which precipi-
tates his death through self-slaughter. This representation of woman as encouraging, even taunting, men to fight and face death is no bright spot or advantage
in the war of the sexes, it turns out. The death-demanding Rajput woman, however demure, is often also shown to be uncompromisingly and frighteningly bru-
tal. This kind of characterization is also to be found in a poem published in a
collection of *dohas*. It portrays a triumphant wife bragging about her husband to
her older sister-in-law when she sees the stolen cows he was pursuing return home
with bloody hooves. The Hindi commentary on this almost koan-like Rajasthani
verse explains that the wife surmises that her husband caught up with the cattle
thieves, defeated them, and then fell to the ground (though not necessarily in that
order), and that the cows, making their way home, trampled the body of her husband, whose blood then stained their feet. Her husband, in short, died a hero's
death, news of which prompts her to rejoice.[58] This is the kind of death, presumably, that the cowardly husband's wife would have wished for him and that the
Cornish daughters recommended for the faint-hearted policemen they sought to
embolden by singing "go to death and go to slaughter!"

Another example of the encouraging, taunting wife is provided in the well-
known story of Balluji Rathor, a mercenary Rajput whose story is told in some
length in *Vir Vinod*. The variant to be presented here, however, was delivered in
Jaipur by the Rajput *thakur* whose Pilva *jhunjharji* account is given above and
who finished off his demure wife's version of the same story by providing ritual
detail. Like the Pilva *jhunjharji* and this narrator who venerates him, Balluji is a
Champavat Rathor, whose shrine near Udaipur is deemed by the narrator a
sacred place of pilgrimage.

---

57. *Father, Son, and Holy War.*

58. There are various collections of 700 verses of heroic poetry, each called *Vir Satsai*. The one with which
I have worked most extensively is Nāthūsinh Mahiyāriyā, *Vīr Satsaī*, sampādak Mohansinh Mahiyāriyā
Mahtābsinh Mahiyāriyā. This verse is on p. 94, v. 207. It provides an interesting reversal of a common ritual
performed on Calves' Twelfth, when cows are covered with auspicious red handprints. The commentary explains in detail the justification for this husband's status as *virpurush* (heroic man), and his attainment of Virgati
after crushing the entire enemy army.

Balluji was a person who died twice.[59] Ballu Champavat Rathor was a very obstinate person, but very brave. He was honored everywhere he went. It would take too long to list everywhere he went, [but] he served Jodhpur, Bikaner, Jaipur, Bundi, and Udaipur. He couldn't stay anywhere permanently because of his short temper.

At last after Udaipur he went into the Moghul service, Shah Jahan's court. When he was in Agra, a big historical incident occurred. Amar Singh Rathor was the brother of the Maharaja of Jodhpur and he was killed in the Moghul court in Agra. . . . [For the sake of brevity, I have deleted an account of Amar Singh's death.] His body was thrown onto one of the towers of the court. This was at evening time. In the night, Amar Singh's wife sent a request to Balluji saying, "I would like to become a *sati*, so please bring back the body."

At first Balluji refused. He was a friend [of Amar Singh's] but they were on bad terms. But then his [Balluji's] wife taunted him [saying], "My husband is a coward" [so] he went there with his men, fifty soldiers.

Early in the morning when the doors of the fort were opened, he rushed in. Before that night, a horse was brought to him as a present from Maharana Jagat Singh of Udaipur. The Maharana had three horses known as the best of those times. Each cost one *lakh* rupees. It was one of those. It reached Agra the same night, so when Balluji was going to get the body, he had it. He told the Maharana's men [who had delivered the horse] "Tell your master, 'Whenever you call, I'll come to your service,'" so he could pay him [the Maharana] back.

Then Balluji went into the fort and picked up the body and jumped off his horse because he couldn't come back through the doors. [But then he remounted and] he jumped down [still riding] on his horse from a rampart, and crossed over the moat. The horse died. Ballu survived but then died on the bank of the Jumna somewhere where his wife was committing *sati*. Guarding her, he became a *jhunjharji* there.

Years later when Aurangzeb attacked Mewar and there was a furious battle in Debari, near Udaipur, during the time of Jagat Singh's son Raj Singh, it came to the Maharana's mind, "If [only] Balluji were alive today!" As soon as he remembered, people saw Ballu on the same horse. He fought there and died again, so the Maharana built a *chatri* at Debari.

In this story two women are to blame for the hero's death, first another's wife, who wants to become a *sati* and desires to die with her husband's body, then the hero's wife, who, to get her way, resorts to taunting.[60] Though Amar Singh's wife

---

59. In another variant of this story, Balluji is said to have died three times, because years later a hair from his mustache was discovered and given a separate cremation ritual.

60. In the version of the story narrated to me by Nahar Singh while working in the City Palace Museum, Udaipur, more than one of Amar Singh's wives demanded his body back. In this variant, Balluji had previously told Amar Singh to call on him if his services were ever needed. Amar Singh's wives took him up on his offer to their husband.

has little to lose by requesting that Balluji retrieve the body, Balluji's wife has everything to lose. Still, she persists in her demand by accusing him of timidity. She is reminiscent of the coward's wife in the frame story. In this Balluji account, however, cowardice is not given as the actual reason for the hero's reticence. The truth is that Balluji is simply annoyed at Amar Singh, who is, according to the narrator, a notoriously difficult person. Nevertheless, even the thought of being represented by his wife as a coward is too much for Balluji, who, having attended his wife's words, goes forth to death and slaughter. Moreover, he becomes a *jhunjharji*, guarding his wife until she can commence immolation.

The two women who want Balluji to retrieve the body despite certain death then become *satis*, manifesting their *sat* and so demonstrating not only their power but also their goodness. Once again the women who demand a fight to the death are also ever-devoted victims of loss. Having demanded Balluji's death, they are still "perfect wives."[61] *Sati* immolation serves as proof of that. Typically wives who take pride in their husbands' martial activities, including and especially death, are represented in poetry as not only satisfied with their husbands' courage but also proud to the extreme. Thus one couplet has a Rajput woman boasting of her husband to Uma (Parvati) and comparing her husband favorably to Shiv.

> It is the warrior's nature to kick a head with his feet;
> Uma, my husband doesn't give the head [of an enemy] respect
> [but] yours wears it as an ornament![62]

Here a Rajput wife takes pride in the contempt with which her husband treats the heads he has severed in battle and holds him up as superior even to the god Shiv, for Shiv wears his enemies' heads as pendants on a necklace, which is too respectful and rather too "soft" or unmanly for her taste.

Even more common than heroic scenarios in which wives celebrate the heroism of their husbands, however, are those scenarios that involve and implicate the selfless martial mothers whose lives are fulfilled by their sons' heroic ends. In general parlance as well as in epic songs and *dohas*, one of the most prolific claims about heroes is that they "make their mothers milk resplendent." This is true of unworshiped heroes like Rana Pratap, about whom Col. Tod makes this very claim, but it is also, and perhaps especially, true in the case of heroes who die in battle.[63] Moreover, the connection between milk and blood is

---

61. On the "perfect wife" and *sati* immolation, see Leslie, *The Perfect Wife*, 1–2.

62. This *doha* was recited to me by N. Tomar Singh Chauhan, interview, February 1, 1985, Tamla House, Udaipur. He attributed it to Nathudan.

63. Tod, *Annals and Antiquities*, vol. 1, p. 265. *Dohas* attributing the son's success as a warrior to his mother abound in *dohas* cited in contemporary sources. Two examples follow. The first, from Hiralal Maheshwari's *History of Rajasthani Literature*, condemns Rajput mothers who support their sons who are unwilling to die. It asks, "Why beget sons who only lose land and keep alive" and then suggests that mothers should have poisoned them when they were born rather than raise them to become cowards. The quoted text is from an English translation that appears without the original text, p. 44. The second is from an article in the *Hindustan Times* by Deokrishna Vyas about heroic poetry in Rajasthan. Entitled "Songs of Valour," it recites several *dohas* about mothers, including one in which a poet says that he offers his regards "to the mother who blesses her child" in her uterus by telling him heroic traditions, so that "no sooner is he born" than he tries to seize the midwife's knife.

omnipresent and is expressed in many ways. A couplet recited to me by the same Rajput nobleman in the context of a discussion on heroism states the matter thus.

> O brave one, you drank your mother's milk, then the [nectar from
>   the] kisses of your wife.
> Now you drink the blood of enemies; such drinking is your work.[64]

Just a few minutes before reciting this *doha* he told me that "Whenever Muslims attacked, mothers would say, 'you've suckled my breast, now fight!'" The heroic death of sons, then, validates their birth from their mother's wombs and their suckling their mothers' breasts, this latter act being traditionally simulated by Rajputs in past centuries before both marriage and battle. Thus Rajput mothers are portrayed in narratives and conversation as demanding that their sons fight, however unlikely their survival in combat may be. As one Udaipur-based *thakur* commented, "It's the mother's job to tell the son to kill, to die, to fight in battle." Sons' blood, shed in battle, reveals the splendor of mothers' milk and confers the mothers' measure of glory.[65]

A good example of the warmongering mother is provided in the story of the heroes Dhanna and Bhinya. I collected two oral variants of their story. One was delivered to me in a few lines by a young married woman who resided in a fort on her husband's family's *thikana* in Mewar. The other, which took the form of several written pages, was narrated by her father, the aforementioned Nahar Singh, in Jodhpur. When a goat is stolen from Bhinya's family, a poor Rajput family reduced to goat herding for a living, Bhinya's mother exclaims to her son and to Dhanna, "If you're sons of mine, you'll get revenge!" Dhanna is said to be Bhinya's uncle, not his brother, but no matter. The inclusion of the phrase bears testimony to its formulaic nature: mothers' sons must get revenge and preserve honor. In this case, the trial demanded by Bhinya's mother leads to their deaths as glorious heroes. Having managed to retrieve the goat from an army of fifty men, they are employed as bodyguards by the much-impressed general, Mukandar, who is Thakur of Pali and Prime Minister for Ajit Singh, Maharaja of Marwar. Later, while in Mukandar's service, they die gloriously. Dhanna uses his head as a battering ram to break through a gate under siege; Bhinya rushes in to avenge the death of Mukandar by killing Mukandar's enemy, Pratap Singh of Chippia. The heroes' sacrificial glory is attested to by a *chatri* in

64. This poem, recited to me by N. Tomar Singh Chauhan, February 1, 1985, Tamla House, Udaipur (who identified its author only as a Caran), clearly identifies the sacrificer drinking blood with the victim, the hero (now deified) to whom this poem gives praise. On this identification in the context of asceticism, see Visuvalingam, "Bhairava's Royal Brahmanicide," 165.

65. Such a depiction of the martial Rajput mother, so vaunted in Rajasthani expressive traditions, reminds one of Thomas Hardy's stark characterization of his tragic heroine Bathsheba: "She was the stuff of which great men's mothers are made. She was indispensable to high generation, hated at tea parties, feared in shops, and loved at crises"; *Far from the Madding Crowd*, 441. The theme of the debt incurred by sons drinking their mother's milk and of the duty to fight entailed by that debt was exhibited in the skit "Dahi ka Karz" (The Price of Milk), a Bollywood spoof performed by some of Connecticut College's South Asian students during their annual Divali extravaganza in 1999. For more on this diaspora spoof, see Harlan, "Reversing the Gaze in America."

the Jodhpur fort. There a sign posted nearby explains that "the maharaja, moved by the loyalty of these heroes, built this *chatri*," and immediately after provides the following couplet.

> Oh brave Bhinya, what a great deed you performed: Mukanda's
> widow wept bitterly at midnight.
> But what a wonder that you killed Pratap Singh and caused his
> wife to weep before dawn!

In this brief testimonial there is no mention of Bhinya's mother, whose demand that the youths retrieve a goat leads them to take heroic revenge and so qualifies them for the service that ultimately takes their lives. This resolute matron is to be contrasted with the couplet's two sobbing wives. In the *doha,* women are featured not as causes but as victims of their husbands' deaths. Its women appear as vulnerable females to be protected by men. They are not the bloodthirsty, celebrated women who demand, like Bhinya's mother, that men put their lives on the line. It is also worth noting that in the snippet of story conveyed by this couplet about Dhanna and Bhinya, no mention is made of their wives (if either had one), just as no mention is made of their mother. The poem's women here are other people's women. One belongs to the lord served so admirably and selflessly by the heroes, whereas the other belongs to lord's slayer, whom one of the heroes slays and through whose death our hero exacts revenge. These women are allowed here to demonstrate pain. Moreover, depicted as grieving, the lord's wife shows the loss that the heroes feel when their master is taken from them, and so indirectly demonstrates his dearness. The enemy's wife is, like the lord's wife, pitiable, but her grief is literally poetic justice. Making her cry by dawn is, after all, evidence of Bhinya's magnificent expeditiousness.

These two women, crying at midnight and before dawn, are thus counterparts opposed by plot but demonstrating the same principle. Deprived of beloved husbands, women may well give themselves over to grief. To women, in their defenseless mode, is assigned the role of expressing sadness and the duty of lamentation. They are enactors or performers of tragic emotion, which men, as a lot, cannot afford to demonstrate publicly, if at all, lest the manifest feeling of loss become an index of vulnerability and weakness.[66]

In short, heroic men are portrayed in many traditions as not fearing loss of life as they face that very prospect; to women is relegated the role of experiencing their loss. It would be silly to say that Rajput men have actually never shown grief over such a loss. Recall Tod's description of his Rajput contemporaries shedding tears while telling of the heroic deaths of Jaimal and Phatta at the gates of Chittor.[67] Nevertheless, principle may often diverge from practice. Moreover, the shedding of tears before Tod most certainly transpired in male company, in which the shedding of tears does not as blatantly cross gender boundaries as it

---

66. For an interesting discussion of the gendered division of emotional labor in the Greek epic context, see van Wees, "A Brief History of Tears," especially p. 14.
   67. *Annals and Antiquities,* vol. 1, p. 265 note 1.

would in the presence of women.[68] In any case, the principle holds that men should stay in control. Thus, as in so many other cultures, but particularly cultures in which there is a stark division of gender roles and locations, women are designated mourners who express and absorb loss. Is this not also, one might ask, poetic justice, as elsewhere their implication in death is made clear?[69]

Another place in which women are depicted not so much as generators but as victims of loss is, as we shall see, in women's *ratijaga* songs. Although typically not concerned with a hero's actions, the songs often include a formula in which female relatives (mother, wife, sister, older sister-in-law, younger sister-in-law, and so on) try to stop the hero from going off to war, usually by pulling on his horse's reins.[70] These scenes foreshadow the hero's tragic end while depicting women as fearing heroic death (which the hero, counterpart of demanding and unfeeling women, should not do) and wanting to preserve a man's life (at which they will regrettably, if profitably, fail). The songs, in short, take up the unfinished or perhaps much avoided business of domestic stories, which tend to de-emphasize or even eliminate pain and suffering.

The only place where typical domestic narratives might be taken to imply the pain felt by women would be in the inclusion of a *sati* following the hero to the afterlife. Again, however, the image of the aggrieved and victimized woman who will not live without her husband quickly shifts to an image of resolute agency. As in the case of the jubilant mother or wife, the *sati* is said to be either serene and determined or else joyous and smiling. In the case of the hero's *sati*, the hero completes his duty and transcends human status, which enables her to do the same.

Women's desire for blood, exemplified in the mother who demands revenge or whose milk is made resplendent, as well as in the wife who taunts her husband into battle or who celebrates bloody cow hooves, appears as a motif initially in the cowardly man incident but also much later the text, in the form of the shadowy "two women" who will not let the hero reenter social space and infiltrate the living. If society and its demand for security is represented as feminine or effeminate (women, cows, and Brahmins being emblematic of the social order) relative to Rajput heroes, they are also depicted as inimical to penetration by a rugged hero who has been sacrificed in battle on its account.[71] In hero narratives (whether recited by men or women), two women can stop a beheaded hero in his tracks: their glance or the exclamation, "he has no head," so neatly paralleling society's prior albeit implicit command, "off with his head," arrests

68. In the *Dhola* epic, Raja Nal is depicted as crying, which serves as one more bit of evidence of his ambiguous Rajput/Jat identity. Susan Wadley, personal communication, May 1999.

69. For easily accessible (translated) couplets that demonstrate this implication of women, see Vyas, "Songs of Valour," 3.

70. An interesting variant on this theme is found in a recitation by a shrine attendant of a story of the cultic hero Tejaji. In his narrative, the hero's mare "doesn't agree" to the hero's decision to set off in pursuit of 350 Mina cattle thieves: she starts bucking. A similar scene is found in *Pabuji*.

71. For a succinct discussion of the "hyper-masculininty" of leaders and the feminization of the masses threatened or violated by outsiders, see Das, "Introduction," 26.

the aggressive, headless hero on the boundary where as divine guardian he can ward off future attacks.[72]

Thus although the narrator may not have intended to compare the coward's wife, whose remark to her maidservant motivates her husband to die, with the anonymous "two women" who cause the death-dealing hero to "drop dead," the women all embody the pervasive social mandate that soldiers sacrifice them-selves for society's sake. The two women express the obvious dilemma that society faces with a sacrificed and bloody hero who desires a homecoming: "what kind of man is this?" The hero who has become a sacrifice and has attained the glory of martial death in battle must know his place on the periphery.[73] His vengeance for human sacrifice must ever be directed outward, and he must serve for eternity as a patroller of the border. The anonymous women who stroll along the border, and so cause the hero to drop at the border, thus share with the hero's women a common agenda and cause.

In one narrative, the roles of wife and strolling women are shown to con-substantial and identical. Told to me by the heavily mustached Rathor Rajput *thakur* who narrated the detailed account of the Pilva *jhunjharji*, then supple-mented his wife's account with a number of current ritual details, the account adds a compelling twist. The hero's new wife, who was just about to enter her husband's village for the first time, requires protection by her husband, who orders her home along with some old people; but in this case, since she has never entered the village with her husband and so completed the marriage ceremo-nies, she refuses to set foot in his territory. She remains at the boundary and thus is neatly situated in the stance of the "two women."

> At the time of Aurangzeb, the Muslim army came to break the temple in Shekhawati. So there was a person, Sujan Singh from a neighboring village but an offshoot of the [family of] the Raja of Kandela. He was coming back from his marriage. On the way, he found out from some shepherds that the army was coming. So back at his village he told his wife and some older people to go home and he went off with the younger lot, fifty of them. When the Moghul army came, they fought bravely and died. He became a *jhunjharji*. After the battle, when his head had fallen, he was still on his horse.
>
> His wife refused to enter his village, saying, "I'm a new bride: how can I enter the village without my husband?" So she stayed out, having stopped her bullock cart.
>
> Later she saw a horseman coming without a head. She got down from the cart and stopped the horse and said, "You're a very simple

---

72. On the banishment of ancient European warriors who "killed enemies of the social order" in battle, that is, "in a condition of lawlessness," see Duerr, *Dreamtime*, 61. See also Georges Dumézil, who speaks of the problem faced by a society greeting a victorious soldier as one of preserving "their force and valor while depriv-ing them of their autonomy"; *The Destiny of the Warrior*, 116. Social security requires a redirection, which in our case means deploying proven killers where they can do good: on the border.

73. On fence straddlers and various types of marginal personae, including the Janus-faced soldiers, see Duerr, *Dreamtime*.

person that you've forgotten to bring your head." She then pulled the body down and became a *sati* there.

Every marriage we go to the *sati*'s place and the *jhunjhar*'s place to bow down. Also at the first hair cutting.

In this story, the wife does not simply observe or remark that the headless warrior is struggling toward home and so bring on his death. Instead, she literally pulls him off his horse, having teased him for being a simpleton. Her teasing is ambiguous, as teasing often is. Expressing affection or frustration or both, the jibe produces the predictable result: his progress is checked at just the right place. Even better for society, his wife joins him in death as a *sati* and so becomes another protective divinity. Like the cultic hero Kallaji, whose wife also sacrifices herself on her husband's pyre, he is worshiped together with his wife. In most hero stories, unlike the Kallaji and Balluji stories, it should be noted, no cremation is mentioned. None is needed, in that sacrificial death in battle, which is a *balidan*, serves as or stands in the place of a *samskar*, a refining ritual transforming substance and status.[74] In this case, and in Kallaji's, however, the wife sacrifices her husband's body on the pyre that serves as the locus of her own sacrifice. In fact, Kallaji's wife cuts up her own body and offers her bloody bits of flesh for oblations.[75] Frequently, warriors' wives who become *satis*, however, do so back at the boundary of society, where immolation at the cremation ground unites the *sati*'s body with her husband's turban. Again, however, this type of detail does not infiltrate heroic narratives, which, as we have seen, tend to end abruptly with death or turn immediately to ritual veneration and placation.

Keeping in mind the shifting imagery of the women in these narratives and other heroic genres while looking back to our first frame story, we see that the frame story, situated where it is and opening up the text that follows, issues two challenges. First, it asks, if also settles, the evidently rhetorical question, which family is superior, the coward's or Maha Singh's? Whereas the Greek cycle may recurrently ask, who is the *best* (of the Achaeans), many domestic Rajput hero stories—again, particularly the stories of Rajput men—aim to establish who is better: it defines relative illustriousness of different Rajput lines and between rival family members who will bring about split family lines.[76]

Second, it discreetly asks who is more martial, or rather who is more ready for men to "go to death and go to slaughter": men or women? And although the answer is clear in the opening paragraph, where the woman incites her husband to kill himself, the two "femmes fatales" motif of the framed story would seem to revisit the matter and reach the same conclusion: women demand and men fall. The "two women" motif also brings closure to the hero's struggle and complements the invitation to death accomplished by the angry wife's insult.

74. David R. Kinsley comments that the *samskars* are "patterned on wishful thinking," and that "blood spilt" may be regarded as "an affront and a threat to the neat vision of the order of *dharma*." Thus the *samskar*, like its battle *balidan* substitute, remains an ambiguous or tentative matter; "Kālī: Blood and Death out of Place," 83. See also Nicholas, "The Effectiveness of the Hindu Sacrament (Saṃskāra)"; and Knipe, "Sapiṇḍīkaraṇa."

75. A version of Kallaji's story and analysis that pays particular attention to this scene is to be found in Harlan, "Tale of a Headless Horseman." On Kallaji's death and purity, see chapter 2, pp. 51–52.

76. On the Greek material, see Nagy, *The Best of the Achaeans*.

At the same time, however, the frame story demonstrates the identification of society and its need for security with the female, appearing in a variety of narrative contexts as wife and mother, or simply (then again, not so simply) as "two women." This identification subtly and ironically aligns women with the enemy, requiring the hero's death for their benefit. The identification is neatly illustrated in the story of Bharat Singh above. In this story, the hero leaves his home at Ladana to fight in Tonk. His head is severed, but he fights for hours before coming across "two girls" at a well. When they point out that he has no head, he drops dead. In this case the two women are located in enemy territory, and they achieve what enemy soldiers could not. Hence the women keep the hero from crossing the border into their (enemy) territory, just as the other sets of "two women" do for the hero's territory.

This is not the end of the story, however. Whereas the hero's head usually remains out in the battlefield (whether in enemy or friendly terrain) as his body makes its way home, in this case the body remains far away and the head makes its way home. It "flies" back to Ladana. Thus the "two women" aligned with hostile forces are associated with a thwarted homecoming. Although the narrative does not indicate whether the head is allowed back into society or whether it is arrested at the border, it may well be that the head is less threatening than the body. Though synecdochically representing hero and serving as a relic to be used in establishing a familial shrine, its arrival does not present an unfelled vengeful hero bearing sword and shield. In fact, in the variant of the *Pabuji* narrative I translated, the hero's mother keeps her son's head in a box while he is off at war and then does something improper (what she did is left unspecified), so that he cannot ever retrieve it. In this case the *bhomiya* is denied by a mother who establishes a "periphery" while staying securely at home![77]

Although the alignment of the female and the inimical is revealed in the framed text that the "cowardly husband frame story" opens up through the motif of the "two women," it is even more blatantly manifested in the multifaceted character of Maha Singh's mother. A Muslim, this woman is marked by identities influencing one another. She is deceitful in a way that is despised in Muslims. As we have seen, Muslim trickery is often shown to illustrate inferior character, whereas Rajput trickery is argued to indicate wit and cleverness: evident resemblance fails to strike or convince. This Muslim mother's masquerade is despicable, as in the truce Ala-ud-din feigns to abduct Padmini, whereas Padmini's deceit is commendable, as is, for that matter, Man Singh's impersonation of Maharana Pratap. Yet in the case of women, who are already imputed to have conflicting interests (in men living and men dying), Muslim identity in itself serves not to mask but to reveal the treacherous motivation whereby women need men to die for them. The mutual implication of the female and the inimical is here manifest.

Whereas this mother's Muslim identity serves to disclose women's hidden motivation, her concealment as a Bhil, as we have seen, reflects badly on her son. If she is hiding her identity, he is hiding behind her and demonstrating

77. Harlan, "Heroes Alone and Heroes at Home."

not the much-rumored Muslim hypervirility, but rather timidity. Given the pervasive notion that a person draws strength and develops character in accord with the quality of his or her mother's milk, this son with a duplicitous mother protecting him comes off as ignominious and inglorious. Whatever the case, the boon she procures through disguise effectively dooms her son. Protected, he beheads his nemesis, the hero, who then deals a vengeful death as a *jhunjharji*. His mother's meddling on his behalf has thus assured that he will die.

If the mother's "Muslimness" confirms and reveals her feminine duplicity, what then is to be made of her masquerade as Bhil? Inasmuch as her inimical identity as a Muslim reflects women's treacherous need for protection, her Bhil identity evinces the fluidity and obscurity of this need. The mother's appearance as a Bhil leads Maha Singh to consider her an ally yet, as allies, Bhils, at least in Rajput characterizations, are not always deemed unwaveringly loyal and law-abiding. Appearing as cattle thieves in many hero narratives, the Bhils are often the enemy engaged by heroes who lose their lives and are then worshiped. If, like Muslims, they constitute a threat to cows protected by Rajputs, Bhils, who are represented as adept at hunting and warfare as well as mercenary and unruly, are comparable to Rajputs. Thus the Bhil disguise is also revealing in two ways. First, it is a "natural" costume to choose given that, as we have seen, Bhils (or other tribals) and Muslims (especially Pathans) are sometimes conflated in hero stories. It discloses the inimical Muslim-like "other" side of Bhils. Second, however, it is a good choice in that Bhil ambiguity (friend/foe) reveals the female ambiguity resulting from women's evidently conflicting agendas. Moreover, just as the Bhil costume reflects badly on women—it shows how low women will stoop to get what they want—it also reflects badly on Muslims, for precisely the same reason.[78] Thus this character, a Bhil and a woman who is a Muslim, is like a kaleidoscope with facets that reflect and inform (and in this case, intensify) the two other facets. Both Muslim and Bhil identities illuminate the duplicity of loving but demanding martial women, men's most intimate others.

Does such a construction of women mean that women as a group are to be understood as "split" into contrasting persons or dueling personae? In one sense, no. As much of the recent scholarship on women and goddesses has argued, sorting females or their characteristics into two groups, one (the "breast" type) represented by the nurturing cow and the other (the "tooth" type) represented by the sexually insouciant mare, is simplistic and misleading.[79] The contrast tends to "peg" female figures, ignore continuities and overlaps between supposedly opposed traits associated with them, and divert attention from mediating or divergent tendencies they exhibit. Moreover, as Ann Gold has argued persuasively, the same female, whether woman or goddess, can embody ten-

78. On the transparently suspicious nature of a jungly woman, see Gold, "The 'Jungli Rani' and Other Troubled Wives in Rajasthani Oral Traditions."

79. Gold, "The 'Jungle Rani' and Other Troubled Wives in Rajasthani Oral Traditions" and "Sexuality, Fertility, and Erotic Imagination in Rajasthani Women's Songs"; Erndl, *Victory to the Mother*, 153–158; and Harlan and Courtright, "Introduction," 8–11. See also Doniger (O'Flaherty), *The Origins of Evil in Hindu Mythology*, 346–349, as well as her *Women, Androgynes, and Other Mythical Beasts*, throughout.

dencies variously valued in different contexts: female cleverness, for example, can cut both ways.[80] Another illustration is to be found in women's votive traditions or *vrat*s, which require self-denial for the sake of husband's health/longevity and also reflect women's self-interest: *vrat* performers hope to get their desires fulfilled.[81] More narrowly, *vrat* performance can also be construed as effecting a sort of life insurance policy. Women want men alive for their own sake. A husband's sickness or death can subject a wife to financial insecurity and vulnerability to aggression by other men, not to mention the sadness that can accompany loss of a loved one.

At the same time, however, women are indeed often represented as split, and the splitting is significant, however whole and complex the split female may appear in other contexts or however ambiguous the splitting may ultimately prove to be.[82] Splitting remains an unstable state that the female being depicted sometimes resists and sometimes embraces, but that frequently leads beyond itself to posit alternative "wholes" and new paradigms. And so these representations of the stalwart Rajput women who facilitate and even boast of their beloved sons' or husbands' tragic ends incorporate both the victim and agent aspects that are "frozen" in different "frames." The women are not divided and neither are the aspects, for they transmute one into another, as do the extremities (beginning and end) in a Möbius strip.[83] Women (as victims) needing protection wind up demanding it (as agents). The mother's milk both feeds the son (literally and ceremonially before battle) and requires (lest it be shamed) that he spill his blood.

The splitting that is apparent in a frozen frame of fluid and sequential cultural expression, be it narrative plot or its performance in ritual, can reveal and accentuate ambivalence. And this is true not only for women but also for men. Although there has been much discussion about depictions of split females, be they women or goddesses, not enough has been said about the split imaging of men.[84] And yet those male attendants of goddesses—the goddesses' henchmen who are sacrificed sacrificers—are venerated heroes alternatively described as

80. Gold, "The 'Jungli Rani' and Other Troubled Wives in Rajasthani Oral Traditions," 119–136.

81. Pearson, *Because It Gives Me Peace of Mind*, 8. On this point and for more on *vrat*s generally, see McGee, "Desired Fruits," 84, and her "Feasting and Fasting"; Narayan, *Mondays on the Dark Night of the Moon*; Reynolds, "To Keep the Tali Strong" and "The Auspicious Married Woman"; Tewari, *The Splendor of Worship*; Wadley, *Shakti* and "Vrats."

82. For insightful reflections of many types of gendered splitting, see Doniger, *Splitting the Difference*, as well as her more recent book, *The Bedtrick*, 71–76, 94–98.

83. On the image of frame as Möbius strip or loop, see Handelman, "Framing, Braiding, and Killing Play"; Hess, "Staring at Frames till They Turn into Loops"; and Doniger, *Dreams, Illusions, and Other Realities*, 159 and 240–249.

84. Wendy Doniger (O'Flaherty) speaks of splitting in the context of Shaivism in *Śiva: The Erotic Ascetic*, as well as in various more recent works. On related paradigms of fissure, both male and female, see also her *Women, Androgynes, and Other Mythical Beasts*. Robert P. Goldman has discussed the splitting of heroes into ego and alter ego in his "Rāmaḥ Sahalakṣmaṇaḥ." This split is also to be found in the Greek epic cycle in the figures of Achilles and Patroklos. I thank Gregory Nagy, whose class at Harvard on Greek heroes I audited during the fall of 1996, for bringing this to my attention. As we shall see in the next chapter, the Hindu deity Bhairava or Bheruji also splits in a similar fashion. On the ambiguity of *guns* (qualities) said to inhere in a goddess, see Cynthia Ann Humes, who discusses a goddess's *rajasik* yet *rajasik-sattvik-tamasik* nature in "Vindhyavāsinī," 67, 69 note 9.

sattvik (pure, good) and *rajasik* (passionate, kinetic), said to embody *shanti bhav* (the feeling of peacefulness) and *ugra bhav* (the feeling of fierceness), and homologized to or identified as Bherujis, who come with dark and light iconographies and incarnations. Heroes come with contrastive identities that may be frozen and isolated or conjoined through song and story.

The next chapter, which begins with an examination of our Maha Singh story's second frame, directly addresses the heroic and masculine identity of heroes whose stories are told in Rajput stories. Whereas this chapter has examined representations of heroes and women in men's and women's narratives, what follows locates domestic texts, such as those we have seen, in discourse about the heroes that associates them with a variety of prominent constructs, beginning with goddesses.

4

Heroic Story Frames

Liberation, Perfection, and Seclusion

Be all that you can be, in the army.
　　　　　—U.S. Army recruitment jingle

Sometimes dead is better.
　　　　　—Stephen King, *Pet Semetary*

Among Rajputs, dying as a warrior has long meant being the best one can be. The result of this accomplishment is realizing the ultimate. Death in battle brings not only glory and fame through song and story but also release from the round of rebirths that binds the vast majority of people. Thus sacrificed, the hero finds *moksh*, liberation from the travail that is human existence. Whether *jhunjharji, bhomiyaji,* or *sagasji,* the hero finds himself transported to Virgati, "The Goal of Heroes," a wondrous abode where he can delight for an eternity in "wine, women, and song." At his disposal will be inebriants, dancing girls, musicians, and a host of other pleasures. Understood to be delivered from the world and ensconced in paradise, the hero is depicted as inarguably better off dead.

This picture of the hero's destiny combines imagery from two very different soteriologies, one the Vedic sort of heaven, where pleasures abound, and the other an Upanishadic sort of liberation, where the senses no longer enslave one to desire. Needless to say, the concepts, though frequently conjoined in heroic discourse, do not work neatly together. Ann Gold has noted that the Rajasthani villagers among whom she worked sometimes used the term *moksh* to refer to liberation from rebirth, but at other times deployed it to designate the peaceful condition of dwelling "in 'heaven' (*svarg*), 'paradise' (*Vaikunṭh*), or 'father realm' (*pitṛlok*)" which are "seen as temporary way stations for the spirit (*pret*) en route to another human body."[1] Nevertheless, for Rajput heroes who have attained their goal—Virgati—there is no question of returning. Self-sacrifice born of martial discipline has liberated them from rebirth, and if this picture of blissful, heavenly liberation departs from that described in the *upanishads*, no matter; here abstinence is rewarded by the fulfillment of desire, not its abandonment.

Linked, however loosely, Virgati and *moksh* reinforce the idea that for the Rajput, dying in battle fulfills warrior duty and removes him from this world and its mere mortals. Just as the virtuous woman (*pativrata*) becomes a "real woman" (*sati*), earning salvation on the pyre, the man (*vir*) becomes the "real man" or hero (*vir*), finding liberation through a violent death that places him beyond death. However conceived or wherever located, his after-death destiny represents cessation of life as we know it, but also a certain continuity that includes as a prominent feature devotion to the goddess to whom his life was given.[2] The hero will eternally serve his goddess as henchman, and will not take up residence in "temporary way stations." Even in cases where the hero is said to have attained Vaikunth, the identification of Virgati with Vaikunth does not rob the hero of his permanent status, which I have never heard doubted. Rather, one must assume, the identification renders Vaikunth consistent with the eternal Virgati, earned through self-sacrificing *bhakti*.

One thing is evident: salvation is a subject from which domestic stories generally steer clear. As we have seen, they prefer to end with the hero's death or with details of hero worship. Soteriology is not an express part of the agenda, which focuses on human experience and struggle. And if the narratives are not consistent or precise as to the afterlife, they are also vague about the matter of when the hero actually dies.[3] Some Rajputs conceive death as synonymous with decapitation, which visibly terminates ordinary human existence. Others describe death as transpiring when the hero's body falls to the ground and becomes motionless. Still others hold that a hero dies twice. Although this claim usually refers to the hero's decapitation and then his fall minutes or hours later, in the case of Balluji the "deaths" are separated by years. Our raconteur stated that he "died twice," once while retrieving Amar Singh's body from Shah Jahan's court and again when fighting Moghuls at Debari.

Whenever the warrior's death occurs, and however else it is conceived, it is presumed to be *dharmik* sacrifice for "god[dess] and country." It is marvelous, a cause for celebration. This should be obvious from the preceding discussion, but it bears repeating in light of the research on hero worship elsewhere and of notions about death that have been generated from work on death in other contexts. Before proceeding further to analyze the hero in the context of commonly associated constructs in Rajasthan—goddess, Bheruji, ancestral spirits,

---

1. Gold, *Fruitful Journeys*, 234–235. She says on p. 263 that elderly pilgrims visiting well-known sites along the Ganges River are especially likely to use the term to refer to their goal of "final release" achieved through detachment from sensual stimuli.

2. On the connection between heroes fighting to the death and goddess worship in nationalist politics in Bengal, see McKean, "Bhārat Mātā," 253.

3. For a discussion of death as a social construct in India, see Justice, *Dying the Good Death*, 12.

ascetics, and criminals—it is necessary to address this scholarship and contemplate its claims.

Good, Bad, and Perfect: Heroic Power and Preference

Analyzing death in Banaras, Jonathan Parry distinguishes between "good" and "bad" deaths.[4] According to Parry, the "good death" of the householder (male or female) is one in which death terminates a long and full life in which duties and desires are fulfilled. At such a point, a person is ready for and desirous of death.[5] Thus "the 'good death' is one to which the individual voluntarily submits his- or herself."[6]

By contrast, the person suffering a "bad death" is unprepared for dying. Says Parry, "the paradigmatic case is death by violence or as a result of some sudden accident; the underlying notion being that the victim has been forced to relinquish life prematurely and with the result that his embittered ghost is liable to return to afflict the survivors unless the appropriate propitiatory rituals are scrupulously observed."[7] Such a death, in Banaras and throughout India, is frequently referred to as *akal mrityu* or "untimely death," which Parry glosses as "uncontrolled death."[8]

In Banaras, Parry's informants "unhesitatingly" identified the death of a hero (*bir*) as *akal mrityu*, though they did not believe that his death causes him to "join the ranks of ordinary ghosts." In fact, Parry renders *bir* "hero ghost" and explains that *bir*s, being more powerful than ordinary ghosts, can control (ordinary) ghosts.[9] Controlling ghosts is a good thing—in cultic contexts this is one of the services that heroes perform—and presumably this mitigates to some extent the negative assessment of heroic death, but Rajputs would take exception to Parry's characterization of heroes as "hero-ghosts" and, more important, they would certainly reject the notion put forth by Parry's informants that the death of heroes is untimely.[10] For a Rajput soldier, death in battle is death in the line of

---

4. *Death in Banaras*, 158–166. Parry also discusses "good death" in "Death and Cosmogony in Kashi," and in "Sacrificial Death and the Necrophagous Ascetic," especially pp. 80–85. The notion is also central to Christopher Justice's treatment of death in Banaras in *Dying the Good Death*, 11–12, and is treated in various works on India, including Helen Lambert's "Medical Knowledge in Rural Rajasthan," 172–177. See also Maurice Bloch and Jonathan Parry, "Introduction," especially pp. 15–18.

5. On desire and death, see also Justice, *Dying the Good Death*, 184, as well as Coccari, "The Bir Babas of Banaras," 16. For a published introduction to her work on *bir*s, see her essay "The Bir Babas of Banaras and the Deified Dead."

6. Parry, "Sacrificial Death and the Necrophagous Ascetic," 82.

7. Parry, "Sacrificial Death and the Necrophagous Ascetic," 83. Coccari also employs this popular distinction, but describes untimely death as merely one of the ways that a man may become a *bir*, in "The Bir Babas of Banaras," 16.

8. Parry, "Sacrificial Death and the Necrophagous Ascetic," 83. For application of the point in other different geographic and temporal contexts, see Knipe, "Night of the Growing Dead"; Long, "Death as a Necessity and a Gift in Hindu Mythology," 76, 90; and Lambert, "Medical Knowledge in Rural Rajasthan," 172–177.

9. *Death in Banaras*, 163.

10. Helen Lambert has noted the unsatisfactory simplicity of the good/bad typology in the Rajasthani case and refers to various categories of the dead, including *bhomiyas*, *jhunjharjis*, and *sagasjis* as "only partially congruent with the typology"; "Medical Knowledge in Rural Rajasthan," 172. For example, based on her

and in fulfillment of duty. As almost any Rajput will tell you, for a Rajput soldier to die while fighting is glorious, whereas to die old and in bed is not.

As for the question of heroes as ghosts, it is true, as we shall see, that heroes technically remain *purbaj* (ancestors) even though they are liberated ancestors, but they are not therefore wandering and menacing *bhuts* (ghosts).[11] According to Coccari, Banarsi heroes have failed not only to be liberated but also to move on to the next incarnation.[12] They remain vexed and jealous of the living. Although such an understanding of heroes as angry, haunting, and jealous might make sense in the Rajput case, given the role society, and more narrowly females, play in bringing about their deaths, I have never heard a Rajput hero's death assessed by Rajputs as anything but beneficial and wondrous, in that it honors the hero's family and enables the hero to metamorphose into a divine family guardian. This kind of death is represented in story and elsewhere as exceptionally good, glorious, and fruitful. An indication of martial greatness and a demonstration of truth and goodness, it manifests *sat* and reaps divine protection for families.

Turning to the matter of voluntarism, it should be emphasized that the hero is credited with choosing his destiny. The choice may be represented as being made when the hero sets off for battle. Typically nondomestic men's traditions such as heroic ballads and *bhopa*'s stories make much of the hero's departure, which the hero typically takes bereft of companionship, an index and omen of his willingness to die. Alternatively, the choice may be made when the hero dons a saffron turban, signifying his ascetic renunciation of life (and women) in the field of battle.[13] All genres of heroic expressive tradition, from epics to tourist tracts, have drawn on this ascetical iconization of hero to a greater or lesser extent. Third, the hero may be depicted as embracing death when he severs his head and offers it to his goddess. Rajput domestic stories, however, seldom contain this type of scene, but rather employ a more "natural" scenario up until the moment of the hero's death, which then manifests the hero's distinctiveness as it reveals his emergent, superhuman power. The choice of death, however represented, is affirmed in many a heroic text by a bloody climax in which the hero demonstrates his *sat* by struggling headlessly while managing to exact revenge.

The hero's choice is neatly illustrated by the first frame story of the Maha Singh narrative analyzed in the previous chapter. In this outermost frame story, as we have seen, a husband chooses life rather than heroism, but because of his cowardice he ultimately loses it in compensatory suicide. Whether or not we agree with the notion that, given evident social pressure, a hero could truly be

work with villagers from various caste backgrounds, she considers the *bhomiya* to belong to a "transformational category between incorporated/good and unincorporated/bad spirits," and says that although the "manner and age of death" of the *bhomiya* correspond to the general Hindu conception of "untimely death, they are "benevolent and auspicious" once settled and worshiped; p. 174. Moreover, in that village the *jhunjharjis* are understood as having foreseen (and so presumably prepared for) their deaths, as have *sagasjis*, who are there understood to be *jhunjharjis* whose identities have been forgotten; p. 175.

11. On the separation of heroes from *bhut-pret* in eastern Rajasthan, see Lambert, "Medical Knowledge in Rural Rajasthan," 173–174.

12. Coccari, "The Bir Babas of Banaras," 18.

13. Donning saffron is typically, though not exclusively, associated with the *saka*, the unwinnable battle in which Rajputs ride into certain death. See chapter 1.

said to choose death is another matter. What concerns us here is the perception among Rajputs that the hero must have chosen, otherwise his heroism makes no sense.[14] Like Dhanna, who offers his head to batter in the enemy's gates, or his nephew Bhinya, who avenges his general's death at the cost of his own life, and like Balluji, who after initial hesitation about taking on the entire Moghul court, decides to retrieve Amar Singh's body, the hero is distinguished because of bravery, which is shown by his decision to confront a worthy foe, and so be prepared to offer up his life.

Hence the Rajput hero's death, in the context of Rajput domestic tradition, is seen to be good. Moreover, it fulfills most of the criteria for goodness set out in Parry's discussion of the "good death." To arrive at this conclusion, let us address individually ways in which Rajasthani heroes diverge from, as well as comport with, the "good death" paradigm emerging from Parry's fieldwork in Banaras. First, the hero's death does not meet the criterion that death terminate a long and full life. Neither, however, does the death of the *sati*, which Parry and Coccari report to be quintessentially good.[15] The *sati*'s case certainly attests to the fact that the good (can) die young, or, to put this less colloquially, the young can die good deaths.

This brings us to the second criterion, which holds that a good death requires that a person die with duties and desires fulfilled. This criterion logically comprises two qualifications. As to fulfilled duties, the Rajput hero's death is again comparable to the *sati*'s: both are made "timely." Unlike the widow, a good woman predeceases her husband or accompanies her husband as a *sahagamini*, literally, "one who goes with" her husband to the afterlife. These deaths are both understood to be in accord with the *dharm* of woman, whereas the *sahagamini*'s death is seen as also in accord with Rajput (or warrior, that is to say "class," i.e., *varn*) *dharm*. Like the *sati*, the hero who dies young dies fulfilling his duty as man and Rajput. He fulfills his *dharm* of protection before he grows too old to fight and avoids the far less satisfactory fate of dying infirm and degenerated.[16] It could be argued that a hero dying young has not necessarily fulfilled his householder duties, but then recall that familial women are represented as needing, if not outright demanding, men to protect them by fighting. In short, duty to caste is made commensurate with and even indistinguishable from familial duty, as the case of Balluji's taunting wife makes clear.

---

14. Intentionality is represented as more explicit in case of *satis* who take a *vrat* (explicit vow) to die on the pyre. See Harlan, *Religion and Rajput Women*, 118–120.

15. Coccari, "The Bir Babas of Banaras," 124. Coccari speaks of the "pure and uplifted character of the Sati," which causes her to have a "lack of ambivalence, the sine qua non of an active local deity," 124. Coccari concludes that this is responsible for the *sati*'s "lacking in the attention and elaboration that one finds in Rajasthan and elsewhere," 124. In my work on *satis*, however, I have argued that the *sati*'s substantial goodness (*sat*), which is anything but one-dimensional, makes her powerful and very attractive in Rajasthan; see *Religion and Rajput Women*, 124–129.

16. Dying in bed is often described as an inglorious and otherwise unsatisfactory end for a heroic Rajput. Diane M. Coccari also resists typifying the hero's death as "untimely" and discusses Sontheimer's contribution to correcting the tendency to interpret all heroic deaths in this way in "The Bir Babas of Banaras," 8, 13. The Rajput case compares nicely to that of the ancient Greeks, for whom a glorious death is far preferable to one after bodily atrophy and decay.

As to fulfilled desires, in a sense desire coalesces with duty. The Rajput is presumed to have desired death in the line of duty, or else he would not have chosen it (in any of the ways discussed above). Although the stories represent the hero as voluntarily dying and even as having donned the ascetic hue as he faces death, it is not at all clear that all his desires are fulfilled. Many a hero continues to fight after death because of unfulfilled desire. In this case, bloody revenge is depicted as the object of desire, and the headless hero both seeks and achieves revenge. Not all heroes, however, are headless. Most *sagasjis*, especially those who are victims of intrafamilial intrigue, keep their heads, and many do not get revenge. They simply die without killing all or even any of the parties responsible. Furthermore, even headless heroes who achieve revenge do not always then achieve fulfillment; they desire a homecoming, which women typically prevent by exclaiming, "Look, he has no head!" Nevertheless, the heroes seem "satisfied" with being barred. They do not proceed further or resist final rest at this point. Having died the perfect death at the right time and place, and so having distinguished themselves from the ungrateful and undeserving dead, they are ripe for settlement. Moreover, their "arrest at the border" is shown to locate them as protectors—and signifiers—of the border. Thus a failure to penetrate the border enables them to remain at the border as divine territorial guardians. In short, although some desires motivate the headless hero to fight but then are satisfied, other desires effectively dissipate when the hero is located (by two women or later by a memorial) on the border. If desires remain, they are the sort that causes no harm, that is to say, the sort thoroughly and endlessly sated in paradise.

Moving on to the next criterion, Parry says of a person who dies a good death, such a person renders his or her body a sacrifice fit for the gods. This rendering occurs as the dying householder fasts "to make himself a worthy sacrificial object free of foul faecal matter" and is completed by the cremation ritual, which includes bathing and tonsure, these activities continuing the process of purifying the body so as to make it a fit for a final sacrifice (*antyeshti*) on the cremation pyre. Parry completes his reflections on the condition that a person be a fit sacrifice by concluding that in the good death, the dying person is a ready and willing victim.[17]

What is to be made of this? First, there can be no argument as to whether the hero's body is a sacrifice fit for the gods. General consensus and a variety of genres, including epic, make it clear that the goddess devours him. Yet the hero is not depicted as preparing for death by fasting, and the cremation ritual is often not performed. Moreover, although hero narratives generally end with the hero's death (in the case of men's stories) or move on to discuss ritual (in the case of women's), cremation is not typically mentioned.[18] Rather, as in the case of the epics *Pabuji* and *Devnarayan*, soldiers' bodies become carrion for bloodthirsty

17. Parry, "Sacrificial Death and the Necrophagous Ascetic," 77–82.

18. This is not true, however, in a poetic version of the Kallaji narrative composed by Shil Sharma, whose treatments of the death of Kallaji reflect Brahmanical concern with purity as well as with the performance of *samskars* (purifying rites of passage), including and especially cremation. See Śil Śarma, *Karmavīr Kallā*, which is analyzed in depth in Harlan, "Tale of a Headless Horseman."

goddesses incarnate as kites or vultures.[19] At times, such heroes are explicitly represented as goats and their deaths as *balidans*. Heroes are, after all, the goddesses' victims, and victims who are sacrificed are deemed to choose death. The Navratri-Dashara goat signals preparedness by shaking, a gesture I have heard explicitly related to the *bhopa*'s trance when welcoming possession by a cultic hero.[20] Such a manifest imaging of hero as goat is found in the following excerpt from the *bhomiya* song that is sung in *Pabuji* and also performed on its own.[21]

> Mounted on your horse
> With a dagger tied on your waist
> As the sun began to rise,
> Bhomiya, having taken some *bhang*
> and tied a turban on your head,
> You went to fight for the cows alone.
> Alone you went to war. . . .
>
> Your knife chewed and spat *pan*.
> Your spear swished and spat blood.
> *The goat was killed.*
> *Vultures screamed above.*[22]
> [emphasis supplied]

The glorious hero who is eulogized in such epic verses is thus the goat who goes off to find sacrificial death in war. Although the ritual of death varies between long-lived householder and short-lived hero, the hero's death fulfills Parry's notion that the dying person is a ready and willing victim. If anything, the sacrificial nature of the saffron-turbaned hero's death is even more explicit. And if the hero is young, rather than the old victim preferred in the cremation sacrifice (which mimics the Vedic god Purusha's self-sacrifice) then so much the better![23] The goddess likes tender victims with juicy flesh, not tough old men. In *Pabuji*, she can barely wait for heroes to die in war, and must be satisfied temporarily with the livers of two self-disemboweled but persevering soldiers— Dhebo and the unnamed *bhomiyaji* resembling him—who must live on long enough to slay their enemies.

That the hero is ready and willing is also shown by his preparation for war as a soldier and by his yearly participation in Navratri slaughters from the time he comes of age. Preparedness to give blood for the goddess is illustrated

---

19. On vultures and kites as forms of the goddess in *Pabuji*, and in worship of the Caran *kuldevi*, Karni Mata, see Hiltebeitel, *Rethinking India's Oral and Classical Epics*, 108–109, and Harlan, *Religion and Rajput Women*, 71.

20. The hero who dies in battle is a goat, a substitution for the buffalo that is slain by Durga in the *Devimahatmya*. That buffalo is also deemed a substitute—for the divine—in some Tamil traditions; see Shulman, *Tamil Temple Myths*, 184.

21. This song, only a small excerpt of which appears here, was performed for me by professional musicians at Komal Kothari's home. For other reflection on it, see Harlan, "Heroes Alone and Heroes at Home," and "On Headless Heroes."

22. *Bhang* is cannabis; *pan* is a betel nut preparation.

23. See, for example, Knipe, "Sapiṇḍīkaraṇa," 111–124.

handily in the case of a Rajput family that lives on a *thikana* in Madhya Pradesh. A Rajasthani noblewoman who hails from this estate reports that on Navratri male family members cut their arms to allow their *kuldevi* to drink their blood. For the Rajput who beheads goats and offers himself to his martial *kuldevi*, preparedness for death takes on an altogether different meaning from freedom from fecal matter, and so forth.

Having wrestled with the criteria for "good death" and "bad death" Parry derived from his fieldwork in Banaras, I have decided that rather than attempting to figure out to what extent or in what ways the hero's death is "good" or "bad," it makes more sense to ask whether the model is apt. Perhaps the hero dies not a "good death" or a "bad death" but rather a perfect death, which is so good as to seem rather too good. Reducing notions of heroic perfection and completeness to mere goodness robs the hero who dies of his subtle complexity and transcendent mystery.

To press this further: perfected, the hero's *sattvik* goodness, again like the Möbius strip, overflows or turns back on itself, so that perfection, realized at the very moment of death, transcends goodness and so appears as awesome and wondrous as well as potentially threatening. We have seen repeatedly how women who need protection (as potential victims) end up demanding (and so being agents of) male demise, and how heroes, willingly giving their lives as victims, are also agents of death not only before but also after their deaths, a frightening state of affairs. In other words, just as good women who are defended have a "dark side," so do heroes dealing death whether merely as soldiers or as deities, whenever their deaths are assessed as having occurred, that is, when struggling headlessly or after falling to the ground. The hero is also potentially menacing after his death if his ire is aroused. His *sat* (essential character or inner "stuff") reflects and fuels his *shakti* (power) and is often deemed inseparable from it, the terms *sat* and *shakti* being used at times interchangeably. That *shakti* can be used to defend but also to harm, to sacrifice. The inseparability of *sat* and *shakti* is most succinctly represented in the perfect moment of death whereby the hero's goodness makes him the sweetest of victims but most explicitly reveals his power as he becomes a divine henchman, who will do what he will do.[24]

The perfect death, then, raises the specter, if you will, of theodicy. The hero who is the goddess's *sattvik* warrior victim is ever a powerful presence whose victimization, as well as his agency, will render him divine and rather frightening, as divinities can, if they wish, exact awful retribution for human transgressions. Thus although I heard myriad times that the divine hero does "good work," I also heard it said that he can be troublesome if crossed. He may cause fevers or simply alarm people by rattling windows so as to get their attention. As one Rajput woman put it:

> If the *jhunjhar* is angry and neglected, he'll throw open and close a
> window or throw a stone. Then one must do something good, like

---

24. On the mutual implication or identification of *sat* and *shakti* in the Gujarati context, see Tambs-Lych, *Power, Profit, and Poetry,* 108–109.

help the poor. If the *jhunjhar* is neglected, he'll give a curse or if he's angered, given some impure thing—if a woman has her period and approaches him, if he's given meat or wine [which] are dirty to him, if someone hasn't had a proper bath—then he'll come in a dream.

If this *jhunjharji* does not receive due respect, if he is given food he does not like (in this rather atypical case, meat or wine), or if a woman is in an impure state, he will curse or complain in a dream. Seldom, by the way, did informants refer to curses given by heroes, though the hero clearly can curse. Unlike the *satis*, who frequently curse before ascending the pyre, the hero prefers to treat disappointments ad hoc.[25] Most commonly he sends an omen, a reminder. Thus, for example, according to a Rajput women, her brother was riding on his horse when he came upon a snake (a form commonly associated with cultic heroes, including Tejaji, Gogaji, and Kallaji); immediately the brother remembered that he had forgotten to pay his respects to the family hero.[26] In most cases, ancestral heroes merely urge descendants to remember them by appearing as soft glowing lights in the night sky or by making mischief, such as curdling milk. In cases where fevers were reported, no mention was made of serious subsequent harm. The fever simply reminds the devotee to stay on course with devotion. One such example is provided by a *jhunjharji* who, dressed in white and riding a white horse, would appear to the informant's mother and grandmother "if they forgot to do worship [*puja*] and give offerings on the sixth day of the bright half of the month [his *tithi*, 'date,' presumably that of his death] . . . Then they would get feverish or a buffalo wouldn't give milk."

The only real damage from a neglected hero that I heard reported by a Rajput did not pertain to the Rajput's family. Rather it involved the aforementioned Baniya family who purchased from Amet *thikana* a property containing a Rajput *sagasji* shrine. The results are recorded in this short narrative, delivered by Prabhuprakash Singh of Amet:

> Baniyas bought the *thikana* granary property. They were Jains. They didn't keep up the *sagasji bavji* worship that used to take place there. Then bad things began to happen. You'd suddenly hear a scream from there in the middle of the night. There was fighting [within the Jain family] and property loss. Then they resumed the veneration and things improved for them. Now during Navratri people pay their respects and give lamps and *sindhur* there.

In this case the Baniyas are beset by family discord, but also by property loss, which would be thought very upsetting to Baniyas, whose traditional profession pursues financial profit. The Baniyas, the narrator indicated, had failed to understand that when they stopped routine veneration of the hero on Navratri (which celebrates the goddess Durga and the *kuldevis* with whom she is identi-

---

25. Cursing is generally left to women and ascetics, whose self-denial during life is typically associated with cursing, an act understood to motivate people to alter offensive behavior.

26. Some heroes, like Gogaji and Kallaji, are said to assume snake forms at times. Here, a snake seems merely to be an omen.

fied) the hero would be incensed. He added that there was a "big public outcry, so many people believed in him," so that these unfortunate Baniyas, who would not typically celebrate a holiday for a blood-consuming goddess attended by their problematic Rajput hero, had to reverse their course and commence Navratri veneration in pursuit of good fortune.[27]

In short, though perfected, the worshiped warrior can demonstrate anger, which is, after all, indispensable to the warrior whose life and identity are very much concerned with and informed by fighting. Moreover, although tending to instruct rather than inflict serious harm on descendants who neglect him through oversight, he can retaliate if malignantly insulted or intentionally denied his due. In such cases, however, the offending party is not a descendant devotee but rather a hostile, ignorant, or haughty outsider. A case in point is the previously mentioned polo player who urinated on a hero stone and then succumbed to fits until convinced to send an offering. Even in this case, recovery follows an apology and veneration. Thus one should not cross a hero, for in a battle with a hero there can be no doubt who will win. At the same time, it should be realized, the hero is not malicious or capricious in the view of familial devotees. Vengeance strikes them as earned, sensible, and predictable.

The same, of course, holds true for other deities, many of whom have never been assessed as malevolent. Even the gentile and kind Lakshmi, goddess of good fortune, will pass by, and so doom, a household that does not invite her in with a collection of oil lamps or that is insufficiently clean and tidy. Neglected or insulted, most gods and goddesses become annoyed and threatening, but their ire should not automatically be taken as indication of a generally malignant disposition.[28]

The attribution of malevolence or benevolence, then, has a lot to do with the identity of informants. Thus villagers from various caste backgrounds, whose territory is protected by a warrior to whom they are not related, may assess a Rajput hero to be more threatening and less accommodating than his descendants do. To the villagers, the hero may well appear to be more like a *bhut* (ghost) and less like someone's glorious forebear.[29] The same holds true for ethnographers characterizing and categorizing deities. Take the example of the avid colonial commentator Crooke, who describes the hero as "a very malignant village demon" who "brings bad fortune." This assessment at least partly reflects the discomfort that colonial observers felt with certain types of so-called "minor" deities such as the *bhomiya*, whom Crooke demotes to mere "godling of the land or soil."[30]

27. As Jains, they were probably vegetarian. I have met some Jains who eat meat, but Jain carnivores are unusual.

28. On malevolence and positionality, see Dumont, *A South Indian Subcaste*, 446.

29. For Coccari's informants, those who do not worship *birs* refer to them as ghosts but those who do worship them refer to them as deities; "The Bir Babas of Banaras," 18. Banarasi *birs* have been rendered so by deaths that include falling from a tree and falling in an oil vat—demises that would render them *purbaj*, not *vir*, in Rajasthan; Coccari, "The Bir Babas of Banaras," 17.

30. Crooke, *The Popular Religion and Folklore of Northern India*, vol. 1, pp. 158, 65. The term "folk deity," demotes heroes just as the term "godling" does. The term "folk" itself has been problematized; for discussion in the context of similarly controversial ethnopoetic terms, see the editors' introduction to *Gender, Genre, and Power in South Asian Expressive Traditions*, edited by Appadurai, Korom, and Mills, 4.

As to the matter at hand, domestic traditions, the hero of Rajput story, it bears repeating, is not conceptualized as a ghost, embittered or otherwise. He belongs to his own class of divinity and has been rendered a member of that class by dedication to family and society but also by devotion to his goddess, deemed by all a very good thing. Thus Rajputs who worship heroes do not characterize them in negative terms or compare them to demons, much less "malignant" ones. Unlike demons and ghosts, these are perfected, sacrificial beings whose lamented deaths bring good news of guardianship.[31]

To understand more fully Rajput assessment of heroic nature and power, we must turn now to investigation of some figures or personae who inform heroic identity. For the sake of avoiding needless repetition (from this and previous works), the *sati* will not be treated as a separate persona here. Nevertheless, extensive discussion of the *sati*, who will emerge as an independent subject in the following chapter, has been integral to the preceding text and will continue to insinuate itself in my treatment of various other personae. First among these is the goddess to whom the Rajput sacrifices himself and whose female identity aligns her in some telling ways with females encountered previously.

Frame Two and Beyond: Goddesses' Consumption, Heroes' Devotion

As *balidan* and as henchman, the hero serves as a paradigmatic devotee of his demanding, blood-loving goddess. Loyal to the point of death and beyond, a hero is shown to be distinguished from all ordinary people (both friend and foe) who do not sacrifice themselves to the goddess. Furthermore, having achieved death in battle as his goddess' sacrificial victim, the hero reveals his perfection in a particular way. Whatever might be said of the after-death destiny of the hero (he achieves *moksh*, Virgati, or both), he is a henchman-devotee, a status that earns him the epithet Bheruji but cannot efface his (*itihasik*) human distinctiveness, which will remain preserved most fully in men's detailed domestic stories and descendants' invocation of and pride in his name.

Choosing a sacrificial death and becoming a Bheruji can be seen as separate moments of transition in the domestic tradition that includes domestic hero stories. In narratives, however, these moments are presumptive: constitutive of identity, they are largely left unspoken. Commonly invoked as epithet in conversations about heroes and in commentaries about heroism in general, they reveal aspects of the same person, for the sacrificial victim and henchmen both serve goddesses' needs, the victim in the human realm, the henchmen in the divine. Hence whereas *balidan* imagery tends to emphasize the victim (albeit willing victim) aspect of sacrifice, typification of the hero as divine attendant or henchman tends to emphasize or promote the hero's agency as an independently venerated figure. Hero worship sometimes occurs in conjunction with goddess

---

31. At least superficial comparison with Jesus Christ seems obvious here. On the development of Christian theology in the context of classical hero devotion, see Wills, *The Quest of the Historical Gospel*, especially pp. 21–50.

worship, as it often does on Navratri-Dashara, and sometimes happens independently, whether calendrically (on a daily, weekly, or annual basis) or in conjunction with auspicious rites of passage (particularly weddings, births, and the tonsure of sons). In addition, both representations, sacrificial beast and henchman, have their source in a single event, death, with its revelation of the hero as perfect devotee yielding his life as an act of faith and a sacrificial gift, a *balidan*.

The second frame of the Maha Singh story makes clear the devotional context of heroic sacrifice. The statement that "Maha Singh went to war and did a lot of *puja* to Shiv and Mataji" may strike some as too cursory a pronouncement to merit designation as a frame. Even if envisioned alternatively, as simply the introductory sentence to the framed text, however, it still stands out as a striking and revelatory contextual comment from which the next sentence follows abruptly. Commanding pause, it stands on its own and opens up the text like a finely honed key. At the same time, it realigns the text so that it does not simply convey the information that Maha Singh gave his life; it also delivers the opinion that his battle had something to do with devotion to the divine.[32]

Given such an opening, the later statements about worshiping Maha Singh's sword and shield at Dashara cannot easily be misconstrued to constitute some sort of extraneous or fleeting observation made in closing. Whether or not an association between liturgical frame and closing is intended, the two references reinforce one another and foreground the religious nature of sacrifice in battle. In the household stories of Rajputs, particularly those of Rajput men, the secular agenda often remains expressed whereas the sacred dimension of sacrifice is left unsaid or, if mentioned, is indexed to the arena of posthumous ritual, where women predominate.

This religious agenda, which identifies the hero with the goddess, particularly in the context of her veneration on Dashara, is explicit in the following narrative, told by a Rajput woman about the Rathor Rajput *thikana* of Baghera, which is located near the city of Ajmer.

> The Marathas and the Baghera ruler had a war. The Marathas attacked and he was doing *puja* in a *chatri*. From a long distance the Marathas noted that he was doing *puja*. From there they shot a bow and arrow. His head was cut. Afterward, he hired a horse and went to fight—outside the village. Without his head he fought. He fought and went a long distance. In the fields two women were walking. They noted that he had no head. At once he fell from his horse. At present there is a *chatri* being made there. On every Dashara we have to go there, offer drink [liquor] and *prasad* [blessed leftovers, in this case sweets], and do *puja*.

In this narrative, it is unclear which divinity is receiving veneration. *Chatris* frequently contain images of divinities as well as images of ancestors. In the

---

32. For recent and intriguing reflections into ways in which frames infiltrate and inform text, see Handelman "Postlude: Towards a Braiding of Frame," and also his essay, "Framing, Braiding, and Killing Play."

narrative, evidently, no identification of the recipient of *puja* at the time of the hero's death is made. What is stressed is the manner of the hero's death, which though said to be by an arrow is specifically rendered a cutting (the verb used was *katna*: to be cut), which evokes the sacrificial action of a sword beheading a victim in sacred ritual space.[33]

The death by cutting is not represented as symbolic; the arrow decapitates in the mode of a sword and renders the devotee a headless hero who wages war after his head falls before the image of some (unmentioned) divinity. And if the cutting is not sufficient to convey a sense of the hero's sacrificial status, the narrative's conclusion surely is. Whatever the significance of the locus of the head's severing at the unnamed *chatri*, there is great significance in the locus of the body's ultimate fall (at the words of two women walking), now commemorated by a new *chatri* where there is worship on Dashara. Thus ritual tempus effects retroflex identification of heroic victim with the goddess worshiped on Dashara as well as confirmation of the hero's identity as divinity: he is offered drink and sweets as a deity in his own right. The hero's ongoing conceptualization and veneration are intrinsically linked to *devi* devotion, which here, as in our Maha Singh narrative, functions as interpretive frame.

It is worthwhile noting that in the context of cultic hero worship, where familial glory is of little concern to most pilgrims and officiants, coming as they do from different castes, the religious aspect of sacrifice is succinctly stressed. For example, hero and goddess images appear side by side in many cultic hero shrines. Moreover, a hero possessing a *bhopa* at a cultic shrine often manifests his presence by giving *dhok* before an image of his goddess, or otherwise venerating the goddess, for whom he once gave up his life. And most tellingly, goddesses frequently appear in *bhopas'* narratives, as they do in heroic epics.

In our text, Maha Singh worships his goddess along with Shiv. How are we to understand this? Although *kuldevi*s are typically depicted and venerated as independent goddesses in the martial context (that is to say in battlefield narratives), they are frequently described as married the domestic context (that is, in narratives about a *kuldevi*'s appearances and the blessings she delivers to members of the household, especially women). Thus in the *kuldevi* narratives told by men and in public iconography, *kuldevi*s are frequently depicted as carnivorous beasts—typically scavenging birds, but sometimes predatory felines such as tigresses. In the narratives told by women and in household shrine iconography, *kuldevi*s are commonly *suhagins*, auspicious wives.[34] The reference to Shiv may reflect the imaginative iconization of a goddess as married (the narrator is, after all, a woman), but it may also reflect the characterization of Shiv as the god of war and as the chosen deity (*ishtadevta*) of the kingdom of Mewar, as well as the vast majority of its *thikanas*.

---

33. *Katna*, the first definition of which is "to be cut, to be wounded (by a blade etc.)" means also "to die in battle." The deployment of this multivalent verb could be thought of as setting the shrine sacrifice within the context of battle, which in any case ensues shortly and is foreshadowed by the sacrifice that engenders a hero; see Mahendra Chaturvedi and Tiwari, eds., *A Practical Hindi-English Dictionary*, s.v.

34. Harlan, *Religion and Rajput Women*, 71.

In heroic narratives, however, the hero's death is understood as a sacrifice not for Shiv but rather for Shakti, the goddess who takes blood sacrifice. Furthermore, these days the god Shiv is typically depicted in local iconography as a *ling* (literally, "mark"; the term here designates a phallic stone) or a detached meditating *yogi*, rather than as the bloodthirsty battle god whom Tod found so appealing. The most common image of Shiv circulating in Mewar is from the Eklingji ("One Ling")temple in Kailashpuri, which is located near Udaipur. With this image the ruler of Mewar is thoroughly identified. The Maharana is understood to be first servant among devotees. He is both patron of the temple and of the *gosains* (ascetics) and other priests who have traditionally administered the temple.[35] The image of Eklingji remains on many of the official communications coming from the palace. In addition, the charter myth for the establishment of the royal dynasty tells of the miraculous revelation of Eklingji to Bappa Rawal.[36] And like the Maharaja of Banaras, also held to be "chief servant," the Mewar Maharana is represented in certain contexts as a manifestation of the deity. Thus during the royal celebration of the festival of Gangaur (now transformed into the Mewar State Tourism Festival), the Maharana once toured Udaipur's Lake Pichola with an image of Shiv's spouse while, some say, the divine ascetic was diverted on shore. Then there is the case of the cultic hero Kallaji, who is held to have been given to his parents as a boon from Shiv and who, as also a celibate incarnation of Shiv, gives his *kuldevi*, Naganechaji, his head on a platter before dying along with the famous heroes Jaimal and Phatta.

Viewed in light of the assumption by Rajputs that the hero's death is a sacrifice to a goddess, the reference to Shiv does not diminish but rather reinforces the proposition that the goddess—who is sometimes represented (particularly in the case of women's *kuldevi* stories) as consorting with Shiv but at other times seen as independent of Shiv—motivates and receives her virile human victims. In keeping with such an interpretation and in accord with the association between Shiv and royalty, along with Shaivite mythology (which often renders Shiv bellicose), it is hardly daring to suggest a homology between Shiv and hero, and in so doing impute to the hero a sort of intimate or conjugal relationship with Shiv's divine counterpart. Devouring her victim, the goddess unites with him and engulfs him; is not coitus suggested here? We need not rely on Freudian theory to hazard the exchange. From ancient times through the present, Indian texts have frequently employed metaphors substituting modes of consumption. The story of that hungry mother Bhukh Mata, who devours fighting *maharanas* one by one, implies a certain predilection for monarchs that recalls the tryst of *maharana* and goddess in the circumnavigations on Lake Pichola during Gangaur.[37] Another example is

---

35. As befits this eminent devotee of Shiv, the "erotic ascetic," the Maharana is located within both the ascetical and householder traditions. Such dual identifications is hardly innovative: the exiled Ram is both ascetic and householder during the period of his forest exile. Later he takes no second wife after banishing his wife Sita to the forest. Furthermore, as previously noted, Pabuji, who is called an ascetic of the desert, is disinclined to marry, but also reluctant to leave his bride.

36. Harlan, *Religion and Rajput Women*, 77–78.

37. On Bhukh Mata, see Harlan, *Religion and Rajput Women*, 107–108.

FIGURE 4.1. The goddess Naganechaji and the heroes Jaimal and Phatta during the celebration of the festival Navratri at the Kallaji memorial, Chittor

Shakti De, a Gujarati Rajput *kuldevi* who eats a monarch limb by limb, then revives him to render him a suitable groom.[38]

Clear association between Shiv and hero is also expressed on royal cenotaphs at Ahar, where memorial stelai for Mewar monarchs portray them as heroes flanked by diminutive *satis*; these husbands and *satis* typically face images of Shiv and his consort Shakti, who are united as *ling* and *yoni*.[39] Although not all the monuments commemorate heroic metamorphoses, their heroic iconography implies a complementary association of monarch and hero and posits an association between both and Shiv. The most explicit association, however, is the imaging of sacrificed heroes as Bheruji, who is often represented either as Shiv or as a manifestation of Shiv's wrath.[40]

In hero narratives, whether or not the hero's identification with or as Shiv is blatant, latent, or absent, the goddess, not Shiv, is the deity understood to demand and receive blood offerings and, more particularly, heroes.[41] Thus, as I have argued, the frame initiated by the narrator's declaration of the hero's routine devotion to Shiv and Mataji is completed (if not simply complemented) by the references to ritual veneration at Dashara, the final day of devotion to Durga (and so *kuldevi*), and the day on which is worshiped the sword that cuts the goddess' goat (itself representing Durga's enemy Mahishasur) during Navratri and that also slices the hero's enemy in war.[42]

Because of this veneration, Dashara is deemed an ideal day for waging war.[43] Pleased with the ritual recitation of the *Durgasaptashati* (the story of Durga's conquest over the demons) and with her blood offerings on Dashara, as well as with the cleaning and veneration of martial instruments (for example, the sword, which is an icon of the goddess and may be infused with her power), the goddess is thought inclined to grant victory.

The Maha Singh text refers to worship in the frame and on Navratri, but it also suggests ritual in its representation of Maha Singh as a sacrificial offering. It holds that he is decapitated by "a single slash of the sword." This is a formulaic phrase that recurs frequently in all manner of heroic tradition in Rajasthan. Recall that cutting a goat with "a single slash of the sword" on Navratri initiates boys into manhood. Slicing enemies with "a single slash of the sword" confirms

---

38. Personal communication, Jaya Singh Jhala, October 3, 1987. The goddesses' revival of the king brings to mind the story I heard about a *thakur* who once asked why he should bother to sacrifice a goat. He asked, "Can the goddess bring it back to life?" The goddess answered his question by bringing back to life the Navratri goat *balidan*—even though it had been killed, cut up, and cooked. Having witnessed the miracle, his family decided not the eat the goats slain this way but to give them to the cook and his family.

39. Shiv's *ling* is his phallus. The goddess is symbolized by her *yoni*, vulva. The *ling* is depicted as united with a *yoni* in many sculpted icons.

40. As is Virabhadra; see Knipe, "Night of the Growing Dead," 123–156.

41. In Andhra Pradesh, the epic hero Katamaraju is also associated with Shiv and promises Ganga, who identifies herself to him on the battleground as his family deity, to give her animal and also human sacrifices. See Narayana Rao, "Tricking the Goddess," 107, 114.

42. On Pottu Raja, another multiform henchman of Mahishasur, see Hiltebeitel, *Rethinking India's Oral and Classical Epics*, 33–34.

43. On Dashara and the display of a king's *digvijaya*, territorial might, and its connection to the Vedic *ashvamedha* sacrifice in the context of Banaras, see Lutgendorf, *The Life of a Text*, 46.

that manhood, and dying by "a single slash of the sword" both confirms that manhood at the final hour and signifies that the hero is identified with his goddess's Navratri goat.

Death by a "single slash of the sword" thus indirectly and ironically, if technically, renders Ranbaj Khan a sacrificer, albeit an unwitting one (as Muslim sacrificer, he presumably intends no sacrifice to a goddess), just as death at the hands of a Hindu Rajput transmutes Muslims into victims suitable for a goddess's consumption. Things are not so neat, however. Ranbaj Khan would never, of course, be seen as a suitable sacrificer by many Rajputs. Recall that the touch of a Muslim's sword was enough to render a Rajput an unsuitable sacrifice, in the words of our young Rajput quoted earlier. Furthermore, in this story a dog is poisoned and dies after drinking Muslim blood. Unfit for a dog, it should surely be unfit for a goddess. And yet, logically speaking, if the hero is said to be sacrificed, and especially if he is said to have been sacrificed "with a single slash of the sword," the enemy must serve the role of sacrificer—even if the hero is also a self-sacrificer. After all, in these *itihasik* narratives shunning self-decapitation, the hero's wielding of the sacrificial sword signals his decision to fight unto death and glory. And so, once again, the Muslim appears in the Rajput's reflection. If the Muslim is in some manner a sacrificer for a goddess, the Muslim sacrificed in battle by a Rajput sacrificer is also made to play the part of the goddess's victim. When it comes to carrion, she prefers the sweet flesh of the hero, but carrion is carrion. A kite consumes all.[44] Thus we have a contradictory situation where, ironically, fit and unfit cohere in the same inimical persona. Ambivalence abounds.

I am tempted to push the argument further: portraying the villain as dealing death with a "single slash of the sword," the text suggests the assailant's manhood, as killing this way would in the case of a Rajput. Thus, to repeat, this enemy's manner of slaughtering rescues him from the utter ignominy associated with having his mother do the real work of confronting the enemy. Again, intended or not, assigning to the otherwise scurrilous enemy this Rajput index of (Rajput) manhood would then connote a certain worthiness as an enemy, which in turn reflects well on the hero. Unlike the Kachvaha ruler who defeats drunken tribals and is demeaned for it by a descendant's Rathor rival, Maha Singh faces a mightily masculine foe.

Naturally, the text does not leave things there. Having represented Ranbaj Khan as worthy to sacrifice the hero, it then demonstrates the hero's superiority with an impressive demonstration of one-upmanship. After Ranbaj Khan decapitates Maha Singh with a single slash, Maha Singh then decapitates him while also bisecting his elephant saddle and elephant. And the narrator's very next sentence indicates that these acts are the basis for worshiping on Dashara the sword striking these blows, along with the shield defending his body.

The sacrificial action framed by these references to deities and worship, that is, the bisection of hero, enemy, and elephant, is more easily contemplated in

---

44. The goddess Kali, who appears not just as a general in the war of the gods with demons, is represented as actually consuming the blood of enemies and not, of course, of her divine companions. On Kali and demon blood, see Kinsley, "Kālī: Blood and Death out of Place."

light of another narrative recounted during the course of my research. During one of many conversations I had with a middle-aged Rajput woman who had married into Dailwara, another of Udaipur's powerful *thikanas* but who lived in an airy and contemporary Udaipur home, I learned a hero story that helps demonstrate the importance and nature of death as sacrifice in the Maha Singh narrative.[45]

> The *thakur* from our family asked the Maharana of Udaipur for leave to go to the *thikana* to sacrifice for Dashara. [The noblemen had evidently been called to perform some duties in the Maharana's court].[46] The Maharana said, "If you're going home, I hope you intend to sacrifice an elephant," meaning "this must be very important if you have to leave and go home." So he took up the challenge given by the Maharana and sacrificed an elephant to the Rathor goddess. . . .
>
> The temple was up on a big hill. The sacrifice was made from that height and the elephant tumbled down. The mahout refused to part with the elephant and so he died with him. On the hill are now two *cabutras* [shrines consisting of stelai on raised platforms]: one for the elephant and one for the mahout.

Deploying hyperbole, the affronted Maharana suggests that if sacrificing is so important to the *thakur*, he had better be sacrificing something much bigger than a goat, for instance, an elephant. The *thakur*, like any legendary Rajput worth his salt, takes up the challenge and literally sacrifices an elephant. Maha Singh's sacrifice of an elephant has the same effect. It demonstrates the seriousness of devotion and the extent of his desire to provide his goddess with sacrifice.

Second, in this Dashara text, the killing of an elephant is identified indirectly with the *thakur*'s honor as a *thakur*. The elephant's sacrifice reflects on him. In effect it is his (self-) sacrifice, which the story represents by way of substitution: the "scape-elephant" for the king or, more precisely, the "scape-elephant" for the scape-goat standing in for the buffalo that represents Mahishasur and is identified with the king![47] Moreover the elephant, like the horse, symbolizes royalty. If the hero's death in battle substitutes for Navratri-Dashara slaughter, Navratri-Dashara slaughter also here substitutes for the soldier's death. The elephant's slaughter can work as a symbol of its master Ranbaj Khan but also of its sacrificer Maha Singh, another king. If this sacrifice is not enough to make the point, we have the elephant's sacrifice leading to the sacrifice of the *mahout*, the king's servant.[48] In any case, here animal sacrifice clearly effects human sacrifice. Both sacrifices are commemorated by *chatris*.

45. This woman was routinely described by other Rajput women as "contemporary," and "progressive." Having been raised outside Rajasthan and having relatives in the United States, she shared an interest in local Rajasthani lore that struck me as ethnographic.

46. When attending the *darbar* (king's court), nobility lived in *havelis*, sprawling mansions, in Udaipur.

47. On identification of the slain king with his elephant and horse, as well as other emblems of royalty, see Filliozzat, "The Giving up of Life by the Sage," 148.

48. This post would typically be filled by a "Daroga" or "Ravan Rajput" (offspring of a Rajput father and a non-Rajput mother), perhaps making the human sacrifice even more dear.

Maha Singh's slaughter of an enemy as well as his own death at the hands of an enemy thus constitute acts that connote and serve as ritual.[49] If killing men in war reaffirms commitment to a goddess, a commitment that is first established when the hero becomes a man by slaughtering a Navratri-Dashara goat, decapitation in war is a *samskar* that can be thought of as bringing closure to the Navratri-Dashara initiation. Hence, like our explicit second frame and the mention of Dashara in the Maha Singh story, Navratri-Dashara ritual often functions as an implicit or elliptical frame that informs domestic hero stories and that expresses what is religious about stories that are seemingly preoccupied with secular achievement, glory way back then and status here and now. Navratri ritual also operates as a complement to the calendrical rituals and rites of passage, which are overwhelmingly organized and overseen by women. Thus in women's stories, sacrificial death becomes not the climax but the beginning of the story that most concerns them, that of the posthumous hero who, like his *kuldevi*, protects the family, guards its health, and above all brings life in the form of fertility, which makes women mothers.

The devotional frame, then, helps formulate the agenda and highlight the subsequent text's religious nature. When, in turn, viewed in the context of religious praxis, the frame demonstrates the hero's identification with Shiv and association with Shakti, while it reveals the sacrality of sacrifice for others. Here, as in the story of the monarch-eating Bhukh Mata, sacrifice for society and sacrifice for his goddess are covalent, if also discrete. Elsewhere these images are hard to express at once: like Wittgenstein's duck-rabbit, which appears as a duck or a rabbit depending on how one focuses at a particular instant, sacrifice "for others" (women, cows, and so on) and for a goddess are aspects of the same action that are seen alternatively or sequentially to occupy the same space.[50]

By this point, one might well ask, if a goddess devours her protégés, what kind of guardian goddess is she? Isn't it her job to protect? As in the case of familial women, the answer is yes, the feminine protects, but not without cost. Up to this point the cost, more than the benefit, has been stressed. Given that the lives of worshiped heroes always terminate in violent death, it is easy to see why: in hero stories the goddesses always get their sacrificial beasts. Nonetheless, it should be emphasized, Rajput devotees of *kuldevis* understand them primarily as preservers, not grim reapers, of life.

The construction of goddess as guardian is neatly illustrated in the following comments of an elderly and respected Rajput about a beneficial relationship with his goddess. The story was told to me by the irrepressible Col. Mohan

49. In Devnarayan's epic, Gujar women address vultures who have come to the "brave, courageous Nevo" and to "brave Bhoj" at the invitation of the "crown prince Nevo," and tell them, "Look, cowry shell [white] vultures, you should come either on the Navrātrā festival of the nine days. Or you should come precisely (on) the night of Daśaharā"; see Miller, "The Twenty-Four Brothers and Lord Devnārāyaṇ," book 2, p. 651. The vultures are told almost immediately thereafter: "There is about to be a battle in the settlements. At that time, you can eat plenty on the battlefield," p. 653.

50. In classes I frequently compare this enigma to that of Jesus Christ, represented in the *New Testament* as both fully god and fully man, a dual nature that religion students frequently encounter with furrowed brows, expressing bafflement. On the duck-rabbit, which Ludwig Wittgenstein attributes to Jastrow, see *Philosophical Investigations*, 194.

Singh about an adventure he had while serving in the army, with the Jodhpur Lancers. Having heard from others tales of the retired army officer's courage and bravado, I now listened to him offer me a mere sliver of his autobiography as we sat in chairs out on the lawn during two visits I made to his comfortable Jodhpur home.

The colonel told me that in 1948 he crossed into Pakistan on a camel to retrieve some cows that had been stolen and taken there. In the process he killed "five or six men" because he "had the goddess's protection." In his narrative, which sounds very much like a typical hero story apart from its first-person narration and happy ending (the narrator lives to tell his tale), the Pakistanis assume the role of cow rustlers from whom the hero is protected by a guardian goddess.

He also told me of another situation in which the goddess saved him.

> In '39 or '40 I was going through some guerrilla training. After a
> long march I was exhausted and the group came to a big river. My
> C.O. ordered me to go across the river. I started in but I knew I was
> too tired. I lost my footing and was falling into the current. Then I
> felt someone grab me and pull me up out of danger where I could
> stand. When I got out, my C.O. asked me what happened there at
> that moment when I was in trouble and I told him. My C.O. told me
> not to tell that to anyone else.

Here Mohan Singh attributes his survival to his goddess, who literally pulls him out of danger and grants him safety. His confidence in the reason for his rescue is, evidently, not shared by his commanding officer. The colonel made it clear to me that the officer was skeptical and was concerned that others might take his account of a religious experience as unacceptable in the modern, secular army. His continued faith in his *kuldevi* was evident in that he had to excuse himself to do his midday goddess *puja*. He explained to me that he worships the *devi* three times a day, so he took his leave after inviting me back to hear more adventures and miracles of protection the following day.

As is clear from various narratives about goddesses and heroes, protection is provided at a cost. The general rule holds true: a goddess guards the *kul* (family), but this is no guarantee of individual life, which must be sacrificed to her (much as individual lives must be sacrificed for a country during wartime). Demanding death or receiving sacrifice, however, can be deemed a good thing for the individual. An act of grace, it brings the individual who complies salvation and confers glory, which is bequeathed to his family.

Like goddesses, women hold the responsibility, and so are deemed to have the power, to protect men's lives. Their weapons are two: devotion to protective deities (including goddesses, but also *satis* and heroes) and preservation of virtue, especially chastity.[51] If a hero dies, however glorious his death may be for the family and however rewarding for the hero, his death implicates her dedica-

---

51. For more on Rajput women's chastity and protection, see Harlan, *Religion and Rajput Women*.

tion and integrity. Self-sacrifice as a *sati* is an expeditious means of exoneration. And yet, given the presumption about women's dangerous and even deadly need, one might speculate as to subtext. However much the *sati*'s death in such circumstances may be said to be probative and wondrous, it may also (like our iron-fearing coward's suicide) be compensatory and purificatory. In short, women and goddesses both require sacrifice, but their protection is finite. Protection by goddesses is limited because of their need for appealing victims, while protection by women is limited, perhaps because of their failures as wives to protect husbands (through *vrats* and other self-sacrificing service), but certainly because of their need for protectors to die for them.

This brings up another matter. Like women, the goddess who protects men requires their protection, and so live male protégés.[52] The Kachvahas, it should be recalled, took away Jamvai Mata from the Minas, and although some may think that she is better off with the Kachvahas than with tribals, the fact remains: having been taken from tribals, she could, theoretically, be taken from the Kachvahas by someone else. Goddesses of weak kings become spoils of war. Thus the Kachvahas claim to have acquired from vanquished Bengali protégés the goddess Shila Mata, to whom they give Navratri blood offerings because Jamvai Mata, their vegetarian *kuldevi*, doesn't accept them. In short, like the princess married to a conqueror by a defeated king, the goddess may leave her abode and protégés to guard a new king and people. Visibly manifest in icon form, a goddess is potentially a flag to be captured.

Before closing this discussion of men and their female associates, I should add that I have noted the frequency with which students of Hinduism ask why, if Indian goddesses are thought so powerful, Indian women are so powerless. By this point it should be clear that bellicose goddesses (the most popular kind among Western feminists) may be depicted as depending on men. At the same time, women have been thought to possess what we might think of as extraordinary powers (*sat*, *shakti*), which is one reason they are assigned responsibility for fending off, or not fending off, their husbands' deaths.[53] Thus, each of the premises expressed in the question's clauses is flawed. As those who have read the literature on gender well know, the situation is complex.

To conclude: understanding Rajput hero stories, where desires for life and death dance an endless and intimate tango, requires some serious reckoning with goddesses and women. Appearing in heroic stories, often in narrative frames, the female may appear as inherently conflicted as well as conflictual. Inhering in one figure, woman or goddess, the twin interests in preserving but sacrificing men who protect women and goddesses reflect unstable, bifurcating, and coalescing constructions of the feminine. These constructions reflect directly on constructions, also shifting, fracturing, and conflating, of men who die as heroes. Fluid, if transcendent, heroic identity is succinctly illustrated in

---

52. On a goddess's need for protection in south India, see Meyer, *Aṅkālaparmēcuvari*, 50.

53. On this question, see Harlan and Courtright, "Introduction," 8–15. On the appeal of the bellicose Kali to Western feminists, see McDermott, "The Western Kālī."

the hero's assumption of the epithet Bheruji, which conveys divine status while positing continued intimacy with goddesses.

Bheruji

Dying as a sacrificial victim, the hero becomes a Bheruji.[54] How do these images compare? From a religious point of view, the hero is not literally a goat, but he is in fact consumed by a bloodthirsty goddess, quite as a goat is consumed by that goddess on Navratri. Digested, the hero becomes a Bheruji. Is this metaphor as well? Yes and no. At some times and from some perspectives and contexts, the hero is identical with Bheruji. At other times and from other perspectives and contexts, he is merely analogous to Bheruji. Particularly in a cultic setting, in which the hero's past is of minimal concern compared to the healing work the hero can do now, heroes (about whose lives little is generally known to devotees) are frequently identified as Bherujis. In fact, some are said to be incarnations of Bheruji from birth.

In Rajput domestic traditions, however, identification is subtler, less literal. Heroes worshiped as heroes rather than gods such as Ram are human ancestors who achieve divine status by fulfillment of their social and sacred sacrificial duties in death. Thus, while Rajputs frequently say that their ancestors are Bherujis, they are not completely and simplistically conflating identities. Rather, such a statement about the hero's after-death identity and destiny needs to be qualified by and added to the soteriological mélange with which we are already familiar. Hence, instead of simply equating hero and Bheruji, it is better to contemplate factors likely to facilitate the association. Aside from the mythic context in which both heroes and Bheruji are connected with beheadings (Bheruji having beheaded the god Brahma in one myth and having been beheaded by the goddess he desires in another), heroes and Bherujis are defenders of perimeters. Both are typically located on and protective of territorial boundaries.[55] Like the *kuldevis* they serve, they are protectors of a territory, along with its inhabitants. Bherujis guarding the perimeter are often identified as or confused with (depending on the devotee with whom one speaks) Kshetrapals ("Guardians of the Field"), some of whom are identified as or confused with Poliyaji, an epithet given some heroes who die defending a gate (*pol*).[56]

---

54. For a handy introduction to Bheruji (Bhairava) as guardian devotee, see Hiltebeitel's introduction to *Criminal Gods and Demon Devotees*, especially pp. 8–11. See also two chapters in the same volume, Visuvalingam's "Bhairava's Royal Brahmanicide," and Erndl's "Rapist or Bodyguard, Demon or Devotee?" Also informative is Guha's "Bhairon." On various Bheruji identities and homologies in Maharashtra, see Sonthcimer, *Pastoral Deities in Western India*. See also Stanley, "The Capitulation of Mani." For a good example of Bheruji's fluidity and transmutability, see Roghair, *The Epic of Pālnaḍu*, 195.

55. See Erndl, "Rapist or Bodyguard," 243.

56. A good example of a Poliyaji is found in a shrine near Shikar Bari, the old royal hunting lodge on the outskirts of Udaipur. In general Polyaji serves as an epithet for heroes who, like Kallaji, Naruji, or Balluji, die defending gates. It is sometimes, however, a nameless guardian who "must have died defending the gates"

In addition, Bherujis serve as guardians at the gates of various temples, especially goddess temples. Iconic or aniconic stone representations of Bherujis are typically located just outside or inside entryways. Here the blood offerings to goddesses are frequently made. Thus the hero's roles as defender of a goddess and as sacrificial victim locate him conceptually, if not literally, on the goddess's threshold.

One more factor that contributes to association is the very proximity of hero and Bheruji images when they are located on territorial boundaries. Crude shrines or *cabutras* may incorporate a number of deities, heroes and Bherujis among them. Multiple heroes and Bherujis may mingle in the crowd.[57] Along this same line, in hero shrines goddess images may be flanked by Bherujis, a situation that reinforces the identification of heroic devotee and Bheruji as henchman.

Then there is the matter of iconography. Many crude roadside-shrine images of heroes are virtually indistinguishable from Bheruji images. Represented as a bust covered with layers upon layers of colorful foil, the identity of hero or Bheruji may remain a matter of speculation for most beholders. Only devotees may know for sure, and even they may disagree. Many busts in which features are actually discernable—eyes, nose, mustache, and turban—are equally enigmatic. Both divinities may be depicted in this way.

Some stelai present a similar problem. Whereas the best-known relief image of the hero, the equestrian figure, can easily be distinguished from Bheruji (though not from certain *purbaj*, that is, non-heroic ancestors), the less popular but still prolific image of standing warrior may not be. Bherujis are frequently depicted as mustached men with club and dog. The standing hero may bear any one of a number of weapons, but is typically not flanked by a dog. Nevertheless, the iconographies invite identification, which is not infrequently made. The Bheruji with dog may be construed as signifying a Rajput warrior, especially as Rajputs are well-known lovers of dogs. The Maha Singh story, with its loyal blood-lapping dog, exemplifies the affiliation, and to this day Rajputs pride themselves on their possession of fine dogs. In fact, Labradors (or "Labradogs" as they are more typically known in Rajasthan) are highly prized hunting dogs. Now that few Rajputs own elephants and horses tend to be exorbitantly expensive, the well-bred dog stands out as an especially visible marker of Rajput status and is often to be found in the back of jeeps, the vehicle of choice for many Rajputs.

The association of identities in cultic shrines and in village icons doubtless contributes to the tendency to associate and even identify heroes and Bherujis among Rajputs. Thus it is not surprising that when Rajput informants spoke to me on the general subject of Rajput heroes, they frequently identified heroes as Bherujis and sometimes included them in the throng of fifty-

---

and who is a Kshetrapal or Bheruji. I have also, though infrequently, heard Bheruji identified with Dharmaraj, another perimeter-guarding deity, but I have never heard of Dharmaraj being equated with a hero, except in the case of Devnarayan, who is explicitly held by villagers I met to be an incarnation of Dharmaraj, just as Pabuji is held to be an incarnation of Lakshman.

57. An example is the Bheruji *sthan* in a compound where there is also a Pabuji *sthan* in Kushelgarh.

two Bherujis who, along with sixty-four *yoginis* (female ascetics), accompany goddesses in battle.[58]

Nevertheless, individual Rajput heroes retain their discrete historical and individual identities, which also tend to distinguish and distance the hero from the Bheruji. Deployment of hero stories in the battle for status with its rewards requires nothing less. Thus even where complete conflation of hero with Bheruji would be an irresistible temptation for others, Rajputs tend to refrain. The following case makes the point well. It involves a historical hero whose name is Bheru and who is worshiped by descendants as the historical Bheru Singh but by the *bhopa* and followers who frequent the hero's thriving cultic shrine as an incarnation of the divine Bheruji. A rendition by a Rajput woman from Bheruji's family goes as follows.

> There's a *jhunjhar* in the *mahasatiyan* [royal cremation ground]. We go there to give *dhok* at weddings. A late *maharana* had this person killed. Bheruji was his name and he was a Sisodiya Rajput [from the royal line]. He was beheaded. His wife's brother wanted to kill him. The person beheaded had five wives and they tried to jump from the rooftop [to become *satis*]. But they were locked in the room. Through their *sat* they became *satis*.

In this account, Bheruji dies because of a scheming brother-in-law, and then his *satis* follow him. The reference to women using their power to become *satis* refers elliptically to a situation made clear in some other accounts, which hold that the *satis* managed miraculously to escape and kill themselves after he became a *jhunjharji* and took revenge on some of his assailants. Still another variant was told to me by Dhruv Singh, an ebullient, now deceased, middle-aged Sisodiya Rajput who belonged to Shivrati and was closely related to the royal family. Evidently annoyed about the assassination and an avid reader of history, he provides further elaboration.

> Bheru Singh was killed by the order of Maharana Bhim Singh. The Marathas wanted to be ruled by a king from Udaipur. Bhim Singh was easy-going and so he asked his nephew Bheru to rule the Marathas. He was too lazy to do it himself. The other *thakurs* became jealous and said bad things to the Maharana. They poisoned his ears. Once when they were sticking a mad elephant, Bheru barely escaped: the king became convinced that he [Bheru Singh] was against him and so he had him murdered. Unable to penetrate his fort to kill him, he bribed Bheru's brother-in-law to kill him. The two queens died [as *satis*].

This rather more *itihasik* account, which gives an especially felicitous rendering of Maratha-Rajput relations, is bent on assigning culpability to the Maharana.

---

58. Based on his research in Maharashtra, Gunther-Dietz Sontheimer associates the fifty-two *virs* with Mhasasur, who "becomes Mhaskobā or Kāḷbhairav" and with Narasimha (an incarnation of Vishnu); *Pastoral Deities in Western India*, p. 200. No such names occurred in references to the fifty-two *virs* I heard. Their names were either left unspecified or consisted of only one name, that of the hero worshiped by the informant.

Like the previous account, it gives Bheruji's name as merely a name and makes
no explicit connection between this living Bheruji and the divinity.

How different is the case in an account rendered by the older brother of
and assistant to the *bhopa* at Bheruji's shrine in Karjali Haveli (the urban Udaipur
mansion once occupied by Bheru Singh's family, now subdivided into many
apartments). In that account, of which but a tiny excerpt is provided here, the
bhopa's brother represents Bheru Singh as an *avatar* (incarnation) of the god
Bheruji, and even credits Bheru Singh's strength to his identity as an incarnation: "When Bheru Singh was asleep, his *sala* [older brother-in-law] took his
turban and bound him to the bed. Then he started to cut him on the legs and
then his head. Bheru Singh was an *avatar* so he killed that *sala* [he was stand-
ing] while still bound to his bed. He did it from his *shakti*." Hence the historical
Bheru easily becomes the divine Bheruji, whose strength enables Bheru Singh
to visit revenge upon his wife's dastardly brother. In cultic worship, the historical and the divine Bherus are not sequential but consubstantial identities. In
this case the identification of human hero and divine lord occurs not at death
but at birth.[59]

Another interesting identification between human hero and divine Bheruji
is made in the case of Kallaji, held by many devotees to be an incarnation of
Shiv. In a widely circulated printed account, this incarnation is instructed from
a young age by his guru, the divine Bheru Nath.[60] Moreover, in a variant related
to me by a *bhopa*, Bheruji imparts to Kallaji divine wisdom, which accords him
the ability to see the future. When his powers are perfected, Kallaji emerges from
Bheruji's cave and goes off to have his final adventures. In this account, the student is metaphorically reborn from his guru when he emerges from the cave.
He is now a householder and goes directly to find a bride. Bheruji is not only a
spiritual father, who gives life to the initiated "twice-born" son Kallaji, however.
He is also associated here with Shiv: he teaches Shiv—a god now possessing
human form (Kallaji) with its various limitations—the divine wisdom that Shiv
ordinarily possesses. Represented elsewhere in mythology as an emanation of
Shiv's anger, Bheruji here serves as an emanation of Shiv's wisdom, which he
imparts to Kallaji.

Though certainly a more meandering association than that made in the
Bheru-Singh-cum-Bheruji account, this story's association provides further
evidence of the ways in which the hero may be subsumed within or infused with
aspects of Bheruji's identity. Thus the cultic context, like village iconography,
reinforces the association between the two, even as the Rajput domestic traditions qualify the association, not the least by making it diachronic. In history
the hero is human, a condition that ends with death. Beyond "the boundaries of

59. This raises the specter of developmental models, typically propounded and debated in the context of
epic development. Blackburn's well-known model, which treats elaborate birth stories as accretions to traditions that commemorate heroic death, is presented in "Patterns of Development for Indian Oral Epics." Alf
Hiltebeitel critiques the model in *Rethinking India's Oral and Classical Epics*, 21–37.

60. On Bheruji and Naths, as well as other ascetic groups, see Visuvalingam, "Bhairava's Royal
Brahmanicide," 157–229.

FIGURE 4.2. Bheru Singh and *satis* at Ahar shrine

the text" lies his "Bherujiness."[61] Invoked most commonly by epithet, Bheruji serves as another "frame," one that does not necessarily open up that which is contained within the text, but one that links the text *in toto* to a wide, religious world of divinities. In other words, the frame points beyond the text's scope while connecting what lies within and beyond as nexus.

Quite apart from the matter of linkage between Bheruji and hero, it is striking how much hero and Bheruji characterizations have in common. Positioned as guardians and associated with a goddess, they also share her tendency to split into contrasting personae and images. Whereas in Rajput myth and iconography the most evident splitting of a goddess is to be seen in her appearances as a domestic bride and a battlefield scavenger, in pan-Indian mythology and iconography the most obvious goddess bifurcation is to be found in the dual Devi (Goddess) incarnations: Gauri, the "Light One" and Kali, the "Dark One." In Rajasthan, as elsewhere in India, Bheruji also divides along color lines. He appears as Goraji, the "Light One" and Kalaji, the "Dark One."[62] Frequently im-

61. This notion is loosely adapted from *The Boundaries of the Text*, edited by Flueckiger and Sears. See also Flueckiger, *Gender and Genre in the Folklore of Middle India*.

62. Kalaji is also associated with Kalabhairava, the "Lord of Time-Death" (*kala*); see Visuvalingam, "Bhairava's Royal Brahmanicide," 160.

FIGURE 4.3. Kalaji-Goraji shrine, Udaipur

ages of the goddess are flanked by both these deities, which often appear solo in mythology and have their own temples.[63]

As in the case of goddesses, or women for that matter, the splitting into these deities does not mean that they are completely and finally dissociated. Rather, one implies the other and they may work together, complementing one another, or else quite often, merging, so that each one, whatever his name, simply is Bheruji and so implicitly subsumes the other. In this respect, Bheruji resembles goddesses. The point is neatly made in the words of a Bheruji *bhopa*, an engaging Khati (carpenter-caste) man with whom I once conversed for most of an afternoon. In a tiny Bheruji temple hidden away in a grove at the end of a field near the royal cremation ground, he told me about his life and his decision to become a *bhopa*. He told me that while he was walking in that secluded spot, he had a vision of a white goddess ("white as you," he emphasized) who revealed herself to be Kali, and who was accompanied by Bholinath (Shiv), over whose head a cobra was poised.[64] Having been possessed by this white Kali, he determined to become a *bhopa*. He is now routinely possessed by Bheruji.

---

63. For a comparative perspective, see Mayer, *Caste and Kinship in Central India*, 188–192. Mayer reports that Shiv's "true" son is Gora, whereas Shiv's second son, Kala, came from Parvati's skin dust; p. 188.

64. The "light side" of Kali reveals the coincidence of opposites among divinities. This is thoroughly discussed in Wendy Doniger O'Flaherty's *Śiva: The Erotic Ascetic*. Perhaps the most famous incident in which a goddess is expressly identified as having both dark and light manifestations is the *Vamana Purana* incident, in which Parvati, embarrassed by her dark skin, sheds her sheath and reveals her light complexion. For commentary on this episode, see Kinsley, "Kālī: Blood and Death out of Place," 79.

Like the *bhopa*, this Bheruji, with no epithet mentioned, serves the goddess who is both dark and light: the bellicose virgin Kali, but also the pacific consort of Shiv. He is simply known as the Bheruji of that place, like so many other Bherujis bearing toponyms.[65] In temples such as the well-attended Bheruji temple located just down the street from the Sarv Ritu Vilas Sagasji Bavji Temple, Sagasji devotees frequently worship Bheruji en route to Sagasji Bavji. In this imposing and vibrant shrine, Bheruji is depicted in adjacent dark and light images but is referred to in the singular, as Kalaji-Goraji. This dual Bheruji is also depicted alongside heroes in the "Hall of Heroes" in Mandore, to which maharajas of Jodhpur must go to pay tribute when they wed. In the hall are shrines dedicated to various well-known heroes such as Pabuji and Gogaji, and also Kalaji and Goraji, each of which escorts the goddess Brahmani Mata, who is represented by two identical icons.[66]

When appearing individually as Kalaji or Goraji, however, Bheruji behaves in ways that one would expect. Goraji is said to be temperate and easygoing, but not as powerful as Kalaji, who is comparatively passionate and forceful. When Goraji possesses a *bhopa*, his mood (*bhav*) is one of peace (*shanti*). The *bhopa* sits quietly and serenely. When Kalaji possesses a *bhopa*, however, his mood is fierce (*ugra*). The *bhopa* then typically hyperventilates, whirls, and shouts.[67]

As we know, these moods are also experienced by *bhopas* possessed by heroes. Unlike Bherujis and goddesses, heroes are not frequently designated light or dark, but heroes who possess *bhopas* in cultic contexts are said by their *bhopas* and devotees to express themselves primarily, if not wholly, in *ugra* or *shanti bhavs*. These moods do not appear in the discourse of descendants venerating ancestral heroes at home, unless the ancestral hero is also the central figure in a hero cult. Even in that case, however, family members tend to dissociate themselves from the common folk and worship in their own ways the hero who has attracted the cult. They tend to do so not at a cult shrine but at their home or cremation ground. For example, when Bheru Singh's descendants pay respect to their deity, they go not to the *bhopa*'s shrine in Karjali Haveli but to the familial memorial at the Ahar cremation ground. Although a second *bhopa* and his followers gather at this shrine, they constitute a small group that comes and goes quickly at times that family members can easily avoid. Accompanying the family, which vehemently distances itself from the cult, is a Brahmin *pujari* who makes the offerings and, needless to say, debunks possession.

The distinction that does appear frequently in the discourse of descendants is that between two qualities: *sattva* and *rajas*. Each hero is said to possess both qualities. The *sattvik* makes the hero good, clear-headed, wise, and just, whereas

65. In Rajasthan, it is common to refer to Bherujis in this way. This is true of local Bherujis, such as Chittoriya Bheruji, and of well-known, potent imports, such as Kashi ka Bheruji.

66. These deities accompany an imposing image of Ganesh, another gate-keeping guardian deity. Despite Ganesh's central position in the shrine containing his image, the shrine's sign reads "Śri Kālāgaurā Bherujū Mandir" (Kalagora's Temple).

67. I still find these behaviors unnerving, especially when the *bhopa* flagellates himself with chains, but devotees are quite used to this behavior and generally pay little attention. Rather, they chat among themselves until it is their turn to approach the *bhopa* and ask for boons or predictions.

the *rajasik* makes him kinetic, fierce, and powerful. Although all Rajputs are said to share these traits, some are believed to manifest one quality more than another. Thus Rajput heroes, like some classical heroes such as the *Ramayan*'s Ram and his brother Lakshman (as well as their brothers Bharat and Shatrughna), are frequently said to exhibit either a more contemplative and quiescent or a more active and hot-headed personality.[68] Predictably, this delineation tends to fuse as much as sever traits. And so, *sat* (essence, pureness), which in the case of the *sati* is also identified with *sattva* or the goodness that enables her to become a sacrificial agent, is often treated as a sort of encompassing category, so that goodness may be rendered goodness at one's duty. In the case of Rajput heroes, this means killing in a most kinetic or *rajasik* fashion, which helps explains the fluid association between *sat* and *shakti*.[69] Thus although the qualities can be, and often are, distinguished in discourse, they also can be, and often are, constructed as noncontradictory. Accordingly, a warrior's *sat* may be exhibited by a hot-headed (*rajasik*) warrior vengefully beheading a victim in battle.

Possession of a relatively cool or hot personality is sometimes demonstrated in ancestral narratives, such as the story of Balluji. Far more typically, however, it is shown in the type of offerings certain heroes desire. Some, like Man Singh of Amet, require very *sattvik* fare; as we know, meat and wine are "dirty" to him. Heroes like him are often fed sweet dishes such as *lapsi* (a pudding). Other heroes prefer offerings that stir the passions and produce heat. Although none that I know of is routinely offered meat, meat does not typically offend, I was repeatedly told; after all, Rajputs are a carnivorous lot. And, of course, meat eating is virtually *de rigueur* on Navratri-Dashara. Because women are most frequently responsible for providing and offering food to the household deities, however, it makes some sense that the offerings would be vegetarian. The majority of women, unlike men, say they prefer vegetarian fare. In many households, only men will cook meat, and because women typically cook, meat is generally eaten only on special occasions, including and especially Navratri-Dashara, when goats are slaughtered.

At that time, *balidan*s for goddesses are often shared by Bherujis. Frequently the sacrifices for goddesses are made directly in front of Bheruji icons. Some Bherujis even receive independent *balidan*s. A few Bherujis are famous for their blood lust, the prime example of such a Bheruji being Raktiya Bheruji, who, as his name would indicate, is fond of blood (*rakta*).

Thus both some Rajput heroes and Bherujis of the Kalaji variety are held to be engaged in the sacrificial ritual and to partake of the sacrificial offerings. In fact the hero, whose death not only enacts battle sacrifice but reenacts festal sacrifice, continues the predeath role of Rajput sacrificer that is in some cases directly connected with Bheruji as well as his divine mistress. The following

---

68. Goldman, "Rāmaḥ Sahalakṣmaṇaḥ." In the epic *Devnarayan*, Nevo is hot tempered while Savai Bhoj is restrained; Miller, "The Twenty-Four Brothers and Lord Devnārāyaṇ," 159. In a course at Harvard on Greek heroes in fall 1996, Gregory Nagy lectured extensively on heroic alter egos, including Achilles and his "other half," Patroklos.

69. On Rajputs and *sat* as "goodness" as well as "goodness at" conforming to Rajput code, see Harlan, *Religion and Rajput Women*, 124–129.

account, in which Tod expresses grave disapproval of sacrifices for the blood-loving Bheruji, gives an extreme example. It narrates the nefarious deeds of one Surthan Singh, a Bheruji devotee from the kingdom of Bundi.

> Rao Surthan succeeded in S. 1591 [A.D. 1525] and married the daughter of the celebrated Shakta, founder of the Shaktavats of Mewar. He became an ardent votary of the bloodstained divinity of war, Kal-Bhairava, and like almost all those ferocious Rajputs who resign themselves to his horrid rites, grew cruel and at length deranged. Human victims are the chief offerings to this brutalized personification of war, though Surthan was satisfied with the eyes of his subjects, which he placed upon the altar of "the mother of war." It was then time to question the divine right by which he ruled. The assembled nobles deposed and banished him from Bundi, assigning a small village on the Chambal for his residence.[70]

It may be surmised from Tod's account that both Tod and ultimately Rao Surthan Singh's followers found human blood sacrifice unacceptable. Like Kali, however, this Kalaji Bheruji is evidently quite pleased with the offerings. Directly tying Bheruji with goddess here is that fact that Kalaji's flesh offerings are "placed upon the altar of 'the mother of war.'" Thus Bheruji, along with his goddess, consumes humans in ritual just as a warrior and his *kuldevi* consume humans in war.[71] For goddesses, Bherujis, and warriors, devouring bloody sacrificial offerings is seen as signifying and effecting strength. Rajputs, like "panthers and tigers," let us recall, "don't eat grass." This blood lust is dramatized with particular clarity in the case of a village Rajput *bhopa* who, I heard from one Rajput man, becomes possessed by his *kuldevi* and "drinks fresh blood from the *balidan* on Dashara."[72]

The connection between meat eating and human sacrifice is made even clearer in the following legend about the Maharana Hamir. It was told to me by Gopi Nath Sharma, who said that after leaving Chittor, Hamir entered a cave, and his *kuldevi* appeared to him and gave him a sword. Sharma then explained that Ban Mata (the *kuldevi*) had wanted to test Hamir, so she "made a boiling cauldron of blood and heads and told him to taste it." He did, "so she handed over the sword to Hamir."[73] Finally, Sharma tied the Rajput king's cannibalism to receipt of a sword for use on Navratri. A reward for tasting human flesh, Hamir's sword continues to be "worshiped as a part of the Navratri ceremonies at the palace."[74] Drinking blood and eating flesh, Hamir mimics the goddess whose blood-lusting invitation he accepts and whose service he will perform in war as well as during

70. *Annals and Antiquities*, vol. 2, p. 280.

71. On human sacrifice for Bheruji and his goddess, see Visuvalingam, "Bhairava's Royal Brahmanicide," 157. The semantic fields of consumption and killing, of course, vary in the context of goddess consumption and warrior consumption. The goddess becomes a kite or vulture to feast on entrails, whereas the warrior eats goats representative of the demons Durga kills in her own battles; he also kills his enemy, thus "consuming" him in the sense of a consumer who does not eat but utilizes something or someone.

72. He claimed to have seen this with his own eyes when he visited the Degana Kalika temple.

73. The story is reminiscent of the *doha* about milk and blood recited in the previous chapter. There the hero is reminded that he drank his mother's milk, so he should "drink the enemy's blood."

74. Second interview with Gopi Nath Sharma, at his home in Udaipur, October 17, 1990.

Navratri-Dashara, when his goddess-given sword will be worshiped.[75] At the same time, his maleness facilitates identification with Bheruji, who also shares his goddess's *shakti*-enhancing victuals.

A narrative offered to me by one Sisodiya woman from yet another of Mewar's *solah thikanas* explicitly identifies the origins of this intimate relationship between the Maharana and this bloodthirsty *kuldevi*: "Ban Mata was a daughter of Cakra Caran in the village of Khod. The Moghuls had taken over Chittor. Hamir knew that she was worshiped by the people. He asked her for his kingdom back and she granted it to him. So everyone—the Sisodiyas—began to worship her as a *kuldevi*."

Thus, as is so frequently the case with Rajput *kuldevi*s, war is the occasion for the adoption of a *kuldevi*, whose power is proven in the capturing of territory and whose appetite for flesh and blood is commemorated as well as demonstrated ritually on Navratri-Dashara, when flesh and blood are offered to the goddesses, then typically consumed by carnivorous Rajputs after a goat has been cut.[76]

Like meat, wine is said to strengthen and embolden. It lowers inhibitions, inflames passions, and makes warriors potent. Elsewhere it is typically classed as *tamasik*, or producing lethargy, inertia, and confusion of the senses. However, in the case of the warrior, who, it is often said, likes his wine or pegs of whiskey before battle, it allows him to fight fearlessly and effectively. Hence the connection with *rajas*.[77] Some cultic heroes, like some goddesses and Bherujis, take alcohol offerings. As we know, taking liquor as an offering and consuming it as *prasad*, alcoholic Rajputs are said to be sufficiently fortified to abandon alcoholism at one well-known cultic hero shrine.[78] The same is true for opium, which few household heroes take, but which many cultic heroes do. (A *bhopa*'s consumption of it typically precedes possession.)

75. In a similar story, the goddess Ashapura tells a Chauhan Rajput boy where he can find and kill an unusually large buffalo that wears a gold ring in his nose. The boy kills the buffalo and obtains the ring, which he, as the founder of a kingdom, and his royal successors are to wear. As instructed by the goddess, he also cuts open the buffalo's stomach and finds a sword, which is also supposed to stay with the ruling head of state through the generations. Here the Rajput boy imitates the goddess Durga's slaying of the buffalo demon, Mahishasur, whose likeness (goat, buffalo, or in one case, as we have seen, an elephant) is slain by a Rajput on Navratri. Thus once again the king is both sacrificer and sacrificed, hungry agent and consumer (of *balidan*), as well as potential (future) victim of a hungry goddess. See Harlan, *Religion and Rajput Women*, 61–63. On buffalo sacrifice as reenactment of human sacrifice, see Biardeau and Malamoud, *Le sacrifice dans l'Inde ancienne*, 148; Herrenschmidt, "Le sacrifice du buffle en Andhra cotier"; and Hiltebeitel, *The Cult of Draupadī*, vol. 1, p. 63. On the complicity of devotee and deity in devouring others in the ancient and south Indian contexts, see Shulman, *The Hungry God*, especially pp. 40–45.

76. As indicated previously, in many stories, the *kuldevi* is captured; in this one, she is adopted from an allied caste. A similar case is to be found in Marwar, where the Caran *kuldevi* has been adopted by some Rathors. For interesting reflection on Caran goddesses, see Weinberger-Thomas, *Ashes of Immortality*, especially pp. 66–67, 157–158.

77. For instruction on the transformative character of *tamasik* substances, I am grateful to McKim Marriot, Conference on South Asia, Madison, Wisconsin, October 1995.

78. The Bheruji *bhopa* who received a vision of the white Kali said that after his vision and when possessed by her he drank twelve bottles of alcohol, which had no effect on him (as Kali herself consumed them, he insisted). Another local Mataji, residing at Biyawar, I was told by a supplicant, "will consume two and a half pegs of whiskey—not more—from every devotee" when she possesses the body of her *bhopa*. Savai Bhoj Bheruji can imbibe "one bottle of whiskey after another," as one informant put it, though this is curious in that Savai Bhoj is typed in *Devnarayan* as the cool complement of the hot-headed Nevo. Typically the cooler heroes/Bherus abstain. In a cultic setting, *bhopa*s of heroes, Bherus, and possessing goddesses also frequently take opium.

In short, although heroes are not categorized as light and dark, they are—like Bheruji and goddesses—in some measure and contexts divisible. To the extent that the hero is understood to be or be like a Bheruji, the predominance of one quality (such as *rajas*) may make it easier to conceptualize him as, or in relation to, a certain Bheruji (in the case of *rajas*, Kalaji). Like heroes, Bherujis have their preferences. As one would expect, Kalaji, along with Bherujis identified with or homologized to him, loves alcohol, whereas Goraji is ever the vegetarian teetotaler.

Moreover, in the case of heroes, offerings, whether domestic or cultic, take the *itihasik* story "further along," demonstrating who he has become while also implicitly commenting on the type of man he was. Deciphering the commentary is difficult, however. Offerings reflect current constructions of heroism, and those constructions at times reflect current preferences of supplicants. Furthermore, although most offerings are represented as comporting with the hero's preferences, if a hero is very *rajasik* he may be offered *sattvik* fare, for *sattvik* fare such as milk sweets are said to cool the body and reduce wrath. In this respect some heroes resemble Shitala, goddess of pustular diseases and heat. She is often given cold food so that her fervor and fever can subside. Nonetheless, asked why heroes take the offerings they do, the same response recurs without further explanation: the heroes "like them." To complicate matters further, whether or not they are said to like non-*sattvik* offerings in their shrines, they are imaged and imagined as enjoying them in Virgati, where all heroes consume warrior fare, no matter what sort of Bheruji they may be identified with.

Up to this point, no mention has been made of one of the better known characteristics of Bheruji: his insouciant lust. What, if anything, does Bheruji's lust have to do with *rajasik-sattvik* Rajput heroes? To begin with, the randy Bheruji in Rajasthan is a Bheruji who either is Kalaji or a locative Bheruji quite like him in his desire for pleasurable and potency-stimulating offerings. Although all Bherujis, like all heroes, are understood as bringing the blessing of fertility, only some Bherujis are said to seduce female devotees.[79] Among Rajputs, whether aristocrats or village Rajputs, and among many other castes, unmarried women are not allowed to visit many Bheruji shrines lest they fall prey to desire. The images of some Bherujis are actually restrained by chains, which are said to keep them from ravishing maidens.

This is not true in the case of Goraji Bheruji, who is considered harmless in this respect and is sometimes styled an ascetic. Moreover, the Bheruji who appeared to the hero Kallaji is referred to as "Nath," a name that could simply mean "lord," as it does when affixed to Krishna at his Mewar shrine Nathdwara, but that certainly also refers to his association with the Nath sect of ascetics, as the epithet does elsewhere in India.[80] Ascetic Naths are a persistent feature of

79. On Kalaji as seducer, see Carstairs, "Patterns of Religious Observances in Three Villages of Rajasthan," 73. On the conjunction of the seductive and "juicy" Kalaji and Goraji in one figure, see Gold, *Fruitful Journeys*, 258.

80. According to Kathleen M. Erndl, Bhairo is depicted in Vaishno Devi myths as a *sadhu* belonging to the Nath order; Erndl, *Victory to the Mother*, 160. See also Visuvalingam, "Bhairava's Royal Brahmanicide," 157–159.

Rajasthani lore, including epics.[81] Although ascetic deities, like Shiv, can be erotic—indeed they gain sexual potency from abstention—this does not detract from the fact that the distinction between ascetic and seductive, like the distinction between Goraji and Kalaji or between *sattvik* and *rajasik* heroes, is frequently made and meaningful to those who make it. Many unmarried girls who would not dream of visiting a Kalaji shrine visit Goraji temples along with their mothers. There they are considered perfectly safe, even as their mothers ask from Goraji the blessing of a child. Goraji is, quite simply, discriminating. Thus Goraji remains distinguishable from Kalaji in terms of epithet and character, but his work impregnating women is considered effective by devotees (though perhaps not by others). The overwhelming majority of Rajput women (villager or aristocratic) visit Bherujis (Kalaji and/or Goraji) at the time of marriage, and many perform the first tonsure of their sons at Bheruji temples, just as others do at hero shrines or still others at *kuldevi* shrines. For example, at the time of marriage, Sisodiya women from the Mewar royal family customarily pay respects to Chittoriya Bheruji (Bheruji of Chittor), and Rathor women from the Marwar royal family attend the Bheruji shrine in the Meghangir Fort in Jodhpur.

Like the composite (Kalaji-Goraji) Bheru character, the hero is both ascetic (like Bheru Nath in the cultic context and like the saffron-donning heroes in both domestic and cultic contexts) and sensuous, as his pursuits in Virgati demonstrate. In domestic narratives, Rajput heroes are by no means lustful types, but many are householders, a status merely assumed in the story or made explicit by details such as the climactic immolation of their wives, who are presumed to love their husbands. Nevertheless, their householdership is suspended or terminated as they take off for war and sacrifice. The saffron turban may or may not be mentioned in such stories, but it is omnipresent in general conversation and is a persistent feature of poetic imagery and iconography. Thus, for example, when "fighting a war" against the government in the case of the Roop Kanwar controversy and also against Muslims in the context of the Ram Janam Bhumi riots, many Rajputs and other Rajasthani men donned saffron, signifying their commitment to renounce their lives or fight to the death rather than give ground on the issues. Intensifying the connection between warrior and ascetic is the fact that in Rajasthan, as in various other places in India, ascetics have taken up arms to fight in battle.[82] Add to this association the aforementioned Rajput admiration for Jain ascetic heroes (the great Mahavir and other *tirthankars*) who proved their perfected renunciatory discipline in self-afflicted death by starvation. In brief, the heroes of narratives are largely householders

81. *Gopichand* and *Pabuji* are prime examples. Sontheimer describes a Bhairav as a "doorkeeper or guardian of Pārvatī . . . in the forest," and notes that "his life outside villages and permanent settlements made him—like Mhasobā—a celibate (*brahmacārī*) despite his propinquity to the *śakti*"; *Pastoral Deities in Western India*, 50.

82. On armed asceticism among ascetics and ascetic warriors, see Lorenzen, "Warrior Ascetics in Indian History," and Pinch, "Subaltern Sadhus?" A version of Pinch's paper, which has good bibliographic references, is published on the web. See also Kolff, *Naukar, Rajput and Sepoy*, especially pp. 74–85; Farquhar, "The Fighting Ascetics of India"; and Orr, "Armed Religious Ascetics in Northern India." For reflections on militancy and asceticism in the Jain context, see Babb, *Absent Lord*.

who terminate their status through ascetic sacrifice. In both endeavors, domestic and martial, they are potently virile, producing progeny on the home front and victims, including themselves, in sacrificial battle.

Women's songs, as we shall see, present a rather different portrait of the sacrificial householder. In these songs, the hero is not simply a family man who dons saffron to fight. He is an object of desire. Like Bheruji, he is seen as enticing and alluring; his role in fertility is connected, as in the case of Kalaji Bheruji, to felicitous carnality. Moreover, the ritual offerings that are presumed to link present hero-guardian with historical ancestor provide continuity between human and divinity in which sensual, if not sensuous, pleasures are indulged. The warrior remains fond of his fare, be it simply sweet or else bloody and/or intoxicating. Continuing to consume household food, he also continues to provide progeny.

It must be clear by now that familiarity with the figure of Bheruji, who splits into light and dark but also fuses into a singular being, is, like knowledge of goddesses, critical for understanding the milieu in which Rajput domestic veneration, in all its complexity, is actually practiced. If every picture tells a story, Rajput hero stories also paint pictures that imply, if they do not overtly demonstrate and manipulate, contextualizing frames such as those supplied by Bheruji epithets and other textual and ritual references.

From this analysis several things should also be clear. First, in India split imagery is not solely reserved for females, whether women or goddesses. It is also employed in the case of males, whether men or gods. Bherujis are divisible in terms of iconography, light and dark, and in terms of the mood (calm, fierce) they express in possession. Heroes do not tend to be explicitly depicted as dark or light, but they are associated with Bherujis, particularly Kala Bheruji, whose violent persona accords well with the warrior who fights and dies by the sword. Moreover, in the cultic context, Rajput heroes who possess bhopas manifest themselves with the same moods that Bherujis and goddesses manifest and with which they possess.

Second, split imagery does not tell the whole story, which is inevitably more complex. However contradictory, variant images can cohere in the same entity paradoxically. Thus Gangama, an unmarried virgin goddess, can wear a *tali*, a necklace that ordinarily signifies marriage, while Kali, a haggard virgin with pointy shriveled breasts, can also be Mother.[83] And, as shown by Ann Gold, women, on whom are imposed different aspects (mare and cow, "dangerous wife" and "sacred sister," and so forth) are not thereby literally bound to live a bifurcated or polarized existence.[84] It is not enough to find the apposite contrast deployed routinely in indigenous discourse. It is necessary to understand the force of the contrast as contributing to an overall understanding that is far more nuanced and intricate than the ever-so-accessible polarity might indicate.

83. I thank Joyce Flueckiger for her comments on Gangama, May 1998.

84. Gold, "The 'Jungli Rani' and Other Troubled Wives in Rajasthani Oral Traditions." Doniger's mare/cow distinction was treated in chapter 3; see her book, *The Origins of Evil*, 346–349. The terms "dangerous wife" and "sacred sister" come from Bennett, *Dangerous Wives and Sacred Sisters*.

In terms of the hero, splitting reveals his dominant qualities, but these qualities cohere in a duplex persona that distinguishes Rajputs from members of other castes; Brahmins are considered predominantly *sattvik* and Baniyas mostly *tamasik*, but Rajputs are conjointly *rajasik* and *sattvik* to the extent that these qualities seem to "transubstantiate," so that "goodness" becomes kinetic, active, and even violent. Thus these males—hero and Bheruji—both split and fuse in ways that reveal the dynamic complexity of the whole being. In the case of the hero, the split persona precedes and follows that perfect moment, sacrifice, where goodness and power, agency and victimization, become united in a perfection that distinguishes the hero from other mere men. This sort of "perfect death" is beyond "good death" and "bad death" and so conventional morality, like the self-termination of the *sati* or the suicide of an ascetic. The *sat*-saturated killer killed is, once again, a Möbius strip turning back on itself, so that "goat" and henchman as well as victim and agent cohere as well as transpose, seamlessly and synchronically, one into the other. In this sense, the hero's story never ends and the hero known through story goes on to be the hero of song and ritually "well-watered graves."

At such a point the story's hero, who was "one of us," is now no longer "one of us," as the "two women" motif so vividly points out; but in the case of Rajput devotees, he will also remain an ancestor, invited home in *ratijaga* ritual. This ancestral linkage is undoubtedly what prompts Parry to conclude, on the basis of his experience with his informants, that the hero is a ghost, but ghosts lack the hero's glory and perfection. Thus the association, while understandable, obscures as much as informs heroic identity. This said, let us examine the subtle context that "ghost" veneration provides.

Ancestors, Ghosts: More Socialized/Unsocialized Beings

The venerated hero belongs to his own class. He is a *jhunjharji*, *bhomiya*, or *sagasji*, however much the actions that earn him the epithet may at times resemble or approximate those appropriate to other categories and to whatever extent and in whatever ways he is homologized to them. Thus predilections associating him with Bheruji do not thereby terminate his status as a hero. He is also, however, a family member who has died and thus literally and logically become an ancestor, the most commonly used words for which are *pitar* (Sanskrit *pitr*) and *purbaj*. Perfected and liberated, he eludes the limitations of run-of-the-mill ancestors, but he remains part of the family and is honored implicitly, and in some families even explicitly, on days on which ancestors are worshiped. On Amavasya (the full moon night) and on Shraddh Paksh (the dark fortnight of Asoj, which is given over to honoring and feeding ancestors) heroic ancestors are not denied their due simply because they are heroes. As I was told repeatedly, to exclude them from such hospitality rituals would cause offense.

The sense that the hero is "from among us" (but not just "one of us") is, as one might imagine, a reason why an ancestral hero who communicates primarily through omens and dreams can so easily be assumed to be a mere ancestor or ghost, be it a *pret* (familial ghost) or *bhut* (someone else's unidentified ghost). Both of these are unperfected and often bothersome beings who may roam about because of envy of or excessive attachment to those who continue to live. Whereas the *bhut* is always a menacing "other," however, the *pret* may stir affection and may be welcomed, albeit temporarily, as a *purbaj*, if he sends helpful omens, comes in dreams, or even appears *sakshat*, directly before the eyes, of family members. He may even be gladly received if he briefly possesses them. Relatively few aristocratic Rajputs report ancestral possessions (as we have seen, many Rajputs tend to view possession as déclassé), but they do report *sakshat* and dream visitations. Among village Rajputs, possessions are more common, especially those by recently departed loved ones. Almost every family has known at least one ancestral revenant. In whatever family such a spirit reveals itself, eventually visitations tend to be deemed troublesome. If so, attempts are made to discern (generally through a *bhopa*) its wish to be permanently settled on some periphery, preferably under a shady tree or by a well, but in any case out of the way. An effigy is sometimes worn as a *putli* (pendant), indicating that the deceased is still close to one's heart, a gesture that is pleasing to the dead. Often, however, these pendants are kept in a box or stored in a temple as the painful memory and problematic nature of the deceased diminish.

Most ancestors, however, do not return. They are incorporated into the family retinue of ancestors, who are venerated together as *pitar* or *purbaj*, the two words often being conjoined in discourse as if hyphenated (*pitar-purbaj*).[85] A family's heroes, however, are not understood as ever being incorporated into and contained within this retinue. It is true that most families worship only one or two heroes whereas many ancestors would have died violently in war—a fact that would tend to lead one to conclude that eventually heroes do in fact become incorporated into the general lot of ancestors. Although the numbers do not add up, heroes who die violently are understood to remain forever distinguished deities, be they *jhunjharjis*, *bhomiyas*, or *sagasjis*. In this respect they differ from a family's *satis*, who are ultimately conceptualized and referred to in the singular (as Satimata).[86]

Let it be noted that some *purbaj* resist incorporation and are never completely settled. Even if located in a cool and pleasant place of their choosing, they may continue to manifest themselves and/or their desires. In such a case, the family may take their ancestor's ashes (euphemistically referred to as "flowers") to a sacred river such as the Ganges, to be submerged and dissipated so that ancestor (and family) may be relieved of restlessness and enabled to find peace.[87] Nevertheless, some ancestors remain permanently attached to their place and will not be persuaded to leave even with the temptation of the Ganges. Having died violent and "untimely" deaths, they will not be removed from the place where they lived. Roaming about, they continue to affect the lives of family

85. On the specifics of *pret* and corporate ancestor worship, see Knipe, "Sapiṇḍīkaraṇa," and also Parry, "Sacrificial Death and the Necrophagous Ascetic," 78–79.

86. This notion is explored more fully in the next chapter.

87. For extensive discussion of "sinking flowers," see Gold, *Fruitful Journeys*, 190–261.

members. Their title *purbaj*, needless to say, does not distinguish them from *purbaj* who have died peacefully and who are more frequently termed *pitars*. By now, however, such imprecisions should hardly bother us. The afterlife, which transcends human experience, is appropriately imprecise, resistant to neat categorization, contradictory, ironic, and paradoxical.

Far more than quiescent ancestors, *purbaj* dying violent deaths are likely to be venerated in a manner that resembles the worship of heroes, who also died violent, albeit sacrificial, deaths. Restive *purbaj* may receive memorial stelai that are virtually indistinguishable from hero stones. Quite common are *purbaj* stelai that depict a *purbaj* sitting astride a horse or standing in front of his wife or wives (in the manner of a *sati*). Despite their untimely demises and their need for continued veneration, some of these *purbaj* may be deemed by family members not to be nuisances or menaces but to be guardians who can be persuaded to serve descendants in a manner consistent with hero guardianship. A good example of such a *purbaj* is to be found in the figure of Devgarh *thikana*'s Chatriya Bavji, a Rajput referred to by all immediate family members as *purbaj* (rather than by heroic epithet), though the circumstances of his death diverge little from those of the deaths of some heroes, especially *sagasjis*.[88] The version of his demise that I present below was narrated by a Rajput woman from one *solah thikana* after she returned home from a visit to Devgarh, another *solah thikana*.[89] She told me that because of her recent journey to the site of his memorial and her closeness to his family, his story was fresh in her mind.[90]

> The son [an ancestor] made his own marriage. He chose his own wife. [Here I asked whether the wife was a Rajput and was told that she was]. The family was very unhappy about this. She used to stay outside the main part of the household. Someone—no one knows who the enemy was but someone—who was living there, put poison in the *prasad*. [*Prasad* is often distributed among friends and relatives after the subtle essence is consumed by a deity. She later told me that the *prasad* comes every night from a Krishna temple nearby.]
>
> His [the *purbaj*'s] wife was very pregnant at that time. That night when the husband came to sleep there [where his wife stayed], they both took the *prasad*. Then in the morning some servant went to wait on them and called at the door but nobody answered. After calling several times he tried the door but they had locked it. The servant called people at the palace and they had the door opened and saw that all three—the husband, wife, and unborn child—had died. Their feet and fingers were all blue from the poison. So they cut the baby

---

88. This ancestor's name derives from *chatri*.

89. I also have far briefer variants, which concur with this more specific account, from interviews at Devgarh. One adds that not only family members but also villagers worship Chatriya Bavji, and that his wife is also worshiped. It also explains that he is routinely worshiped on the fourteenth day of the dark half of the month (Anderi Chaudas) and that the deaths occurred "about a hundred years ago."

90. The same informant narrated the lengthy version of the Man Singh narrative given above.

from the mother and burned the husband and wife. They buried the child according to custom.[91]

Since then that *maharaj kumar* [heir apparent, oldest son] comes [as a spirit] and people have a lot of faith in him. Whatever he says, that will come true.

In this case a revenant has become a benefit: he reliably forecasts the future, which is useful. Moreover, he continues to be worshiped by family members including, I was told, then Prime Minister V. P. Singh, who married the Devgarh Rao Sahib's (*thakur's*) sister.

Aside from the evident benefit accruing from this victim's death, one fact deserves special attention. Chatriya Bavji dies from poisoned *prasad*, which is significant in that it indicates death in the context of devotion to a deity, in this case, Krishna. Death while worshiping or in some way that is connected to worship is, as in the case of the sacrificed hero, a good thing. Remember that in the case of the Pilva *jhunjharji*, who is beheaded in a manner suggesting *balidan*, death is related to attending a *Pabuji* performance. In the variant I provided, his wife joins the plot against him because she suspects that instead of or in addition to going to *Pabuji* performances regularly he is sleeping with a strumpet. Thus the Pilva *jhunjharji* is, as it were, doubly blessed, by heroic death as *balidan* and by death related to worship of the deity Pabuji. This is the case in another *jhunjharji* narrative in which the hero dies while worshiping:

> Babo Sahib Fateh Singh died fighting the Bundi people who were fighting Jaipur. They killed him from behind when he was worshiping Ram Lalaji. He got on a horse and went six miles cutting people before one woman said, "look, he's fighting without a head" and he fell down. There's a fair during [the month of] Magh. Lots of people come but only Rajputs can go right to the *chatri*. [The story continues, with more details about ritual and blessings.]

Then there is the story of Dhanna and Bhinya, who—their future patron Mukandar points out to his men—might well have killed him while he was worshiping in close proximity to the slaughtered goat they were bent on retrieving from his men. This close call both indicates Mukandar's goodness as devotee (despite his men's goat theft) and foreshadows his sacrificial death in battle.

Like death in battle, then, dying in worship is recognized as particularly desirable and reveals not regrettably unfortunate but exquisitely fortunate timing. This manner of dying appears as one of the ways in which deities come into being, as is indicated by its inclusion, along with death in battle and various other demises, in the folk deity chart found in Udaipur's folklore museum, the Bharatiya Lok Kala Mandal.[92] Venerated by family members who give offer-

---

91. Children who die young are buried rather than burned, as their incarnation is considered incomplete. Some petitioners venerate the child.

92. The museum's terminology for dying at worship is *prārthnā karne mṛtyu ko prāpt*.

ings, the *purbaj* Chatriya Bavji, like various Rajput heroes, has generated a cult that draws various nondescendant devotees.

A further similarity between this *purbaj* and venerated heroes is revealed by the following variant, told to me by an aristocratic woman, a devotee closely related to the Devgarh family's celebrated *purbaj*. Her version resembles the "political intrigue" narratives we have encountered, but with a twist. In this case what irks is not succession but a certain marital alliance.

> The Devgarh family's son married a girl from a small *thikana*, but servants and others in the family had wanted him to marry a woman from a big *haveli* [i.e., from a prominent *thikana*]. People from that *haveli* that wanted its daughter married there sent some *prasad* with poison in it for the wife. The husband used to take his meal with the men. He came to the *zanana* only to sleep. When he came, she was waiting with the *prasad*. She was seven/eight months pregnant. The two ate and they both died. Now his spirit comes to a *bhopa* and what he says really comes true.

This account varies from the previous account in some evident ways. The first assigns blame for the association to someone, "no one knows who," who was living at the estate. The narrator's imprecision points to Devgarh's responsibility, but also, as in the case of the *thakur* who assassinated his servant for squeezing a coin, softens the charge, this time by leaving the exact identity of the culprit a mystery. The "somebody" could have been a family member or a servant. The second account, however, blames another *thikana*, whose hopes of a beneficial alliance had been dashed by the "love marriage." Thus interfamily politics were to blame, although the disappointment of "servants and other members of the family" is made clear. The deflection would seem to suggest that the *purbaj*, if annoyed, would be primarily or exclusively annoyed with those "other people" who were responsible, not with family members, who are devotees and who represent him as dear to them and helpful because "what he says really comes true."

Despite the similarities with Rajput heroes, one important dissimilarity remains: this *purbaj* is not thought to be a hero. Like this *purbaj*, a number of *sagasji*s die at home rather than in battle, but the heroes struggle with attackers. They do so either with or, like *jhunjharji*s and *bhomiya*s, without heads. Their struggle makes for martial sacrifice and, however doubtful it may appear to us, these heroes are understood as having some determination in the matter. At the very least, they are all represented as mighty struggling soldiers and death-dealing agents, if also victims.

This said, some heroes, such as Sarv Ritu Vilas Sagasji Bavji's brother, Sardar Singh, and his uncle, Arjun Singh (another Udaipur *sagasji* who was killed after getting on the wrong side of the Maharana), are poisoned, rather than cut. These poisoned *sagasji*s, however, are still represented as struggling agents. Arjun Singh, for example, does not die quietly. Enraged, he runs a great distance while poison (*halahal*) racks his body and burns him from inside out. He

FIGURE 4.4. Arjun Singh's shrine, Udaipur

stops only when he arrives at a well, where his image is now located near the base of a long staircase.

Chatriyaji, however, is painted as a tragic, tender victim. Although no explanations were forthcoming for why the *purbaj* bears that title rather than a heroic one, I suspect that because he died in his sleep, the requisite reaction and resistance are lacking. Deprived of agency, he is what he is, a *purbaj*.[93] He is not, however, a difficult *purbaj*, despite his youthful demise. His worship is actually indistinguishable from hero worship. If imperfect, he is understood to be helpful despite this "bad death"; his presence bears wondrous fruit. Whether because goodness accords with his human personality or whether it results from the lavish attention he receives at his shrine, one sees how the category of *purbaj* can, in some instances, overlap with that of hero. This overlap, however, does not necessarily require "demotion" of the ancestral hero to some roaming, dissatisfied spirit. Rather, it may involve "promotion" of an ancestor who is dear and well disposed despite violent death.

93. Asking this type of leading question is, in any case, fruitless. It is like asking why an orange isn't like an apple. Only obvious dissimilarities, if any, tend to emerge in response.

The positive valences of the term *purbaj*, combined with the hero's consumption of a share of ancestral offerings, help explain how it is that in the ritual context the term is sometimes substituted for "hero." Thus as yet another aristocratic woman told me in a brief discourse on heroism: "We do a *ratijaga* for *vir-shahid*, meaning *purbaj*, every year [on his *tithi*]. . . . We use the term *purbaj* for *vir* and only do *puja* for them. Both *vir* and *satimata* are worshiped on this day. A *jhunjhar* is a *shahid*, a struggler."

If this use of the term and the treatment of *purbaj* such as Chatriya Bavji can be taken loosely to signify a sort of elevation, it should be recognized that in some contexts, as we have seen, a demotion of the heroic can also be possible. Just as one man's *purbaj* (or *pret*) is another man's *bhut* (the lack of blood relation rendering a spirit ominous), the Rajput's hero may well be another man's *bhut* (or demon, for that matter). Our domestic stories, like the songs we will discuss in the next chapter, do not reflect the beliefs and fears of nonrelatives who live in a *vir*'s vicinity. Pilgrims to cultic shrines, whatever their castes, may see a Rajput hero as benign and well disposed (which is why they approach him), but villagers who are stuck with a Rajput guardian on their village's border may, we know, find the *vir* fearsome. Like Parry's informants, a nondescendant villager may well think the hero who dies violently to be not a blessed guardian but a potential, even persistent, terrorist. Veneration of the hero may feel as if it were coerced, the result of perceived extortion from Rajputs, who, if formidable in life may be may seem positively irascible after death, as Ann Gold's work suggests. In a village that comprises numerous castes, it would hardly be surprising to find the sort of conflations between troublesome ancestors and heroes that Gold found in the village in which she worked.

Gold's work, by the way, reveals another salient identification. For the villagers whom Gold knew, the term *jhunjharji* "no longer implied a noble warrior's death." For them *jhunjharji*s are the spirits of dead children, who, as Gold notes, "emerge" among washermen as well as Rajputs.[94] Gold is aware how radically different this identification is from the definition of *jhunjhar* found in Sitaram Lalas's multivolume dictionary. Although it makes no reference to headlessness, the dictionary's definition of *jhunjhar* as a "person killed in battle for the benefit of others and who is later worshiped," comports fully, as we have found, with the general understanding of Rajputs today. It also squares with usage hundreds of years ago, according to Norman Ziegler, who in his study of "middle-period" Rajasthan defines the *jhunjharji* as "an individual of great strength and power who fought until death in battle in the assistance of others and who was afterwards worshiped for his death."[95]

Despite the definition Gold took from villagers belonging to a variety of castes, not all the *jhunjharji*s with which Gold's informants were familiar were children. In fact, she explains that *jhunjharji* was first defined for her by infor-

94. Gold, *Fruitful Journeys*, 65. On the metamorphosis of a dead child into a Virabhadra, understood as an incarnation of the rage of Shiv after he was excluded from Daksha's sacrifice, see Knipe, "Night of the Growing Dead."

95. See *Rājasthānī Sabd Kos*, s.v. and Ziegler, *Action, Power, and Service in Rajasthani Culture*, 67–68. Both are cited in Gold, *Fruitful Journeys*, 64.

mants as "one who died in battle (*jujh; yuddh*), had not received release, and therefore caused trouble."[96] This definition, however, provides an obvious linkage with the current village usage of *jhunjharji* as a departed child. According to the informants' perspectives, the *jhunjharji* killed in battle "had not received release and therefore caused trouble." "Release" here is envisioned in an interesting way. The warrior fails not only to achieve final release (from reincarnation) but also to receive release from this incarnation, which is why he "causes trouble." Such a person is a problem indeed, and it is quite understandable how he can be conflated with or homologized to the spirits of children who feel cheated of the opportunity to live full lives and who feel jealous of the living experience of relatives and descendants. To placate these juvenile "*jhunjharjis,*" speculates Gold, they are called *pattar* (*pitar*), a more flattering epithet. This usage turns the Rajput usage on its head, for according to Rajputs, to style the *pitar-purbaj* as a *jhunjharji* (through funerary iconography, worship, and so on) flatters the *purbaj*. The conflation between warrior spirits and children is surely enhanced by the singing of *jhunjharji* songs such as the two Gold supplies. Filled with martial imagery, they tell about heroes of yore in the context of placating today's dead children.[97]

To summarize, as in the case of Bherujis, *pitar-purbaj* share much, including at times identity, with fallen Rajput heroes. For Rajputs, the hero whose story continues to bring glory "becomes" a Bheruji and "inherits" Kalaji-Goraji iconization, but is still historically distinctive and very much a forebear receiving hospitality due deceased family members who, unlike him, have not received release. He also merits more. He needs special fare, whether predominantly *sattvik* or *rajasik*, and the individual attention it requires, for as a hero he is distinguished from ordinary ancestors. His distinctiveness is prefigured in his exceptional achievement of heroic death, and is fully reflected in the adamant contention rehearsed over and over with regard to the heroic scenario that precedes death: the hero struggled alone.

Heroic singularity is represented in two ways. First, the hero is represented as being literally alone. As in the case of the song of the *Pabuji* epic's *bhomiya*, who is said to have "set off on a deserted path" and of whom is sung, "You went for the cows alone; alone you went to war," the Rajput hero is often represented as fighting in seclusion and single-handedly. Bereft of company (like Balluji as he retrieves Amar Singh's body), the hero is also frequently said to end up decapitated and struggling by himself. In women's songs and epic, the formula *eklo eklo junjhiyo* ("alone, alone he struggled") finds frequent expression. Moreover, in the *bhomiya* song in *Pabuji*, the hero, who has hosted a party in which all guests are inebriated, is the only one to take up the challenge to retrieve cows stolen from his village. While his compatriots continue to lounge on his carpet, the *bhomiya* sets off unescorted.

Second, the hero is singled out from his companions through a sort of "zoom lens" imaging, so that although there may be mayhem all around, only the hero

96. Gold, *Fruitful Journeys*, 64.
97. Gold, *Fruitful Journeys*, 76–77.

and his enemy (whether individual or horde) are present. Good examples are Maha Singh, who confronts directly and immediately Ranbaj Khan, leader of the Muslim forces, and Kallaji, who at the gates of Chittor struggles headlessly alone (after Jaimal dies), while Moghul soldiers pursue him and one by one meet their fate. In stories of familial intrigue occurring outside the battlefield, singularity as a struggler initially results from location within an ostensibly benign environment that actually requires a sacrificial goat. Thus through poetic design and also historical circumstance, the singular goat is separated from the herd. Fighting single-handedly, the hero, a man alone, dies in isolation.

This distinction from others, whether inimical forces or ancestors, thoroughly informs Rajput heroic identity and is a concomitant of perfection, which others lack. Singularity, resulting from what Romila Thapar calls "an act of self-assertion that the [hero] stone captures for eternity" also links him to two other independent figures who follow their own paths: the ascetic and the criminal.[98] Unlike Bheruji and *pitar-purbaj*, neither figure is commonly conflated with the Rajput hero in Rajput discourse. Nevertheless, as we have seen, the ascetic and the criminal do inform the identity of Rajputs as well as Rajput heroes.[99] Thus in closing I offer a brief treatment of these figures, both of whom are "loners" who, like warriors, transgress and transcend conventional social codes. Much could be said about these tangential constructs in connection with cultic hero worship. Here our interest in them is limited to the domestic context and focused on the ways in which they reflect and reinforce the trope, hero-maverick.

More Loners: Ascetic and Criminal Motifs

Let us begin with ascetics, a subject about which much has been said already. To address fully the connections between asceticism and martial life would require an inexcusably long digression from our analysis of domestic stories, where asceticism appears as a subtle but potent contextual motif (such as Bheruji as Nath) and not a dominant or determinant ingredient in stories that Rajputs tell their descendants. In terms of the agenda here, five points come to the fore.

First, the warrior's saffron turban, which links martial and ascetic disciplines, stands out as a potently charged icon in fundamentalist discourse. Like headless struggling, it has come to identify the Rajput who sacrificed himself in an unwinnable battle (*saka*) centuries ago with any Hindu who participates in contemporary communalist struggles. Given this political milieu, the saffron turban often renders the hero a "freedom fighter," although, as we know, in Rajput heroic narrative traditions heroes frequently die at the hands of Hindus in opposing armies or political factions.[100]

98. "Death and the Hero," 309.
99. Ascetic associations are treated in my ongoing work on traditions of cultic veneration.
100. See Harlan, "On Hero Worship." Pabuji is born in a plot of saffron, and his horse, an incarnation of his mother, has a kind of saffron for a name.

Second, Rajputs frequently represent heroes as "taking *samadhi*," a phrase commonly used to describe the achievement of enlightenment by an ascetic. For the ascetic, taking *samadhi* while leaving behind his bodily form is considered the ultimate yogic achievement, the culmination of years of ascetic discipline. Whereas the phrase is often used euphemistically to refer to the death of any loved one, in the context of hero worship it is typically deployed in conjunction with the term *moksh*, which then associates the hero's *samadhi* with the attainment of liberation, characteristically achieved by an ascetic.[101]

Third, both ascetic and martial disciplines are thought to produce extraordinary power. Because of this empowerment, ascetics, who are dedicated to pursuing liberation in isolation, become magnets for devotees seeking benefits and miracles.[102] Thus even before liberation, power accrued through self-denial distinguishes the ascetic, whose mastery is proven in the context of interaction with devotees. The same is true of the hero, whose period of manifest power begins only when he has determined or commenced to make himself a sacrifice. Like the ascetic and also the *sati*, who is empowered after taking an oath (*vrat*) to abandon life, the hero can confer blessings. Moreover, like the ascetic and the *sati* about to mount the pyre, he can also curse. As we have seen, however, unlike the *sati*, who typically curses to instruct errant family members, the hero rarely curses family members, or others for that matter. Engaged in battle, rather than a ritual procession such as *sati*s make as a prelude to cremation, heroes seldom take time out to instruct, harm, or give specific blessings to others. But then, of course, heroic death, like the *sati*'s, is itself considered a boon to family members.

Fourth, the association of the hero with the ascetic, who gives up family life to pursue liberation on his own, surely reinforces the image of hero as solitary renouncer. The hero who is worshiped, the hero who dies, is finally separated from his family the moment he begins to struggle. This moment is sometimes actually identical, rather than prior, to the moment of his decapitation, which begins his headless fighting.

Fifth, there is the convergence of ascetic and martial disciplines in the form of celibacy. For the ascetic this celibacy is supposedly total, though as Shaivite mythology and stories about ascetics from ancient to modern times have shown, ascetics have been known for their sexual potency and potential for deviating temporarily from celibacy. For the soldier it is temporary, during times of battle and on Dashara, when weapons worship is performed. This dual identity of householder-ascetic is made manifest in the epic hero Pabuji, who, like the cultic hero Kallaji, leaves his wedding to fight, as it is in other South Asian contexts, for example the epic hero Katamaraju, a married ascetic trickster from Telegu folklore.[103]

101. On the semantic range of *samadhi* in the ascetic context, see Coccari, "The Bir Babas of Banaras," 27 note 6. According to Coccari, some *bir*s are represented in shrine images as "martial ascetics," p. 21. For general discussion on the conflation of ascetics and *bir*s in Banaras, see also pp. 20–22, 35. Says Coccari, "the city's image-sellers . . . admit to offering the same general image to patrons wishing to establish an ascetic's *samadhi* [shrine commemorating the ascetic's enlightenment] or the *sthan* ["place," memorial] of a Bir"; p. 35.

102. For a wonderful discussion of ascetic isolation, power, and magnetism, see Narayan, *Storytellers, Saints, and Scoundrels*.

103. Narayana Rao, "Tricking the Goddess," 116.

In the case of Rajput heroes, the self-sacrificing ascetic is one more identity that, like Bheruji and ancestor, works at certain times and in certain contexts as metonym and at other times as homonym. None of these constructs aurally impinge upon ancestral stories recited. Rather, they inhere as frames that we might otherwise wish to conceive of as "deep background."

The same is not true, however, for the final construct to be mentioned in this chapter, that is to say the criminal or dacoit, whose image is today so persistent in the imagination of those Rajputs who feel frustrated, limited, or belittled by the imposition of democratic governance. We have explored the way the image of Rajput is informed by the alienated and swashbuckling brigand, whether in centuries past or in contemporary times. In fact, if the Rajput strikes the outsider as epitomizing romance, the dacoit strikes many Rajputs as doing the same.[104] I do not wish to convey the impression that Rajputs are somehow preoccupied with the illicit and transgressive. Rather, my purpose is to demonstrate yet another motif that sometimes serves as frame of reference for Rajput domestic traditions. Like asceticism, this motif seems to be subtly linked with the image of the Rajput who struggles against political dominance, or at least certain aspects of it, including the controversial constitutional protections for minorities. Thus, to continue this line of speculation, the criminal, like Robin Hood, becomes a vehicle of justice or retribution and a nostalgic reminder of Rajput "glory days" when Rajputs ruled or served kingdoms.

Generally speaking, admiring reflections on dacoits, such as those incorporated into chapter 2, arose during discussions I had with Rajputs about Rajput heroes who were not dacoits. In the following case, however, the Rajput hero is not simply likened to the criminal; he is a criminal. Like the image of the ascetic who severs himself from society, the following heroic figure leaves society, and in his solitary existence as bandit earns a sacrificial demise befitting his name Pratap, "Glory."[105] As one might expect, in Rajasthan Pratap is a tremendously popular name. Unfortunately for the reader, it is the name of not only the hero but also of most of the characters in this account of Rajput banditry and bravado.

This story was related by the aforementioned Col. Mohan Singh. I present here a translation of his rather long and wandering account. I have chosen to stick with translation rather than summarization to be consistent with what I have presented so far and to convey a sense of the unhurried storytelling style of the narrator, who is well known as a consummate and commanding raconteur. For the sake of brevity, however, I have excised two stretches, one appearing about half-way through the narrative and one at the end; both digress from the matter at hand. I do, however, summarize what is excised.

> There were two *thakur*s in Osian, and whenever there's a situation
> like that, there's bound to be lots of fights. The *thakur* with whom
> our family was allied, Ravat Singhji, was a quiet man, but very good.

---

104. On the fantasy of "outlaw" in identity formation among the Pardis, once a scheduled tribe and now reclassified as a backward caste, see Kakar, *The Colors of Violence*, 90.

105. The name is comparable to that of the *Iliad*'s slaughtered hero Patroklos, "Glory of the Forefathers."

The other *thakur* had a Baniya working for him. One time the Baniya
went out riding on a camel and then just left the camel in a field.

Pratap's father, who was related to the first *thakur*, went to the
Baniya and asked him what he was doing [by just leaving the camel
in the field, where he didn't belong]. The Baniya, who was young,
became very rude and insulted him.

Pratap's father had only one son and so [when he saw Pratap] he
insulted him [the implication: a son should see to it that a father is
not insulted or that any insult to his father is avenged].[106] Pratap was
hot tempered, so when he heard his father's words, he quickly
finished the food he was eating, washed his hands, and left.

Pratap went to see our *thakur* and asked how this could happen
[how a servant of the other *thakur* could feel free to express disdain this
way]. Our *thakur* said, "What the other *thakur* is doing [allowing] is not
right." Now Pratap was not educated, but there was a lot of discipline in
those days: he asked his *thakur*'s permission to go to the other *thakur*
[to air his grievance]. Ravat Singh said, "yes, go, but don't be rude."

So Pratap went to the other *thakur* and said, "your *kamdar*
[Baniya servant] has done thus [caused offense]," but the *thakur* said,
"It doesn't matter." So Pratap went to the *kamdar*, who abused him.
Then Pratap killed him with a stick and became a dacoit. There is no
other option when you kill someone. Otherwise the police catch you.

Pratap formed a party [gang] with other bandits and became
their leader.

At this point the narrator digresses to discuss various matters, including
the skills acquired by people who live full-time in the desert. One is ascertain-
ing the exact location of animals by listening to their voices. Another is becoming adept at nocturnal travel. The story resumes.

There was a man who was a *hakim*, a position kind of like a *tehsildar*
[a kind of governor]. My own real auntie was married to him.[107] His
name was Sir Pratap and he looked after the state.[108] My aunt told
her husband that it wasn't Pratap's fault that he did what he did
[killed the Baniya]. Sir Pratap told her that Pratap should surrender.
My aunt sent a message to Pratap saying that he should come and
talk. Pratap answered, "You're . . . like my mother. [True,] he's Sir
Pratap and a very big man, but I'm also Pratap ["Glory"] and not a

---

106. A number of stories I recorded included lines such as this one from a Rajput account of Dhanna
and Bhinya, important heroes in Jodhpur: "If you're sons of mine, you'll get revenge." The son is expected to
avenge an insult to his father. Deokrishna Vyas's article "Songs of Valour" reports that avenging one's father's
death is a rite of manhood; at the age of twelve a boy of a murdered father is expected to take revenge of his
father's death; p. 3.

107. "Real auntie" is used to distinguish a blood relative from an honorific auntie, someone called "auntie"
as a term of endearment.

108. Sir Pratap served from 1873 to 1922 as regent of Jodhpur during the minorities of his nephews Sardar
Singh, Sumer Singh, and Umaid Singh. See Rudolph and Rudolph, with Mohan Singh Kanota, *Reversing the
Gaze*, especially pp. 9, 474.

sheep that I should surrender." Sir Pratap then said, "I'll give 25,000 rupees and some land to whoever catches Pratap alive."

Now there was a *kiledar*, an in-charge [superintendent] at [the fortress of] Phalodi, which is on the way to Jailsamer. The in-charge was Pratap's *dharam-bhai* [dear friend] but he wanted the money so he invited Pratap for a meal.[109] Pratap's guide, Pratap Puri, who was wise like a *sadhu* [ascetic] though he had a wife and children, heard the animals talking and he saw a kite that didn't seem right [a very bad omen].[110] So he told Pratap, "the in-charge will deceive you." Pratap was hot-tempered and said, "He's my *dharam-bhai*! How would he go against me!"

The guide, Pratap Puri, left Pratap.[111] When Pratap reached the fort [at Phalodi], the people there gave him drinks and got him tight. In the village there are huts; ladies don't come out [to meet guests] so you have to have separate huts for meeting visitors. Pratap and his hosts were in one of these huts. They were having drinks and there was a goat cut and vegetables prepared for dinner. After dinner they went to sleep, but the people there took away Pratap's water pot. When he awoke and was thirsty he went out to find water but the hut door had been closed. When he opened it, there were five hundred soldiers there. They started shooting.

Pratap was wounded but he made it over to his camel, which was his favorite camel, and he chopped the camel's head off so that no other man could ride it. Then he said to the in-charge, "You did a foul thing to me; now only deer will inhabit this place." He meant that the whole village area would become a jungle.

Pratap was wounded badly in the chest, but still he didn't fall. So someone took out a sword and chopped off his head. Even then he didn't fall, but kept on fighting. In our history, most people who died [fighting] died without their heads. Finally someone sprinkled Holi powder on him and he died.

The narrator then went on to say that afterwards Pratap appeared in the dreams of his wife and father or "maybe he just appeared to them *sakshat*." He also told me that there is a Langa (Muslim musician) who composed a song about Pratap, which, he said, "was excellent." He also mentioned a female drummer (Dholhin) who is a devotee, lives nearby, and plays for him regularly. Moreover, he informed me that if one goes to Pratap's shrine at Divali, one can see him appear along with his gang of bandits.

A number of things are worth noting about his lengthy and rich narrative. First, it begins with an insult, not to the hero but to his father. If Pratap is to be

---

109. *Dharam-bhai* translates literally as *"dharm* brother."
110. An omen of death and battle; also, as we have seen, a theriomorphic form of the *kuldevi* in war.
111. Here it is unclear whether he left because of the bad omen or because he was insulted by Pratap's inattention to his advice as a guide.

worthy of his name, he must avenge the slight. As is clear from the text, an insult to the father is insulting to the son, who is succinctly reminded of this by his father. Bloody vengeance will signify glory as Pratap becomes a resplendent *jhunjharji*.

Second, Pratap is distinguished from the offending Baniya, and implicitly the unapologetic *thakur* employing the Baniya, by his evident refinement and civility. Unlike the Baniya, portrayed as rude and insulting, Pratap is characterized as courteous and refined, despite his twice-mentioned hot-headedness. Scolded by his father, he finishes his meal and washes his hands before setting off to consult with the "good *thakur*," who admonishes him not to be rude. A better picture of the restrained and *sattvik*, yet impulsive and *rajasik*, Rajput could hardly be found. The contours of ideal Rajput comportment are effectively highlighted by the Baniya's base behavior.

Third, Pratap is sufficiently outraged at betrayal by his so-called *dharam-bhai*, whom he defended against condemnation by Pratap's sagacious "*sadhu*" guide, that even when he is wounded and bleeding he takes time out from his struggling and sacrificing to curse him. Now no domesticated animals will graze at that fort. It will be desecrated and revert to deer-inhabited jungle.[112]

Fourth, the glorious Pratap is, in his own words, "no sheep." Rather, he is subtly identified in the story with his last meal, a "cut goat," which like the kite (the bloodthirsty goddess incarnate) spotted by his guide, serves as an omen of slaughter. His death is, in short, sacrificial, as his headless struggling confirms. Its sacrificial nature is emphasized by his sacrifice of his camel. He will not have his vehicle defiled by the touch of another; instead, it will remain forever his. The episode is reminiscent of other sacrificed companions who accompany sacrificial victims (Balluji's horse, Maha Singh's dog, and, in that interesting case of reversal, the Navratri elephant's mahout.)

Finally, Pratap, who puts up an impressive struggle first as a bullet-ridden camel sacrificer then as a headless "beast," dies when the soldiers sprinkle Holi powder on him. In this case Holi powder (*gulal*) accomplishes what the "two women" do. It stops him cold. Although rare, termination by Holi powder does occur in several other hero stories I collected, as does termination by *nil* (bluing, indigo), which is generally thrown by Muslim cloth printers (Chipas) on rampaging heroes. In the song of Sati Godavari, a Chipa tries to throw it on a *sati* from the Sadh caste but through her *sat*, she manages to make him spill it on himself.[113] Unlike the sight of two women strolling, which is auspicious, contact with *nil* is considered extremely inauspicious. Although I never found anyone who could explain why or how two women or *nil* would be able to stop a hero, it seems likely that the two auspicious women serve to defend their terrain against inauspiciousness by keeping at bay the beheaded *jhunjharji*, whose failure to become a divine guardian of the border and whose untransformed

---

112. For a parallel case of a disloyal *dharam* sister being cursed, this time by a *sati*, see Harlan, "Satī: The Story of Godāvarī," 229. There the perfidious friend is contrasted with a loyal *dharam* (fictive kin) father, who brings her a disco band, p. 230.

113. Harlan, "Satī: The Story of Godāvarī," 229. On *nil* in the context of *sati* immolation, see Weinberger-Thomas, *Ashes of Immortality*, 24–34.

presence in the village would be unfortunate indeed for those inhabiting it. The inauspicious liquid keeps the doomed hero *cum* metamorphosing guardian from completing his journey home to hearth and kin. Thus the women defend auspiciousness by their own embodiment of it, whereas the *nil* thrower preserves it by drenching and cooling off the red-hot-blooded hero with blue liquid that is inherently inauspicious.

But what about Holi powder, the brightly colored substance that Hindus throw by itself or mixed with water on the festival of Holi? How does Holi powder cause Pratap to die? Again I received no answer to these questions from raconteurs and others. I did, however, encounter an intriguing reference to Holi powder as a symbol of bloody death in a conversation with another aged and well-known Rajput aristocrat, who was a prominent participant in and organizer of the annual Jauhar Mela. Passionately discussing Akbar's sack of Chittor, he explained that on the eleventh of the dark half of the month of Cait, Chittor burned. Then on the twelfth, the gates were opened. Ten thousand men, he continued, went out but no one wanted to live after all the women and children died in the *jauhar*. "All," he said, "were slaughtered," and he then went on to say, "People say that Akbar was great, but what he did was a massacre. On the thirteenth we play *phag* (throw Holi color) to remember the blood that flowed on that day. Just at Chittor they do it, thirteen days after Holi, nowhere else, in remembrance of that blood."

Perhaps in this account lies the connection we need to understand the final moments of the renegade Pratap. Throwing *gulal*, which is typically deep pink to red (and is frequently depicted in Rajasthani miniature paintings in rose to crimson hues) may well represent scattering blood in battle.[114] In epic iconization, the headless hero spurts blood from his neck, from which sprouts a lotus (while eyes appear on his chest). In Pratap's case, however, because of the Holi powder, which fights blood with "blood" or "fire with fire," his blood disperses and ceases to animate the previously struggling "hot-headed" warrior whose *sat*, if you will, has previously set blood "boiling," quite as a *sati*'s *sat* causes her spontaneous combustion.

There is one other aspect of Holi powder, however, that should also be noted. In the Rajasthan village in which Ann Gold has worked it is customary to place Holi powder on a corpse as it sets off for the pyre. The custom, says Gold, is in line with the practice of placing the powder on pilgrims setting off on their route. Thus the Holi powder also expedites, as it redirects, Pratap's final journey, his pilgrimage to Paradise.[115] It brings about transcendence, which transvalues tragedy, while keeping society safe from warrior fury so powerful as to impel this outlaw's headless body.[116]

For whatever reasons, these three things—women, bluing, Holi powder—serve to seclude the hero finally and to confirm his distinction from other

114. For discussion of the correlation between *gulal* and *gulabi* (rose-pink), I thank Susan Wadley, private correspondence, July 11, 1998.

115. Ann Grodzins Gold, private correspondence, July 12, 1998.

116. George Dumézil speaks of two ways in which myths and rituals handle warriors who have killed and thus posed problems to society. Where the warrior's fury threatens society, he must be cooled by water or diversion in female form; *The Destiny of the Warrior*, 134–135. Where the warrior's crime causes despair, he must be lured back to society and made to rekindle his *tejas* (energy) for useful purposes; pp. 124–126.

human beings. In this case, Holi powder puts an end to a period of struggling headlessly, but also a long period of outlaw activity, during which the hero was relentlessly pursued by Sir Pratap in his constabulary capacity. In fact, by the end of the story, the initial antagonism between rival *thakurs* along with their supporters is displaced by the battle of the Prataps in a zoom-lens, close-up isolation that reminds one of the Maha Singh versus Ranbaj Khan duel to and beyond death. In the end, the hero Pratap loses his life but proves his *sat* by sacrificing his camel despite his bullet wounds and by fighting on despite decapitation. Like so many Rajput stories, this is another beloved tale of victorious defeat, in this instance, of a perfected sacrificial victim. In death the hero is left alone in his perfection, which transcends ordinary human experience. The criminal who has left society and dies violently (like the alleged "*jhunjharji*" smuggler who died on his motorcycle) achieves liberation, just as the ascetic who has left society and leaves his body (takes *samadhi*) achieves liberation. In the end, they are alone in their fulfillment and complete in their achievement of their goal, whether characterized as the indescribable *moksh* or as the quality-filled heaven where life is a perpetual party.

Reflecting back on the narrative a while later, the raconteur spoke of the music composed and performed for the hero, who has made posthumous appearances to beloved relatives.[117] He also discussed sightings of Pratap cavorting with battle companions during Divali. In this respect, Pratap's manifestations comport with those of various *virs* in Udaipur, who are said occasionally to be seen or to be heard conversing over music and the jingling of dancers' anklet bracelets. Some devotees of heroes worshiped as ancestors by family members, but by others in cults led by *bhopas*, have had visions in Mewar's royal cremation ground at Ahar; they have described the heroes as playing *caupad* (a board game), dice, or cards while drinking liquor or opium drinks. The appearances also accord with Divali-night sightings of myriad heroes and others slaughtered at Chittor. Although sometimes loosely called a *bhut mela* (literally, ghost festival) because of the various types of unrelated spirits who congregate on that night, this gathering is generally described as a celebration and not some menacing haunting, on this most auspicious night when the dead celebrate the arrival of Lakshmi, the goddess of good fortune. Typically Rajputs perceive Divali as a relatively unimportant holiday, but the occurrence of the *bhut mela* (which no Rajputs I knew ever attended or mentioned as important in terms of their ancestor worship) would seem to indicate that the *mela* is not generally perceived as ominous but rather joyful and playful, the way Divali is for living human beings.[118]

---

117. The narrator also said that he may have possessed descendents. "May" is to be stressed here, as he then qualified his speculation with the words "or maybe he just appeared before them." The mention of the possibility of possession may reflect the narrator's seniority: perhaps in times past possession by ancestral *jhunjharjis* was far more common an occurrence among Rajputs.

118. In some places in Rajasthan, Divali is also associated with Bheruji, an aniconic stone image of whom "is taken round each village at night" so that devotees can "propitiate him to guard the village for the new year"; *Rajasthan District Gazetteers: Dungarpur*, 1974, 74. The association of Chittor victims and Bherujis at Divali once again brings together Bherujis and heroes, albeit in the company of other Chittor victims (*satis*, children, and other men).

Taken together, the visitations demonstrate the tendency for the isolated and perfected individual who is severed from society to form his own heavenly society after his demise. At whatever point death is deemed to occur, it leads to a sort of splitting of perfected character into qualities (*sattvik* and *rajasik*) along with a sorting out of preferences (certain types of offerings), but also to a sharing of identity with other perfected beings reinvested with qualities. Perfection, then, is not simply the end of an individual's story but the beginning of socialization along new lines and with different rules. Death resocializes the hero in a way that makes him less alien, removed, and threatening, despite enforced marginality. He associates with his goddess, his gender complement and the divine corollary of women who need him, but also with liberated men in heaven, frequently imaged or imagined as a royal assembly or court. Thus his isolating perfection and perfect isolation are unstable and entropic. Perfection and seclusion ultimately conduce toward differentiated, delimited personae and long-term endearing relationships. They invest the postsacrificial hero with mindfulness of, and engagement in, life with its chaotic and phantasmagoric multiplicity. Unlike Jain spiritual heroes who permanently transcend qualification and so are "out of station" or beyond reach, these liberated yet sensual heroes are as close as the family shrine.[119] Whether or not seen, heard, and felt by familial devotees, their desires can be ascertained and satisfied, which sustains a fruitful relationship.

Continuing the relationship with the hero singled out by death, which is the logical and pervasive terminus of many domestic stories (particularly, as we have seen, those told by men), are recurrent familial rituals, particularly and especially the *ratijaga*, in which hero songs are sung by women. Whereas Navratri-Dashara, with its goddess worship and commemoration of heroes who have sacrificed themselves to their goddesses, tends to rehearse and appropriate the hero's sacrificial death long ago, the rituals women perform typically push the story forward, beyond the hero's sequestered and perfected sacrifice to his present and future life as family guardian, whose story and power continues to manifest through time. The benefits of ritual veneration motivate women to sing praises to heroes and invite them, along with other important family deities such as *kuldevis*, *satimatas*, and Bherujis, to important family occasions. To these *ratijaga* "epilogues" we now turn.

---

119. On the *gati* (goal) of Jain *tirthankars*, see Babb, *Absent Lord*.

5

Heroic Song

End of the Story and Beyond

Jhunjharji, come to my *ratijaga*.
Jhunjharji, come and bring your friends.
Jhunjharji, come to my *ratijaga*.
Jhunjharji, bring grain, wealth, and good fortune.
Jhunjharji, I am waiting for you.

Jhunjharji, come to my *ratijaga*.
Jhunjharji, come and bring your friends.
Jhunjharji, I am having *lapsi* cooked for you—it's thick and sticky.
Jhunjharji, there's hard candy and sugar.

Jhunjharji, come to my *ratijaga*.
Jhunjharji, I'm having rice cooked for you—white rice.
Jhunjharji, I'm having thick *khir* made for you.

Jhunjharji, come to my *ratijaga*.
Jhunjharji, I am having *laddu*s cooked for you—ones with crumbs
    on them.
Jhunjharji, I am offering a *thali* for you.
Jhunjharji, come to my *ratijaga*.

In this song, a woman invites an ancestral hero to attend the *ratijaga*
she has organized.[1] All that remains of this hero's story is an epithet
that distinguishes him from unheroic men and ancestors but not
from other heroes who bear the same epithet. Whereas becoming a

---

1. The offerings in this song are various sweet dishes. Like *khir*, *lapsi* is a pudding; *laddu*s
are dry, round sweets. In a personal communication, R. S. Ashiya suggested the gloss "thick and
sticky" for *laclaci* and commented on the way in which *lapsi* sticks to the lips. More generally, the
term means "elastic, springy"; see Chaturvedi and Tiwari, eds., *A Practical Hindi-English Dictionary*, s.v. A *thali* is a round metal tray on which foods are served and eaten. This chapter does not

jhunjharji is a climactic moment toward which the hero's story leads teleologically in many men's stories, and after which the hero's story typically transmutes into a discussion of ritual detail in many women's stories, here the epithet removes any trace of individual identity and equates the *jhunjharji* with the decapitation-and-struggle scenario enacted by all *jhunjharjis*.

Furthermore, the hostess makes it clear to the *jhunjharji*, whatever his name might be, that he should bring his friends, presumably other heroes with whom he cavorts in Virgati. And so, the hero who once "went on a deserted path" and "struggled alone" is now a resocialized being who keeps good company and is good company. He enjoys hospitality and comes bearing gifts of "grain, wealth, and good fortune."

Thus initiated by death into this exclusive society of heroes, he is also now welcomed at home, and by women! Whereas in the vast majority of hero stories that state the cause of a hero's fall women are the "kiss of death," here women sing eager invitations to join female celebrants at the *ratijaga*, from which men are excluded. Once arrested at the border by women, the hero is lured to the innermost apartments of the home, where he can socialize with women and their various divine guests.[2]

This chapter looks at the verbal iconization of heroes in women's songs, which overwhelmingly relocate the hero from past to present and articulate his role as guardian. What little emerges in these songs from the events of a hero's life appears as fleeting flashbacks, intertextual references that link the past, in which the hero died in battle and earned the glory bequeathed to his family, to the present, in which he safeguards and fortifies familial welfare. Let us begin by looking at various ways in which women's songs represent heroes, and in doing so contemplate how the representations are inherently if transparently framed by those found in other *ratijaga* songs, especially those about Bherujis, ancestors, *satis*, and goddesses. This allows us to appreciate fully hero songs' inevitable and unmistakably gendered intertextuality.

The Hero as Good Company: Sociability, Generosity, and Desire

Women perform *ratijagas* as part of important family occasions, especially marriages and births. Bringing along small children, they gather to sing the praises of their host family's gods by way of inviting them to the ceremonies. Rajput men do not participate directly but can, of course, hear the songs that women sing. In Rajput families, women are invariably accompanied by musicians, especially women whom they call Dholhins, female drummers who some-

---

attempt a broad analysis of the *ratijaga* genre *per se*, but utilizes relevant songs from the genre. Treatment of the genre is to be found in my article "Women's Songs for Auspicious Occasions," and also in an article I will be writing for a volume on women's rituals now in the planning stage and being organized by Tracy Pinchman.

2. The luring of the now divine and helpful heroes to earth by human women who seek blessings is reminiscent of the luring by Saci (if also Agni) of her husband Indra from his despair in the ocean, to heaven, where he was needed to serve as king; Dumézil, *Destiny of a Warrior*, 124–125. In both instances, if on different planes, the hero is transformed from potentially threatening murderer to powerful (but beneficent) protector of society.

times also play harmonium as they sing songs for the family's deities. Also attending and singing are various female servants, some who are currently in the family's employ and some who have taken jobs elsewhere but still participate in *thikana* celebrations. Among these are women who call themselves Rajputs but are termed by many others Darogas.[3] The maidservants and Dholhins tend to provide constancy in the Rajput wedding celebrations; they sing while Rajput friends and relatives are busy providing and receiving hospitality, chatting about recent events and, sometimes, nodding in and out of sleep. Rajput women I came to know regularly suggested that I should listen to Dholhins or Darogas if I wanted to hear songs that were complete.[4]

After hearing many songs at a *ratijaga*, I decided to record the *ratijaga* songs that might be relevant to this project. Rajput women I knew well introduced me to elderly maidservants (so-called Darogas) who had sung at their *ratijagas* for many years. One performed for me in the palace of a Mewar *solah thikana*. Her family has been employed by the *thikana* for generations, and although she is eighty years old at the time of this writing, she continues to perform when she is called for *ratijagas*, both at the *thikana* palace and in Udaipur. The other, an elderly woman who recently expired, performed for me at the urban residence of another *solah thikana*. Because these women had attended many weddings and birth celebrations over the years, they knew many *ratijaga* songs and knew them well. Although these women were quite willing to be recorded, they did express concerns about making mistakes that would be preserved by the tapes and about the quality of their aged voices, which, both suggested modestly, were unworthy of recording. These worries were alleviated when I guaranteed the women the same anonymity I had promised Rajput women. Because of my promise, I will refer to them here as the "palace" and the "Udaipur" singers, these designations referring not to any status differentiation but to the location of their recorded performances.

Once we began recording, any lingering wariness of the microphone quickly receded as the singers sang to the evident satisfaction of the small audiences of household servants and relatives that gathered around them. Clearly everyone ended up having a good time during these sessions. It was also evident that everyone in the audience was familiar with the lyrics being sung, and that the presence of others rendered the singers' performances something other than purely individual. The audience was also performing actively, as audience: members encour-

---

3. "Daroga," as noted previously, designates descent from a Rajput father and a woman from another caste. Although the term is regularly used by Rajputs and other members of high-ranking communities, it is seldom utilized in front of the designated people, who contest the appropriateness of the designation and generally refer to themselves as Rajputs or as Ravan Rajputs. I use the term only to describe the (etic) perspective of Rajputs. I am somewhat reluctant to designate these women, to whom I promised anonymity, as "maidservants," as if this designation somehow sums up their identity. I have chosen it, however, because it at least designates a position they acknowledge—of being a female servant. I have decided against pseudonyms because I have no wish to name people who have names of their own, particularly since every name carries connotations I have no desire to introduce. The term "Dholhin" is also frequently contested, though commonly used to designate caste members. We will see an example of contestation presently.

4. Their designation of these women as their representatives is reminiscent of the ways in which prominent people, especially people from the upper echelons of society, often appoint spokespeople to represent them.

aged the singers, indicated their approval, and sometimes joined in the singing, if intermittently and almost silently. Their presence helped mitigate the strangeness surely experienced by singers who were charged with performing solo lyrics ordinarily sung in chorus within a social—ritual—context.

In addition to taping these household servants, I also decided to tape a performance by an experienced musician employed throughout her career by various aristocratic families in Udaipur. She sang with great relish the lyrics in the *jhunjharji* song above. Although all the people I knew referred to her as a Dholhin by the name of Mangi Bai, she characterized herself differently. A boisterous, rotund woman with great energy and humor, she told me that people refer to Dholhins as "Bai" (the honorific "sister") and that some of them call her Mangi Bai, but that she was really not so much a Dholhin as a Rajgahik ("royal singer") because she sang for royal and noble families. She refers to herself as Mangi Devi Arya, and explained to me (in no uncertain terms) that she has become very famous, which I had already gathered from the Rajput woman who had graciously arranged for a performance in her home and who intermittently attended the performance and oversaw its progress.[5] This singer's fame was later confirmed by folklorist Komal Kothari, who was well acquainted with her work. Unlike the servants, this extremely self-confident, professional singer was happy to have her name appear in print, and repeatedly suggested that I might want to call her to the United States to perform for some functions there, some time after she returned from a recital she was to be giving in Kolkata.[6]

Another woman who performed many *ratijaga* songs for me was a young woman who lived with her family in a modest apartment in a converted *haveli* near the City Palace. I had come to know her when I used to record *bhajans* (devotional songs) in the Jagdish Temple, which is near her home.[7] She described herself as belonging to a *chota bhai* ("little brother") Rajput family (that is to say, a family descended from a little brother of a Rajput oldest son, who inherited through primogeniture), most of whose members live on their farm near Udaipur. Her family was not known by local members of the erstwhile aristocracy, however, and some women to whom I mentioned my association with her presumed Daroga provenance. Fortunately, it is not necessary to settle the matter here.[8] With

5. She was thus positioned as another patron of the performance that was arranged not for some typical reason but rather for my edification.

6. When I explained that there were no functions I could think of that would call for this kind of music, she replied that maybe I should start a trend. She explained that she had performed for many important people, including foreigners, and that she was about to go off to Kolkata (or as it used to be called, Calcutta) to perform. She made it clear to me that I should be impressed by her talent. After every song, she leaned forward and, with a broad grin demanded, "How did you like *that!*" The Rajput woman at whose home this concert was given remarked that the songs, which were played on harmonium rather than on the more traditional drums, sounded "modern" to her. The harmonium, but also the singer's style, was evocative of "filmi music," or songs from Bollywood musicals. On a recent trip to a *sagasji* shrine, I heard songs she had recorded in this style and the word "filmi" was used by a devotee to describe them. The lyrics she sang, however, were consistent with those I heard in other performances.

7. I did this as a hobby. It turned out to be a wonderful way of meeting many women outside the Rajput community during the earliest days of my first major research stint in Rajasthan.

8. Nor could the matter be settled here, even if we were have access to family records. On the complexity of Rajput identity politics—including matters of inherited/earned Rajput status and Rajputization—see chapter 2.

one exception, I heard similar versions of all the other songs she sang from Rajputs, maidservants, and musicians, in well-known Rajput households.[9] Moreover, the exceptional song, which I will analyze shortly, I use to demonstrate succinctly a characteristic that is evident, if diffuse, in various songs sung by women who belong to these groups.

All the songs in these various recordings are vastly superior to the songs recorded during rituals, where the crowd noises made them intermittently unintelligible. I still found my recordings of groups valuable as records that help to expand the scope of comparison and allow for greater confidence in making judgments about typicality. Some of the songs in each collection overlap with songs in other collections, as they do in the case of the last singer, whose repertoire of songs was extremely useful as a comparative resource.

My final sources are published collections of *ratijaga* songs that are available for purchase in Udaipur. One is a pamphlet of *ratijaga* songs that I found in small religious bookstalls in Udaipur bazaars and was shelved alongside works belonging to other typically female genres such as women's *vrat kathas* (stories [*kathas*] told in conjunction with routine performance of vows [*vrats*] of devotion to deities). Others are published and bound volumes of Rajasthani songs. Some of lyrics found in these various written sources shed light on those found in recorded lyrics and are cited below for comparison and emphasis. In short, the analysis that follows draws on a variety of texts, some oral, some written, and all representing in various ways the voices of women inviting deities to come and receive their hospitality as hostesses. Let us turn, then, to the *ratijaga* songs that tell us about heroes and the ways in which they are conceptualized.

One of the most obvious things about *ratijagas* is that the presence of professional musicians contributes to the tendency to render household heroes nameless and generic. After Mangi Devi had finished singing hero songs and was about to begin singing some goddess songs, I asked her if she sang special songs for individual *kuldevis*, like Naganechaji and Ban Mata. She said yes, she did, and that she sang Ban Mata songs for Bari Sadri. When, rather timidly, I objected that Bari Sadri is a Jhala Rajput *thikana* and so should have songs for their *kuldevi* Ad Mata, her eyes twinkled and she laughed, saying, "All *kuldevis* are the same: they're all Matas and Mata is one, just as Bheruji is one." She was clearly amused that I knew this little bit about *kuldevis* and, if she felt at all embarrassed by my question, she did not show it. Although her response to me can be construed as rationalization, it can also be seen as an indication of the way a professional musician with diverse patronage can contribute to confluence, homogenization, and perhaps, over time, change in the conceptualization of deities.

In the context of heroes, it should observed that the songs this singer sings for one family's *jhunjharjis* she also sings for *jhunjharjis* belonging to other families. And the same holds true for songs she sings for other categories of beings,

---

9. I also attended a *ratijaga* for one of her relatives and heard many of the *ratijaga* songs she knew sung then—by relatives, Dhohins, and also a male musician who played a harmonium.

including other categories of heroes. Even when women do not rely on professional musicians and, with or without servants, sing their own songs, however, they typically refer to familial heroes in the same generic way and do not name them. Many women not living in the household (whether distant relatives or nonrelated friends) could hardly be expected to know the household heroes' names (which even many familial women do not know), much less the heroes' individual stories. Participation in *ratijagas* by these women reinforces the lack of specificity found in women's stories, which so often cut to, or even begin with, the chase, that is to say the hero's struggle and fall, before moving on to matters of ritual, in which lie their predominant interest and expertise.

Men also have interest and expertise in ritual, as we know, but they lie chiefly in performance of Navratri ritual, which is devoted primarily to the goddess Durga as well as to the familial *kuldevi* to whom she is homologized, and in the activities of Dashara, during which they venerate vehicles and implements of war and battle sacrifice. Thus although the hero and Navratri-Dashara sacrificer are identified in many narrative contexts, the holidays are not prima facie hero festivals. *Ratijagas* are also, of course, not first and foremost hero events; they simply include heroes in the ever-shifting constellation of familial divinities invited to attend.[10] Nevertheless, in the context of *ratijagas*, heroes are explicitly venerated, which is not typically the case in Navratri-Dashara rites. In some families, a hero is also given special worship on his death anniversary, but this typically consists of offering some favorite foods to supplement the routine fare prepared and provided overwhelmingly by women as part of regular (usually daily) *puja* of household deities in their domestic shrines. In the cultic context, this anniversary frequently occasions a fair, to which pilgrims of both sexes throng to ask blessings and witness miracles. At home, however, ritual veneration of heroes is overwhelmingly the province of women, though both men and women routinely pay respects when passing their familial hero shrines.

As with the routine *puja* that women perform, the offering of praise in a *ratijaga* song is primarily concerned with pleasing deities so that they will bring about fruitful consequences. Thus in one *jhunjharji* song sung by the "palace singer," the *jhunjharji*, who is repeatedly addressed as "my merry struggler" or "my saffron-donning struggler," is asked for a variety of more specific benefits than those requested in the opening song.

> My merry Jhunjharji—take *pan*.
> My saffron-donning Jhunjharji—take *pan*.
> The king worships you—take *pan*.
> Lord, my sons' wives and grandson's wives grasp your feet—take *pan*.
> My ruddy Jhunjharji—take *pan*.
> The king's son worships you—take *pan*.
> Lord, make our bangles and red saris indestructible.
> My saffron-donning Jhunjharji—take *pan*.
> My ruddy Jhunjharji—take *pan*.

10. Individuals, especially brides, import deities as *ishtadevtas*.

Lord, make our bangles and red saris indestructible.
My saffron-donning Jhunjharji—take *pan.*
My ruddy Jhunjharji—take *pan.*
Lord, in the forest you fought alone—take *pan.*
Lord, the king worships you—take *pan.*
Lord, to the brothers give long life—take *pan.*
Lord, make our bangles and saris indestructible—take *pan . . .*
The grandsons worship you—take *pan.*
Lord, give the children and adolescents long life—take *pan . . .*
Lord, make our eyes and knees long-lasting—take *pan.*[11]

Represented in the song are anonymous singers, who let the *jhunjharji* know
that all family members worship him, offer him *pan,* and ask for "bangles and
red saris" that are "indestructible." In other words, they request husbands who
will outlive them, for only married women may wear bangles and red saris. The
women singing this song also ask for long life for brothers, sons and grandsons, children and adolescents. Emphasizing the importance of male longevity
(which is also stressed in other women's traditions, including *vrats*), the singers
effectively outline the current generations of the *kul* (patriline), out of which daughters, and into which wives, marry.[12] Living husbands mean security for the family, including and perhaps especially wives marrying into it, for wives' value to
the family derives overwhelmingly from their connection to their husbands and
their contribution of sons. Thus the song is not exclusively preoccupied with the
welfare of men, as the women's request for "eyes and knees" that are "long-lasting"
attests. These women want good health in addition to long life.

By pleasing heroes, women hope to get what they want—benefits that come
to them and to the people who make up the families in which they live. As with
the first song, in this *"pan* song" almost nothing is said of past events. Along
with the designation *jhunjharji* there is the reference to donning saffron, which
implies the hero's intention to leave society behind and sacrifice his life. Then
there is the reference to being "ruddy," which probably refers to a face flushed
by intoxication. A ruddy complexion is acquired by intoxication, whether it results from consuming intoxicants at a feast or is the metaphorical "intoxication"
that attends bloodthirsty slaughter. Goddesses, in particular, are known for this
kind of battle intoxication, though they are often depicted as literally drinking
the (red) blood of victims. The unambiguous flashback, however, is the line "in
the forest you fought alone," a formula that frequently reverberates in women's

---

11. The words I translate "merry" and "ruddy" are *rangraliyo* and *rangbhariyo.* Both terms have as their
first element *rang,* which is not only a Rajasthani (both Marwari and Mewari) term but also a common one in
Hindi. Its primary meaning is "color," but it also has many other denotations, including "gaiety," "whim," or
"merriment." The *Rājasthānī Sabd Kos* translates *rangraliyo* as *mauj; āmod-pramod* and *rangbhariyo* as *rasik;
maujī, ānandī.* Though roughly synonyms, I decided to gloss one as "merry, " but the other "ruddy," a gloss
that conveys the high color (*rang*) of "enjoyment," construed in different contexts. For more on these terms,
see Laḷas, ed., *Rājasthānī Sabd Kos,* s.v. For the Hindi *rang,* see Chaturvedi and Tiwari, eds., *A Practical Hindi-
English Dictionary,* s.v.

12. On Rajput *kuls* and other segmentation units, along with the problems they present, see Harlan,
Religion and Rajput Women, 26–33.

songs. Inserted in the midst of the body of this text, it serves as another temporal reference point, which, when combined with the others, constructs the most rudimentary and economical of scenarios: the hero donned saffron, became ruddy (intoxicated, glowing), fought in the forest alone, and died struggling as a *jhunjharji*. These actions are references outward and beyond the text, to every *jhunjharji*'s story. In the context of any particular *ratijaga*, however, the familial stories of a *jhunjharji* or some *jhunjharji*s (whether known to individual singers or not) serve as background, foundation, or—to deploy the prevailing and more flexible metaphor—frame, in this song the frame being verily "braided" into the text or serving as explicit "framework," for the members of the host family, who may know well of whom they sing.[13]

Thus although little is said, the actions of the scenario are broadly sketched. Not sketched, however, are the specifics of any historical situation, such as embattlement by an emperor or assassination by a relative. Some songs are somewhat more specific in that they refer, for example, to dying in battle (as opposed to being assassinated). Nonetheless, in these, little of past life intrudes on the "story" with which women are overwhelmingly concerned. This story is less occupied with remembrance of a glorious individual way back when than it is with interaction with an eminent supernatural persona in the world women know right here and right now. Moreover, rather than establishing or negotiating status, women's songs, like this one, are directed toward obtaining material, tangible, and palpable results. They are overtly focused on the fruit (*phal*) arising from ongoing communion with and placation of the divine.

And so, as in the "merry *jhunjharji*" song above, temporal referents to story are, to say the least, elusive. Moreover, where they do appear, they are often marvelously ambiguous. Regarded from one angle, they presume and suggest a death scenario, but viewed from another, they function as iconic elements (such as weapons wielded) that point as much, if not more, to who the hero *is* (protector) than to what he *did* (die fighting). In other words, to a supplicant at an image the iconography signifies identity and power, rather than merely memorializing past heroic achievement, beyond which, in any case, the perfected hero has progressed and because of which he has been able to appear and be helpful to petitioners through time. In fact, in women's hero songs, it is hard to tell whether the hero who is described is the hero living in the past or manifesting in the icon they behold now, for, as is so often the case with religious ritual, the then and now conflate in lyrics employing present tense.[14] Women's songs may thus be purposefully ambiguous, their descriptions of the hero serving as dual references to parallel or merged sequences: the hero going forth to face sacrificial death and the hero returning to family members. This is most evident in the many hero songs that follow the convention of describing a deity head to toe. The following song, sung by the maidservant who performed for me in Udaipur, is a typical example.

---

13. On the concept of braiding in the context of frames, see Handelman, "Postlude: Towards a Braiding of Frame."

14. On this well-known aspect of sacred time, see Eliade, *The Sacred and the Profane*.

Jhunjharji, you wear a fine turban.
On the turban a lovely ornament is attached.

You wear a very fine pearl ornament.
 Over the pearl lovely clusters of lalas [glass pendants] are attached.

You wear a very fine necklace.
Jhunjharji, over the necklace a fine neck ornament is attached.

Jhunjharji, you wear a very fine bracelet.
To the bracelet a lovely watch is attached.

Jhunjharji, you sit on a very fine horse.
Jhunjharji, on the horse is seated a very fine rider [that is, you].

Jhunjharji, you wear fine shoes,
And your feet are stained with henna.

This song, which contains no hint of action other than epithet, crafts a characteristic verbal icon that combines features of two types of imagery: the equestrian relief that adorns so many hero stelai and the more rudimentary hero bust, adorned with vibrant markings and foil. In either case, the icon suggests parallel points of departure. From one perspective this hero is the ideal warrior, decked in his finest, mounted on a noble steed, and ready to die in battle. From another, however, the hero is not, at the moment, a warrior set to become a headless, bloody trunk but rather an oh-so-lovely bridegroom. The wedding albums of Rajput men often show them in similar attire, resplendent with various ornaments including a dangling pearl (over the forehead) and brightly hewn lalas framing the face below the pearl.[15] Not only attire but also vehicle suggest parallel sequences. In times past many prominent Rajput grooms arrived for their weddings on elephants, but in recent years the vast majority of Rajputs have arrived on horses. Both animals, of course, are martial vehicles, but the heroes are especially identified with their equestrian mounts.[16] The coincidence of martial and matrimonial imagery is reinforced by the many stories of various heroes who, like Pabuji and Kallaji, leave brides at the altar and rush away from their weddings on horseback to do battle, die on the battlefield, and sate their goddess's appetite.[17]

The hero who appears to women, then, is strikingly attractive. Many women's songs stress the hero's beauty, which is indicated both by description of his lavish shringar (ornamentation) and by overt praise of his loveliness. The following song for Sagasji, sung by Mangi Devi, is a case in point.

15. In Rajasthan, wedding albums remain overwhelmingly a male concern. Until recently, women's faces were not typically displayed in photo albums, which are shown to people outside the family. This has been slowly changing, and in some less conservative families weddings are now videotaped—even women's ceremonies in which faces are revealed.

16. So thoroughly are Rajputs identified with horses that many express resentment that members of other castes allow grooms to arrive at their brides' homes on horseback.

17. The attractiveness of fighting a battle is recognized, albeit metaphorically, in Phillip Roth's novel Deception, where the main male character says to his cancer-ridden ex-lover, "When the fight's still in you, you look pretty good," 142.

FIGURE 5.1. Bedecked groom and bride, from a Rajput wedding album

You are lovely and handsome, O Lord of the Hindus, Giver of Grain
    [Anndata].
You are lovely and handsome, Sagasji Bavji.
You are the basis of the breath in my heart, O King.
You are the basis of the breath in my heart, O King.
Lovely and handsome, lovely and handsome,
    Sagasji Bavji, O King.
You are the basis of the breath in my heart.
O man from Mewar, you are the basis of the breath in my heart.

Your turban is striking, Sagasji Bavji, O King.
Your turban is striking, Sagasji Bavji, O King.
Giver of Grain, your turban is beautiful.
Lovely and handsome, lovely and handsome,
    Sagasji Bavji, O King.
Giver of Grain, you are the basis of the breath in my heart,
    Sagasji Bavji, O King.

Giver of Grain, your *lala*s are shapely. . . .

The song continues on from head to toe, continually revealing and emphasizing Sagasji's beauty while scanning his physique and dwelling on particularly appealing items of manly ornamentation. One of these merits special attention: the "attractive watch," sported by this *sagasji*, as by the *jhunjharji* in the previous song.[18] This detail functions as an anachronistic, formulaic element in this vision of a hero poised for sacrifice in the past (which though indeterminate, is a bygone time of equestrian warfare between the Lord of Hindus and others) and also, more logically and easily, as a nice touch in this contemporary divinity's elegant sartorial statement.[19] By way of context, I should add that during the time of my research, fashionable watches, as well as clocks, were all the rage in Rajasthan, as in the rest of India. Rolex spin-offs were to be found in abundance in city bazaars, as were colorful art deco and modern clocks of diverse design.[20] In one remote cultic *jhunjharji* shrine, which required a seemingly endless and sometimes treacherous drive over rocky, sandy terrain and then a long walk after motoring proved impossible, three such vibrant clocks were prominently displayed around the central icon. Whatever the impetus for inclusion in this head-to-toe depiction, here a timepiece itself indicates temporal co-location and suggests this hero's presence here and now. His appeal is as immediate as it is intimate.

Enhanced by lavish ornamentation, the hero's masculine beauty is reflected in the attractiveness of the petitioning woman's appearance, signified in song by her own *shringar*. In the following song sung by the "palace singer," a woman asks the hero for feminine ornamentation, and invites him to "linger" in each jewel as a memory.

> Bring a hair ornament for my head, Jhunjharji.
> In the ornament on my hair part linger as a memory.
> Take a scarf with beads on it.
> I am coming to your balcony, I am coming, Jhunjharji.
> Please tell me what my heart wants to know, Jhunjharji.
> Send away the worries of my heart, Jhunjharji.
> Take a scarf with beads on it.
>
> Bring earrings for my ears.
> In the earrings linger as a memory. . . .

The song continues, describing a woman's ornamentation from head to toe and asking the hero to stay in various pieces of jewelry, which will serve as lovely mementos. Wearing these accessories, the petitioner will remember the *jhunjharji* and so wish to be with him (serve him, please him) regularly. Here memory is laced with desire (as it is in the Sanskrit *"smara"*) and connotes long-

---

18. In another *ratijaga* song I came across, the *jhunjharji*'s watch is said to be worth one and a quarter *lakh* (125,000) rupees. This number is formulaic. See, for example, a narrative description of Maharaja Jai Singh's turban, said to be worth one and a quarter *lakh*s, in Mayaram, *Resisting Regimes*, 128.

19. On the tendency to envision *vir*s as "freedom fighters" battling Muslims, whatever the particulars of their individual stories, see Harlan, "Deploying the Martial Past."

20. Colorful watches and clocks abounded in Udaipur's Bappu Bazaar shops, as in stores in Delhi's trendy Jan Path bazaar.

ing and reflection, actions frequently intimately conjoined in devotional poetry, particularly in some Vaishnava poetry, where remembering Krishna invites playful (re)union with him.[21] Although drawing the comparison is misleading, in that the song's use of memory as a vehicle for intimacy is subtler here than in the case of so much Krishna poetry, the simile does convey a shared sense of delightful transgression with the transcendent. This sense is enhanced by the specific form that requests take: the petitioner asks the hero to both bestow and inhabit pieces of jewelry, which typically come from a husband. Lingering in her jewels, the hero's presence is intimate indeed.

Thus the struggling hero who is isolated, sacrificed, and ostracized in narrative is beckoned as a handsome, elegant, and desirable guest in songs. To entice these heroes and reward them for coming, women serve various sorts of milky and sugary concoctions such as those mentioned in the first poem. There is "thick and sticky" pudding as well as other varieties of luscious temptations, including candies and pastries. Called away from paradise, where the hero's senses are continually and maximally indulged, women's cooking is still alluring. Two circumstances conspire to make it so.

First, there is nothing like home cooking. If the devotee is "remembering" the hero, the hero is also "remembering" home, or at least the place that once was home.[22] Being called as a guest for a *ratijaga* feast does not in itself distinguish him from members of other categories of supernatural guests, such as goddesses, gods, and ancestors. What does distinguish him is that he belongs to a class summoned by women after women sent him away. Home cooking epitomizes the very welcome that was denied by narratives' married women, who establish and enforce social boundaries. Having dispatched a hero to Virgati, they entice him back home now that he has regained the head he lost.

Second, as in the case of Odysseus and other Greek adventurers, the hero's homecoming is explicitly connected to longing for a woman. Like the singers, women characters are represented in *ratijaga* lyrics as luring the hero with "thick and sticky pudding." And as elsewhere, eating luscious food connotes consummation of sexual desire.[23] It is also connected with fertility, as are visitations by ancestors, whose deaths are inevitably followed by and associated with (re)birth, and who are sometimes said to be reborn (typically as a grandson) within the family. Unlike the *pitar-purbaj*, however, the *vir* is depicted as a perfected predecessor, whose life and death are temporally distant from the singers' and whose glorious sacrifice has rendered him incomparably potent or, quite literally, virile. Thus cultic hero shrines, like some Bheruji shrines, are often draped with baby cradles given by devotees in return for impregnation. Women's *ratijaga*

---

21. Of Krishnite devotional poems, Jayadeva's *Gitagovinda* is perhaps the best known to students of Indian culture.

22. In remembering home, these heroes are unlike Greek heroes, who are remembered but do not remember (Achilles being a notable exception).

23. Associations between food and sex have been observed and analyzed by many scholars of Indian lore. For examples, see Narayan, "Singing from Separation," 36, and Trawick, *Notes on Love in a Tamil Family*, 105–106.

songs often allude to "lady pilgrims" satisfied in this way by their familial heroes at cultic shrines.

The "thick and sticky" milk pudding, it should be noted, not only expresses but also conjoins maternity and sexuality, which are so often imaged in the contrasting female icons or personae (cow/mare) of which we have spoken. The alchemical nature of milk, transmuting from breast secretion to semen emission or even saliva exchange, contributes to the song's erotic (*madhurya bhav*) charge.[24] Like the *doha* beginning, "O brave one, you drank your mother's milk, then (the nectar from) your wife's kisses," it accomplishes what divinity so often does: fluid transmutation of logical or mundane oppositions.[25]

This connection with sexuality-fertility is especially, though once again subtly, evident in the following hero song, which tells of just one such visitation. Here, however, the linkage between sex and birth is conveyed not only through milk but also through seed imagery.[26]

"O Jhunjharji, you bathed and washed your *dhoti*.[27]
O Jhunjharji, you bathed and washed it and adorned yourself."
Lord Ram's invitation came to you.

"O lovely lady, I washed my *dhoti* at the tank.
Lovely lady, under a *banyan* tree I adorned myself."
Lord Ram's invitation came to you.

"O Jhunjharji, you ate a cucumber in the field and dropped its seeds in
    the planting row.
O Jhunjharji, you dropped seeds in the planting rows."
Lord Ram's invitation came to you.

"Lovely lady, I ate the cucumber at the row.
Lovely lady, I threw the seeds on the ground."
Lord Ram's invitation came to you.

"O Jhunjharji, you left the row and went to your chambers.
O Jhunjharji, you left the row for your parlor."
Lord Ram's invitation came to you.

"Lovely lady, laughing I went to the chambers.
Lovely lady, smiling I went to the parlor."
Lord Ram's invitation came to you.

24. This charge is also found in cultic settings. For example, one song sung for the *jhunjharji* Bheru Singh (before his *bhopa* becomes possessed) compares a young woman's mother-in-law to a watchman. The woman beseeches the *jhunjharji* to hurry and meet her (before she gets caught).

25. For reflection on the associations of love, lovemaking, and milk in the Nepali context, see March, "Two Houses and the Pain of Separation in Tamang Narratives from Highland Nepal," 163–166. On milk, semen, blood, and sweat associations, and also fertility and sexuality in north India, see Alter, *The Wrestler's Body*, 148–149, 157–159; and Sax, *Mountain Goddess*, 129–148. For a south Indian example, see Shulman, *Tamil Temple Myths*, 90–110.

26. For examples of reflections on blood sacrifice and fecundity, see Shulman, *Tamil Temple Myths*, 91; Hart, *The Poems of Ancient Tamil*, 31–40; and Sax, *Mountain Goddess*, 148.

27. A *dhoti* is a long piece of cloth men wrap around their waists, which covers the thighs and sometimes the lower legs.

"O Jhunjharji, having played in the planting row, you left.
O Jhunjharji, you left the planting row to see your wife."
Lord Ram's invitation came to you.

"Lovely lady, laughing and laughing I left my playing children.
Lovely lady, smiling I left my wife."
Lord Ram's invitation came to you.

"Lovely lady, if one turns back, the *kul* (family) is shamed.
Lovely lady, one shames his mother's breast."
Lord Ram's invitation came to you.

Sung by the "Udaipur singer," this song is suffused with potency and fecundity. Its repartee places in contact with the hero a "lovely lady," who inhabits the text but is identifiable as any *ratijaga* singer. A dialogical format is common in hero songs, and sometimes appears in *ratijaga* songs for other deities. This song's lyrics, however, distinguish the hero from most guests invited by *ratijaga* songs in that they detail a homecoming by a deity who once lived a human life, one with land, wife, and children. Only the *satimata* compares in this respect.

The banter is especially intriguing as it serves to establish a second parallel, that between the lovely lady with whom he is visiting and the woman he once married. Along with land and children, he visits his wife, who is generally the one to ask a hero to "turn back" rather than go off to war. Here the question of whether to leave for war or go back home is implicitly offered by the lady who recounts the hero's visit to his wife, for the *jhunjharji* tells this lady, as he would tell a mother of his children, that were he to turn back, he would shame his family, and especially his mother.

Thus the lyrics artfully effect synchronicity, collapsing the gap between then and now in a time-warping act of visitation, construed variously. Regarded as a story sung by contemporary *ratijaga*-singing women or by some unknown lovely lady and as recalling right now the agricultural pursuits and conjugal relations that the hero had with his wife before his death—that is to say, in the past as described to the lovely lady—that past abruptly terminates as the song constructs a present moment of conversation between hero and lady in the final verse with its implicit promise of death lurking in an imminent future, and so even greater fertility in the more remote future. Like so much ritual, what happened way back when (*in illo tempore*) is made to happen here and now (*hic et nunc*) so that ritual practitioners participate in the sacred events represented in myth and commemorated by ritual.[28]

Alternatively, that moment can be viewed as transporting the singers back in time, so that they are there back then (as a lady) at the crucial and original moment of heroism; this reverses the narrative, so that the death, the subject of the

---

28. These terms are borrowed, of course, from Mircea Eliade's well-known phenomenology articulated, for example, in *The Sacred and Profane*. A comparable example from Christian lyrics is to be found in the Christmas carol whose first line is: "We three kings of Orient are."

final verse, logically precedes and explains the hero's (posthumous) visit to well, wife, and children. This, of course, comports with the way in which *ratijaga* songs take up where stories leave off. From this perspective, the song transports singers to the past, again, not through its use of past tense but by its deployment of the present tense and sense at the moment when the hero's death is predicted. In brief, from this retrospective reading, the song ends with what is typically the point of departure for *ratijaga* ritual: the hero's death, which makes him capable of conferring not simply mundane but also supermundane fertility.

The song's preoccupation with fertility links agricultural fertility to human fertility in a poetic, if blunt and blatant, way. Having bathed and washed his *dhoti*, the hero deposits his cucumber seeds into the soil, or "planting row," where it will bear new generations of cucumbers. This seed-spitting reads as a description of agricultural endeavor but also as metaphor for human procreation. In Rajasthani folklore the seedy cucumber is a well-known signifier for sperm-filled phallus. The metaphor plays on the notion prevalent in Rajasthan and throughout India that human conception occurs when a man plants his seed, basically a homunculus, in a woman's nourishing "soil" or womb. The father thus contributes the child to the line, whereas the mother sustains him in utero as well as after birth, when her milk continues the service that her soil began.[29] Her milk will be shamed if the hero does not fight and die, as mother's milk has given him the strength and will to be manly: it is responsible for this physical and mental potential and potency.[30] The hero's traditional (mimetic) suckling of his mother's breast when departing for marriage and war dramatically conveys this conviction.

The cucumber seed scene, which follows suggestively on the alluring washing-and-dressing by water episode, thus suggests and anticipates the scene that follows. Having left the planting row, the hero, "laughing" and "smiling" goes to his chambers and visits his wife, whom he evidently enjoys. This enjoyment in turn suggests and anticipates the next scene where, "laughing and laughing," he leaves his "playing children," who are in the next line reassociated with his wife. Visited in this way, she may produce more.[31]

The song concludes by stating the hero's reason for leaving his family: he must accept Lord Ram's invitation. The invitation, which is both battle order and death sentence, comes from Lord Ram and identifies the hero's battle with one that Ram fights in the *Ramayan* epic. The phrase is also used in a general way to indicate "meeting one's maker," but the literal meaning of the phrase, which recurs as striking refrain, inserts a telling dash of Vaishnavism into the mix. Many women, who, as we have seen, are more likely than their husbands to prefer vegetarian fare to meat, take Ram or some other Vaishnava deity as their *ishtadevta*. Despite the heavily Shaiva-Shakta orientation of Rajputs, particularly those in western Rajasthan, Ram and Krishna (as well as Vishnu, of

---

29. For interesting reflection on field/seed analogies, see Doniger, "Begetting on Margin."
30. See also Alter, *The Wrestler's Body*, 148–149, 157–159.
31. In one *ratijaga* pamphlet, a wife sends her husband and *jhunjharji* a letter asking him to "adorn" her bed.

whom both are incarnations) are hardly shunned. Although Rajputs sometimes express disdain for people who are first and foremost worshipers of Vishnu in his various forms, they often have images of Vaishnava deities in their homes and make pilgrimages to the much celebrated Carbhuja, Dvarakadesh, and Shri Nathji temples, which are located near Udaipur. Their deities appear along with Shiv (as Eklingji) on local lithographs and on the yearly calendars published by the Udaipur's City Palace. Moreover, in the context of the Ram Janam Bhumi agitation of the past decade, the proliferating appeal of Ram should not be dismissed or discounted.

The last point to be made about this song is that its hero "played" (*khel gyo*). This is a clear indication that the text is to be understood as an account of not only visitation in the past but also theophany in the present. The line can be read as referring to the hero's departure from the planting row where he played as a child, but it can also be imagined as a place to which he returns after death to play for a time before visiting his wife. Grown men do not "play," but children, gods, and spirits do. The hero in the fields, the one who plays, is clearly, if also, the divine revenant who is patently happy to have a lovely, if previously denied, homecoming. Furthermore, unlike the hero in the *doha* that distinguished the hero as a child who "plays alone" from the coward who requires company, this returning deity is pleased to play amid the best of company, his family, whose line now offers praise.

In a nutshell, through visitation and as evidenced by visitation, the hero is resocialized in a *bhakti* relationship with household women, and through them, with household men. Expressing and evoking desire, the hero's beauty, a subject notably neglected in men's domestic narratives, conspires with the tragedy of his death to make him a powerful and also wanted presence in the household he is to serve as guardian. Thus his death, which distinguishes him from other men, becomes a beginning for a new relationship with women that will, women hope, lead to satisfaction of women's wants, expressed with amatory nuance, and hoped-for fulfillment as well-being including, and especially, fertility.

This resocialization amid women presumes and parallels the hero's resocialization in Virgati, the reward of sacrifice and the goal that also serves as conclusion to many stories of heroic transformation. It is the locus obliquely referenced in the first *ratijaga* recited above. The song asks the hero to bring his friends, which indicates that he is not permanently isolated from men but rather thriving among other men who have accomplished the heroic scenario. Thus the hero resides in paradise, which functions as a sort of homogenizing realm where one heroic profile resembles another, much like idealized faces of heroes on Greek urns.

Enjoying themselves in the heroic *darbar*, heroes are assuredly less threatening than they would be were they required to remain solitary, their condition while struggling unto death. Rather, isolation in story initiates them into divine society, where they thrive perpetually with those they resemble.[32] It is not surprising that heroes end up enjoying company. As penal systems everywhere

---

32. Romila Thapar has observed that "heroic rituals emphasized the aggregation of the hero into the community rather than the separation, despite his deification; "Death and the Hero," 309.

recognize, isolation is a form of punishment. In India, where being alone is less possible, and arguably less desirable, than in less populated countries with nuclear families, isolation stands out as an especially disturbing prospect.

Moreover, in other contexts in India, aloneness connotes a certain illicitness.[33] It is no novel insight that in cultures where shame plays a substantial role in enforcing code, the absence of audience provides opportunities that may be scintillating or menacing. Here the insight should not be raised to the level of grand theory. It is not meant to lead to the superficial and overdetermined conclusion that India is "essentially" a shame culture.[34] Rather, it is to emphasize that in India, aloneness often connotes potential or actual transgression, as it does in the case of the solitary ascetic who in abandoning society is no longer bound by its strictures (the particularly transgressive Aghori ascetic serves as a notable case in point), or in the case of the courtesan, who is left to her own devices.

Resocialized in heaven, the hero distinguished and segregated from the living through perfection is not, then, lonely. Rather, he is satisfied by male as well as female company. Visits to his family home are therefore not returns from seclusion by a poor soul desperate for social intercourse. At routine *pujas* and *ratijagas*, heroes are welcomed as guests who are imagined as anything but pathetic, menacing, or intrusive lonely hearts.

The hero is associated not only with Virgati denizens and family members, but also with the other deities and ancestors who are *ratijaga* guests. All come to claim offerings graciously offered by the singers of their songs. In one Sagasji Bavji song, in fact, the power of some other deities attending the *ratijaga* renders the hero immortal in the first place. The following excerpt attributes the hero's divinity to Shiv, Shri Nathji (Krishna), and Mewar's tutelary goddess, here addressed by the epithet Jogmaya.[35]

> Bravo, bravo for your womb, mother-in-law!
> You delivered Sagasji Bavji.
> Shri Nathji, make him immortal, I ask you.
> Eklingji Nath [Shiv], make him immortal, I ask you.
>
> Bravo, bravo for your womb, mother-in-law.
> You delivered the King of Mewar.
> Jogmaya make him immortal. . . .

Performed by Mangi Devi, this song gives a new twist to the hero's indeterminate and shifting soteriology. Death has made him a *sagasji*, but the power of the gods has made him divine. Although I found this notion of empowerment by other deities articulated nowhere else in the many *ratijaga* songs I collected, it does lend support to the notion that the hero is no stranger to other divinities. He is a well-known and divinely recognized denizen of the beyond.

33. This is most apparent to lone female travelers on an overnight train. They are often asked the question, "You travel alone?" which is not so much interrogation as invitation to intimacy.

34. On the problematization of shame, see Herzfeld, "Honour and Shame."

35. Jogmaya: loosely, "She Who Has the Power of Illusion."

Like the previous *sagasji* song above, the song is also atypical in that it refers to a particular *sagasji* (Sarv Ritu Vilas' Sagasji Bavji), whose shrine is not
far from her home. What gives his identity away, however, is not his name but
the reference to his mother as delivering the Mewar king, a title he would have
inherited had he lived long enough. Later on (and again, like the previous *sagasji*
song), the song also refers to him as Hindupat, "Lord of the Hindus," which
also designates him as Maharana, for the Maharana is frequently imaged in
Mewari lyrics as foremost defender of Hindu *dharm* against Muslim invaders.[36]
In designating identity (which is suggested subtly, even ambiguously, in the
previous *sagasji* song) the song for an ancestral Sisodiya Rajput hero departs
from other hero songs sung by Rajput women but resembles the *ratijaga* songs
sung by devotees of cultic heroes such as Pabuji and Tejaji.[37] These songs are
to be found along with diverse songs for gods, goddesses, and ancestors in the
printed *ratijaga* pamphlets that are readily available in religious bookstalls. Although the songs for designated cultic heroes tend to incorporate more *itihasik*
particulars than the hero songs Rajput women sing of their heroic ancestors at
home, the cultic hero songs too are often overwhelmed by the singers' agendas,
as the following excerpt from a Tejaji song from the pamphlet *Ratijaga ka Git*,
illustrates.

> In the family are two big flowers.
> One is the sun, the other the moon, O Basag's Tejaji.[38]
> The sun spreads out beams.
> On a clear night the moon shines.
>
> In the family are two big flowers.
> One is the earth, one the sky.
> One rains down.
> The other grows up as fruitful barley. . . .[39]

The song continues to present a vision of paired and complicit prosperity, including cow and horse, goat and sheep. Aside from the agrarian indices of prosperity, there are signs of familial welfare, beginning with fertility but extending
to social relationships. The mother gives birth, then the father raises the child.
The brother gives his married sister a scarf, but the husband rules as lord. The
sister gives her married sister a blouse, but the husband's sister gives her
brother's wife a blessing. These pairings express an ordered social vision that is
manifestly hierarchical. According to conventional wisdom, the husband raises
the child; as socializer, he will enable his son to play his part in society. Thus
his job is "higher," as is the husband's role compared to the brother's and the
sister-in-law's compared to the sister's. The priority of marital relations over natal

---

36. This role was most visibly enacted in recent times when the previous Maharana, Bhagwat Singh,
served as president of the Vishva Hindu Parishad. For more on this, see McKean, "Bhārat Mātā," 256.

37. One maidservant who sang for me said that she knew there were songs for named heroes such as
Devnarayan, Pabuji, and Tejaji, but that these songs were not sung by Rajput women in their *ratijagas*.

38. Basag: the snake who bites Tejaji on his tongue and renders him a divinity.

39. *Rātījagā kā Gīt*, sampādak Sarasvatī Devī Bhensālī evam Jnāndevī Telī. 12.

ones is made especially clear in the last pairing, in that the sister gives only a blouse, whose sleeve is easily torn, whereas a sister-in-law gives a blessing, which "lasts forever."

In short, connected with cosmic order (sun and moon, earth and sky) are agricultural fertility (rain and barley) and social success, beginning with fertility but including domestic order. So prominent are these concerns that the prominent cultic hero Tejaji is almost completely eclipsed from sight. His name is invoked only once. His story explains his connection with fecundity and familial harmony, but is rolled up in his name, which serves minimally to evoke his story, as heroic epithet does in many Rajput songs of household heroes. The hero's death is cause for bounty and order—what more need be said?

The same conclusion is reached in another hero song from a different pamphlet, a modest collection of Marwari songs printed in Maharashtra.[40] Here a nameless *bhomiya* is beseeched by women to appear to them (give *darshan*) at the beginning and end of the song. The remainder of the song, however, is a conversation in which the specifics for growing ginger and chickpeas are discussed at length. It details where to plant them, how to water them (in this case with milk!), how to cut and transport them, how to pot them, and how to grind them.

In song the hero, resocialized into the household through ritual and into the heavenly cohort of gods through soteriology, is himself an agent of socialization. A participant in *ratijaga* ritual and a guest with other divinities, the hero is classed with a group whose presence brings together and affirms relationships between members of the household. Whether appearing in Rajput women's songs or songs printed in *ratijaga* pamphlets, lyrics frequently list, as well as enlist, the family members by their role designations. This is evident in the following excerpt from a *ratijaga* song I recorded from the young woman who, as I mentioned, described herself to me as a "little brother Rajput." Although it is not a hero song I include it here because its sole mission is to indicate the familial roles of women attending a Rajput *ratijaga*. Whatever the background of the singer, the names in the song make it clear that what is represented in the song are the voices of Rajput women.

> "Who put the wick in the lamp?
> Whose wife filled it with *ghi* (clarified butter)?"
> Light the lamp for the four watches of the night.
>
> "Bhagvat Kanvar put the wick in the lamp.
> Mahavir Singh's wife filled it with butter."
> Light the lamp for the four watches of the night. . . .

The song goes on to include all the female relatives participating in the *ratijaga* ritual. In this way they are counted as present and represented as participating in the ritual that many divinities and ancestors are attending. The song thus reads as a register of sociability in which everyone works together for the benefit of family

---

40. *Rājasthānī Lokgīt (Rātījāgā evam Vivāh)*, Bhāg 1.

and for the procurement of blessings. Furthermore, because these women are referred to not only by their own names but by their husbands', the song also underscores the fact that the activities that women are performing are intended to benefit both women as individuals and others, particularly husbands. Familial designations such as these were also evident in the "long-lasting eyes and knees" song above, where the women include as intended beneficiaries of blessings not just themselves but also various categories of household members. They are also to be found in songs for other supernatural beings.

My argument here is not that ritual generally orders social relations and creates social solidarity within the patriline, but that it *can* do so or at least be understood to do so by practitioners; this *ratijaga* song illustrates consciousness of this type of desired conviviality.[41] It represents women—designated by name but also set in their roles by virtue of marriage to their husbands—as working together harmoniously to light lamps (invite supernatural guests) so as to procure blessings. The song envisions women as embodiments and agents of familial cohesion.

This depiction indirectly but powerfully challenges the pervasive and simplistic notion that women threaten the stability and harmony of the patriline. Daughters, who as elsewhere in India are frequently referred to as "guests," marry out of the family. Coming into families as wives, they bring along their diverse ways and possibilities for conflicted loyalties. Seeking to claim the affection of their husbands, they are often represented as potential or active disrupters of loyalty to blood relations. Unrelated to other household women, whose way of doing things they may not share, they are also regularly typed as quarrelsome. In our *ratijaga* song, however, women represent themselves as constituting a cohesive structure and effecting a united purpose.

This vision of women working together in this way is prominent in Rajput women's hero songs. The following song, sung by Mangi Devi, is a good example.

> Jhunjharji's body is on the ground.
> Jhunjharji's body is on the ground.
> His feet are imprinted [on the earth].[42]
> O my dear Purbaj![43]
> Truly the *jhunjhar* fought.
>
> Your mother stops you, your mother stops you.
> "Obey my order," she says.

---

41. Rituals *can* also express and create social rifts and fault lines, of course. I am thus not presenting an unqualified Durkheimian view of ritual as expressing social effervescence. For concise discussion and illustration of ritual as potentially divisive in India, see Hanchett, "Ritual Symbols." See also various essays in Raheja and Gold, eds., *Listen to the Heron's Words*.

42. Although in combination with the image of a body on the ground, the image of the feet's last impressions suggests that the hero's struggling has stopped, the imaging of the feet as auspicious footprints foreshadows the worshiping of the hero at this site. Like ascetics, heroes are sometimes represented by their footprints, just as *satis* are represented by their handprints. Footprint images of this type are to be found at the *mahasatiyan* at Pokran.

43. Discussion of this apparent slip follows shortly.

O my dear Jhunjharji!
The *jhunjhar* struggled [fought] well.

Jhunjharji, your sisters stop you.
"Heed what we say."
O my dear Jhunjharji!
Truly the *jhunjhar* fought.

Jhunjharji, your brothers' wives stop you.
"Obey our order."
O my dear Jhunjharji!
Truly the *jhunjhar* fought.

Jhunjharji, your mother's sisters stop you.
"Obey our order."
O my dear Jhunjharji!
Truly the *jhunjhar* fought.

The song continues with various other classes of familial women attempting to stop him. No women, it seems, want to the hero to fight—even his mother. In fact, women are united in trying to stop the much-praised *jhunjharji* from becoming a *jhunjharji*. What is to be made of their efforts to preserve the life of this wondrous and useful hero-to-be?

To answer this, let us bear in mind that *ratijaga* songs please the deities, as do the food offerings accompanying them. The invitations illustrate the ever-present assumption that guests will feel indebted and come bearing gifts for the hostess, who will distribute them among family members. At the same time, however, hero songs serve as recognition of the hostesses' prior indebtedness. In one sense, at least, the invitation is a "payback" for the gift (demanded by "hardy little lasses") of unselfish heroic sacrifice.[44] Being female, the participants are members of a class whose members have already, figuratively at least, feasted on the hero now being invited back home for a feast. In league with their prior and foremost guardian, a bloodthirsty goddess, they have his blood on their hands, and she has it on her lips. Thus by *ratijaga* ritual, as well as by women's routine veneration, is completed a picture of the sacrificial hero who, along with the goddess, drinks enemy blood (that, as the *doha* explained, is his "his work"), as is also represented during Navratri-Dashara by blood sacrifice. This is made especially clear by the example of the Rajput who habitually drinks the Navratri victim's blood, but in hero worship the hero's devouring extends after he is devoured.

In sum, women working together to greet, reward, and ingratiate the hero thus reveal a certain complicity in the hero's death. The nature of this complicity, which emerges in stories, is further negotiated and qualified by women's *ratijaga* songs. Whereas stories and songs concur in their conclusion that women send heroes off to war, some songs demonstrate a dimension to this send-off

---

44. On the now commonplace association of gifting and indebtedness, see Mauss, *The Gift*. For reflections on Mauss's theory in the Indian context, see Raheja, *The Poison in the Gift*.

that is lacking in domestic heroic stories: female protest against the hero's death. This protest can be read at least two ways.

Taken in the context of story, it serves as recognition of indictment but also of desired exculpation: women are not to blame for the hero's death. This claim, voiced in the commands of various household women, can, however, be read as protesting too much and so implicitly recognizing complicity. It is, in fact, reminiscent of the various attempts by villagers in the song of Sati Godavari to prevent this non-Rajput woman from burning herself on her husband's pyre. Although it might well be in their interest to have a *satimata* in their community and receive her blessings, they repeatedly interfere with her plans and claim that they are worried she might burn down their village should she lose her nerve on the pyre and run about ablaze.[45] They also say that they fear police retribution for letting her die as a *sati*, a crime in contemporary India. The villagers, perhaps, protest too much. Reading against the grain, one might sense an interest in having her die but without appearing to have her blood on their hands.[46]

Although such a reading is sensible in the current context, it is also possible to read women's claims as revealing a desire to protect the hero from his fate and keep him alive in the family fold. Conveying the idea that woman may need, and even want, men to die as heroes, songs such as the one above also demonstrate ambivalence. Women want men, or more specifically *their* men, not to go to war, even if as these women, being women, require that men go.[47] They try to stop the hero, who succeeds despite their efforts. Hence the song imputes to women in the past affection now reflected in present admirers. After all, the hero's death is tragic, even if benefits the family.

Commanding the hero not to leave, these women point toward a convention voiced in contemporary epic and implied in the hero's recognition of his mother's milk at the time of departure. Theoretically, sons go to battle only by their mother's leave. Thus in *Pabuji*, when the warrior Harmal wishes to go to Lanka on an espionage mission for Pabuji, he travels a long distance to obtain his mother's blessing.[48] The request for leave-taking, however, turns out to be a formality. When Harmal's mother withholds her permission, he goes anyway. The same holds true for our song's hero, who goes ahead despite women's protest. The reason: he owes it to his mother's milk. His mother's denial of leave-taking is of little consequence, as are the protestations of various other women. The song above has it that he knows what she really wants or needs. Mothers, it turns out, are not very different from Dhanna-Bhinya story's matron, who commands her son to get back her livestock or die trying. Thus the matter of what

45. On benefits, including financial benefits, of *sati* immolation, see Nandy, "Sati as Profit versus Sati as a Spectacle," and also Oldenberg's response to it, "The Continuing Invention of Sati Tradition."

46. Harlan, "Satī: The Story of Godāvarī," 228–230.

47. Pabuji leaves his wedding to go to war, but his wife Phulvanti clings to his stirrup trying to prevent him; Smith, *The Epic of Pābūjī*, 423. Alf Hiltebeitel has commented on the ambivalence of the goddess in this epic: she both seems allied with Pabuji's wife and determined to take her husband away as a victim of sacrifice in battle; *Rethinking India's Oral and Classical Epics*, 107. Hiltebeitel makes a further claim: ambivalence "is itself an ironic trope" in this epic, p. 95.

48. Smith, *The Epic of Pābūjī*, 350.

women desire or require is not at all straightforward and simple in this women's song. Like life, the hero's death is figuratively, if also literally, messy.

This motif of women's thwarted prohibition is prolific in the *ratijaga* songs I recorded. I also found it in a printed source, a collection of folksongs that was published in Udaipur and contains a song that employs the same formula of protest, but associates it not only with various women but also with a man.[49]

> Sitting on the wall, your father stops you.
> "Don't go to battle, son!"
> Bhomiya, you struggled in the fight.[50]
> "I won't open my waistband.
> My mother's milk would be shamed."
> The Hindu struggled in the fight.
>
> Siting in the kitchen, your mother stops you.
> "Don't go to battle, son."
> Anndata struggled in the fight.
> "I won't undo my waistband.
> My mother's milk would be shamed."
> The Hindu struggled in the fight.
>
> Bhomiya struggled in the fight.
> His head fell and he fought as a headless trunk.
> A stream of red opium drink [blood] flowed and flowed.
> The Hindu struggled in the fight.

This song represents an interesting extension of reticence to the father, whose command, like the mother's, a good son is supposed to heed. Nevertheless, the hero-to-be disobeys him, just as he does his mother. The reason for disobedience remains the same as in the previous song: by declining to fight, the young man would shame his mother's milk. In this song, turning back from war is represented as opening a waistband, in which is secured the hero's dagger. Thus women are once again prominent in motivating, if also lamenting, a hero's leave-taking.

This song is entirely focused on two things. The first is the hero's departure for war, presumably war with Muslims, as his identification as a Hindu suggests. The second is death, about which it provides grisly details atypical of lyrics in women's songs. At the same time, it does point to an auspicious future in that his blood, represented as opium drink—which as we have seen is consumed by some heroes before war and imbibed by some cultic *bhopas* before possession—"flowed and flowed." The flowing liquid is a matrix of transition (the hero's transformation) and of fruition, for this liquid will nourish the soil and bear forth fruit. In fact, the notion that the hero's blood admixes with earth, sanctifies it, and nourishes it is a common one in *dohas* and cultic worship. If women's tears water heroes' graves in "Pirates of Penzance," here the hero's

---

49. *Rājasthānī Lokgīt*, Bhāg 2. *Sampādak, Śivsinh Coyal.*
50. "Struggled in the fight": *junjiya jhagade.*

own liquid, blood, "waters" the soil, which is enhanced and enriched even as the women he leaves behind weep for him.[51]

Whether seen as causes of death or protesting and lamenting victims of the hero's death, women are represented in *ratijaga* songs as blessed by the hero and receiving from him the ability to extend and order family life. Singing hero songs, women enlist the hero who, having sacrificed his life, becomes an agent who catalyzes sociability, starting with familial concord. Women's rituals are seen to effect this sociability, which begins at home and proceeds outward to the community, in a way that parallels and supports the socializing role that men play, as the Tejaji song indicates.

Given this fact, we should not be surprised to find that women's *ratijaga* songs often paint a picture of communal cooperation and harmony. This theme is prevalent in other *ratijaga* songs, particularly those for Bheruji, whose worship is performed in a cultic setting by people from diverse backgrounds, though it is relatively muted in hero songs, perhaps because Rajput hero worship is so closely associated with family rather than cult in the Rajput context. Nevertheless, the theme is found in Sarv Ritu Vilas's Sagasji Bavji song above. This hero's profile as a cultic (as well as household) deity, together with his status as son of the Maharana, may help explain the salient expression of cohesive community. Having exclaimed "bravo, bravo" for the womb of the mother-in-law who bore the hero, and having asked Shri Nathji, Eklingji, and Jogmaya to grant him immortality, the song continues:

> "Buy some flowers from the gardener's [Mali's] store.
> Call the gardener, the gardener clever and wise."
> The servant brought the flowers.

Mangi Devi's song then proceeds to describe the contributions made by members of other communities, such as lavish ornaments from the goldsmith and *pan* from the *pan*-seller, who are both "clever and wise." Thus these various classes of people, whose wares are ingredients in hero worship in any context, are represented in the most positive terms: they are all clever and wise. They are good devotees now, as they were good subjects of their king, described as "Lord of the Hindus," back then. The effect is a utopian vision of caste relations with a Rajput god who requires their service and effects cooperation among them as they ply their trades. Thus, to summarize, the hero who has been removed from society through story is represented in song as restored, resocialized, and reintegrated into a slew of social relationships that he renews, socializes, and integrates.

This brings us to the second task before us, which is to construe the heroes of song in the context of other figures with whom they are affiliated in women's *ratijaga*s. Having gained familiarity with some of these in the chapters on nar-

---

51. In heroic poetry, soil mixed with heroic blood (which is often said to "flow in rivers") is sometimes imaged as reddish *khicadi*, a moist combination of rice mixed with lentils. On the wrestler's sweat (and other transmutable liquids) nourishing soil, see Alter, *The Wrestler's Body*, 148–149, 157–159.

rative, we are now prepared to appreciate ways in which lyrics indicate additional or divergent representations of the heroes, whose songs are connected through *ratijaga* ritual sequencing to other songs sharing motifs and formulae. The list will diverge in certain respects from the one in the previous chapter because it reflects my desire to analyze intertextual dynamics of women's songs within the *ratijaga* context. Thus, for example, there is no discussion of ascetic elements, which are patently absent in women's *ratijaga* songs. Nor is there discussion of criminal elements, though the transgressive is certainly suggested; here, however, transgression is linked to the absence of asceticism and the presence of patent sensuality. The order of characters who are common contextual referents will also differ between this and the second narrative chapter, simply because a desire for symmetry between chapters loses out to a strategy of exploring in depth internal frames of reference in *ratijaga* songs. Nevertheless, I will pursue points of comparison with narrative as they arise in discussion of some of the nonhero songs serving as these frames of reference. Let us begin with those most "near and dear" to *ratijaga* performers: ancestors.

Ancestors: Commingling *Pitar-Purbaj*

Perhaps the best way to begin is to note the anomalous and unrepeated invocation of *jhunjharji* as *purbaj* in a *jhunjharji* song already investigated. Recall the song's beginning.

> Jhunjharji's body is on the ground.
> Jhunjharji's body is on the ground.
> His feet are imprinted [on the earth].
> O my dear Purbaj!
> Truly the *jhunjhar* fought.

The singer, who refers to the hero as Jhunjharji three times in the verse, also addresses him, "O my dear Purbaj." One may look at this little discrepancy as an unintentional slip, which in large part it may be, but as in what have been commonly and (often too) loosely called Freudian slips, it is telling. As we know, women's songs effectively eradicate fearsome individuality and render the hero a socialized and sociable being who, it is hoped, will bring his friends to the *ratijaga*. A sufficiently affable being, the hero no longer stands apart from the family, or from others for that matter. Thus it is by no means startling that his ancestral status would be stressed and his heroic identity closely connected with *purbaj*, along with whom heroes are worshiped in many families on the new moon night. In fact, in many if not most songs, ancestors are overwhelmingly summoned together as a group, from which they are not individually distinguished.

> Under a mango branch beside Lake Pichola,
> My ancestors enjoy themselves.
> "Come for your *ratijaga*.

> For your *ratijaga* we feed our *gotra* (lineage) members the cold and the
>   warm [food].
> Relatives come and wait for you.
> Come, *putaran* (sons) for your night wake."
>
> Under a mango branch, beside Lake Pichola,
> My ancestors enjoy themselves.
> "Come, sons, for your night wake.
> For your *ratijaga* we feed our lineage members the cool and the warm.
> Married women are coming and waiting on you.
> Come, sons, for your *ratijaga* . . ."

The song then repeats the last stanza, substituting *satimata* for ancestors and then moving on to invite other *ratijaga* guests. As Mangi Devi, who sang it for me (but grew tired of it after singing just two verses because she had already sung for an hour on a hot afternoon) explained, "this song is long and wide." She said the song could be adapted to accommodate different families' *ishtadevtas* or "chosen deities."

In addition to the obvious fact that all the ancestors from the *gotra* are invited together, several other things are worth noting. First, like the song of the cucumber-spitting *jhunjharji*, it begins with a water scene. As is the case with heroes, ancestors are often placed in a pleasing, shaded spot near water and so that they can enjoy themselves, feel comfortable, and remain pleasant. Satisfied with their location and with routine veneration by descendants, they are expected to interfere minimally with family affairs, unless asked. This particular song represents female relatives of ancestors as awaiting their arrival for a sumptuous *ratijaga* feast. Thus, although they are summoned by song from *pitarlok*, the "world of the ancestors" where they reside until reincarnation, they are called from the site of their earthly settlement.[52]

Second, in this song the *pitars* are addressed as *putars*, sons. This is no mere slip. The song clearly images these ancestors as sons of the patriline. The effect is twofold. First, it effectively represents these ancestors as young. Employing the word *putar* (Sanskrit *putr*), it suggests youth, which sheds further light on the first "slip" mentioned above, the substitution of *purbaj* for *jhunjharji*. As we saw from Ann Gold's work, villagers often conflate *jhunjharji* and *purbaj* categories so that those whom villagers usually call *jhunjharji*s are youths who die before marriage. According to Gold, calling a *jhunjharji* a *purbaj* flatters the *jhunjharji*, whereas in our context calling a *jhunjharji* who has died in battle a *purbaj* is a considerable demotion, as it would be in the case of a *satimata*.[53] The equation may have arisen from the singer's experience performing for people other than Rajputs, who are very particular about retaining the martial

---

52. Dual location is common in religions. For example, many Christians who believe that their departed dear ones dwell in heaven may also visit them at graves.

53. That likening those who died unheroic deaths to heroes flatters the unextraordinary dead is also recognized in Tamil Cankam literature, which describes the mutilation of corpses to provide the appearance of death in battle. Private communication from David Shulman, August 20, 2000.

context for attainment of the title *jhunjharji*. More probably, it simply points out that it would be unthinkably rude to exclude heroes from the feast that celebrates and propitiates forebears.

The second effect is to limit the category of *putar* to males. This points to a telling ambiguity. Although *pitar-purbaj* songs are sometimes referred to as "*pitar-pitrani*," that is, "male and female ancestor" songs, female ancestors simply seem to vanish in these songs. Female revenants tend to be assigned to other categories such as *satis*, who merit their own *ratijaga* songs, and as various other sorts of problematic and not easily pleased female spirits, who do not receive *ratijaga* songs and are not welcome during auspicious occasions. Among these are women dying in childbirth (who may trouble pregnant women, cause miscarriages, and harm newborns) and dead women whose husbands remarry (and find that their new brides suffer various mysterious maladies). Troublesome women like these are usually rendered benign by the same measures that are used for the male ghosts, at which point they are subsumed within the general (masculine) category of *purbaj*.[54] This subsuming of gender has a familiar analogue in genealogy. Generations ago, male genealogists and bards, who are thought of as recording family history, typically recorded the deeds of Rajput men, but not of Rajput women. Like the English pronoun "he," the classification of ancestral songs, which theoretically includes women, tends to erase them or dispatch them to another marked category. Some Rajput families employed Ranimangas, genealogists who recorded the names of familial women, but as patronage has declined and genealogists have overwhelmingly been forced to take "day jobs," finding Ranimangas has become a daunting endeavor.

Having noted how patrilineal genealogy both encompasses and overwhelms female gender identity (even) in women's songs, let us turn to ways in which women's *ratijaga* rituals juxtapose and assess the heroes vis-à-vis the *purbaj*. As the songs above have shown, heroes are idealized and thrilling figures, alluringly attired. Garbed as stunning bridegrooms with dangling *lalas* and flashy watches, these heroes have died perfect deaths at the very peak of human potential, the age of marriage, when one is no longer growing as a child but not yet growing old and decaying. Depicted as utterly ripe and at the cusp of manhood, the generic hero of whom women sing is akin to the divine playboy Krishna, for example, in Jayadeva's *Gitagovinda*, a Sanskrit rendering of the relationship between Krishna and Radha, who is both "babysitter" told by Krishna's father Nanda to take Krishna home and nubile playmate with whom he has a tumultuous erotic relationship. Ancestors, however, are not imaged as ripe and alluring. They are lineage sons, waited on by married women. Whether literally young at death (which may mean greater reluctance to move on in the cycle of transmigration) or metaphorically young (as with the American Revolution's "Sons of Liberty"), the dominant image of son in ancestor songs conveys an affection that is not erotic.

54. On the rare phenomenon of patently active female ancestors, see Gold, *Fruitful Journeys*, 67–68.

Lacking the *jhunjharji*'s "nice pants and attractive pajama string," ancestors are connected with fertility, which is evident in the following very popular ancestor song, of which I collected many variants. This particular song, which singles out a *purbaj* but does not identify him, renders him not a son but a "brother" responsible for various types of progeneration.

> My ancestor came to the gullies near my house.
> I spread flowers, *campa* flower buds.[55]
> My ancestor was welcomed.
>
> My ancestor came to my cow pen.
> The cows gave birth to a white bullock and she-calf.
> My ancestor was welcomed.
>
> My ancestor came to my buffalo pen.
> One of the buffaloes gave birth to a brown she-calf.
> My ancestor was welcomed.
>
> My ancestor came to my horse stable.
> One of the horses gave birth to a sweet little colt.
> My ancestor was welcomed.
>
> My ancestor came to my elephant stable.
> The elephant gave birth to a virile [*mast*] calf.
> My ancestor was welcomed.
>
> My ancestor came to my daughters' houses.
> A daughter gave birth to my dutiful grandson.
> My ancestor was welcomed.
>
> My ancestor came to my daughters-in-law's quarters.
> A daughter-in-law gave birth to a beloved grandson.
> My ancestor was welcomed.
>
> My ancestor came to my home's storage room.
> He brought crops, wealth, and good fortune [Lakshmi].
> My ancestor was welcomed.
>
> My ancestor came to my stove and water-storage area.
> The boiled milk overflowed.
> My ancestor was welcomed.
>
> My ancestor came to my son's cradle.
> My son was playing and he started to cry.
> My ancestor was welcomed.
>
> "My ancestor, do you have unfulfilled desires?
> Or did you fight alone in a deserted forest?"
> My ancestor was welcomed.

---

55. *Campa* flowers, from the tree *michelia campa*, are light yellow to white and are known for their sweet fragrance; see Chaturvedi and Tiwari, eds., *A Practical Hindi-English Dictionary*, s.v.

"My sisters, I did not fight in the forest.
And I do not have unfulfilled desires."
The ancestor was welcomed.

These lyrics, known to all the singers who performed for me but performed here by the "palace performer," identify salient elements of the good life. To begin with, there are abundant progeny. After the ancestor visits various places, females give birth to offspring of the most valuable sex in each category. Both bullock and cow are desirable, but with buffaloes, there is preference for the she-buffalo, which can lactate as well as work. Also wanted are male elephants and horses, which are stronger and bigger than their female counterparts. And then, of course, there are the ever-desirable grandsons, born to daughters and to daughters-in-law.

The song then presents one of the most common metaphors for overall plenty: overflowing milk. This image follows and essentializes the benefits described in the previous stanzas: offspring, crops, wealth, and good fortune. Serving the same purpose is another convention that frequently appears in *ratijaga* songs, that of doubling. After a visitation, the supplicant finds that various resources have multiplied in this way. This common convention is also illustrated by verses from a *pitar* song in a printed *ratijaga* pamphlet, which attributes the doubling to the crowds of ancestors. In this song a woman says she cooked *lapsi* (here not called "thick and sticky") for her *pitars*, who "came all together" and then, "having finished eating and washed their hands . . . were satisfied" and so doubled the volume of what was previously in her *lapsi* pot. She then offered them *kesar-kumkum* (saffron-rouge), which they accepted for *tikas* (auspicious forehead markings). Satisfied with these, they doubled them. The song then zooms in one of the ancestors, a "little *pitar* boy" and asks for the boon that the family will multiply and "spread like the *nim* tree," "like the *bel* bush," and "like green coconuts hanging down in chains."[56] Once again plenty is associated with lots of ancestors, but in this printed song the singer singles out one particular boy to ask for a blessing. And again we see the *ratijaga* singers relating to ancestors as honorific contemporaries, in this case, dear sons.

By contrast, the last verse of the song translated above identifies the singers as "sisters," thus envisioning the ancestor as brother, and so either focusing on the relationship between daughters born to the family and their brothers in the patriline or distancing the ancestor from in-marrying women, who are reconfigured as "sister" rather than sexually active wife—or perhaps both. In any case, the ordinary ancestral "brothers," among whom are recently deceased male relatives, are not easily or comfortably deemed alluring, however much their visitation may be tied to fertility (green coconuts and the like). With the help of deceased "sons" or "brothers," generations proliferate.

Having emphasized the benefits of ancestral cooperation, however, we should note a discordant note in the translated "doubling" song. After express-

---

56. *Rātijagā kā Gīt*, p. 3.

ing gratitude for so many blessings, the song describes an ancestor's visit to a baby, who cries in his cradle when the ancestor appears. Tears are a completely understandable response to what is, after all, a sort of haunting. When the ancestor's visit produced good results, the "ancestor was welcomed." From the song, however, it is unclear whether the welcome preceded or succeeded the blessings: both worshipers and ancestors return gifts in a cycle of blessings and hospitality, and, as always, indebtedness fuels any such cycle. Whatever the case, the ancestor was evidently not welcomed by the child, who seems to have acted like the fabled boy who pointed out that the emperor wore no clothes. The child reflects uncertainly about visits by ancestors who, as the next line indicates, might have "unfulfilled desires" and so wander about restlessly, causing mischief because they envy the living. As an offering, the *ratijaga* song welcomes the ancestor and stresses repeatedly that he has been welcomed: it constitutes ritual placation. Properly attended, he should be favorably disposed to supplicants. *Ratijaga* songs do not portray ancestors as being other than beneficent. Properly attended, they should be favorably disposed to supplicants. Hence, as it is bound to turn out, this particular ancestor is represented as having no unfulfilled desires, a foregone conclusion in lyrics designed to please and pacify. Inquisition does not end here, however. The song asks whether the ancestor "fought alone in the forest," an ascription commonly found in hero songs. The ancestor, however, denies that he fought and died alone; as the lack of heroic epithets already makes clear, he is not a hero.

The song presents "dying alone in the forest" and "having unfulfilled desires" as two separate matters, as indicated by the use of the word "or." Nevertheless, the juxtaposition of questions serves to reveal the potential for association or identification illustrated elsewhere. In the following and final ancestral song, sung by Mangi Devi, the potential is actualized.

> "Where did you wash your *dhoti*, O Muga [ancestor]?
> Where did you stay in the deserted forest?
> Where did you wash your *dhoti*?"
> "I washed it at the tank.
> I dried it on the wall."
> "Why did you stay in the deserted forest?"
>
> "Where did you eat a cucumber?
> Where did you throw the seeds, O Lord?
> Where did you eat a cucumber?
> Where did you throw the seeds?
> Why did you stay in a deserted forest?"
>
> "I ate the cucumber at the tank.
> On the wall I threw the seeds down.
> I washed my *dhoti* at the tank
> I dried it on the wall. . . ."

This song should sound familiar. It is in many respects similar to the *jhunjharji* "cucumber song" encountered above. Moreover it asks, "Why did you stay in the deserted forest?" This time it does not ask whether the ancestor was alone but rather why he was alone, presuming that in fact the ancestor did die alone. No mention of fighting is made, however. The circumstances of the ancestor's death are mysterious, which is not, in general, a good thing. Dying alone may mean dying without suitable preparation for death and without proper attention after death, which is troubling in the case of a nonheroic and thus nonsacrificial death.[57] This means that the ancestor might not have been rendered a *proper* sacrifice by the cremation *samskar*, a word that connotes completion, transformation, and perfection. These circumstances are troubling, given the prevalent typology of timely/untimely death. In the case of heroes, we saw, the typology is problematic. This song demonstrates the transparency of the line between good and bad death in the case of ancestors. As in the case of the woman whose husband predeceases her although she dies a *suti*, and so is referred to as a *sahagamini* (one who "goes with" her husband), an ancestor whose terms of death are evidently troublesome can be rendered a beneficent *pitar* through ritual. Ceremonially settled in a comforting spot and then duly attended, he may be rendered an asset. He will then be interpreted not as a ghost who wanders about tormenting people but rather, like Chatriya Bavji, as a source of supermundane power that can be channeled in a constructive and positive way. In our song, the ancestor is located near a tank and by a wall, that is to say, at a property's periphery. He is placed at a pleasant place, where he can do his laundry and also spread his seeds.

Although the song speaks of *dhoti* and cucumber, both clearly associated with fertility as they were in the *jhunjharji* "cucumber song," here there is no spicy and suggestive banter between man and "lovely lady." Nor is there any "laughing and smiling" visitation. As is typically true of visiting ancestors (and frequently untrue of heroes and Bherujis), fertility overshadows, if it does not substitute for, sexuality. In this song both seed and *dhoti* connote human (if also agricultural) conception, but the song lacks the bridegroom-hero songs' breathy innuendo.

In all of the ancestor songs above, little distinguishes the ancestors of Rajputs from those of many other castes who perform *ratijaga* songs. Questions as to the circumstances faced at death point to the possibility of heroic death, which is a stronger possibility with Rajputs than others given Rajput caste *dharm* and martial history, but Rajput ancestors who die not as *virs* but as victims of accident or illness are sung to, as are ancestors propitiated by members of other castes performing *ratijagas*. Moreover, Rajput or not, many nonheroic ancestors are flattered with memorials that deploy hero iconography. In the neighborhood where I lived during various research trips, there was a large shrine to a (nonheroic) ancestor in the Dhobi (washerman) caste. Then there are the royal cenotaphs at Ahar, where kings merit hero-type stelai whatever the circumstances of their deaths. And let us not forget the reputed Rajput smuggler who

---

57. "A man dying alone" is described in the Bharatiya Lok Kala Mandal's chart of people worshiped after death as belonging to a category of ancestor.

died in an accident, not in battle, but whose legend has begun to reconfigure him as "road warrior," a process facilitated by the deployment of heroic iconography on his memorial stone. Whatever the possibilities for identification and the development of legend, deities are categorized by song, even as they reveal the fluidity of designation in interrogatories such as: did you die alone in a deserted forest? We know that the deity invited to the *ratijaga* belongs to a certain category by virtue of the fact that he is being sung a particular type of song—a hero song, a *pitar-purbaj* song, and so on. Nevertheless, the use of shared formulae as well as questions about the circumstances of death point to the inadequacy or fuzziness of all conceptual categorization. Things are never as neat as they should be, and here is expressed a measure of anxiety. Moreover, the child who cries when a blessing-bestowing ancestor arrives indicates what everyone knows: ordinarily, at least, the dead do not belong among the living. Perfected or not, they should limit their stays to short and useful visits. Like living guests, they can wear out their welcome, especially if they do not contribute to hostesses' families in some way.

Another point of similarity between hero songs and ancestor songs is that like hero songs, ancestor songs portray a picture of ideal social relations. In the following song sung by the "Udaipur singer," familial harmony is signified by appearances made by an ancestor in various familial gardens, that is to say, pieces of land that belong to a woman's male relatives. The image of the verdant garden as a place for a *purbaj*'s visit conjoins social cohesion with horticultural bounty, each of which contributes to or reflects the other.

> "In my paternal grandfather's garden, O King,
> Flowers are spread, my King,
> *Mogra* buds, O Purbaj, O King."
> "Expensive or cheap, bring them; they'll do nicely."
> "A rupee for a half *ser*, O King."
>
> "In my paternal uncle's garden, O King . . . "

The song goes on with other verses that substitute different male relatives, including brother, maternal uncle, elder sister's husband, maternal grandfather, and so forth, for paternal grandfather and uncle. Thus once again we see the way in which the *ratijaga* song lays out a social map of the female singer's world. Although presenting a socially conservative image of family with all male relatives (who own land or might inherit it) being privileged over women, it simultaneously goes against the grain in that like some hero songs, it includes in its list of relations to be supernaturally blessed not only members of the husband's family but also members of their fathers' and mothers'. The inclusion displays loyalties to blood relatives that are maintained after marriage. This sort of representation can strike male members of the patriline at times as revealing a conflict of interest. I say "can" because the impression of conflict of interest may depend on whether a man is thinking of himself at any given moment as a husband or a brother. The loyalty of sisters to their natal families, and especially their dear, protective brothers, may seem appropriate to brothers, but the loyalty of the same men's wives to their brothers may seem inherently disloyal.[58]

Although perhaps not patently revolutionary, the inclusion of names from women's families effectively, if subtly, recenters kinship configuration and problematizes the representation of married women as "other" to their blood relations.[59] Family is not imaged simply as the patriline with women moving across margins. Instead, it is constructed from the perspective of a woman in the center with men from various related families constituting her rather fluid or alchemical social margins. The ancestors who frequent women's lyrics thus preserve generations of families sketched on this map from the perspectives of women singers performing auspicious ritual traditions that often conjoin, as well as distinguish, social constellations and demonstrate loyalties outside the realm of in-laws.

To sum up, familiarization with women's ancestral songs as well as with hero songs provides entry into the present-tense world of women's ritual veneration, in which fecundity, fertility, and prosperity for women and their relations are key concerns addressed by quite present revenants. This is a very different world from the realm of heroic story, where the details of what happened to and among predecessors as they met death is of concern and can be deployed to garner glory and support status. In ancestor songs, as with hero songs, death is imaged typically not as the climax of life but rather as a point of departure for worship, from which milk is made to overflow.[60]

Moreover, in the case of ancestors, as well as in the case of heroes, women's songs tend to deemphasize individual identity and emphasize social roles or genres. Ancestors are depersonalized through epithet and their tendency to throng in crowds. The same holds true for heroes, but with heroes, homogenization also occurs through idealization. The hero's unworldly (*alaukik*) beauty serves to join heroes into their own society of incomparably beautiful martial men. The virility manifest in the perfected heroic persona prompts a lyrical steaminess that belies the saffron turban. Having died alone and maybe even in a deserted place, the hero now has his homecoming in the form of women's breathy *bhakti*. Little wonder then that the hero's songs share much with the songs women sing for the sexually precocious trickster Bheruji.

Bheruji: Frolicking in the Garden

Kalaji has come playing, Goraji is frolicking.
The potter's daughter is his friend, she's bringing a golden pot.
Bheruji is in the garden, Bheruji is in the garden.
Kalaji has come playing, Goraji is frolicking about.

58. On dual positioning and shifting solidarities, see Raheja, "Negotiated Solidarities."
59. See also Raheja, "Negotiated Solidarities," 181.
60. For further examples of milk imagery in ancestor songs, see Gold, *Fruitful Journeys*, 72–75.

Bheruji is in the garden, Bheruji is in the garden.
The potter's daughter is his friend, she's bringing two pots.
Bheruji is in the garden, Bheruji is in the garden.
That lustful Bheruji is in the garden, Bheruji is in the garden.

Kalaji has come playing, Goraji is frolicking about.
Bheruji is in the garden, Bheruji is in the garden.
The gardener's daughter is his friend, she's bringing a garland.
Bheruji is in the garden, Bheruji is in the garden. . . .

This song, sung by Mangi Devi, goes on to repeat this final verse but substitute women from various other castes and professions, including the goldsmith's daughter bringing necklaces, the pan-seller's daughter offering *pan*, the carpenter's daughter carrying chairs, the sweet-seller's daughter providing delectables, and the liquor seller's daughter toting spirits.

As in the case of one hero song we reviewed, this popular Bheruji song, of which I collected various close versions, links together members of the community in a utopian model of organic solidarity. Under Bheruji's direction, everybody works together on designated tasks, and society prospers. At the same time, however, we have in these songs a socially transgressive Bheruji, who is a consummate trickster. Although the song splits Bheru into Kalaji and Goraji, which calls attention to Bheruji's double persona, Bheruji is also hailed in the singular and described as cavorting in the garden with various young girls he "befriends" after receiving their pots, connoting fecundity and prosperity, as well as other delights, such as *pan*, sweets, and liquor. In women's songs, this lustful Bheruji dominates the renunciatory Bheruji who appears, for example, as Bheru Nath in the Kallaji hero cult traditions, and simply as Goraji in Bheru cult traditions as well as in women's songs. Thus the Bheruji featured in *ratijagas* is the Bheruji most directly associated with sexual desire, dalliance, and reproduction.

Whereas the Bheruji of so many songs is coarse and randy in comparison with the perfected and idealized hero, he is described in at least one song I recorded as sharing the hero's sartorial style:

"Oh Bheruji Bavji, your turban is striking.
Oh Bheruji Bavji, your turban is striking.
Oh Giver of Grain, let me see your turban ornament all night."

"Gujar girl, I can't stay the whole night.
Gujar girl, I can't stay the whole night.
Oh Candraval Gujar girl, my temple is empty."

"If your temple is empty, send a *bhopa*.
If your temple is empty, send his assistant (*hazuriya*)."

"With a silken cord I will bind you.
Bheruji Bavji, your turban pearl is lovely.
Bheruji Bavji, your necklace is lovely.
Let me see your *lala*s all night. . . ."

In this head-to-toe description in a *ratijaga* song sung by the "Udaipur singer," Bheruji is praised for his lovely turban, turban ornament, necklace, *lalas*, bracelets, pajama string, horse, and shoes. The verbal icon makes him a dead ringer for the Rajput ancestral hero. Both Bheruji songs, however, describe a Bheruji who differs from domestic heroes, and markedly so. The first song depicts a devotee's relentless longing for a union that she expects Bheruji will grant because, despite his associations with asceticism (through his Goraji epithet) this Bheruji (as Kalaji) has "befriended" all sorts of girls. The ancestral hero, however, is portrayed as favoring the women of the line from which he came and to which he lends luster.

The second song acknowledges a woman's longing for a tryst with Bheruji, but denies the woman an opportunity. Bheruji will not stay the night because of his concern (feigned or not) for his cult. Thus Bheruji puts her off repeatedly, protesting that if he stays with her, his shrine (*devra*) will be empty. She tells him to send a *bhopa* to represent him or, if the *bhopa* is busy, to send the *bhopa*'s assistant. Nevertheless, he continues to complain that his temple needs him. Thus eroticism in the song is both admitted and thwarted, which, if anything, seems to extend and intensify the longing.

This song is sung by Rajputs, and also for them by Dholins and maidservants, yet it describes a dialogue between Bheruji and a Gujar girl, a patently brazen Gujar girl. Thus in this case at least, no Rajput women are directly implicated as "frolicking" with Bheruji, any more than they are in the previous song, which sings of liaisons between Bheruji and various low-caste girls.[61] Thus Bheruji's base carryings on are described as occurring elsewhere, even as the benefits of Bheruji worship are claimed by the Rajput women who participate in *ratijagas*. Despite the relationship between *ratijaga* singers and Bheruji that the song finesses, he is very much the cultic Bheruji attended by a plethora of castes, including and perhaps especially the relatively low castes enumerated in the "befriending" song.

The following song about another locative Bheruji makes the point about cultic commonality well. Sung by Mangi Devi, it deploys no surrogates from lower castes to express longing. Although a cultic figure, this Bheruji is like the ancestral hero in that he receives a direct petition from a woman with whom the singer is, as in so many hero songs, implicitly but poignantly identified. It employs the familiar food-as-sex euphemism that synchronizes and identifies two "playing in the garden" scenarios: eating and "eating." Taken together with songs that enlist surrogates (however transparent), it demonstrates the ambivalence that women who hold modesty dear feel about Bheruji worship.[62] The song represents a shift in perspective whereby desire wins out over decorum. Its longing woman asks Bheruji to come to her, and then reports the results to a friend.

---

61. Ann Gold recorded a Kala-Gora song that begins with an encounter between a "very juicy" Bheruji and a Brahmin girl, then mentions "Gardener, Wine seller, Washerwoman, Potter, and Rajput"; *Fruitful Journeys*, 258. Gold does not identify the singer(s) but, given my experience among Rajputs, I would guess that members of other castes would be more likely to include Rajputs than Rajputs would.

62. On the "fuzzy borders" of desire and shame in women's songs, see Gold, "Outspoken Women," 109.

O Saffron-donning One, appear to me (give me *darshan*).
O Intoxicated One (Matvala), appear to me.
When you appear, give me refuge, keep me from pain and affliction.
O Bheru, intoxicated one, appear to me.

Today, O friend, I saw Bheruji in the garden of Bundi fort.
Pomegranates, raisins, sweet limes, he tore open, playing in the
    garden. . . .

Whereas the first verse of this song depicts a woman asking Bheruji to manifest himself and deliver her from vague, potential difficulty, the second is more suggestive. It describes him as tearing open pomegranates and other "fruits," metaphors no more subtle than seedy cucumbers. Later the song makes transgressive sexuality even more obvious as the nameless narrator describes her nocturnal tryst with Bheruji, which, she says, must be a secret from her mother-in-law. (How different this situation is from that of Rajput hero songs' resocialized hero, whose presence among [familial] women is represented as steamy but not secretive.) Thus, however cautious and veiled some *ratijaga* songs sung by and for Rajputs may be, others portray petitioning women as libidinous (Gujar girl- or *gopi*-like) revelers. Thus the identification of women shifts according to context; some songs preserve the singers' modesty (*laj*) while attributing lust to lower-caste people, and other songs represent all female singers as abandoning modesty to unrestrained desire.

The gendered solidarity effected by the lack of caste names in a song about a cultic Bheruji reflects, in any case, the unison effected by the fact that Rajput women do not sing alone and by themselves. Musicians' and maidservants' voices admix with Rajput women's; thus, for example, all voices intermittently coalesce in the first person narrative about "playing in the garden." In the wee hours of the morning, Rajput women's voices become fewer and fewer—and those of servants and musicians, also inviting Rajput family deities, become comparatively stronger—as hostesses and guests increasingly drift into slumber. And although, it is true, the joining of voices in a crowd can also be construed to distance Rajput women from the desire expressed most steadily by professional, lower-caste musicians and maidservants, it is also true that many Rajput women know, sing, and lay claim to these sexy Bheruji songs, just as they do hero songs.

This brings us to the matter of resemblance between our last Bheruji song and hero traditions encountered so far. That Rajputs identify divinized heroes and Bherujis in some contexts helps explain and support this song's utilization of formulae found in various hero traditions. The song begins, "Oh Saffron-donning One," an image that combines with intoxication, described in the next line, to make this Bheruji resemble the "saffron-donning . . . ruddy struggler" or *jhunjharji*, discussed above, or any hero for that matter. At the same time, it evokes the ascetic aspect of Bheruji and hero, which has already been thoroughly explored. Patently ambiguous and shifting, Bheruji the warrior-ascetic, like the hero and so many Shaiva deities, turns out to be a terrible tease.

The connection between the two divinities, which is so prevalent a presumption in informal social discourse, I also found in the collection of Rajasthani *ratijaga* songs printed in Maharashtra. In this text, the hero and Bheruji songs share telling formulae. One *jhunjharji* song, in which devotees address a cultic *jhunjharji* worshiped at a temple, proclaims "pilgrims come to you . . . Jhunjharji." It then describes these ladies as bringing their "newborn sons" to the hero's temple and giving offerings of one-rupee coins and sweets.[63] The implication is that the *jhunjharji* is to be thanked and rewarded for giving these women their little boy babies. Then in a Bheruji song from the same pamphlet, we find once again that female pilgrims come to Bheruji's temple and that (in a subtle variation) they have "babies with new hair" who are "sitting on their laps."[64] Here Bheruji functions as a hero functions, that is, to produce offspring, and so the two are implicitly likened through shared motifs and formulae. In the printed songs, unlike Rajput women's songs, however, the hero is explicitly rendered a cult figure, which makes his blessings available to nonfamilial women, as are the blessings of the cultic Bherujis of whom both Rajput and non-Rajput women sing.

It is interesting that the connection between the songs sung by socially privileged Rajput women and the songs sung by other women, including those who might happen to buy a song pamphlet, is suggested in the Maharashtra collection. It contains another Bheruji song, one that does not share the "lady pilgrims" formula with the *jhunjharji* song in which lady pilgrims are featured, but does share another element: in both songs, the king is said to have made [donated] the temple's (two-*gaj*, "yard") foundation.[65] In this song, in which Bheruji asks the liquor-seller's wife to bring him a cup of liquor, the oil-seller's wife to bring him oil, and so forth, the diversity of communal involvement is stressed, as it is in the songs sung by Rajput women; at the same time, it issues an order to tell the non-Rajput women of the king's household to sing *ratijaga* songs. Thus having begun with the line "The king said, 'dig a . . . foundation,'" the song ends, "Tell the maidservants to sing auspicious songs." Here the singing of auspicious songs by maidservants in the king's household is featured as a paradigm for emulation by other women. When maidservants sing these songs in a Rajput home, we know, familial women do so as well. Moreover, whether maidservants accompany Rajput women or vice versa, familial women are the primary patrons of these maidservants and the hostesses of the deities that the songs invoke. In any case, the song portrays the palace as the primary, or at least the prior, place for all women's celebration of this distinguished Bheruji with his diminutive shrine.[66]

63. *Rājasthānī Lokgīt (Rātījagā evam Vivāh)*, Bhāg I, 31–32. A text for general consumption would, of course, depict a cultic, not a domestic, hero, who would bless those who sing his printed songs.

64. *Rājasthānī Lokgīt (Rātījagā evam Vivāh)*, Bhāg I, 40–41.

65. A similar assessment is to be found in an ancestor song recorded by Ann Gold in a village. The song describes a *pitar* as playing "Beneath mother's father's castle," in the various rooms, and on the porch; these details reinforce the image of a grand residence, where the ancestor would be worshiped by royal women; *Fruitful Journeys*, 74–75.

66. See Gold, *Fruitful Journeys*, 74–75. The point remains valid even if the palace is construed as merely a metaphor for anyone's home, as in "a man's home is his castle." In various castes wives are poetically referred to as "queens" and their husbands as "kings."

The conceptualization of Rajput women as the premier hostesses for deities is also to be found, albeit in an elliptical way, in the epic of *Pabuji*, whose male, lower-caste (Nayak) singers sing *"ratijaga* songs" when narrating the weddings of Pabuji and of Gogaji, a hero with his own narrative but who also appears in *Pabuji* as the suitor of Pabuji's sister.[67] I use quotation marks around *"ratijaga* songs" because the songs represented by Nayak singers as royal women's songs for familial deities bear little resemblance to the *ratijaga* songs I recorded or the ones I collected in printed pamphlets. Rather, they are filled with the very sort of narrative detail that women's songs so poignantly omit.[68] One such song, a Bhomiyaji song, serves as a sort of epigraphic summary or *mis en abyme* of the epic; its hero, like Pabuji, is born, is nurtured, grows up, cavorts with friends, sets off to war, and dies a sacrificial victim to a hungry goddess.[69] Both the printed *ratijaga* pamphlet and *Pabuji* have singers who reference the royal hospitality of Rajput women, which is thought authoritative, even definitive. Representing Rajput women as inviting and venerating the deities through the lyrics male Nayak performers actually sing, these lyrics underscore the legitimacy of the deities they celebrate and of the ritual that women's singing constitutes.

In short, in the Rajput songs, as in the pamphlets available for purchase in Rajasthani bazaars (and also, evidently, in epic), there are obvious intertextual linkages that defy the sequential or diachronic performance of ritual and suggest association and even interpenetration of divine identities. As we have seen, these exist among heroes, ancestors, and Bherujis. I have also found, in printed pamphlets, widely scattered associations between heroes and other male deities, including Balaji and some well-known cultic and epic heroes including Tejaji (mentioned above), Pabuji, and Devnarayan. I have not found them, however, among songs sung for and by Rajputs. My exploration of Bheruji and *pitar-purbaj* lyrics here is not intended to cull all possible associations, but rather to suggest the ways in which heroic traditions construct perfected male identity from a variety of sources, which are themselves at least partially constructed by heroic and other traditions. The perfection of the liberated man, is, after all, and as the *upanishad*s recognize, an inconceivable subject, upon which both nothing and yet everything can be said; discussion can go on and on until someone's head falls off from excess verbiage.[70] Heroic lore is sufficiently saturated by the exemplary frames (*purbaj*, Bheruji) I have selected that I could hardly pass over them, but they are by no means the end of the story.[71] Printed pamphlets are especially rich in terms of intertextuality, as they are not limited by the deities dominant in a particular caste, family, or place.

---

67. See Harlan, "Heroes Alone and Heroes at Home."

68. See Peter Lamarche Manuel on the masculinization of women's genres when imported into the realm of men in India, in *Cassette Culture*, 175.

69. For extensive reflection on the operation of *mis en abyme* in *Pabuji*, see Harlan, "On Headless Heroes." On this song, see also above, chapter 4.

70. This is the consequence of which exasperated gurus warn their persistent, questioning students, such as the celebrated female student Gargi (*Brihadaranyaka Upanishad* 3:6, 3:8) and poor Vidagdha Shakalya, whose head fell off and whose bones were mysteriously stolen (*Brihadaranyaka Upanishad* 3:9).

71. Hence the opportunity for a sequel on cultic worship, a work in progress.

The associations among the male personae we have discussed parallel *ratijagas'* implicit interidentification of various women singing and inhabiting *ratijaga* lyrics. This interidentification is most obvious in written *ratijaga* collections, which are intended for purchase by anyone and which represent women with names indicating membership in various castes; but it is also evident, as we know, in Rajput women's *ratijaga* rituals, where Rajput women's voices commingle with those of female relatives from other places, as well as with those of musicians and maids. In and through song, women variously situated interact with different male personae, including heroes, ancestors, and Bherujis, in the context of ritual transactions and lyrics that interrogate and praise supernatural beings.

If women (singers, characters) interact with these personae as gendered others, what, then, is to be said of major female personae that are associated with heroes in general parlance, narrative, and some iconography? How are figures such as these—figures with whom women directly identify themselves and their desires—constructed in *ratijaga* ritual? Let us begin with the perhaps obvious fact that the divine female personae petitioned and honored in lyrics do not function as homologies enriching, infiltrating, and complicating male heroic identity. Because of this, songs about females less frequently deploy the same formulae as hero songs. Absent, for example, are the ubiquitous inquiries about dying alone in a deserted place. Also lacking, as one would expect, are descriptions of male *shringar*. Rather more common than formulaic links that interlock integral textual units are contextual links that connect *ratijaga* song to the realms of narrative and ritual, such as the Navratri-Dashara ritual, about which so much has been said already. Thus, for example, a *sati* song may not associate the *sati* with any *jhunjharji*, *bhomiya*, or *sagasji*, but like hero songs, it picks up where narrative leaves off. This is true both of the narratives that feature *satis* receiving worship independently of husbands, whose importance in the narrative context is circumscribed and left behind with narrative, and of hero narratives that mention *satis*.

Our analysis of female personae begins with the *sati*. As we have seen, many narratives make no mention of *satis*, and narratives that do mention *satis* tend to do so fleetingly and typically deploy *sati* immolations as indices confirming and enhancing the hero's glory. In hero stories, *satis* bring closure and completeness, as frames often do. They also, however, open up the text and allow for a shift of perspective, which suggests that ultimately completion of heroic identity may lie in complementarity, in this case the ideal complementarity of male and female, characterization of which is contemplated outside the hero "text." Thus the isolation of the hero whose body is felled by one or more women (often unidentified) is suspended, in some cases at least, by reunion with conjugal women, *satis*, who initiate during their final hours as living wives the task of resocialization effected fully in the divine realm by denizens of Virgati and in the human realm by women singing *ratijaga* songs, which portray women interacting with heroes after their deaths.

Having treated *satis*, we turn to address the other predominant female personae in *ratijaga* songs: goddesses. Discussion of these divinities renders much richer the notion of hero as gendered other. It also brings us full circle, arriving back at two prominent notions that guide the conceptualization and development of ancestral hero narratives: heroic sacrifice, which is required and lamented by women, and ultimate consumption by goddesses for whom heroes are henchmen.

Satis: From Addendum to Independent Divinity

This section treats Rajput *sati* songs not as an independent subject but as another context or situating frame for our topic, Rajput hero worship.[72] *Satis* are like goddesses and Bherujis in that they are sometimes paired with males for whom they are consorts and sometimes imaged and imagined independently. In *sati* narratives that Rajput women tell about *satis* in their families (their husbands' families, their father's families, and sometimes also their mother's natal families) *satis* are represented as *pativratas* (women devoted to their husbands), but their husbands appear in the narratives fleetingly. Typically, husbands simply die, which sets their *satis'* stories rolling. Although *satis* immolating themselves are often said to confirm their devotion to their husbands and to earn eternal union with them, *sati* stories steer clear of the subject of eternal union. There are surely many reasons for the ellipsis, but the one most relevant here is that women's narratives are overwhelmingly concerned not with the husbands to whom *satis* were devoted as *pativratas* but with divine *satis*, who—like heroes—become family guardians, their husbands typically receding into the background as practically irrelevant consorts.

In narratives, the discrete death scenarios of individual *satis* are passed on to succeeding generations, so that any given *sati's* auspicious death, which confirms her *sat* (truth, essential goodness) as a *pativrata*, will be commemorated. At the same time, familial *satis*, who once enacted the ritual scenario of immolation, are identified with one another and amalgamated into a corporate *satimata*, so that the collection of (*kuldevi*) pendants worn by individual *satis* around their necks when their husbands were alive is typically stored after *sati* immolation in a single box and referred to as a singular persona, "Satimata" (Sati Mother) or just plain "Mata," the epithet often given to goddesses.[73] How different this situation is from that of divine heroes, who resemble each other in their perfection but, having "gone on a deserted path" and "struggled alone,"

---

72. For extensive treatment of *sati* songs, see Harlan, *Religion and Rajput Women*, 112–181, and "Perfection and Devotion." For bibliography on *sati* immolation and various issues connection with it, see Hawley, ed., *Sati*, and on the web, the archives of Religion in South Asia (RISA) server. Examples of interesting recent treatments are Hiltebeitel, "Fathers of the Bride, Fathers of Satī"; Weinberger-Thomas, *Ashes of Immortality* or the original French, *Cendres d'immortalité*; Hawley, ed., *Sati*; and Courtright, *The Goddess and the Dreadful Practice.*

73. Jonathan Parry has also noted the tendency of *satis* to be amalgamated in Banaras. He says, "Though today there are many *sati* shrines in the city, these appear to be treated as general repositories of a generalised power, and almost every trace of the individuality of the specific woman whose death is commemorated has been obliterated"; *Death in Banaras*, 52. See also p. 211 and Hawley, "Introduction," 14.

retain conceptual discreteness and integrity, even as they are socialized to eradicate any potentially threatening individuality.

Commemoration also, we know, takes the form of icon construction and veneration. Iconography on commemorative stelai often associates the hero and *sati* traditions formally, even where praxis segregates them. Whereas some stones show only heroes (a number of whom may have had no wife or wives, much less *sati*s), and some stones show only *sati*s (all of whom have a husband or fiancé, but not necessarily a heroic one), some stones conjoin hero and *sati*, resulting in a challenge of conceptualization; the stones are called "hero stones" or "*sati* stones" depending on the perspective, position, and interest of the beholder, whether devotee or scholar.[74] On some stones the husband (hero or not) is foregrounded and attended by diminutive *sati*/s in the background. On others, husband and *sati*/s stand side by side. Hero or not, the husband of a *sati* is rendered glorious for the reasons already given. The conjunction of these male and female icons, hewn of stone or imprinted on the imagination, serves to render a vision of the perfect relationship, with *vir* as "real man" and *sati* as "real woman." At the same time, the challenge of terminology for hero/*sati* stones and the problem of perception that underlies it point toward the inevitable detachment or entropy of relationship.[75] Like Escher's birds and fish, the foregrounding of one tends to effect the recession of the other.[76] Thus relationship is sustained diachronically, even if the contiguity of images expresses simultaneity, a metamessage also conveyed in Rajasthan by the presence on stelai of sun and moon, which are emblematic of constancy and eternity.

Given the ephemerality of connection in iconography and narrative, it is not surprising to find disjunction in song. *Sati*s and heroes receive their own songs, or more precisely, songs celebrating the class of characters to which *sati*s and heroes individually belong. Nevertheless, the songs can be taken to inform each other in performance, as do the notes in different parts of a score, in our case a partially improvised score, as we find song variants competing and merging in a *ratijaga* performance utilizing no set sequence and attended by women from various families and places.[77]

The representations of *sati*s made by women in *sati* songs reveal some interesting things about the ideal, if evanescent, complementarity of heroes and *sati*s worshiped by Rajput devotees.[78] First, song gives voice to the presump-

---

74. An example of the problem with identifying hero stones with *sati*s is found in Gunther Sontheimer's "Hero and Satī-Stones of Maharashtra," where the author separates out *sati* stones for separate treatment under the heading "Satī," but then refers to some of the stones that depict *sati*s as hero stones. For examples of more struggles with terminology, see also the other essays in Settar and Sontheimer, eds., *Memorial Stones*.

75. This same principle is visited in the Krishna-*gopi* tradition, which requires lovers to separate so that the relationship can be maintained.

76. I refer here to M. C. Escher's famous painting, *Sky and Water* (1938). Wittgenstein's duck-rabbit example also works here.

77. Singing for goddesses usually comes first, as goddesses invite other deities. Last comes a song for the dawn and/or the cock that announces daybreak. For an example of one family's sequence of *ratijaga* songs, see Harlan, *Religion and Rajput Women*, 147 note 60.

78. Here it bears repeating that Rajput heroines are not worshiped as *viranganas* (heroines). Heroines who die as *sati*s are worshiped, but as *sati*s.

tion that the *sati*, who as *pativrata* cleaved to her husband and derived her identity from him, gains, in ritual praxis, independence from him, so that the story
of her glory begins with his death, even as her story will converge with other
satis' stories and effect incorporation. This individuation-incorporation is evident in the following song, which both separates individual immolation from
and also connects it with veneration of (the centripetal, generic) Mata.

> At the edge of the village, O Mother,
> At the edge of the village, O Mother,
> Appeared a bundle of pearls.
> News of the *sati* came to me, O Mother.
>
> At the edge of the village, O Mother,
> At the edge of the village, O Mother,
> Came a bundle of ornaments.
> News of the *sati* came to me, O Mother.
>
> At the edge of the village, O Mother,
> At the edge of the village, O Mother,
> Came a bundle of cloth.
> News of the *sati* came to me, O Mother. . . .

Having sung these three verses, Mangi Devi informed me that the song tells
of these and other *parcas* (miracles, proofs).[79] Like so many hero songs, it al-
ludes to past action but also links and collapses past and present with telling
ambiguity. The refrain, "News of the *sati* came to me, O Mother," indicates that
the miracles attest to the powers of a *sati*, news of whom came to a woman, who
passes it on to Mata, the corporate Satimata. At the same time, the miracles affirm
that the *sati* is a *sati*, a woman possessing *sat*, and so the *parcas* themselves constitute the news of immolation. The *parcas* produce an abundance of treasures
at the edge of the village, where *sati* stones would typically be located or where
satis' red handprints might well adorn a gate. Venerated as effigies, prints such
as these are made by a *sati* as she leaves her home or village for the cremation
ground. They locate and signify the *sati's* metamorphosis from wife to Mata.
The song distinguishes the new *sati* from the (generic, amalgamated) Mata, while
also associating the two through the fact of the recently immolated woman's
metamorphosis into Mata. Thus the lyrics of this seemingly simple little song
introduce a sequence of incorporation—the wife dies, then immolation and
miracles prove her status as a *sati*, ergo Mata—that defies itself in that this Mata
is the very figure being told of herself, much as the hero is told of himself by
way of praise in devotional songs and epic performances.

This incorporation of females into a single female Mata persona should not
surprise anyone who has read about female divinities in India. Much has been
written about the tendency of goddesses to fuse into, if also to split from, a single
goddess, often invoked as Mata, as well as Devi (Goddess). Predictably, diverse
conclusions about human psychology have been drawn and have incited fer-

79. Rajasthani: *parcos.*

vent debate.[80] Here I do not want to say more than I already have about splitting and fusing, but rather to state the fluid identity of satis in sati songs, which
sometimes allude to the death of an individual, though unnamed, living sati but
typically identify the individual sati with the Satimata embodying and signifying the sati scenario. The term Mata in this context allows for a fluidity of association that from one perspective joins all satis, but from another makes all satis
women with whom one's own sati can be identified and so with whom all devotees can identify.

Although Rajput women consider satimatas to belong to a category of being
distinct from goddesses (devis), the affixing of mata to sati effectively stresses
divinity of a female, who is conceptualized as Mata. This association is already
present, we have seen, in the utilization of Shiv and Devi images in memorials
that commemorate satis, including those found in Ahar.[81] Moreover, although
Rajput women rarely link their sati traditions to the pan-Indian tradition of Shiv
and his consort Sati, whose decaying body he carried around India after she died
fighting for his honor (sorely bruised after her father Daksha failed to invite him
to a sacrificial feast), they are familiar with it.[82] This familiarity can only facilitate association.[83]

There is one other aspect of association that bears special mention, given this
book's concern with issues of gender. We have explored at length domestic traditions' expression of the complicity, however ambivalent, of females—women and
goddesses—in effecting Rajput hero sacrifice. In this song, a sati, who prior to
becoming a sati was a wife with a living husband, is called Mata, a divinity. In
effect, the song brings together the wife who, if Rajput, demands, if also dreads,
"death and slaughter" and Mata, the "Mother" who is divine. I have argued previously that becoming a sati can be thought of as a "solution" to the problem of the
woman who is devoted to her husband but fails to protect him.[84] "Going with"
the husband as sahagamini, the woman demonstrates by death and miracles that
she was ever committed to a man, who was the husband she was supposed to
protect but also a member of a martial caste whose duty is self-sacrifice.

My reading here is admittedly speculative, but although the song does not
prove the association of human wife and divine devourer of sacrifice, it can
conveniently be used as a textual emblem for this merging of protecting/demand-
ing wife and protecting/demanding, friendly/inimical, human/vulturine goddess. On the ideological level, the highest dharm of the soldier is represented as
death in battle and consumption by a goddess, which leads to incarnation as
divine henchman, and the highest dharm of a woman is devotion, represented

80. A good example of controversy is reaction to Stanley N. Kurtz's claim expressed in the title of his
controversial book All Mothers Are One. Another is scholarly debate about how and when to invoke a "Great
Goddess" tradition. Scholarship on this is prolific. A few relatively recent examples are Erndl and Hiltebeitel,
"Introduction," 11–23; Hawley, "Prologue," 3–9; Pinchman, ed., Seeking Mahādevī and The Rise of the Goddess in the Hindu Tradition; and Kinsley, Hindu Goddesses, especially pp. 4, 132–150.

81. It is also present in linkages made by members of the Mewari caste in their celebration of Rani Sati,
who is identified as Devi. See Hardgrove, "Sati Worship and Marwari Public Identity in India."

82. For discussion of this, see Hawley, "Introduction," 14.

83. On this point, see Hawley, "Introduction."

84. Harlan, Religion and Rajput Women, 112–181.

in Rajput traditions as most powerfully articulated in the figure of the "good woman" whose devotion to husband leads to incarnation as Mata.[85]

The *sati* is represented as quintessentially good in Rajput traditions, but if one reads traditions against the grain, one sees that this conviction suggests ambivalence. Labeling a particular human woman as a *sati* is an affirmation that expresses realization of female duty (*stri dharm*), but *sati* traditions hint at the difficulty people who believe in the notion of a divine Satimata have in believing that any individual, living, breathing woman can be selfless enough to become a *sati*.[86] In this way the individual *sati* is comparable to a saint, who, as the adage goes, is unrecognized in his (or her) own time. The doubt that any individual wife can perfect her *dharm* is demonstrated and bolstered by representations of wives as conflicted and conflictual in both men's and women's folklore genres, from epic to women's songs.[87]

A glimpse of this uncertainty and anxiety about the relationship between the divine Mata with whom past *sati*s have been identified and individual *sati*s at any moment when an individual *pativrata* faces immolation is to be found in women's *ratijaga* songs. Looking at two songs together gives voice to both faith in the divinity invoked by song and equivocation about attaining divinity at any particular time.[88]

The first, which succinctly rehearses ideology, affirms the relationship between *pativrata* and *satimata*. The second, however, demonstrates doubt about the relationship and portrays disruption between the temporal act and the atemporal ideal, represented iconographically as the corporate Satimata or Mata. These songs are to be analyzed in turn. Here then, is song one:

> "Buy me a forehead ornament—do it quickly, little brother-in-law.
> I will follow my husband [as a *sati*].
> Dear younger brother-in-law—yes dear little brother-in-law!"
> Cool the *sati* under a shady *banyan* tree. . . .[89]

The song continues, substituting for forehead ornament various other items of the *sati*'s *shringar* in head-to-toe order. In this song sung by the "palace singer," the *sati* asks her *devar* (younger brother-in-law) to hurry up and bring to her the very finest things so that she can proceed to the pyre. The *sati* is impatient and the *devar* is not quick enough for her, perhaps because of his affection for her. The relationship between a wife and her *devar* is portrayed as one of endear-

---

85. See Paul Courtright, drawing on remarks by Agananda Bharati, on *sati* immolation as the "wringing out" of *pativrata dharm*; Courtright, "Sati, Sacrifice, and Marriage," 184–189.

86. See Harlan, "Truth and Sacrifice."

87. Recognition that women are represented in folklore as both experiencing and causing conflict is now commonplace. For excellent treatment of these ideas and bibliography, see Raheja, "Negotiated Solidarities," and her "Introduction," 1–22, as well as Raheja and Gold, "Introduction," to *Listen to the Heron's Words*, 1–29.

88. A parallel equivocation is to be found in Ashis Nandy's controversial essay, "Sati as Profit verses Sati as a Spectacle," where Nandy relegates praxis to the mythical past.

89. See also Harlan, "Women's Songs for Auspicious Occasions," 271–273, which provides extended discussion of the notion of cooling (the verb *sīlaṇo*) as a wonderfully ambiguous element that allows for dual temporal perspectives.

ment in Rajasthani folklore, as in folklore elsewhere in India. In this song the *sati* displays no hesitation; if there is uncertainty, it belongs to someone else.

Compare these lyrics with the following ones, which locate hesitation within the person of the *pativrata*.

> Satimata, take a forehead ornament and wear it.
> Oh, take a forehead ornament and wear it.
> Why the delay for the forehead ornament, Satimata?
> Your husband's litter is waiting under the balcony.
> Your husband's litter is waiting under the balcony.
> Waiting under the balcony, waiting under the balcony windows. . . .

As in the preceding song, this one, sung by the "Udaipur singer," goes on to describe the wife's *shringar:* there are earrings, a nose ring, a necklace, a saffron-colored sari, and toe rings. Ultimately these lyrics do not express doubt that this *sati* did indeed become a *satimata*. They constitute a *ratijaga sati* song and invoke the woman dressing for immolation as Satimata. It differs from the first song, however, in that it asks the woman herself why there is a delay, when her husband's corpse lies waiting for her in the shade of the balcony. This could well suggest recognition that an individual woman may not rush to embrace unequivocally the prospect of following her husband into flames. Perhaps here women singing to Satimata identify with the enormity of the decision to make a vow (*vrat*) to sacrifice life out of devotion to a husband. After all, purposely embracing fire as a *sati* is unimaginable and frightening. In this song a *sati* may enact reticence, if not outright fear, about immolation, which is normally excruciating.[90] *Sati* narratives told by the faithful typically describe women as going to the pyre serenely or smilingly, but this song can be taken to interrogate gently the prevailing ideology by portraying the *sati* as dawdling; her husband, she is repeatedly admonished, is waiting, waiting, waiting.

Looking back at the first song in light of the second, one wonders whether the delegation of hesitation to the *devar* might not also work as projection or displacement. He is allowed to experience the reticence that ideology denies to *satis*. It renders this junior male a sort of surrogate. Whereas women are usually expected to express grief (their own and that felt by self-controlled men) at funerals, here perhaps, we have a junior male serving as stand-in for the *sati* (who is not shown here as equivocating or feeling), for other women (whom the *sati* is leaving), for senior men (in relation to whom the dawdling *devar* is feminine), or for some or all of the above.

Before leaving these songs, let us ponder briefly two more things. First, there is the matter of the way in which the second song, although expressing equivocation about the relationship between ideology and practice or the general principle and particular instance, expresses the ideal complementarity of saffron donners, male and female. In this song, the word I gloss "husband" (*kesariya*) is actually "saffron one" or "saffron-donning one," an image that the song offers

---

90. See Sunder Rajan, "The Subject of Sati."

along with that of the *sati* wearing a saffron-colored *sari*. Thus it expresses the ideal union of two bodies, male and female, sacrificed on a flaming pyre. The hue expresses renunciation of life, as it does in the context of the hero charging into a *saka*, and subtly renders the husband, whoever he was, a hero in relation to this *sati*, who merits a suitable match. The imaging of the husband thus suggests what the *sati*'s sacrifice makes clear: he is glorified.

Second, like so many songs before, the first song conjoins past and present in a refrain that expresses transparent ambiguity. "Cool the *sati* under the shady *banyan* tree," can be read as reference to the manifestation of *sat* in the *sati*'s metamorphosing body.[91] *Sat*, which is not only a quality but also a substance (as in "the right stuff"), manifests as heat and, according to widespread belief, causes the *sati*'s body to ignite spontaneously. This manifestation parallels the manifestation of *sat* in the *"pan* song" about the "ruddy struggler," the reddened, intoxicated, and dutiful *jhunjharji* who dies a hero's death.

The refrain can also be read as a description of posthumous location and veneration. The line could refer to the *sati*'s stone, situated, like so many ancestral memorials, under the shade of a tree.[92] From this perspective, the song praising the *satimata* by commemorating her metamorphosis also describes ongoing glorification through memorialization.

A similar ambiguity is found in the following *sati* song I recorded. It brings together in verse the *sati*'s preparation for immolation and after-death miracle working, but also, as in the case of Bheruji worship, demonstrates an ideal picture of organic society with Rajputs in charge. Unlike the Bheruji song, however, members of the community are depicted less as worshipers and more as suppliers.

> With a golden bar and a silver plate the scale balances.[93]
> With a golden bar and silver plate the scale balances.
> The perfume seller weighs his perfume generously [unequally].
>
> With a golden bar and a silver plate the scale balances.
> With a golden bar and silver plate the scale balances.
> The perfume is weighed generously.
>
> The perfume is weighed; Satimata has it weighed.
> The perfume is weighed generously.
> The perfume is weighed generously. . . .

In subsequent verses, the song sung by Mangi Devi substitutes for perfume various items of *shringar*, beginning with pearls.[94] It describes the generosity of various merchants selling different items of the *shringar*. Whether the song is read as recording the items to be purchased for a *sati* preparing for the pyre or for posthumous veneration, the song describes everyone as being "generous,"

91. See Harlan, "Women's Songs for Auspicious Occasions," 270.
92. Harlan, "Women's Songs for Auspicious Occasions," 270.
93. *Sona ri dandi . . . rupa ra cera (Sonā rī ḍāṇḍī . . . rūpā rā cerā).*
94. A similar song about a golden-silver scale is sung about a *pitar* in the pamphlet *Rātījagā kā Gīt,* 3.

which reflects the utopian view of communal relations but also, perhaps, a sense that this unbalanced generosity is something of a miracle. The providers, including merchants who are so frequently typed as miserly, are voluntarily relinquishing resources to facilitate veneration of the Rajput divinity. Moreover, they weigh the ingredients with impressive scales, made of gold and silver.

Then again, we could read this generosity as utilitarian. Rajputs typically portray *satis* as their affair, but as the crowds of people who flocked to Roop Kanwar's death site (*sati sthal*) evinced, perhaps the benefits of veneration accrue to others as well. Perhaps the *sati* herself has rendered their scales silver and gold. Certainly the presence of non-Rajput women at *ratijagas* could help bolster this belief in a widened field of fruition. This extension is implied in a *sati* song found in the "Rajasthani Folklore" collection of *ratijaga* songs.[95] From whatever source the collection takes the song, the pamphlet renders the lyrics applicable to women, and *satis*, from various communities.[96] The song itself suggests that the *sati* becomes enshrined in the individual women who worship her.

The song takes the form of a dialogue between devotee and *satimata*. Having promised to build the *satimata* a "small temple," the devotee asks what kind of bricks, mud, and whitewash she should use. The *satimata* then responds: "bricks of the body," "mud of the mind," and the "wash of love." The devotee then asks what kind of lamp, wick, and light are needed and receives the same response (body, mind, and love). Thus the devotee is a walking shrine to Satimata, even as the song goes on to specify the specific items of *shringar* that accord with the *sati*'s preference.[97] The song provides vivid illustration of the internalization of *satimata* veneration that effects identification of the *pativrata* with the *satimata*.

What distinguishes *pativrata* from *satimata* is power realized, as in the case of the hero, through commitment to self-sacrifice. This power is manifested most palpably in *sati* narratives (including Godavari Sati's narrative) through curses and blessings that a *sati* gives as she approaches the pyre, if also her enforcement of curses and continuing history of bestowing blessings after her immolation. *Sati* songs, however, pass over the curses, which, being specific to individual *satimatas*, are unlikely to appear in generic *satimata* songs and have little to do with the purpose of veneration, including the singing of *ratijaga* songs. That purpose is receiving blessings from *satis*, who, like heroes, grace their families, and sometimes others, with manifestations of power, including both material rewards and faith-enhancing appearances.

Sati songs overwhelmingly describe appearances as blessed and welcome events. As we have seen, some *pitar-purbaj* songs also give glowing accounts of

---

95. *Rājasthānī Lokgīt (Rātījagā evam Vivāh)*, Bhāg. 1, pp. 10–11

96. This commonality is also to be found in *Rātījagā kā Gīt*. which describes offerings for ancestors being weighed on a gold and silver scale. The sharing of this unit emphasizes the idea of generic *satis* comprehended as generic ancestors. In this song the evidently non-Rajput Citarmal is identified as the buyer and the non-Rajput Phulchand the weigher; p. 3.

97. This characterization of body as temple reminds one of Lingayat devotion.

after-death visits, but the conceptualization of heroes and satis as realized or perfected beings distinguishes their appearances from ordinary ancestors' in that familial satis and heroes are not construed as envying the living and threatening some potentially serious harm. As we have also seen, the ancestral songs for ancestors make much of the fact that ancestors are welcome. This sort of affirmation is evidently unnecessary in the case of heroes and satis.

One last song, sung by the "Udaipur singer," makes clear the conceptualization of sati appearances as benign. It begins by asking, "Why are there kesar [saffron] footprints in my courtyard?" It then asks why there are turmeric footprints, kanku (Hindi kumkum; English rouge from saffron paste) footprints, and menhdi (henna) footprints. Together these four lines conjoin saffron (as a yellow-orange powder) and turmeric, which share the hue of renunciation, with kanku and menhdi, both of which are red, the color of auspiciousness. The song goes on to invite this Mata to come sit on a throne, and then launches into a head-to-toe description. It characterizes the sati as having loose hair, a line of saffron on her forehead, eyes outlined in lamp black, teeth decorated with gold, lips red with pan, hands colored with menhdi, and feet scented with perfume and adorned with ankle bracelets. Thus we have a vision of loveliness that, like the footprints, conjoins and admixes the colors of asceticism and auspiciousness.

At the same time, the song suggests that this sati is not, or is no longer, a demure dependent. She has loose locks, signifying that she is a female beyond male control.[98] Here is a woman dressed as a pativrata but with the hairstyle of a woman unattached and unbound. The image of black flowing hair surrounding a face with eyes outlined in black adds a third hue to the colors of sati. Like the goddess Kali, whose very name means "black," this satimata, the song hints, has a dark or "wild side" that suggests her independent power as a divinity. This power is the power of deliverance, as is clear in the final line, which repeats the invitation to the ratijaga: "In this degenerate age, O Satimata, come and be my guest."[99] Thus the power of this satimata is the same power frequently attributed by devotees to their chosen deities, such as Krishna, Shiv, Kali, and Durga. And if the yellow and red combine to express the goodness-auspiciousness of this sat-filled divinity, unbound hair (as well as its color) suggests transcendence and the power that is often conveyed by the term shakti and signified iconographically by flowing hair, such as that worn by Kali.

Hence, whereas the perfected hero is homologized to or otherwise identified with Bheruji, who is so frequently enlisted as guardian of and companion to goddesses, the satimata is imaged as independent (a characteristic emphasized by this depiction of flowing hair), while also wearing the shringar that typically comports with that worn by auspicious, self-sacrificing wives.

---

98. Analysis of the connection between bound/unbound hair and controlled/uncontrolled women and goddesses has been given by many. For examples, see Harlan and Courtright, "Introduction," 11; Erndl, Victory to the Mother, 107; Sax, Mountain Goddess, 31–32; Hiltebeitel, "Draupadi's Hair"; Obeyesekere, Medusa's Hair; and Hershman, "Hair, Sex and Dirt."

99. Degenerate age: kaliyug.

In this duplex conceptualization, the married but independent *satimata* of song resembles Rajput *kuldevi*s, with their distinctive dual iconographies: *pativrata* and beast. The connection is subtle and tentative, but does little to belie the previously discussed association between women, who as demanding wives and mothers require protection that may leave heroes without heads (though hardly emasculated), and goddesses, who eat heroic entrails.[100] Moreover, the "real woman" or *sati* who becomes a powerful Mata complements the sacrificed heroic man, synonymous with the "real man," *vir*, who is a denizen of Virgati with its "wine, women, and song," and who becomes in some contexts Bheruji, the salacious, virile trickster, serving, inter alia, as guardian of goddesses.

This brings us to the final female personae to be explored in *ratijaga* songs: goddesses. When I asked singers to sing hero songs for me, they inevitably asked whether I didn't also want to hear goddess songs, just as they did for *sati* songs. Given that the hero's death is a *balidan* for his goddess, his ultimate gendered other, it is fitting to conclude this study of henchmen with a look at how goddesses are represented in *ratijaga* ritual by women, that is to say, men's most immediate gendered others.

Goddesses: Ultimate Observations on Females Making Their Men

Like *sati* songs, goddess songs are largely (and by this point unsurprisingly) timeless songs of praise that contain few if any references to *itihasik* events.[101] Moreover, like *sati* songs, they almost never make direct connections to heroic traditions. Thus although the songs tell us a lot about constructions of feminine divinity, studying them is helpful to this project only insofar as they can be construed as informing and so helping to constitute an ultimate (if often unspoken and implicit) frame for heroic sacrifice. This goddess frame is so evident and so habitual a presumption as to function as transparency.[102] Its lucidity gives focus and meaning to heroic scenarios rendered in various media, including narratives and rituals. Because heroic sacrifice is widely understood as a *balidan* for a *devi*, it is the sort of frame that is "always already" there when any particular narrative or ritual sequence is initiated.[103]

Given this "always already" feature that transforms a human man into a divine henchman, let us look at some specific ways in which women's *ratijaga*

---

100. Simplistic application of the "upward displacement of the genitals" notion could erroneously represent the hero as emasculated, degendered, or regendered. If one were to insist on beheading as emasculation, one would still have to take seriously a goddess's consumption of the hero, which, whether taken literally or equated with coitus, transforms the hero into a henchmen identified as Bheruji, with the sexual charge that such an identification delivers.

101. On the issue of *itihas* in the epic song of the Himalayan goddess Nanda Devi, see Sax, *Mountain Goddess*, 25.

102. See Handelman, "Postlude: Towards a Braiding of Frame."

103. On frames that are there "always already," see Gold, "Whoever Hears God's Wedding Song Has All Their Sins Removed," and Hiltebeitel, *Rethinking India's Oral and Classical Epics*, 44.

rituals portray worship of goddesses.[104] *Ratijaga* rituals typically contain songs for a number of goddesses. Good examples are songs for Chink Mata, "Sneeze Mata," who is worshiped so that bad consequences will not ensue if someone sneezes during a ritual, and for Bijasan, like Bayasan a collective designation for the Saptamatrikas, who are typically attended by Bheruji and associated with various Rajput *kuldevis*.[105] Many Rajput women wear gold pendants that depict both. Printed collections include songs for these and for a wide spectrum of goddesses, including such well-known goddesses as Shitala Mata and Parvati. Then there are songs for all sorts of less well-known goddesses with largely local reputations. Although there is no separate category of *kuldevi* song, goddesses such as Amba Mata are often explicitly identified with *kuldevis* in *ratijaga* performances. *Kuldevis* are represented as a group (in Bijasan songs), but also individually in their association with various individual goddesses.

I am aware of the richness of these goddess songs, which could be analyzed to address a variety of issues debated by scholars of goddess worship, but I am interested here in the ways in which goddess songs sung in Rajput *ratijagas* frame Rajput hero traditions. I will limit my discussion to three goddess songs I recorded, in order to bring to a conclusion this study of domestic hero worship. I use the first song to demonstrate the fluidity of association among various goddesses identified with Rajput *kuldevis*, who are homologized to the Saptamatrikas as well as to Durga on Navratri-Dashara, and who are conceptualized as the consumers of hero flesh in *balidans* transforming tasty soldier sacrificial victims to divine henchmen. I use the second to illustrate the identification of goddesses with female devotees, whose adornment or *shringar* they share.

Both songs are for Amba Mata, or "Mother Mother," a goddess with a name so encompassing that she is easily identified with various goddesses known throughout India and also some important less famous ones. Here is the first.

> Reveal yourself again and again, O Amba.
> Reveal yourself again and again.
> Bhavani, reveal yourself again and again.
> When you reveal yourself, I am happy, Avada.[106]
> When you reveal yourself, I am happy.
> Amba, reveal yourself again and again.

---

104. Here I am not interesting in proposing a grand new theory of the divine feminine. Rather, I am interested in exploring some specific ways in which goddesses named in *ratijaga* ritual add to what we know about the connections between heroes and goddesses explored so far. Together with the understanding of heroic death as *balidan* and connections between Navratri sacrifice and death and battle, the characterizations of goddesses explored here are intended to fill in and round out our understanding of heroism in Rajput domestic traditions. In my next book project, I show how the connection between heroes and goddesses that is so elusive in Rajput narratives and so indirect in Rajput women's goddesses songs is made explicit in cultic narrative and veneration.

105. For an illuminating discussion on these seven goddesses as Bijasan in the Rajasthani context, see Lalas, *Rajasthani Sabd Kos*, s.v.

106. This refers to Avadi Mata, also invoked as Avadi Rani below. Her name also appears in English as "Avari." Variant transliterations derive from variant spellings of the final consonant (ḍ, ṛ).

Your forehead ornament is beautiful, Amba.
Your forehead ornament is beautiful, Amba.
It is intricately inlaid, Jagadamba.[107]
Oh, the forehead ornament is inlaid.
Mother Bhavani, reveal yourself again and again.

When you reveal yourself, I am happy.
Yogmaya, when you reveal yourself, unhappiness vanishes.[108]
Amba, reveal yourself again and again.

Amba, the necklace on your breasts is beautiful.
Amba, the necklace on your breasts is beautiful.
Your earrings are fully inlaid, your earrings, Avadi Rani.
Your earrings are inlaid, inlaid, O Bayan Rani.
Reveal yourself again and again.
Oh Sukh Devi, reveal yourself again and again. . . .

Like so many other *ratijaga* songs, this Amba Mata song, which was sung by Mangi Devi, goes on to describe prominent elements of enhancement.[109] It invokes Amba Mata at the beginning, at the end, and throughout the song, but as it describes her from head to toe, it deploys, quite strikingly, names for other goddesses, who come to constitute her. Like the *satimata* songs, it identifies and unifies various divine females, but unlike the *satimata* songs, it also names various females and so invokes different and often distinctive and enduring mythologies of goddesses who appear "again and again." The verbal icon crafted head to toe is literally a corporate goddess with parts forming but also overflowing and expanding the whole, summarized by the name "Amba Mata." Here we have a goddess's multiplicity and unity conjoined in an image that constructs a feminine entity but simultaneously exceeds the construction by invoking epithets with rich intertextual referents. In other words, the epithets for this Amba shift semantically and transform into proper names for goddesses enacting divergent scenarios in various mythologies and so in other mythological times and spaces.

Whereas some of the epithets/names given to/going beyond Amba Mata (such as Bhavani, Jagadamba, and Yogmaya) point beyond Mewar to widely dispersed traditions, some refer to deities closely tied to territory and circumscribed by relatively immediate environs. One is Avada, or Avadi Mata, a Mewar goddess with a sizeable temple and constant flow of pilgrims, many of them going to or coming from Chittor. Another designation is Sukh Devi, Bedla *thikana*'s "Goddess of Happiness," who is also the *ishtadevta* for many members of the Chauhan Rajput family that once ruled Bedla. Of course, "Sukh Devi" also works as a general epithet—what goddess isn't supposed to give happiness at least some of the time?—but the reference also locates the goddess of happi-

---

107. The inlay mentioned here and below is typically of gems or ivory.
108. Yogmaya: Jogmaya.
109. As is evident from this text, the singer loses her place and has to back up to describe earrings after a necklace. Moreover, she buys time to order the pieces of jewelry by repeating lines when necessary. This is a particularly unpolished performance.

ness in a specific place in Mewar, as does as the reference to Avadi Mata. The links to place also connect locality to identity (of Mewaris) as well as authority, in this case Rajput authority, as they often do elsewhere in India.[110]

Telling in this regard is the invocation of Bayan Rani, or Queen Bayan, who is also called Ban Mata, the *kuldevi* of the Sisodiya family to which Mewar's Maharana belongs. Thus the singer customizes the song to invoke the royal family's *kuldevi* and so make it the Sisodiyas', as well as Mewar's, own.

Yet this particular goddess, like so many others, also suggests the multiplicity that arises from her power (*shakti*). Ban or Bayan Mata is represented by the Bijasan (Bayasan) pendant worn by Sisodiya women. She is at once one of the seven *kuldevi*s and the collective Mata, the mother whose wholeness the number seven conveys. Thus, like any *kuldevi*, her nature is uniform and manifold. The dual iconographies of *kuldevi*s (*pativrata*, theriomorph) thus turn out to be only one aspect of distinction/multiformity. Through epithets and other intertextual images, each *kuldevi* is connected, in women's songs but also narrative traditions and the Bijasan pendant, with a phantasmagoric array of identities. The association of *kuldevi*s with Bijasan, for example, invokes and contributes to a mythological legacy that includes traditions from many sources, including those protean Sanskrit *puranas*.[111] According to the *Rajasthani Sabd Kos*, Bijasan (or Bayasan) is, inter alia, "one kind of Saptamatrika" devoted to curing illnesses, and refers as well to the collective of Mothers who raise the war god Skand, son of Shiv. This dictionary then identifies different lists of Mothers and refers to *laukik* (local) and *pauranik* (Sanskritic) variants.[112] These Mothers are identifiable at times with the bellicose and bloodthirsty *shakti*s who appear on battlefields and devour the dead and soon-to-be dead, as Rajput *kuldevi*s typically do. Each one of these goddesses has a persona resembling the ring impelled outward by a raindrop on a pond. As its periphery expands, it intersects and shares interiority with other peripheries impelled by other drops, and it contributes to greater complexity of design. Epithets proliferate, with some becoming increasingly generic or encompassing. For example, in our second song, to be examined presently, Amba Mata is at one point invoked simply as Devi, "Goddess," the most inclusive designation possible. The name "Mother Mother" is almost as encompassing, yet, unlike "Devi," it is also very specific: it establishes this effulgent divinity as the very deity whose temple is prominent in Udaipur and to whose temple each newly anointed king and each bride marrying into the royal family must pay respects, as they do for other prominent deities including Ban Mata and Eklingji. In other words, this Mother Mother is not only a corporate goddess but also a goddess alongside other goddesses, such as Sukh Devi, Avadi Mata, and Ban Mata—popular deities with influential patrons and celebrated temples in Mewar. Her specificity, her manifestation as a

---

110. See, for example, discussions of the Himalayan goddess Nanda Devi, locality, and royal authority in Sax, *Mountain Goddess*, 72–77, 160–208. For treatment in a south Indian context, see Shulman, *Tamil Temple Myths*, 40–55.

111. Myth compendia that also often include other genres.

112. Lalas, *Rājasthānī Sabd Kos*, s.v.

goddess of Mewar, is rendered apparent by her icon, guarded, as one would expect, by Kalaji-Goraji but also by her insertion into (exceedingly economical or condensed) narrative within *ratijaga* lyrics. Thus in the second Amba Mata song (performed by the same musician), the lyrics, which first ask Amba Mata for support and deliverance from harm, then go on to invoke Durga and Shakti (as epithets, identities) and to describe timeless ritual offerings, poignantly disrupt their representation of timeless myth and ritual by asserting temporal exigency. Calling on Devi, it exclaims:

> O Goddess, Akbar Badshah has come.[113]
> Someone left the drums [*naupat*] in the temple and set forth [to fight].

The song concludes by repeating a formula that asks vaguely for deliverance several times, but now we have a real sense of clear and present danger.

Thus this song of invitation and praise, it would seem, inserts *itihas* into its midst. It states, ever so simply, "Akbar Badshah has come." Once again, however, the reference to a historical event turns out to be temporally ambiguous, and tellingly so. Unquestionably, the line refers to the moment when the *naupat* drums were played just before the king's army set out to defend Mewar against Akbar's siege. But the reference to Akbar's assault works also as a metaphor for any contemporary challenge that devotees must meet by fighting some modern-day, or Akbaresque, nemesis. Like remembering the Alamo, remembering Akbar is synonymous with striving or struggling despite daunting odds.[114]

The reference to drums played in a goddess temple before soldiers set forth to battle Akbar discretely associates this Amba Mata with Mewar's Amba Mata, on whom the Maharana's authority and power depend. Thus the song economically and strikingly reveals the limpid religious frame for heroic sacrifice, described in so many narratives. What begins in Amba Mata's temple ventures outward and leads into battle sacrifice, and so once again, but this time relatively explicitly, goddess worship provides the cosmological and ultimate frame in which human travails are to be situated and through which they are to be given ultimate (theological, soteriological) purpose and meaning.

If this song posits fluid association among divine females, whose veneration is linked to *balidan*—the martial sacrifice men make to their goddesses—the last song to be examined suggests association of female divinities and their female devotees.

> I am your servant, Ambaji.
> I am your servant, Ambaji.
> Sword and trident adorn your hands.
> Sword and trident adorn your hands.
> You sit upon a lion, Ambaji.
> You sit upon a lion, Ambaji.

---

113. Akbar Badshah: the emperor Akbar.

114. On the politics of memory in a Rajput context, see Harlan, "Deploying the Martial Past: Reflections of Hero Worship."

FIGURE 5.2. Amba Mata Temple, Udaipur

> On your forehead is a wonderful ornament.
> On your forehead is a wonderful ornament.
> The ornament on your hair part is fully inlaid.
> Ambaji, the ornament on your hair part is fully inlaid. . . .

The song, again sung by Mangi Devi, then continues head to toe, irregularly repeating the refrain: "I am your servant, Ambaji [Amba Mata]." The repeated line emphasizes the duality of mistress and servant, deity and devotee. Duality is also asserted by the goddess's trident (which identifies her as divinity, as it does Shiv) and by her sword (a weapon associated in human society with men and so distinguishing the divinity, though female, from women, who share her gender). From this point on, however, the enumeration of elements of *shringar* asserts mutual identification of goddess and women, as both female identity genres share most elements of *shringar*. The specific items detailed in this goddess song would have been bought from craftsmen who generally sell commodities (jewelry, cosmetics) for gifts to women. Moreover, the items worn by the goddess are items typically worn by women when they don their fanciest dress, usually at weddings. More specifically, whether conceived as a description of a material icon or as *sakshat* manifestation, the song's *shringar* indicates a goddess resembling an auspicious human bride (who is represented in wedding ritual as the embodiment of Shiv's spouse), just as the *sati*'s does.

Here let us recognize that the *sati*, the good woman, embodies the temporal connection and transition between human and divine female. Wearing the
shringar of a bride when she circumambulates the wedding fire, the *sati* becomes
through immolation a divinity who protects the family, as does a *pativrata*, or
Amba Mata, or any other chosen *devi*. Represented as the corporeal realization
of *pativrata dharm*, she is invested with the perfection of female gender quite as
the bridegroom-hero is invested with the perfection of male gender as he metamorphoses into divine henchman, the eternally feted *vir* who is also his *devi*'s
devoted Bheruji.

At the same time, we have seen, the self-sacrificing woman, who as the
embodiment of *dharm* is represented as the "secret of Rajput honor," is also a
"hardy little lass" who requires and even encourages (typically more subtly than
Hadi Rani) the self-sacrifice of men.[115] Though *vir-sati* are rendered complementary in discourse, narrative, and many (material and lyrical) icons, the representation of heroes as henchmen points to acknowledgement, or at least
suspicion, that from one perspective—from the perspective that views perfected
heroes as doing more than lounge around in Virgati where their senses are sated
by women, music, and intoxicants—perfected men serve females (women and
devis) whose need has mandated their deaths. Like Hamir in that they share
*balidan*s with *devi*s, the Rajput hero-victims become sustenance for "death-and-
slaughter"–demanding females, who feast them during *ratijaga*s.

If *sati* immolation provides a temporal nexus between human and divine
female on an individual level, society suggests nexus in a more general way. As
we have seen, society, along with the *dharm* on which it is predicated, is epitomized in some discourses by the Brahmin standing (through synecdoche) for
the whole, and epitomized in some other discourses (as well as memorial stelai
iconography) by the cow. In both cases it is rendered feminine in comparison
with the warrior and hero. Society is also identified with the soil, which sustains it vividly in feminine constructions such as Bharat Mata.[116] Thus the females demanding sacrifice and shedding tears watering their heroes' "graves"
are themselves indicative of the predicament faced by society, which (like Bhukh
Mata) sacrifices men for its, or rather her, survival and maintenance.

This book has reflected on ways in which various representations of heroic
sacrifice by men express ideas about gender, both masculine and feminine. These
representations have been Rajput constructions of a past in which ancestors
gained glory (bequeathed to descendants) while earning themselves salvation
(liberation, Virgati, union with Devi as henchman or Bheruji) and supernatural
power, which also benefits descendants. As we have seen, however, Rajputs are
not the only ones to worship heroes. Like prominent *sati*s, many heroes, even

---

115. This is illustrated unambiguously in the case of Pema, the wife of Pabuji's enemy but also Pabuji's
sister and auntie of Rupnath, whose mother (wife of Pabuji's brother, Buro) cuts him out of her stomach before she becomes a *sati*. Pema provides the information necessary for her nephew Rupnath to kill her husband
(with whose head he plays hockey) and for her to become a *sati*. See Smith, *The Epic of Pābūjī*, 458–477.

116. Bhu Devi (Earth Goddess) is another obvious example.

and especially Rajput heroes, have attracted devotees from a variety of backgrounds, a fact frequently referred to in *ratijaga* songs. Because heroes are patently "mirrors of experience," they clearly reveal some ideals cherished, anxieties suffered, and fruits desired by devotees situated variously in society with its complex, and often ambiguous and shifting, social ranks. Thus at this juncture we need to move from examining gender to considering other indices of social location, including caste, another dominant, complex, and variously contested genre that differentiates social code or *dharm*.[117] But that is beyond the scope of this volume, the contours of which have been shaped by abiding interests in gender and the ways in which Rajput devotion to ancestral heroes reveals constructions and commitments that tell us about gender representation.

117. The whole story of cultic worship by variously situated others is, as I have mentioned, a work in progress.

Glossary

ahimsa (*ahiṃsā*): Noninjury; nonviolence.

Amba Mata (Ambā Mātā, Ambājī): A goddess with a well-attended shrine in Udaipur.

anndata (*anndātā*): Literally, giver of grain; an honorific.

Avadi Mata (Avaḍi Mātā): A goddess whose temple near Chittor is a popular pilgrimage place.

balidan (*balidān*): Sacrifice, typically the sacrifice of an animal to a god; used to describe the death of a soldier in war, as his death constitutes a sacrifice of self to his tutelary goddess (*kuldevi*).

Balluji (Ballūjī [also Balūjī]): A Champavat Rathod Rajput who died while retrieving Amar Sinh's body from Agra, and later appeared to defend Udaipur during Aurangzeb's siege.

Ban Mata (Baṇ Mātā [also Bāyāṇ Mātā, Bāyāṇ Rāṇī]): Sisodiya *kuldevi*.

Baniya (Baniyā): Member of a merchant caste.

Bharat Mata (Bhārat Mātā): "Mother India"; a goddess.

bhav (*bhāv*): Feeling, emotion; a term referring to the possession of a person by a deity, ancestor, ghost, demon, etc.

Bhavani (Bhavānī): A goddess widely worshiped in Rajasthan.

Bheru Singh (Bheru Sinh): A *jhunjharji* from Karjali.

Bheruji (Bherujī, Bhairva): A fierce deity that is often associated with goddesses; a posthumous hero.

Bhil (Bhīl): A populous tribal group.

Bhinya (Bhīnyā): A hero who died fighting in Jodhpur.

bhomiyaji (*bhomiyājī*): A hero; *jhunjharji*; a term often used in Marwar to refer to a worshiped hero.

bhopa (*bhopā*): A medium who becomes possessed by a hero or some other deity.

Bhukh Mata (Bhūkh Mātā): "Hungry Mother," a goddess who devoured many Mewari princes.

bhumi (*bhūmi*): Land, earth.

bhut (*bhūt*): Ghost; a term referring to ancestors of people not belonging to one's family.

Bhut Mela (Bhūt Melā): "Ghost Festival," which occurs at Chittor on the holiday of Divali.

Bijasan (Bijasāṇ): Group of goddesses, often collectively conceptualized as a single goddess; goddesses identified at times with the seven *matrikas*.

bir (*bīr*, *vīr*): Hero who dies violently.

cabutra (*cabutra*, *cabūtra*): Elevated platform supporting stelai of heroes or other deities.

Caran (Caran, Cāraṇ): Member of a caste of panegyrists.

Carbhuja (Cārbhuja): A form of Krishna.

Chatriya Bavji (Chatriyā Bāvjī): An ancestral spirit worshiped in Devgarh.

chatri (*chatrī*): Funerary pavilion.

Chetak (Cetak): Maharana Pratap's heroic horse, which saved his life in the battle of Haldighati.

Chink Mata (Chīṅk Mātā): "Sneeze Mother," a goddess who wards off the inauspiciousness.

darbar (*darbār*): Literally, the royal court; epithet for a king.

Daroga (Dārogā): Offspring of a Rajput father and a non-Rajput mother: Ravan Rajput.

darshan (*darśan*): Divine sight; seeing and being seen by a deity, often present in the form of an icon.

Dashara (Daśharā): A holiday called "The Tenth," which comes after the festival of Navratri, or "Nine Nights," and celebrates the conquest of the goddess Durga over demons as well as the conquest of demons by the god Ram.

Devi (Devī): "Goddess"; an epithet of goddesses.

Devnarayan (Devnārāyaṇ): A well-known hero with a well-known epic.

Dhanna (Dhannā): A hero who died fighting in Jodhpur.

dharm (*dharm*): Duty, law, custom, religion, morality.

dharmik (*dharmik*): Pertaining to duty, law, custom, religion, morality.

Dhebo (Ḍhēbo): A hero from the epic *Pabuji*.

Dhobi (Dhobī): Member of the washerman caste.

dhok (*dhok*): Respect.

Dholin (Ḍholhin): Female member of the caste of drummers; singers who also play drums and perform at *ratijagas*. The term is often used by members outside the community but increasingly rejected by members who prefer other terms, such as *rajgahak* (royal singer).

dhoti (*dhoti*): A garment that covers the lower body; cloth that is wrapped around the waist and hangs to the ground, or is tucked up in back at the waist.

Divali (Divālī): A holiday that celebrates good fortune and is devoted to the goddess Lakshmi; the festival of lights.

doha (*dohā*): A couplet, which often celebrates martial valor.

Durga (Durgā): A goddess worshiped on Navratri and Dashara: slayer of the buffalo demon Mahishasur.

Dvarakadish (Dvakaradīś): A form of Krishna.

Eklingji (Ekliṅgjī): A form of the god Shiv, whose temple at Kailashpuri is associated with the royal family of Udaipur.

eklo (*eklo*): Alone.

gaddi (*gaddī*): Throne.

gali (*gālī*): Insult: a genre of insulting songs sung by women.

Gauri (Gaurī): The "Golden One," a goddess married to the god Shiv.

Godavari: The *sati* whose story is sung in a ballad bearing her name.

Gogaji (Gogājī): A hero who appears in the epic *Pabuji*, but who also has his own story.

gopi (*gopī*): Milkmaid: one of the sylvan consorts of the god Krishna.

Goraji Bheruji (Gorājī Bherujī): "Light Bheruji"; the light and gentle form of the god Bheruji.

Gujar (Gūjar): Member of an agrarian caste.

gulal (*gulal*): Powder thrown during the celebration of the holiday Holi.

gun (*guṇ*): Quality; one of the three basic constituents of phenomenal reality.

haveli (*havelī*): Urban mansion.

Hindutva (Hindutva): "Hinduness."

Holi (Holī): A holiday devoted to the god Krishna; a day in which people throw colored powder and water at each other as a form of *lila* or "play."

ishtadevta (*iṣṭadevta*): Chosen deity; either one's personally chosen deity or the deity chosen by a family as its special protector.

Itihasik (*itihāsik*): Literally, "historical," though this term refers also to mythological events.

Jagdish (Jagdīś): "Lord of the World"; a form of the god Vishnu.

jagir (*jagīr*): Estate granted by a king.

Jaimal (Jaymal): General whom Kallaji is said to have lifted on his shoulders to fight after the emperor Akbar shot him in the foot.

Jamvai Mata (Jamvāī Mātā): A tutelary goddess (*kuldevi*) of the Kachvaha Rajputs.

jati (*jāti*): Caste.

jauhar (*jauhar*): Mass immolation of women when the men who protect them go out to certain death in a patently unwinnable battle.

jauhar Mela (Jauhar Melā): Festival celebrating the three *jauhar*s of Chittor.

Jhala (Jhālā): A line (*kul*) of Rajputs.

jhunjharji (*jhũjharjī, jūjharjī*): A hero who continues to fight after being decapitated.

jin (*jin*): Spiritual conqueror; a term from Jainism that refers to those who have won salvation; *tirthankar*.

Jogmaya (Jogmāyā, Yogmāyā): "One possessing the power of illusion"; a goddess.

Kachvaha (Kāchvahā): a line (*kul*) of Rajputs; the line of the royal family of Jaipur.

Kalaji Bheruji (Kālāji Bherujī): The "Dark Bheruji," whose complement is Gora Bheruji.

Kallaji (Kallajī, Kalajī): A hero with a large cultic following.

Kali (Kālī): The "Dark One," a goddess known throughout India as the conqueror of various demons.

kamdar (*kāmdār*): Bookkeeper; accountant; Baniya.

kanku (*kaṅkū*, Hindi *kuṅkūm*): Auspicious red powder used as a cosmetic.

Karni Mata (Karnī Mātā): A Caran kuldevi who is also worshiped by pilgrims from other castes at her temple in Deshnok.

kesar (*kesar*): Yellow powder; saffron.

khelna (*khelnā*): To play.

khir (*khīr*): A sweet milk pudding.

Krishna (Kṛṣṇa): A god worshiped in various forms such as Shri Nathji, Carbhuja, and Dvarakadish; a form of the god Vishnu.

Kshatriya (Kṣatriya): Warrior: a member of the warrior class (*varn*).

Kshetrapal (Kśetrapal): "Protector of the field"; a guardian deity; term applied to various Bherujis and associated with posthumous heroes.

kul (*kul*): Line; kinship unit comprising smaller units such as *shakh* (branch) and *nak* (branch-tip; twig).

kuldevi (*kuḷdevī*): Familial goddess; goddess of the *kul*.

laj (*lāj*): Modesty: shame.

lakh (*lākh*): 100,000.

Lakshman (Lakṣmaṇ): Brother of Ram, hero of the *Ramayan*.

Lakshmi (Lakṣmī): Goddess of good fortune.

lala (*lālā*): Glass turban pendants.

Langa (Lāṅgā): Muslim musician caste.

lapsi (*lapsī*): A sweet dish.

ling (*liṅg*): "Mark"; phallus; a form of Shiv.

Maha Singh (Mahā Sinh): A hero slain by Ranbaj Khan.

Mahabharat (Mahābhārat): A massive epic known in variant forms throughout India and beyond.

maharana (*mahārānā*): "Great king"; epithet of the king of Mewar.

mahasatiyan (*mahāsatiyāṇ*): Cremation ground.

Mahishasur, Mahish (Mahiṣāsur): A demon slain by the goddess Durga; buffalo demon.

Man Singh (Mān Sinh): A *jhunjhari* from Amet, who was slain by his father.

mardana (*mardānā*): Men's quarters in a house that observes strict separation of the sexes or *parda*.

Mata (Mātā): "Mother," epithet of a goddess.

matrika (*mātṛkā*): *See* Saptamatrika.

menhdi (*menhdī*): Red paste (henna) applied as a cosmetic, especially to the hands.

Mer (Mer): Member of a tribal group.

moksh (*mokṣ*): Liberation from rebirth.

mundan (*muṇḍan*): Tonsure.

Musalman (Musalmān): Muslim.

Naganechaji (Nāgānechājī): Goddess or *kuldevi* of the Rathod Rajputs.

Naruji (Narujī, Naḷujī): A hero who died defending Udaipur against the army of Aurangzeb.

Nath (Nāth): "Lord," member of a sect of renouncers.

Navratri (Navrātrī): The festival of "Nine Nights," which celebrates the victory of the goddess Durga over the demons and also of the god Ram over the demons.

nil (*nīl*): Bluing; indigo, an inauspicious blue color.

Pabuji (Pābūjī): Hero with an epic that is particularly popular in the Marwar region of Rajasthan.

pan (*pān*): A concoction of betel nut and spices wrapped in a leaf and chewed.

parca (*parcā*, also *parco*): Proof; miracle.

parda: (*pardā*): "Curtain"; the seclusion of women in the household; purdah.

pativrata (*pativratā*): A devoted wife; literally. "one who has taken a vow [of devotion] to her husband."

phal (*phal*): "Fruit"; consequence.

Phatta (Phattā): Jaimal's and Kallaji's kinsman who died with them at Chittor.

pihar (*pīhar*): A woman's natal family.

pir (*pīr*): A Muslim hero; may refer to a battle hero or to a great teacher.

pitar (*pitar, pitṛ*): A male ancestor.

pitrani (*pitrānī*): A female ancestor.

Pitrlok (Pitṛlok): The abode of ancestors; heaven.

Poliyaji (Poliyajī): A guardian deity.

prasad (*prasād*): What remains of offerings given to a deity after it consumes their subtle essence.

Pratap (*Pratāp*): A *jhunjhari* who died fighting the forces of Sir Pratap.

pret (*pret*): Ghost.

puja (*pūjā*): Ritual worship.

pujari (*pujārī*): Officiating priest.

purana (*purāṇā*): Collection of myths and other materials such as royal genealogy.

purbaj (*pūrbaj*): Ancestor.

putar (*putar, putṛ*): Son.

putli (*putlī*): Embossed pendant.

rajas (*rajas*): The quality of kinesis and passion; one of the three basic constituents of phenomenal reality.

rajasik (*rajasik*): Pertaining to the quality of kinesis and passion.

Rajput; Rājpūt: Member of a martial caste.

Ram (Rām): Hero of the *Ramayan* epic.

Ramayan (Rāmāyaṇ): The story of Ram; an epic known in various forms throughout India and beyond.

Ramdev (Rāmdev): A hero whose temple near Jaisalmer is a popular place of pilgrimage; a hero worshiped by Hindus as a *vir* and Muslims as a *pir*.

Rana Pratap (Rāṇā Pratāp): The ruler (Maharana) of Mewar who fought the Moghul Akbar.

Ranbaj Khan (Raṇbaj Khān): Enemy of the hero Maha Singh.

Rathor (Rāthoḍ, Rathauḍ): A line (*kul*) of Rajputs; the *kul* of the royal family of Marwar.

ratijaga (*rātijagā*): Literally, "night wake," a night-long session of singing in which women invite various deities and ancestors to an auspicious occasion, especially a rite of passage such as a birth or wedding.

Ravan (Rāvāṇ): A demon; nemesis of Ram, hero of the *Ramayan* epic.

ravanhattha (*rāvaṇhatthā*, also *rāvaṇhatto*): Stringed instrument common in the Marwar area.

riti rivaj (*riti rivāj*): "Norm and custom"; lifestyle.

sadhu (*sādhu*): Renouncer; ascetic.

sagasji (*sagasjī*): A classification of hero.

sagati (*sagati, śakti*): Power: the power of activation often associated with goddesses and women; a goddess.

sahagamini (*sahagāminī*): Literally, "one who goes with"; a wife who burns on the pyre of her deceased husband; *sati*.

saka (*sakā*): an unwinnable battle in which warriors don saffron, the hue of renunciation, when they go out to meet their enemies.

sakshat (*sākṣāt*): Literally, "before the eyes"; an apparition of a supernatural being or deceased ancestor to a person who is awake.

samadhi (*samādhi*): Death; liberation.

samskar (*saṃskār*): A purifying rite of passage.

sanatan dharm (*sanātan dharm*): Universal law.

sapha (*sāphā*): A style of turban.

Saptamatrika (Saptamātṛkā): a member of a group of seven goddesses; sometimes these are identified as spouses of well-known deities.

Sardar Singh (Sardār Sinh): Prince killed by Maharana Raj Sinh; a *sagasji* who is the brother of the *sagasji* worshiped at Sarv Ritu Vilas.

Sarv Ritu Vilas (Sarv Ṛtu Vilas): Temple for Udaipur's most famous *sagasji*.

sat (*sat*): Inner goodness and truth; moral fuel, which propels a warrior to sacrifice his life in battle and which erupts into flames when a *sati* mounts the pyre of her deceased husband.

sati (*sati*): "Good woman"; a woman who immolates herself on the pyre of her deceased husband.

Sati Godavari (Sati Godāvarī): A *satī* who cursed many people trying to stop her from burning on her husband's pyre.

satimata (*satīmātā*): A *sati* who has become divine after immolating herself on her husband's pyre.

Satimata (Satīmātā): A *sati* worshiped as a goddess.

sattva (*sattva*): "Truth"; one of the three qualities constituting phenomenal reality.

sattvik (*sattvik*): Pertaining to the quality of truth.

shahid (*śahīd*): Muslim martyr.

shakti (*śakti*): *See sagati.*

Shakti De (Śakti De): Gujarati *kuldevi* who married her Jhala Rajput husband, a king, after consuming his body bit by bit.

shanti bhav (*śanti bhāv*): Peaceful mood; quiet form of possession.

Shila Mata (Śilā Mātā): Goddess with a temple in the Amber fort, Jaipur.

Shitala Mata: (Śītala Mātā, Sītalā Mātā): Goddess of pustular diseases.

Shiv (Śiv): A god: as Eklingji, the chosen deity of the Sisodiya Rajputs belonging to the royal family of Mewar.

Shri Nathji (Srī Nathjī): A form of Krishna worshiped in Nathdwara, near Udaipur.

shringar (*śṛṅgār*): Ornamentation, including cosmetics, jewelry, and other accessories.

Shudra (Śudra): The lowest class of castes; typically a member of a service caste.

shur (*shūr*, also *sūr*): Hero; *vir*.

Sir Pratap (Sir Pratāp): Regent of Jodhpur State from 1873 to 1922.

Sisodiya (Sisodiyā): A line of Rajputs: line to which the royal family of Mewar belongs.

Sita (Sītā): Wife of the hero Ram in the *Ramayan*.

solah thikana (*solaḥ ṭhikāna*): A "sixteen *thikana*"; a *thikana* belonging to the group of estates ranked highest.

sthan (*sthān, thān*): Literally. "place"; site of a sacred icon; *sthapana*.

sthapana (*sthāpaṇā, thāpaṇā*): A sacred spot; site of a sacred icon.

suhagin (*suhāgin*): Devoted wife; *pativrata*.

Sukh Devi (Sukh Devī): Goddess of happiness.

sur (*sūr*, also *shūr*): Hero: *vir*.

Surtan Singh (Surtān Sinh, also Suḷtan Sinh): Prince killed by Maharana Raj Singh; the *sagasji* worshiped at Sarv Ritu Vilas.

svadharm (*svadharm*): Caste duty.

svarg (*svarg*): Heaven.

tamas (*tamas*): The quality of inertia and torpor; one of the three qualities constituting phenomenal reality.

tamasik (*tamasik*): Pertaining to the quality of inertia and torpor.

Tejaji (Tejājī): A hero.

thakur (*ṭhākur*): Ruler, lord.

thikana (*ṭhikāṇā*): Estate granted by a king.

tithi (*tithi*): Date; birthday; anniversary.

tirthankar (*tirthaṅkar*): A Jain ascetic who has achieved liberation from rebirth and who is venerated by many Jain ascetics and laypersons.

ugra bhav (*ugra bhāv*): Fierce mood: violent form of possession.

Vaikunth (Vaikuṇṭh): Heaven.

Vaishya (Vaiśya): Member of the merchant class.

vamsh (*vaṃś*): Family: a large kinship unit comprising lesser units such as *kul*, *shakh*, and *nak*.

varn (*varṇ*): Class; one of the four classes, each of which comprises many castes or *jatis*.

vir (*vīr*, *bīr*): Hero.

virangana (*vīrāṅganā*): Heroine.

Virbhumi (Vīrbhūmi): Literally, the "land of heroes"; Rajasthan.

Virgati (Vīrgati): Literally, "the goal of heroes"; warrior heaven.

virta (*vīrtā*): Courage, bravery.

Vishnu (Viṣṇu): A god who has many incarnations, including Krishna and Ram.

vrat (*vrat*): Vow.

yogini (*yoginī*): Female ascetic.

yoni (*yoni*): Symbol of a goddess; vulva.

zanana: (*zanānā*): Women's quarters in a household that observes the strictest form of sex segregation or *parda*.

Bibliography

BOOKS, ARTICLES, AND FILMS

Alter, Joseph S. "Celibacy, Sexuality, and the Transformation of Gender into Nationalism in North India." *Journal of Asian Studies* 53, no. 1 (February 1994): 45–66.

———. *The Wrestler's Body: Identity and Ideology in North India.* Berkeley: University of California Press, 1992.

Amar Singh Diary, Jaipur, July–December 1933. Manuscript in the library of Mohan Singh, Kanota.

Appadurai, Arjun, Frank J. Korom, and Margaret A. Mills. "Introduction." In *Gender, Genre, and Power in South Asian Expressive Traditions*, edited by Arjun Appadurai, Frank J. Korom, and Margaret A. Mills, 3–29. Philadelphia: University of Pennsylvania Press, 1991.

Apple, R. W., Jr. "India: Asia's Epic Adventure." *Town and Country*, April 1997, 82–95.

Babb, Lawrence A. "Rejecting Violence: Sacrifice and the Social Identity of Trading Communities." *Contributions to Indian Sociology*, n.s., 32, no. 2 (1998): 387–407.

———. *Absent Lord: Ascetics and Kings in a Jain Ritual Culture.* Berkeley: University of California Press, 1996.

Balmer, Randall. "American Fundamentalism: The Ideal of Femininity." In *Fundamentalism and Gender*, edited by John Stratton Hawley, 47–62. New York: Oxford University Press, 1994.

Bandit Queen. Directed by Ashok Mehta. Film Four International and Kaleidoscope Production. Distributed by Evergreen Entertainment, Los Angeles. 1994.

Banerjee, Sikata. "Masculine Hinduism, the Shiv Sena, and Political Mobilization." Paper delivered at the annual meeting of the Association of Asian Studies, Chicago, March 13–16, 1997.

Basu, Amrita. "Engendering Communal Violence: Men as Victims, Women as Agents." Paper delivered at the workshop "Rethinking

South Asian History, Re-visioning South Asia's Future," Center of South Asian and Indian Ocean Studies, Tufts University, May 10, 1997.

———. "Feminism Inverted: The Gendered Imagery and Real Women of Hindu Nationalism." In *Women and the Hindu Right: A Collection of Essays*, edited by Tanika Sarkar and Urvashi Butalia, 158–180. New Delhi: Kali for Women, 1995.

Beck, Brenda E. F. *The Three Twins: The Telling of a South Indian Folk Epic.* Bloomington: Indiana University Press, 1982.

———. "The Hero in a Contemporary, Local Tamil Epic." *Journal of Indian Folkloristics* 1, no. 1 (January–June 1978): 26–39.

Bennett, Lynn. *Dangerous Wives and Sacred Sisters: Social and Symbolic Roles of High-Caste Women in Nepal.* New York: Columbia University Press, 1983.

Biardeau, Madeleine. "Brahmans and Meat-Eating Gods." In *Criminal Gods and Demon Devotees: Essays on the Guardians of Popular Hinduism*, edited by Alf Hiltebeitel, 19–33. Albany: State University of New York Press, 1989.

Biardeau, Madeleine, and Charles Malamoud. *Le sacrifice dans l'Inde ancienne.* Paris: Presses universitaires de France, 1976.

Blackburn, Stuart H. "Patterns of Development for Indian Oral Epics." In *Oral Epics in India*, edited by Stuart H. Blackburn et al. 15–32. Berkeley: University of California Press, 1989.

———. *Singing of Birth and Death: Texts in Performance.* Philadelphia: University of Pennsylvania Press, 1988.

———. "Death and Deification: Folk Cults in Hinduism." *History of Religions* 24, no. 3 (1985): 255–274.

———. "The Folk Hero and Class Interests in Tamil Heroic Ballads." *Asian Folklore Studies* 37, no. 1 (1978): 131–149.

Blackburn, Stuart H., Peter J. Claus, Joyce B. Flueckiger, and Susan S. Wadley, eds. *Oral Epics in India.* Berkeley: University of California Press, 1989.

Bloch, Maurice, and Jonathan Parry. "Introduction." In *Death and the Regeneration of Life*, edited by Maurice Bloch and Jonathan Parry, 1–44. Cambridge: Cambridge University Press, 1982.

Bok, Sissela. *Lying: Moral Choice in Public and Private Life.* New York: Pantheon, 1978.

Brenneman, Walter L., Jr. "Serpents, Cows, and Ladies: Contrasting Symbolism in Irish and Indo-European Cattle-raiding Myths." *History of Religions* 28, no. 4 (1989): 340–354.

Burman, J. J. Roy. "Hindu-Muslim Syncretism in India." *Economic and Political Weekly*, May 18, 1996, 1211–1215.

———. *The Twice-Born: A Study of a Community of High-Caste Hindus.* Bloomington: Indiana University Press, 1967.

———. "Patterns of Religious Observances in Three Villages of Rajasthan." In *Aspects of Religion in Indian Society*, edited by L. P. Vidyarthi, 59–113. Meerut: Kedar Nath Ram Nath, 1961.

Chatterjee, Partha. *The Nation and Its Fragments: Colonial and Postcolonial Histories.* Princeton: Princeton University Press, 1993.

Chattopadhyaya, B. D. "Early Memorial Stones of Rajasthan: A Preliminary Analysis of Their Inscriptions." In *Memorial Stones: A Study of their Origin, Significance and Variety*, edited by S. Settar and Gunther D. Sontheimer, 148–149. Dharwad: Institute of Indian Art History, Karnatak University, and Heidelberg: South Asia Institute, University of Heidelberg, 1982.

Chaturvedi, Mahendra, and Bhola Nath Tiwari, eds. *A Practical Hindi-English Dictionary*, eighth edition. New Delhi: National, 1983.

Chauhan, Brij Raj. *A Rajasthan Village*. New Delhi, Vir, 1967.

Claus, Peter J. "Heroes and Heroines in the Conceptual Framework of Tulu Culture." *Journal of India Folkloristics* 1, no. 2 (1978): 27–42.

———. "The Siri Myth and Ritual: A Mass Possession Cult of South India." *Ethnology* 14, no. 1 (1975): 47–58.

Coccari, Diane M. "The Bir Babas of Banaras and the Deified Dead." In *Criminal Gods and Demon Devotees: Essays on the Guardians of Popular Hinduism*, edited by Alf Hiltebeitel, 251–269. Albany: State University of New York Press, 1989.

———. "The Bir Babas of Banaras: An Analysis of a Folk Deity in North Indian Hinduism." Ph.D. dissertation, University of Wisconsin, Madison, 1986.

Cohn, Bernard S. "The Changing Status of a Depressed Caste." In *Village India*, edited by McKim Marriott, 53–77. Chicago: University of Chicago Press, 1955.

Coomaraswamy, A. K. "Atmayajna: Self-sacrifice." *Harvard Journal of Asiatic Studies* 6 (1941): 358–398.

Cort, John E. "Introduction: Contested Jain Identities of Self and Other." In *Open Boundaries: Jain Communities and Cultures in Indian History*, edited by John E. Cort, 1–14. Albany: State University of New York Press, 1998.

———. "The Bell-Eared Great Hero: Tantric Worship in Jainism." Paper presented at the Annual Conference on South Asia, University of Wisconsin, Madison, October 17–19, 1997.

Courtright, Paul B. *The Goddess and the Dreadful Practice*. New York: Oxford University Press, forthcoming

———. "Satī, Sacrifice, and Marriage: The Modernity of Tradition." In *From the Margins of Hindu Marriage: Essays on Gender, Religon, and Culture*, edited by Lindsey Harlan and Paul B. Courtright, 184–203. New York: Oxford University Press, 1995.

Crooke, William. *The Popular Religion and Folklore of Northern India*. 1896. 2d edition. Delhi: Munshiram Manoharlal, 1968.

———. *Races of Northern India*. 1907. Reprint, Delhi: Cosmo, 1973.

Daniélou, Alain, trans. *Shilappadikaram*, by Prince Ilangô Adigal. New York: New Directions, 1965.

Das, Veena. "Introduction: Communities, Riots, Survivors—The South Asian Experience." In *Mirrors of Violence: Communities, Riots and Survivors in South Asia*, edited by Veena Das, 1–36. Delhi: Oxford University Press, 1990.

Davis, Marvin. *Rank and Rivalry: The Politics of Inequlity in Rural West Bengal*. Cambridge: Cambridge University Press, 1983.

Davis, Richard H. *Lives of Indian Images*. Princeton: Princeton University Press, 1997.

Devi, Mahasweta. "Paddy Seeds." In *Of Women, Outcastes, Peasants, and Rebels: A Selection of Bengali Short Stories*, edited and translated by Kalpana Bardhan, 158–184. Berkeley: University of California Press, 1990.

deVries, Jan. *Heroic Song and Heroic Legend*. Translated by B. J. Timmer. London: Oxford University Press, 1963.

Dirks, Nicholas B. "Homo Hierarchicus: Caste Politics and the Politics of Caste." Paper delivered in South Asia Seminar, Center for International Affairs, Harvard University, April 23, 1997.

———. *The Hollow Crown: Ethnohistory of an Indian Kingdom*. Cambridge: Cambridge University Press, 1987.

Doniger, Wendy. *The Bedtrick: Tales of Sex and Masquerade*. Chicago: University of Chicago Press, 2000.

————. *Splitting the Difference: Gender and Myth in Ancient Greece and India*. Chicago: University of Chicago Press, 1999.

————. *The Implied Spider: Politics and Theology in Myth*. New York: Columbia University Press, 1998.

————. "Begetting on Margin: Adultery and Surrogate Pseudomarriage in Hinduism." In *From the Margins of Hindu Marriage: Essays on Gender, Religion, and Culture*, edited by Lindsey Harlan and Paul B. Courtright, 160–183. New York: Oxford University Press, 1995.

————, trans. *The Laws of Manu*. New York: Penguin, 1991.

————. *Dreams, Illusions, and Other Realities*. Chicago: University of Chicago Press, 1984.

————. (O'Flaherty). *Women, Androgynes, and Other Mythical Beasts*. Chicago: University of Chicago Press, 1980.

————. *The Origins of Evil in Hindu Mythology*. Berkeley: University of California Press, 1976.

————. *Śiva: The Erotic Ascetic*. Oxford: Oxford University Press, 1973.

Dube, S. C. *Indian Village*. New York: Harper Colophon Books, 1967.

Duerr, Hans Peter. *Dreamtime: Concerning the Boundary between Wilderness and Civilization*. Translated by Felicitas Goodman. Oxford: Basil Blackwell, 1985.

Dumézil, George. *The Destiny of the Warrior*, translated by Alf Hiltebeitel. Chicago: University of Chicago Press, 1970.

Dumont, Louis. *A South Indian Subcaste: Social Organization and Religion of the Pramalai Kallar*. Delhi: Oxford University Press, 1986.

————. *Homo Hierarchicus: The Caste System and Its Implications*. Chicago: University of Chicago Press, 1970.

Eliade, Mircea. *The Sacred and the Profane: The Nature of Religion*. Translated by Willard Trask. New York: Harcourt Brace Jovanovich, 1957.

Engineer, Asghar Ali. *Communalism in India: A Historical and Empirical Study*. New Delhi: Vikas, 1995.

Erdman, Joan L. "Becoming Rajasthani: Pluralism and the Production of *Dhartī Dhorāṅ Rī*." In *The Idea of Rajasthan: Explorations in Regional Identity*. 2 vols. Vol. 1, *Constructions*, edited by Karine Schomer, Joan L. Erdman, Deryck O. Lodrick, and Lloyd I. Rudolph, 45–79. New Delhi: Manohar and the American Institute of Indian Studies, 1994.

Erndl, Kathleen M. *Victory to the Mother: The Hindu Goddess of Northwest India in Myth, Ritual, and Symbol*. New York: Oxford University Press, 1993.

————. "Rapist or Bodyguard, Demon or Devotee? Images of Bhairo in the Mythology and Cult of Vaiṣṇo Devī." In *Criminal Gods and Demon Devotees: Essays on the Guardians of Popular Hinduism*, edited by Alf Hiltebeitel, 239–250. Albany: State University of New York Press, 1989.

Father, Son, and Holy War. Directed by Anand Pathwardan. First Run/Icarus Films, Los Angeles, 1994.

"Favourite of Puppeteer." *The Hindu*, January 3, 1991.

Filliozat, Jean. "The Giving up of Life by the Sage: The Suicides of the Criminal and the Hero in Indian Tradition." In *Religion, Philosophy, Yoga: A Selection of Articles by Jean Filliozat*, translated by Maurice Shukla, 135–159. Delhi: Motilal Banarsidass, 1991.

Filliozat, Pierre. "The After-Death Destiny of the Hero According to the Mahābhārata."
In *Memorial Stones: A Study of Their Origin, Significance, and Variety*, edited by
S. Settar and Gunther D. Sontheimer, 3–8. Dharwad: Institute of Art History,
Karnatak University, and Heidelberg: South Asia Institute, University of Heidel-
berg, 1982.

Flueckiger, Joyce Burkhalter. *Gender and Genre in the Folklore of Middle India*. Ithaca:
Cornell University Press, 1996.

Flueckiger, Joyce Burkhalter, and Laurie J. Sears, eds. *The Boundaries of the Text:
Epic Performances in South and Southeast Asia*. Ann Arbor: Center for South
and Southeast Asia, University of Michigan, 1991.

Fox, Richard G. "Family, Caste and Commerce in a North Indian Market Town."
Economic Development and Cultural Change 15 (1967): 297–314.

Galey, Jean-Claude. "Reconsidering Kingship in India: An Ethnological Perspective."
In *Kingship and the Kings: History and Anthropology*, No. 4, edited by Jean-
Claude Galey, 123–187. London: Harwood Academic Publishers, 1989.

———. "L'État et le lignage." *L'Homme* 13 (1973): 71–82.

Geary, Patrick J. *Furta Sacra: Thefts of Relics in the Central Middle Ages*. Princeton:
Princeton University Press, 1978.

Gilbert, W. S. *The Pirates of Penzance*. London: G. Bell and Sons, 1911.

Gold, Ann Grodzins. "Whoever Hears God's Wedding Song Has All Their Sins
Removed." Paper delivered at the conference "Framing: Narrative,
Metaphysics, Perception," Academy of Sciences and Humanities, Jerusalem,
May 1999.

———. "Outspoken Women: Representations of Female Voices in a Rajasthani
Folklore Community." *Oral Tradition* 12, no. 1 (1997): 103–133.

———. "The 'Jungli Rani' and Other Troubled Wives in Rajasthani Oral Traditions."
In *From the Margins of Hindu Marriage: Essays on Gender, Religion, and
Culture*, edited by Lindsey Harlan and Paul B. Courtright, 119–136. New York:
Oxford University Press, 1995.

———. "Gender, Violence, and Power: Rajasthani Stories of Shakti." In *Women as
Subjects: South Asian Histories*, edited by Nita Kumar, 26–48. Charlottesville:
University Press of Virginia, 1994.

———. "Purdah Is as Purdah's Kept: A Storyteller's Story," in *Listen to the Heron's
Words: Reimagining Gender and Kinship in North India*, edited by Gloria
Raheja and Ann Gold, 164–181. Berkeley: University of California Press,
1994.

———. "Sexuality, Fertility, and Erotic Imagination in Rajasthani Women's Songs."
In *Listen to the Heron's Words: Reimagining Gender and Kinship in North
India*, edited by Gloria Raheja and Ann Gold, 30–72. Berkeley: University of
California Press, 1994.

———. *A Carnival of Parting: The Tales of King Bharthari and King Gopi Chand as
Sung and Told by Madhu Natisar Nath of Ghatiyali, Rajasthan*. Berkeley:
University of California Press, 1992.

———. *Fruitful Journeys: The Ways of Rajasthani Pilgrims*. Berkeley: University of
California Press, 1988.

———. "Spirit Possession Perceived and Performed in Rural Rajasthan." *Contributions to Indian Sociology*, n.s., 22, no. 1 (January–June 1988): 35–61.

Gold, Ann, and Lindsey Harlan. Raja Nal's Mistake: Epic Themes in Rajasthani
Women's Ritual Narratives." In *Folklore in Modern India*, edited by Jawaharlal
Handoo, 151–162. Mysore: Central Institute of Indian Languages, 1998.

Goldman, Robert P. "Rāmaḥ Sahalakṣmaṇaḥ: Psychological and Literary Aspects of the Composite Hero of Vālmīki's Rāmāyaṇa." *Journal of Indian Philosophy* 8 (1980): 11–51.

———. "Fathers, Sons, and Gurus: Oedipal Conflicts in the Sanskrit Epics." *Journal of Indian Philosophy* 6 (1978): 325–392.

Gottschalk, Peter. *Beyond Hindu and Muslim: Multiple Identity in Narratives from Village India*. New York: Oxford University Press, 2000.

Guha, K. "Bhairon: A Śaivite Deity in Transition." *Folklore* (Calcutta) 1 (1960): 207–222.

Hanchett, Suzanne. "Ritual Symbols—Unifying and Divisive: Observations on the Relation between Festivals and Political Processes in South Asia." In *Religion in Modern India*, edited by Giri Raj Gupta, 131–150. Delhi: Vikas, 1983.

Handelman, Don. "Postlude: Towards a Braiding of Frame." In *Behind the Mask: Dance, Healing, and Possession in South India*, edited by David Dean Shulman and Deborah Thiagarajan, forthcoming.

———. "Framing, Braiding, and Killing Play." In *Focaal: The European Journal of Anthropology*, no. 37 (2001): 145–156.

Hansen, Thomas Blom. *The Saffron Wave: Democracy and Hindu Nationalism in Modern India*. Princeton: Princeton University Press, 1999.

Hardgrove, Anne. "Sati Worship and Marwari Public Identity in India." *Journal of Asian Studies* 58, no. 3 (1999): 723–752.

Hardy, Thomas. *Far from the Madding Crowd*. New York: Penguin, 1978.

Harlan, Lindsey. "On Headless Heroes: *Pabuji* from the Inside Out." In *Valuing History: Culture and Society in the Study of Rajasthan*, edited by Varsha Joshi, Michael Meister, and Lawrence Babb. New Delhi: Rawat, 2002.

———. "Nala and Damayanti's Reversals of Fortune: Reflections on When a Women Should Know Better." In *Nala and Damayanti: Context as Narrative in South Asia*, edited by Susan S. Wadley and Joyce Flueckiger, forthcoming.

———. "Truth and Sacrifice: *Satī* Immolations in India." In *Sacrificing the Self*, edited by Margaret Cormack. New York: Oxford University Press, 2002.

———. "Reversing the Gaze in America: Parody in Divali Performance at Connecticut College." In *South Asians in the Diaspora: Histories and Religious Traditions*, edited by Knut A. Jacobsen and Pratap Kumar. Leiden: Brill, forthcoming.

———. "Battle, Brides, and Sacrifice: Rajput *Kuldevi*s in Rajasthan." In *Is the Goddess a Feminist?: The Politics of South Asian Goddesses*, edited by Alf Hiltebeitel and Kathleen M. Erndl, 69–90. Sheffield: Sheffield Academic Press, 2001.

———. "Deploying the Martial Past: Reflections of Hero Worship." Paper given at the annual meeting of the American Academy of Religion, Nashville, Tenn. November 18–21, 2000.

———. "Heroes Alone and Heroes at Home: Gender and Intertextuality in Two Narratives." In *Invented Identities: The Interplay of Gender, Religion, and Politics in India*, edited by Julia Leslie and Mary McGee, 231–251. Delhi: Oxford University Press, 2000.

———. "On Hero Worship: Reflections on Rajput Identity." Paper given at the conference "Empire, Culture and Globalization," Middlebury College, Vermont, April 2000.

———. "On Being Framed in a Rajput Hero Narrative." Paper given at the conference "Framing: Narrative, Metaphysics, Perception," Academy of Sciences and Humanities, Jerusalem, May 1999.

———. "Tale of a Headless Horseman: Kallaji Rathor." Paper presented at the annual Conference on South Asia, University of Wisconsin, Madison, October 17–19, 1997.

———. "Satī: The Story of Godāvarī." In *Devī: Goddesses of India*, edited by John Stratton Hawley and Donna Marie Wulff, 227–249. Berkeley: University of California Press, 1996.

———. "Abandoning Shame: Mīrā and the Margins of Marriage." In *From the Margins of Hindu Marriage: Essays on Gender, Religion, and Culture*, edited by Lindsey Harlan and Paul B. Courtright, 204–227. New York: Oxford University Press, 1995.

———. "Women's Songs for Auspicious Occasions." In *Religions of India in Practice*, edited by Donald Lopez, 269–280. Princeton: Princeton University Press, 1995.

———. "Perfection and Devotion: Sati Tradition in Rajasthan." In *Sati, The Blessing and the Curse: The Burning of Wives in India*, edited by John Stratton Hawley, 79–99. New York: Oxford University Press, 1994.

———. *Religion and Rajput Women: The Ethic of Protection in Contemporary Narratives*. Berkeley: University of California Press, 1992.

Harlan, Lindsey, and Paul B. Courtright. "Introduction: On Hindu Marriage and Its Margins." In *From the Margins of Hindu Marriage: Essays on Gender, Religion, and Culture*, edited by Lindsey Harlan and Paul B. Courtright, 3–18. New York: Oxford University Press, 1995.

Hart, George L. III. *The Poems of Ancient Tamil*. Berkeley: University of California Press, 1975.

Hawley, John Stratton. "Prologue: The Goddess in India." In *Devī, Goddesses of India*, edited by John Stratton Hawley and Donna Marie Wulff, 1–28. Berkeley: University of California Press, 1996.

———. "Hinduism: Satī and Its Defenders." In *Fundamentalism and Gender*, edited by John Stratton Hawley, 79–110. New York: Oxford University Press, 1994.

———. "Introduction." In *Sati, The Blessing and the Curse: The Burning of Wives in India*, edited by John Stratton Hawley, 1–26. New York: Oxford University Press, 1994.

———, ed. *Sati, The Blessing and the Curse: The Burning of Wives in India*. New York: Oxford Unversity Press, 1994.

Hawley, John Stratton, and Wayne Proudfoot. "Introduction." In *Fundamentalism and Gender*, edited by John Stratton Hawley, 3–44. New York: Oxford University Press, 1994.

Haynes, Douglas, and Gyan Prakash. "Introduction: The Entanglement of Power and Resistance." In *Contesting Power: Resistance and Everyday Social Relations in South Asia*, edited by Douglas Haynes and Gyan Prakash, 1–22. Berkeley: University of California Press, 1991.

Heesterman, J. C. *The Broken World of Sacrifice: An Essay in Ancient Indian Ritual*. Chicago: University of Chicago Press, 1993.

———. *The Inner Conflict of Tradition: Essays in Indian Ritual Kingship and Society*. Chicago: University of Chicago Press, 1985.

Herrenschmidt, Olivier. "Le sacrifice du buffle en Andhra cotier: le 'culte de village' confronté aux notions de sacrifiant et d'unité de culte." *Puruṣārtha: sciences sociales en Asie du Sud* 5 (1981): 137–177.

Hershman, Paul. "Hair, Sex and Dirt." *Man*, n.s., 9, no. 2 (1974): 274–298.

Herzfeld, Michael. "Honour and Shame: Problems in the Comparative Analysis of Moral Systems." *Man*, n.s., 15, no. 2 (June 1980): 339–351.

Hess, Linda. "Staring at Frames till They Turn into Loops: An Excursion through Some Worlds of Tulsidas." In *Living Banaras: Hindu Religion in Cultural Context*, edited by Bradley R. Hertel and Cynthia Ann Humes, 73–101. Albany: State University of New York Press, 1993.

Hiltebeitel, Alf. "Fathers of the Bride, Fathers of Sati: Myths, Rites, and Scholarly Practices." *Thamyris* 6, no. 1 (Spring 1999): 65–94.

———. *Rethinking India's Oral and Classical Epics: Draupadī among Rajputs, Muslims, and Dalits*. Chicago: University of Chicago Press, 1999.

———. *The Cult of Draupadī*. Vol. 2, *On Hindu Ritual and the Goddess*. Chicago: University of Chicago Press, 1991.

———. *The Ritual of Battle: Krishna in the Mahābhārata*. Albany: State University of New York Press, [1976] 1990.

———. *The Cult of Draupadī*. Vol. 1, *Mythologies: From Gingee to Kuruksetra*. Chicago: University of Chicago Press, 1988.

———. "Draupadī's Hair." *Puruṣārtha: sciences sociales en Asie du Sud* 5 (1981): 179–214.

Hitchcock, John T. "The Idea of the Martial Rājpūt." In *Traditional India: Structure and Change*, edited by Milton Singer, 10–17. Philadelphia: American Folklore Society, 1959.

Humes, Cynthia Ann. "Vindhyavāsinī: Local Goddess yet Great Goddess." In *Devī: Goddesses of India*, edited by John Stratton Hawley and Donna Marie Wulff, 49–76. Berkeley: University of California Press, 1996.

Jamison, Stephanie W. *Sacrificed Wife, Sacrificer's Wife: Women, Ritual, and Hospitality in Ancient India*. New York: Oxford University Press, 1996.

———. "Draupadī on the Walls of Troy: Iliad 3 from an Indic Perspective." *Classical Antiquity* 13, no. 1 (1994): 5–15.

Jason, Heda. *Ethnopoetics: A Multilingual Terminology*. Jerusalem: Israel Ethnographic Society, 1975.

Justice, Christopher. *Dying the Good Death: The Pilgrimage to Die in India's Holy City*. Albany: State University of New York Press, 1997.

Kakar, Sudhir. *The Colors of Violence: Cultural Identities, Religion, and Conflict*. Chicago: University of Chicago Press, 1996.

———. "Some Unconscious Aspects of Ethnic Violence in India." In *Mirrors of Violence: Communities, Riots and Survivors in South Asia*, edited by Veena Das, 135–145. Delhi: Oxford University Press, 1990.

———. "Lord of the Spirit World." In *Shamans, Mystics, and Doctors: A Psychological Inquiry into India and Its Healing Traditions*, edited by Sudhir Kakar, 53–88. Boston: Beacon, 1982.

———. "Soul Knowledge and Soul Force: The Pir of Patteshah Dargah." In *Shamans, Mystics, and Doctors: A Psychological Inquiry into India and Its Healing Traditions*, edited by Sudhir Kakar, 15–52. Boston: Beacon, 1982.

Khadgawat, Nathuram, ed. *Rajasthan through the Ages*. Vol. 1, *From the Earliest Times to 1315 A.D.* Bikaner: Rajasthan State Archives, 1966.

Kinsley, David R. "Kālī: Blood and Death out of Place." In *Devī: Goddesses of India*, edited by John Stratton Hawley and Donna Marie Wulff, 77–86. Berkeley: University of California Press, 1996.

———. *Hindu Goddesses: Visions of the Divine Feminine in the Hindu Religious Tradition*. Berkeley: University of California Press, 1986.

Klausner, Samuel. "Violence." *The Encyclopedia of Religion*, edited by Mircea Eliade, vol. 15: 268–271.

Knipe, David M. "Night of the Growing Dead: A Cult of Vīrabhadra in Coastal Andhra." In *Criminal Gods and Demon Devotees: Essays on the Guardians of Popular Hinduism*, eidted by Alf Hiltebeitel, 123–156. Albany: State University of New York Press, 1989.

———. "Sapiṇḍīkaraṇa: The Hindu Rite of Entry into Heaven." In *Religious Encounters with Death: Insights from the History and Anthroplogy of Religions*, edited by Frank E. Reynolds and Earle H. Waugh, 111–124. University Park: Pennsylvania State University Press, 1977.

Kolff, Dirk H. A. *Naukar, Rajput, and Sepoy: The Ethnohistory of the Military Labor Martket in Hindustan, 1450–1850*. Cambridge: Cambridge University Press, 1990.

Kothari, Komal. "Performers, Gods, and Heroes in the Oral Epics of Rajasthan." In *Oral Epics of India*, edited by Stuart H. Blackburn, Peter J. Claus, Joyce B. Flueckiger, and Susan S. Wadley, 102–117. Berkeley: University of California Press, 1989.

Kulke, Hermann. "Ksatriyaization and Social Change: A Study in the Orissa Setting." In *Aspects of Changing India: Studies in Honour of Prof. G. S. Ghurye*, edited by S. Devadas Pillai, 398–409. Bombay: Popular Prakashan, 1976.

Kurtz, Stanley N. *All Mothers Are One: Hindu India and the Cultural Reshaping of Psychoanalysis*. New York: Columbia University Press, 1992.

Kurup, K. K. N. *The Cult of Teyyam: Hero Worship in Kerala*. Calcutta: Indian Publications, 1973.

Laḷas, Sītārām, ed. by *Rājasthānī Sabd Kos*. Jodhpur: Caupāsnī Śikṣā Samiti, 1978.

Lambert, Helen. "Medical Knowledge in Rural Rajasthan: Popular Constructions of Illness and Therapeutic Practice." Ph.D. dissertation, Wolfson College, Oxford University, 1988.

Lapoint, Elwyn C. "The Epic of Guga: A North Indian Oral Tradition." In *American Studies in the Anthropology of India*, edited by Sylvia Vatuk, 281–308. New Delhi: Manohar, 1978.

Leslie, I. Julia. "A Problem of Choice: The Heroic Satī or the Widow-Ascetic." In *Rules and Remedies in Classical Indian Law*, edited by I. Julia Leslie, 46–61. Leiden: Brill, 1991.

———. *The Perfect Wife: The Orthodox Hindu Woman According to the Strīdharmapaddhati of Tryambakayajvan*. Delhi: Oxford University Press, 1989.

Lincoln, Bruce. *Death, War, and Sacrifice; Studies in Ideology and Practice*. Chicago: University of Chicago Press, 1991.

———. *Priests, Warriors, and Cattle: A Study in the Ecology of Religions*. Berkeley: University of California Press, 1981.

Lodrick, Deryck O. "Rajasthan as a Region: Myth or Reality." In *The Idea of Rajasthan: Explorations in Regional Identity*." 2 vols. Vol. 1, *Constructions*, edited by Karine Schomer, Joan L. Erdman, Deryck O. Lodrick, and Lloyd I. Rudolph, 1–44. Delhi: Manohar and the American Institute of Indian Studies, 1994.

Long, J. Bruce. "Death as a Necessity and a Gift in Hindu Mythology." In *Religious Encounters with Death: Insights from the History and Anthropology of Religions*, edited by Frank E. Reynolds and Earle H. Waugh, 73–96. University Park: Pennsylvania State University Press, 1977.

Lorenzen, David N. "Warrior Ascetics in Indian History." *Journal of the American Oriental Society* 98, no. 1 (1978): 61–67.

Ludden, David, ed. *Contesting the Nation: Religion, Community, and the Politics of Democracy in India.* Philadelphia: University of Pennsylvania Press, 1996.

Lutgendorff, Philip. *The Life of a Text: Performing the Rāmcaritmānas of Tulsidas.* Berkeley: University of California Press, 1991.

Madan, T. N., ed. *Way of Life: King, Householder, Renouncer.* New Delhi: Vikas, 1982.

Maheshwari, Hiralal. *History of Rajasthani Literature.* New Delhi: Sahitya Academi, 1980.

Mahiyāriyā, Nāthūsinh. *Vīr Satsaī. Sampādak Mohansinh Mahiyāriyā and Mahtābsinh Mahiyāriyā. Rājasthān Sarkār Dvārā Purskṛt.* Dillī: Shrī Gopināth Seth, Navon Pres, 1977.

Manuel, Peter Lamarch. *Cassette Culture: Popular Music and Technology in North India.* Chicago: University of Chicago Press, 1993.

March, Kathryn. "Two Houses and the Pain of Separation in Tamang Narratives from Highland Nepal." *Oral Tradition* 12, no. 1 (1997): 134–172.

Marriott, McKim, and Ronald B. Inden. "Towards an Ethnosociology of South Asian Caste Systems." In *The New Wind: Changing Identities in South Asia,* edited by Kenneth David, 227–238. The Hague: Mouton, 1977.

Mauss, Marcel. *The Gift: Forms and Functions of Exchange in Archaic Societies.* Translated by I. Cunnison. London: Cohen and West, 1966.

Mayaram, Shail. *Resisting Regimes: Myth, Memory and the Shaping of a Muslim Identity.* Delhi: Oxford University Press, 1997.

Mayer, Adrian C. *Caste and Kinship in Central India: A Village and Its Region.* Berkeley: University of California Press, 1960.

McDermott, Rachel Fell. "The Western Kālī." In *Devī: Goddesses of India,* edited by John Stratton Hawley and Donna Marie Wulff, 281–313. Berkeley: University of California Press, 1996.

McGee, Mary. "Desired Fruits: Motive and Intention in the Votive Rites of Hindu Women." In *Roles and Rituals for Hindu Women,* edited by Julia Leslie, 71–88. London: Pinter, 1991.

———. "Feasting and Fasting: The Vrata Tradition and Its Significance for Hindu Women." Th.D. dissertation, Harvard Divinity School, 1987.

McKean, Lise. "Bhārat Mātā: Mother India and Her Militant Matriots." In *Devī: Goddesses of India,* edited by John Stratton Hawley and Donna Marie Wulff, 250–280. Berkeley: University of California Press, 1996.

———. *The Divine Enterprise: Gurus and the Hindu Nationalist Movement.* Chicago: University of Chicago Press, 1996.

Mehta, Gita. *A River Sutra.* New York: Doubleday, 1993.

Meyer, Eveline. *Aṅkāḷaparmēcuvari: A Goddess of Tamilnadu, Her Myths and Cult.* Stuttgart: Steiner Verlag, 1986.

Miller, Joseph Charles, Jr. "The Twenty-Four Brothers and Lord Devnārāyaṇ: The Story and Performance of a Folk Epic of Rajasthan, India." Ph.D. dissertation, University of Pennsylvania, 1994.

Monier-Williams, M. *Sanskrit-English Dictionary.* New Delhi: Munshiram Manoharlal, [1899] 1976.

Mumhta Naiṇsī rī Khyāt, ed. *Acarya Jinvijay Muni.* Jodhpur: Rajasthan Oriental Research Institute, 1960.

Nagy, Gregory. *The Best of the Achaeans: Concepts of the Hero in Archaic Greek Poetry.* Baltimore: Johns Hopkins University Press, 1979.

Nandy, Ashis. "Sati as Profit versus Sati as a Spectacle: The Public Debate on Roop Kanwar's Death." In *Sati, The Blessing and the Curse: The Burning of Wives in India*, edited by John Stratton Hawley, 131–149. New York: Oxford University Press, 1994.

———. *The Intimate Enemy: Loss and Recovery of Self under Colonialism*. Delhi: Oxford University Press, 1983.

Narayan, Kirin. *Mondays on the Dark Night of the Moon: Himalayan Foothill Folktales*, New York: Oxford University Press, 1997.

———. "Singing from Separation: Women's Voices in and about Kangra Folksongs." *Oral Tradition* 12, no. 1 (1997): 23–53.

———. *Storytellers, Saints, and Scoundrels: Folk Narrative in Hindu Religious Teaching*. Philadelphia: University of Pennsylvania Press, 1989.

Narayana Rao, Velcheru. "A Rāmāyaṇa of Their Own: Women's Oral Tradition in Telugu." In *Many Rāmāyaṇas: The Diversity of a Narrative Tradition in South Asia*, edited by Paula Richman, 114–136. Berkeley: University of California Press, 1991.

———. "Tricking the Goddess: Cowherd Kāṭamarāju and Goddess Gaṅga in the Telugu Folk Epic." In *Criminal Gods and Demon Devotees: Essays on the Guardians of Popular Hinduism*, edited by Alf Hiltebeitel, 105–121. Albany: State University of New York Press, 1989.

Nicholas, Ralph W. "The Effectiveness of the Hindu Sacrament (Saṃskāra): Caste, Marriage, and Divorce in Bengali Culture." In *From the Margins of Hindu Marriage: Essays on Gender, Religion, and Culture*, edited by Lindsey Harlan and Paul B. Courtright, 137–159. New York: Oxford University Press, 1995.

Nutt, Alfred. "The Arayan Expulsion-and-Return Formula in the Folk and Hero Tales of the Celts." *Folklore Record* 4 (1881): 1–44.

Obeyesekere, Gananath. *Medusa's Hair: An Essay on Personal Symbols and Religious Experience*. Chicago: University of Chicago Press, 1981.

O'Hanlon, Rosalind. "Recovering the Subject: Subaltern Studies and the Histories of Resistance in Colonial South Asia." *Modern Asian Studies* 22, no. 1 (1988): 189–224.

Oldenberg, Veena Talwar. "The Continuing Invention of the Sati Tradition." In *Sati, The Blessing and the Curse: The Burning of Wives in India*, edited by John Stratton Hawley, 159–173. New York: Oxford University Press, 1994.

———. "The Roop Kanwar Case: Feminist Responses." In *Sati, The Blessing and the Curse: The Burning of Wives in India*, edited by John Stratton Hawley, 101–130. New York: Oxford University Press, 1994.

Ortner, Sherry B. "Is Woman to Nature as Man Is to Culture?" In *Women, Culture, and Society*, edited by Michelle Zimbalist Rosaldo and Louise Lamphere, 67–87. Stanford: Stanford University Press, 1974.

Pandey, Gyanendra. "Community and Violence: Recalling Partition." Paper delivered in the South Asia Seminar, Center for International Affairs, Harvard University, April 14, 1997.

———. "The Colonial Construction of 'Communialism': British Writings on Banaras in the Nineteenth Century." In *Mirrors of Violence: Communities, Riots and Survivors in South Asia*, edited by Veena Das, 94–134. Delhi: Oxford University Press, 1990.

Parry, Jonathan P. *Death in Banaras*. Cambridge: Cambridge University Press, 1994.

———. "Death and Cosmogony in Kashi." In *Way of Life: King, Householder, Renouncer*, edited by T. N. Madan, 337–365. New Delhi: Vikas, 1982.

———. "Sacrificial Death and the Necrophagous Ascetic." In *Death and the Regeneration of Life*, edited by Maruice Bloch and Jonathan Parry, 74–110. Cambridge: Cambridge University Press, 1982.

Pearson, Anne Mackenzie. *"Because It Gives Me Peace of Mind": Ritual Fasts in the Religious Lives of Hindu Women*. Albany: State University of New York Press, 1996.

Pet Semetary [sic]. Directed by Mary Lambert. Paramount Pictures, 1989. Based on the novel by Stephen King.

Pinch, William R. "Subaltern Sadhus? Towards a Military Genealogy of North Indian Asceticism." Paper delivered at the conference "Rethinking South Asia's Past, Revisioning South Asia's Future" at Tufts University, May 9–10, 1997. A version of this paper is published on the web at http://www.virginia.edu/soasia/symsem/kisan/papers/sadhus.html.

———. *Peasants and Monks in British India*. Berkeley: University of California Press, 1996.

Pinchman, Tracy, ed. *Seeking Mahādevī: Constructing the Identities of the Hindu Great Goddess*. Albany: State University of New York Press, 2001.

———. *The Rise of the Goddess in the Hindu Tradition*. Albany: State University of New York Press, 1994.

Prakash, Gyan. "Becoming a Bhuinya in Eastern India." In *Contesting Power: Resistance and Everyday Social Relations in South Asia*, edited by Douglas Haynes and Gyan Prakash, 160–174. Berkeley: University of California Press, 1991.

"PM Takes Part in Rathore Celebrations." *Indian Express*, December 30, 1990.

Qanungo, Kalika Ranjan. *Studies in Rajput History*. New Delhi: S. Chand, 1960.

Raheja, Gloria Goodwin. "Negotiated Solidarities: Gendered Representations of Disruption and Desire in North Indian Oral Traditions and Popular Culture." *Oral Tradition* 12, no. 1 (1997): 172–225.

———. "The Paradoxes of Power and Community: Women's Oral Traditions and the Uses of Ethnography." *Oral Tradition* 12, no. 1 (1997): 1–23.

———. "Introduction: Gender Representation and the Problem of Language and Resistance in India." In *Listen to the Heron's Words: Reimagining Gender and Kinship in North India*, edited by Gloria Goodwin Raheja and Ann Grodzins Gold, 1–29. Berkeley: University of California Press, 1994.

———. "India: Caste, Kingship, and Dominance Reconsidered." *Annual Review of Anthropology* 17 (1988): 497–522.

———. *The Poison in the Gift: Ritual, Prestation, and the Dominant Caste*. Chicago: University of Chicago Press, 1988.

Raheja, Gloria Goodwin, and Ann Grodzins Gold, eds. *Listen to the Heron's Words: Reimagining Gender and Kinship in North India*. Berkeley: University of California Press, 1994.

Rajasthan District Gazetteers: Dungarpur. K. K. Dehgal Directorate, District Gazetteers. Jaipur: Government of Rajasthan, 1974.

Ramanujan, A. K. "'A Flowering Tree': A Woman's Tale." *Oral Tradition* 12, no. 1 (1997): 226–243.

———. "Toward a Counter-System: Women's Tales." In *Gender, Genre, and Power in South Asian Expressive Traditions*, edited by Arjun Appadurai, Frank J. Korom, and Margaret A. Mills, 33–55. Delhi: Motilal Banarsidass, 1994.

———. "Repetition in the Mahābhārata." In *Essays on the Mahābhārata*, edited by Arvind Sharma, 419–443. Leiden: E. J. Brill, 1991.

―――. "Two Realms of Kannada Folklore." In *Another Harmmony: New Essays on the Folklore of India*, edited by Stuart H. Blackburn and A. K. Ramanujan, 41–75. Berkeley: University of California Press, 1986.

Ramusak, Barbara N. "Tourism and Icons: The Packaging of the Princely States of Rajasthan." In *Perceptions of South Asia's Visual Past*, edited by Catherine B. Asher and Thomas R. Metcalf, 235–255. New Delhi: Oxford and IBH, 1994.

―――. "The Indian Princes as Fantasy: Palace Hotels, Palace Museums, and Palace on Wheels." In *Consuming Modernity: Public Culture in a South Asian World*, edited by Carol A. Breckenridge, 66–89. Minneapolis: University of Minnesota Press, 1995.

Rana Pratap. Bombay: Amar Chitra Katha, n.d., no. 24.

Reynolds, Holly Baker. "The Auspicious Married Woman." In *The Powers of Tamil Women*, edited by Susan Wadley, 35–60. Syracuse: Maxwell School for Public Affairs, Syracuse University, 1980.

―――. "To Keep the Tali Strong: Women's Rituals in Tamilnad, India." Ph.D. dissertation, University of Wisconsin, Madison, 1978.

Richman, Paula, ed. *Many Rāmāyaṇas: The Diversity of a Narrative Tradition in South Asia*. Berkeley: University of California Press, 1991.

Risley, Sir Herbert. *The People of India*. Edited by William Crooke 1915. Reprint: Delhi: Oriental Books Reprint Corporation, 1969.

Roghair, Gene H. *The Epic of Palnāḍu: A Study and Translation of Palnāti Vīrula Katha, A Telugu Oral Tradition from Andhra Pradesh India*. Oxford: Clarendon Press, 1982.

Roth, Phillip. *Deception*. New York: Vintage International, 1997.

Rowe, William. "The New Chauhans: A Caste Mobility Movement in North India." In *Social Mobility in the Caste System in India*, edited by James Silverberg, 69–77. The Hague: Mouton, 1968.

Roy, Asim. *The Islamic Syncretic Tradition in Bengal*. Princeton: Princeton University Press, 1983.

Rudolph, Lloyd I. "Self as Other: Amar Singh's Diary as Reflexive 'Native' Ethnography." *Modern Asian Studies* 31, no. 1 (1997): 143–175.

Rudolph, Susanne Hoeber, and Lloyd I. Rudolph. "The Political Modernization of an Indian Feudal Order: An Analysis of Rajput Adaptation in Rajasthan." In *Essays on Rajputana*, edited by Susanne Hoeber Rudolph and Lloyd I. Rudolph, 38–78. New Delhi: Concept Publishing, 1984.

―――. "Rajput Adulthood: Reflections on the Amar Singh Diary." In *Essays on Rajputana*, edited by Susanne Hoeber Rudolph and Lloyd I. Rudolph, 177–210. New Delhi: Concept Publishing, 1984.

Rudolph, Susanne Hoeber, and Lloyd I. Rudolph with Mohan Singh Kanota, eds. *Reversing the Gaze: Amar Singh's Diary, A Colonial Subject's Narrative of Imperial India*. New Delhi: Oxford University Press, 2000.

Sax, William S. *Dancing the Self: Personhood and Performance in the Pāṇḍav Līlā of Garhwal*. New York: Oxford University Press, 2002.

―――. "Fathers, Sons, and Rhinoceroses: Masculinity and Violence in the Pāṇḍav Līlā." *Journal of the American Oriental Society* 117, no. 2 (1997): 278–294.

―――. *Mountain Goddess: Gender and Politics in a Himalayan Village*. New York: Oxford University Press, 1991.

Scott, James C. *Weapons of the Weak: Everyday Forms of Peasant Resistance*. New Haven: Yale University Press, 1985.

Settar, S., and Gunther D. Sontheimer, eds. *Memorial Stones: A Study of Their*

Origin, Significance, and Variety. Dharwad: Institute of Art History, Karnatak University, and Heidelberg: South Asia Institute, University of Heidelberg, 1982.

Sharma, S. R. *Maharana Raj Singh and His Times*. Delhi: Motilal Banarsidass, 1971.

Shulman, David Dean. *The Hungry God: Hindu Tales of Filicide and Devotion*. Chicago: University of Chicago Press, 1993.

————. "Outcaste, Guardian, and Trickster: Notes on the Myth of Kāttavarāyan." In *Criminal Gods and Demon Devotees: Essays on the Folklore of Popular Hinduism*, edited by Alf Hiltebeitel, 35–65. Albany: State University of New York Press, 1989.

————. "Battle as Metaphor in Tamil Folk and Classical Traditions." In *Another Harmony: New Essays on the Folklore of India*, edited by Stuart H. Blackburn and A. K. Ramanujan, 105–130. Berkeley: University of California Press, 1986.

————. *The King and the Clown in South Indian Myth and History*. Princeton: Princeton University Press, 1985.

————. *Tamil Temple Myths: Sacrifice and Divine Marriage in the South Indian Śaiva Tradition*. Princeton: Princeton University Press, 1980.

Shyāmaldās, Kavirāj. *Vīr Vinod*. 4 vols. Privately published by the Mewar Darbar, ca. 1884. Reissued Delhi: Motilal Banarsidass, 1986.

Singh, Munshi Hardyal. *The Castes of Marwar*. First printed by order of the Marwar Darbar, 1894. Reissued Jodhpur: Books Treasure, 1991.

Singhji, Virbhadra. *The Rajputs of Saurasthra*. Bombay: Popular Prakashan, 1994.

Sinha, Mrinalini. *Colonial Masculinity: The "Manly Englishman" and the "Effeminate Bengali" in the Late Nineteenth Century*. Manchester: Manchester University Press, 1995.

Sinha, Surajit. "State Formation and Rajput Myth in Tribal Central India." *Man in India* 42, no. 1 (1962): 33–80.

Smith, Frederick M. "The Disappearance and Recovery of Possession in Sanskrit Literature." Book manuscript in progress.

Smith, John D. *The Epic of Pābūjī: A Study, Transcription and Translation*. Cambridge: Cambridge University Press, 1991.

————. "Scapegoats of the Gods: The Ideology of the Indian Epics." In *Oral Epics in India*, edited by Stuart H. Blackburn, Peter J. Claus, Joyce B. Flueckiger, and Susan S. Wadley, 176–194. Berkeley: University of California Press, 1989.

Sontheimer, Gunther-Dietz. *Pastoral Deities in Western India*. Translated by Anne Feldhaus. New York: Oxford University Press, 1989.

————. "Hero and Satī-Stones of Maharashtra." In *Memorial Stones: A Study of Their Origin, Significance, and Variety*, edited by S. Settar and Gunther D. Sontheimer, 261–281. Dharwad: Institute of Art History, Karnatak University, and Heidelberg: South Asia Institute, University of Heidelberg, 1982.

Staal, J. F. "Sanskrit and Sanskritization." *Journal of Asian Studies* 22, no. 3 (1963): 261–275.

Stanley, John. "The Capitulation of Maṇi: A Conversion Myth in the Cult of Khaṇḍobā." In *Criminal Gods and Demon Devotees: Essays on the Guardians of Popular Hinduism*, edited by Alf Hiltebeitel, 271–298. Albany: State University of New York Press, 1989.

Stern, Henry. "Le temple d'Eklingji et le royaume du Mewar (Rajasthan), (rapport au divin, royauté et territoire: sources d'une maîtrise)." *Puruṣārtha: sciences sociales en Asie du Sud* 10 (1986): 15–30.

———. "Le pouvoir dans l'inde traditionelle: territoire, caste et parenté." *L'Homme* (1973): 50–70.

Sunder Rajan, Rajeshwari. "The Subject of Sati: Pain and Death in the Contemporary Discourse on Sati." *Yale Journal of Criticism* 3, no. 2 (1990): 1–23.

Tambs-Lyche, Harald. *Power, Profit and Poetry: Traditional Society in Kathiawar, Western India.* New Delhi: Manohar, 1997.

Tewari, Laxmi G. *The Splendor of Worship: Women's Fasts, Rituals, Stories and Art.* New Delhi: Manohar, 1991.

Thapar, Romila. "In History." *Seminar* 342 (1988): 14–19.

———. "Death and the Hero." In *Mortality and Immortality: The Anthopology and Archaeology of Death,* edited by S. C. Humphries and Helen King, 293–315. London: Academic Press, 1981.

Tod, James. *Annals and Antiquities of Rajasthan.* 2 vols. 1829. Reprint, Delhi: M. N. Publishers, 1978.

Trawick, Margaret. *Notes on Love in a Tamil Family.* Berkeley: University of California Press, 1990.

van der Veer, Peter. *Religious Nationalism: Hindus and Muslims in India.* Berkeley: University of California Press, 1994.

van Wees, Hans. "A Brief History of Tears: Gender Differentiation in Archaic Greece." In *When Men Were Men: Masculinity, Power and Identity in Classical Antiquity,* edited by Lin Foxhall and John Salmon, 10–53. New York: Routledge, 1998.

Varshney, Ashutosh. "Contested Meanings: India's National Identity, Hindu Nationalism and the Politics of Anxiety." *Daedalus* 122 (1993): 227–261.

Visuvalingam, Elizabeth-Chalier. "Bhairava's Royal Brahmanicide: The Problem of the Mahābrāhmāṇa." In *Criminal Gods and Demon Devotees: Essays on the Guardians of Popular Hinduism,* edited by Alf Hiltebeitel, 157–230. Albany: State University of New York Press, 1989.

Vyas, Deokrishna. "Songs of Valour." *Hindustan Times,* February 2, 1991, Saturday section, p. 3.

Wacziarg, Francis, and Aman Nath. *Rajasthan: The Painted Walls of Shekhavati.* New Delhi: Vikas, 1982.

Wadley, Susan S. *Raja Nal and the Goddess: Inscribing Caste and Gender in the North Indian Oral Epic Dhola.* Book manuscript in progress.

———. *Struggling with Destiny in Karimpur, 1925–1984.* Berkeley: University of California Press, 1994.

———. "Vrats: Transformers of Destiny." In *Karma: An Anthropological Inquiry,* edited by Charles F. Keyes and E. Valentine Daniel, 146–162. Berkeley: University of California, 1983.

———. *Shakti: Power in the Conceptual Structure of Karimpur Religion.* Chicago: Department of Anthropology, University of Chicago, 1975.

Wagoner, Phillip B. "'Sultan among Hindu Kings': Dress, Titles, and Islamicization of Hindu Culture at Vijayanagara." *Journal of Asian Studies* 55, no. 4 (1996): 871–874.

Weaver, Mary Anne. "India's Bandit Queen." *Atlantic Monthly* 278, no. 3 (November 1996): 88–104.

Weinberger-Thomas, Catherine. *Ashes of Immortality: Widow-Burning in India.* Chicago: University of Chicago Press, 1999.

————. *Cendres d'immortalité: la crémation des veuves en Inde.* Paris: Éditions du Seuil, 1996.

Wills, Lawrence M. *The Quest of the Historical Gospel: Mark, John, and the Origins of the Gospel Genre.* New York: Routledge, 1997.

Wittgenstein, Ludwig. *Philosophical Investigations.* Translated by G. E. M. Anscombe. Oxford: Basil Blackwell, 1972.

Wolcot, Peter. "Cattle Raiding, Heroic Tradition, and Ritual: The Greek Evidence." *History of Religions* 18, no. 4 (May 1979): 326–351.

Zelliot, Eleanor, and Maxine Berntsen, eds. *The Experience of Hinduism: Essays on Religion in Maharashtra.* Albany: State University of New York Press, 1988.

Ziegler, Norman Paul. "Action, Power, and Service in Rajasthani Culture: A Social History of the Rajpūts of Middle Period, Rajasthan." Ph.D. dissertation, University of Chicago, 1973.

Žižek, Slavoj. "Eastern Europe's Republics of Gilead." *New Left Review* 183 (1990): 50–62.

PAMPHLETS

Rājasthānī Lokgīt (Rātījagā evam Vivāh). Bhāg 1. Yavatmāl, Mahārāṣtra: Sau. Aparājitā Caukhāṇī, 1984.

Rājasthānī Lokgīt. Bhāg 2. Sampādak, Śivsinh Coyal. Udaypur: Sāhitya Samsthān, Rājasthān Vidyāpīṭh.

Rātījagā Kā Gīt. Sampādak Sarasvatī Devī Bhensālī evam Jnāndevī Telī. Ajmer: Sarasvatī Prakāśan, S. 2041.

Śarma, Śil. *Ārati: Śrī Jagadambājī evam Kallaji Rāthauḍ ki.* Udaypur: Samdhaj Kalla Rāthauḍ Sāhitya Prakāśan Samiti, 1981.

————. *Karmavīr Kallā: Sarv Siddhidāyak Lokdevtā Śrī Kamdhaj Kallā Rāthauḍ Stuti-Vandan evam Sanksipt Jīvan Paricay.* Udaypur: Kamdhav Kallā Rāthauḍ Sāhitya Prakāśan Samiti, 1981.

Index